SOVEREIGN DEBT AT THE CROSSROADS

SOVEREIGN DEBT AT THE CROSSROADS

Challenges and Proposals for Resolving the Third World Debt Crisis

Edited by
Chris Jochnick
Fraser A. Preston

2006

OXFORD

UNIVERSITY PRESS

Oxford University Press, Inc., publishes works that further
Oxford University's objective of excellence
in research, scholarship, and education.

Oxford   New York
Auckland   Cape Town   Dar es Salaam   Hong Kong   Karachi
Kuala Lumpur   Madrid   Melbourne   Mexico City   Nairobi
New Delhi   Shanghai   Taipei   Toronto

With offices in
Argentina   Austria   Brazil   Chile   Czech Republic   France   Greece
Guatemala   Hungary   Italy   Japan   Poland   Portugal   Singapore
South Korea   Switzerland   Thailand   Turkey   Ukraine   Vietnam

Published by Oxford University Press, Inc.
198 Madison Avenue, New York, New York 10016

www.oup.com

Oxford is a registered trademark of Oxford University Press

Library of Congress Cataloging-in-Publication Data
Sovereign debt at the crossroads : challenges and proposals for resolving the third world
debt crisis / editors, Chris Jochnick & Fraser A. Preston.
p.   cm.
Includes bibliographical references and index.
ISBN-13 978-0-19-516800-6; 978-0-19-516801-3 (pbk.)
ISBN 0-19-516800-3; 0-19-516801-1 (pbk.)
1. Debts, External—Developing countries.   2. Debt relief—Developing countries.
I. Jochnick, Chris.   II. Preston, Fraser A.
HJ8899.S68 2005
336.3'435'091724—dc22   2005004309

9 8 7 6 5 4 3 2 1

Printed in the United States of America
on acid-free paper

To Charlie, Devon, Martin, Mateo, Nico, Paulina, Piper and Rebeca for their love and support.

Thanks to Alberto Acosta and Paulina Garzon for planting the seeds of this book and to Stephen McGroarty and David Palmer for seeing it through.

In memory of Nate Osborne.

Dedicated to the millions of poor who suffer the burden of debts they had no part in creating.

FOREWORD

Reading the essays in this excellent collection leaves one with a single over-whelming impression of the handling of sovereign debt crises and debt reduction: "too little, too late." Sovereign debt crises have been an episodic feature of international finance for centuries. The current round stems mainly from the early 1980s, when dozens of developing countries nearly simultaneously fell into an external debt crisis. Since then, debt relief has been episodic, uneven across countries and over time, gradual and grudging, and far from complete as of 2005. Even the finance ministers of creditor governments have repeatedly acknowledged in recent years that the poorest of the poor sovereign debtors need more relief.

My personal baptism by fire with these issues came 20 years ago when I advised Bolivia on debt cancellation following its struggle with hyperinflation. No sooner had the country stabilized the economy than the IMF began to demand a resumption of debt servicing on external debt. It was clear to me that restarting debt servicing would destroy the political, fiscal, and social basis of the stabilization. I took up the cause of debt cancellation as opposed to debt servicing, arguing that both creditor and debtor interests would be improved by canceling a mountain of unpayable debt. Fortunately, after tough negotiations, Bolivia won substantial relief in the form of a comprehensive "buy back" of debt at approximately ten cents on the dollar.

Yet my and others' proposals for more comprehensive approaches to the developing-country debt crisis since that time have more often than not met with resistance of creditors and international institutions. Proposals for bankruptcy-like approaches have been repeatedly resisted by powerful interests. That resistance has delayed, though not stopped, the process of debt relief, so that in place of a decisive and timely solution, the world has lurched from crisis to crisis. Debt-distressed countries have tended to receive creditor attention and eventual debt relief on the basis of their importance to the foreign policies of creditor nations, the concerns accorded by private markets, and (occasionally) the depth of suffering in the debtor nation itself.

The results have therefore been sporadic and highly uneven. It's fair to say that, overall, Africa has suffered "last service" while creditors have prioritized larger and more financially salient middle-income debtor countries. Relief for the poorest of the poor has come in dribs and drabs, with a gradually increasing acknowledgment by officialdom that most or all of the debts would have to be cancelled. That realization, which could have been reached at least a decade ago with careful analysis, has been delayed for years at the cost of profound suffering in these impoverished countries.

The essays in the collection make clear that we still lack a systematic consensus on how to handle sovereign debt and how to design more permanent institutions to address the problem effectively. Specific proposals for international bankruptcy-like procedures, whether a bankruptcy code like U.S. Chapter 9 (for municipal governments), or the IMF's own Special Debt Reduction Mechanism (SDRM), are meritorious, but have been repeatedly stymied by creditor opposition led by the U.S. Government which often appears to operate on behalf of U.S. private-sector creditor interests. The push for general concepts such as the principle of "odious debt," which would relieve debtor countries of the obligation to repay debts incurred by dictatorial regimes, have made little headway, though the essays here give strong conceptual arguments in favor of such an approach. While some essayists argue that sovereign debtors and private creditors are already negotiating pragmatic solutions in practice, this does not resolve the problem of debts owed to official creditors, nor do these arguments prove that current "pragmatic" approaches are timely, relatively efficient, and attentive to the needs of the poor.

Several of the essays clearly underscore the tremendous imbalance of power of rich and poor in the global system, and the failures of the international institutions like the IMF to represent the needs of their poor members adequately. The poor may owe financial debts to the rich, but the rich also owe tremendous debts to the poor—for ecological destruction, the practice and legacy of colonialism, unfair trade and financial rules of the game in a system largely set by powerful nations, and other misuses of power. Yet these hidden debts of the rich to the poor are off the balance sheet, and are not acknowledged by powerful creditor nations.

The essay on Jubilee 2000 reminds us that social justice, as well as more efficient approaches to the overhang of sovereign debt of impoverished countries, has come through social activism as well as intellectual debate and practical experience. The debt issue involves a complex mix of institutional design, market failures under imperfect information and contract enforcement, the uses of political power, the challenges of collective action, and the international standards of fairness and justice. It will be solved by political logic and dictates of global ethics, as well as by economic rationale.

I hope that this fine volume will advance two important causes: a short-term urgent need and a longer-term project In the short-term, deeper relief is essential for the world's poorest countries, where millions of people struggle for survival each day, and where the overhang of bad debts weighs heavily and adversely on that struggle. It is a tragedy, and a travesty, to be collecting debt servicing from impoverished African countries that need these financial resources (and much more) to extend urgent health, sanitation, education, and other public services.

The longer-term challenge is to settle on a set of international processes and institutions which can offer practical and workable correctives to imperfect information, distorted politics (of both borrowers and lenders), and significantly incomplete contracting and risk spreading that typifies the market for sovereign debt. Sovereign borrowers are prone to run into financial problems, as they have periodically throughout history. Trouble can arise from unsavory leadership in debtor countries, from unanticipated shocks in international markets against which there are no contractual contingencies, from financial contagion, or from simple financial misjudgment. When trouble comes, institutions are needed to handle the resulting financial log-jam with fairness, attention to the urgent needs of the poor, and efficiency. We are still waiting for practical solutions internationally, even decades or centuries after such solutions have been found (even if imperfectly) in domestic financial markets. The compelling essays in this volume urge us to reach those long-term solutions as well.

Jeffrey D. Sachs

CONTENTS

CONTRIBUTORS

Serkan Arslanalp is from the Department of Economics, Stanford University (serkan@stanfordalumni.org).

Jack Boorman is the former Counsellor to the IMF. Dr. Boorman served the Fund for over 27 years in various capacities, including Director of the Policy and Review Department. Dr. Boorman joined the IMF in 1975 and served as the Fund's Resident Representative in Indonesia, as well as holding different roles in the Asian and European Departments.

Fantu Cheru is Professor of African and Development Studies at the School of International Service at American University in Washington, DC. He currently serves as a member of the UN Secretary-General's Panel on International Support for the New Partnership for African Development (NEPAD) as well as Convenor of the Global Economic Agenda Track of the Helsinki Process on Globalization and Democracy.

Jose Echague holds a degree in Economics from the University of Buenos Aires, Argentina. Between 1998 and 2003 he worked as an economist for Argentina's Secretary of Finance. Since 2003, he has worked as a senior economist and portfolio strategist for AGM Finanzas in Buenos Aires.

Joseph Hanlon is a senior lecturer at the Open University, Milton Keynes, England. Dr. Hanlon was policy officer for Jubilee 2000 and has written extensively on international debt. His other areas of research are on the roots of civil wars, and on Mozambique. He can be contacted at j.hanlon@open.ac.uk.

Peter Blair Henry is Associate Professor of Economics in the Graduate School of Business at Stanford University and a Faculty Research Fellow in the International Finance and Macroeconomics and the Corporate Finance Programs of the National Bureau of Economic Research. Professor Henry received his Ph.D. in economics from the Massachusetts Institute of Technology (MIT) in 1997. He is the author of numerous articles and working papers.

Seema Jayachandran is an Assistant Professor of Economics at UCLA. During 2004–2006 she is the Robert Wood Johnson Foundation Scholar in Health Policy Research at the University of California at Berkley. She is a research affiliate with the Bureau for Research and Economic Analysis of Development and has published a number of papers, working papers, and articles on the topics of debt and development.

Chris Jochnick is the Director of Private Sector Engagement at Oxfam America. He is a graduate of Harvard Law School, a former MacArthur Fellow, and currently an adjunct associate professor of human rights and development at Columbia University. He is the co-founder of the Center for Economic and Social Rights (NY) and the Centro de Derechos Economicos y Sociales (Ecuador).

Michael Kremer is currently Professor of Economics at Harvard and Senior Fellow at the Brookings Institution. He has been a National Fellow at the Hoover Institution at Stanford University (1994–1995) and a recipient of both a Mac-Arthur "genius" fellowship and a Presidential Early Career Award for Scientists and Engineers. Dr. Kremer's recent research includes work on the evaluation of health and educational programs and incentives for research and development on malaria, tuberculosis, HIV, and other diseases affecting developing countries.

Daniel Marx is currently a partner of AGM, a financial advisory firm based in Argentina. Previously, he was in charge of debt negotiations of the Republic of Argentina between 1987 and 1993 and became Secretary of Finance in 2000–2001. He has also worked in banking and developing investment opportunities in Latin America.

Ann Pettifor is a Director of Advocacy International Ltd, which advises low-income-country governments. She was a co-founder of the international Jubilee 2000 campaign, and leader of the British campaign. She is editor of the *Real World Economic Outlook* published by Palgrave in 2003, and the author of numerous articles on debt and international finance.

Arturo C. Porzecanski is Scholar of International Finance in Residence at American University and Adjunct Professor of International Affairs at Columbia University. His chapter was written when he was Managing Director and Head of Emerging Markets Sovereign Research at ABN AMRO, New York.

Kunibert Raffer is Associate Professor, Department of Economics, University of Vienna and Senior Associate, New Economics Foundation (London). He was consultant to UNIDO (1979–1980; 1983–1984), Visiting Fellow, Institute of Development Studies, University of Sussex (1989, academic sponsor: Sir Hans Singer), Honorary Research Fellow, Department of Commerce, University of Birmingham UK (1990–1993).

William K. Reilly is president and chief executive officer of Aqua International Partners, an investment group that finances the purification of water and wastewater in developing countries, and invests in projects and companies that serve the water sector. From 1989 to 1993, he served as the seventh Administrator of the U.S. Environmental Protection Agency. Prior to becoming EPA Administrator, he held five environment-related positions over two decades. He was President of World Wildlife Fund (1985–1989) and President of The Conservation Foundation (1973–1985). Reilly has written and lectured extensively on environmental issues.

David Roodman is a Research Fellow at the Center for Global Development, where he is chief architect and project manager of the Commitment to Development Index and co-author of "New Data, New Doubts: Revisiting Aid, Policies, and Growth," published in 2004. In addition, he is the author of *The Natural Wealth of Nations: Harnessing the Market for the Environment*.

Guido Sandleris is an Assistant Professor of International Economics at Johns Hopkins University. He holds a Ph.D. in Economics from Columbia University. He has written a number of papers on sovereign debt issues. He was an advisor to the Argentine Ministry of Economics.

Andrew Simms is policy director of NEF (the New Economics Foundation), an award-winning independent British think tank. He studied at the London School of Economics, led campaigns for several major aid and development agencies and was one of the original organizers of the Jubilee 2000 debt campaign. He is on the board of Greenpeace UK and The Energy and Resources Institute (TERI) Europe and has written widely on issues ranging from disasters to development, and corporate accountability to climate change.

J. E. Stiglitz has taught at Princeton, Stanford, MIT, and was the Drummond Professor and a fellow of All Souls College, Oxford. He is now University Professor at Columbia University in New York. In 2001, he was awarded the Nobel Prize in economics. Dr. Stiglitz was a member of the Council of Economic Advisers in 1993–1995, during the Clinton administration, and served as CEA chairman from 1995 to 1997. He then became Chief Economist and Senior Vice-President of the World Bank, 1997–2000.

SOVEREIGN DEBT AT THE CROSSROADS

INTRODUCTION

The ten years between 1995 and 2004 were not kind to the developing world. Although the 1990s began in the midst of a celebration of the world's "emerging markets," by the end of the decade many of those countries had become submerged in a tide of overindebtedness and economic stagnation. The decade witnessed the devaluation of the Mexican peso and the ensuing crisis throughout Latin America, the 1997 devaluation of the Thai baht and the subsequent "Asian Flu" that triggered seven Asian currency devaluations, three bailouts led by the International Monetary Fund (IMF), the impoverishment of millions of first-generation arrivals into the Asian middle class, the 1998 default by Russia, which ended with the sudden and painful devaluation of the Brazilian real, and finally the devaluation, default, and near self-destruction of Argentina in 2002.

Setting aside the periodic crises and stunted development caused by over-indebtedness, the real cost of sovereign debt is paid in tiny installments every day by people without access to health care, education, and clean water, whose livelihoods are crimped by crumbling public infrastructure and faltering economies. The facts of debt speak for themselves. In Zambia, life expectancy is 33 years, less than it was in Europe during the Middle Ages at the height of the bubonic plague. The average life expectancy in IMF-designated "heavily indebted poor countries" (HIPCs) is 51 years. In eight HIPC countries, child mortality rates are more than 2000% higher than that of the United States. (In Niger, nearly one of every five children die before their first birthday.) Fifty million children in HIPC countries do not attend school—leaving an entire generation without a future. In Ecuador, the government in 2000 spent approximately $160 (U.S.) per person to service its sovereign debt, as compared with $36 per person on education and social services. Argentina's default and subsequent economic crisis sliced per capita gross domestic product (GDP) in half in less than 12 months.

As one of this book's authors points out, to describe the current situation of highly indebted low- and middle-income countries as a "crisis" is to ignore history. The existence of overindebtedness throughout most of the developing world for decades defies the implication of immediacy and urgency that normally defines a "crisis." Responses to the debts have varied over time, from the invasion of defaulting states by creditor governments to internationally arbitrated forgiveness. Often, creditors and debtors have avoided short-term defaults by restructuring debt with reduced principal and/or longer amortization. In recent decades, creditors have securitized debt as bonds and sold them to the public through the so-called Brady program and have partially forgiven the debts of the very poorest countries through the HIPC programs. These efforts have met with mixed success. Although countries such as Chile have grown and even prospered following debt relief, many others continue to struggle under marginally improved burdens, having simply postponed an inevitable reckoning. Following two decades of global initiatives—the Brady Plan, HIPC I, HIPC II, and myriad reschedulings—the average ratio of debt to GDP in Africa, the Middle East, and Latin America still hovers around 50%, an overwhelming obstacle to growth for these countries.

This book is an attempt to unite under one cover various components of, and approaches to, the problem of overindebtedness. It brings together academics, international bankers, representatives of civil society, and the multilateral financial institutions and practitioners of debt relief. The book is broken into three parts: part I offers a background to the problem of sovereign overindebtedness, its history, its impact, and its challenges. Part II makes the legal, ethical and practical cases for debt relief and/or repudiation, and part III offers a range of proposals for redressing past debts and avoiding future crises.

In part I, David Roodman sets the stage with an overview of the past 25 years of sovereign-debt initiatives. Roodman examines the programs devised by creditors, namely the World Bank and IMF, during the 1980s and 1990s that have aimed at addressing the mounting problem of developing-country debt. Roodman discusses the "austerity" lending of the 1980s and the "structural adjustment programs" of the 1990s, and he criticizes the inherent failings that characterized those efforts, including reduced public investment, which has led to economic stagnation.

In the Brady Plan of the late 1980s and early 1990s, Roodman finds an example of success that should form part of future debt-reduction efforts. The heavy writeoffs lenders accepted under the Brady program reflected the economic value of the debt and allowed private investment and inward capital flow to resume. This lesson, Roodman argues, is lost under the HIPC program, which relies too much on government reforms and not enough on reducing debts to levels from which they will not quickly rise again.

Fantu Cheru, the former United Nations special expert on sovereign debt, takes Roodman's historical assessment home to Africa, where he argues that IMF and World Bank "structural adjustment" policies have since the 1970s worsened an already bad situation. Strangling demand through import substitution strategies, the international financial institutions insisted on export-oriented growth, which resulted in collapsed global commodity prices, leaving countries with increased proportions of their internal resources devoted to bringing devalued products to the world market.

Cheru also takes aim at multilateral creditors: "For twenty-five years, the guiding principle of official debt-relief has been to do the minimum to avert default, but never enough to solve the debt crisis." Contrasting debt-relief efforts in Africa with the successful Brady program in Latin America, he argues that African debtors were presented with less attractive, and ultimately less successful, debt-relief terms. Similarly, the HIPC initiative relies on overly optimistic projections of economic growth and therefore provides debt forgiveness that will ultimately prove inadequate for setting deeply indebted African countries on a path to sustainable economic growth.

In chapter 3, Daniel Marx—the former finance minister of Argentina—Jose Echague, and Guido Sandleris provide a context for debt crises by approaching them through the lens of the international capital markets, which both reflect and determine countries' economic strengths and weaknesses. These markets have played an integral role in the overindebtedness of middle-income countries by generating procyclical waves of lending and retrenchment that exaggerate the economic volatility of developing economies and make them more vulnerable to the effects of endogenous shocks.

The authors recommend a number of reforms to the international financial architecture, including a more consistent approach to dealing with countries in crisis and better communication on the part of the IMF, but are most concerned with the role of sovereign borrowers. Governments of developing countries need to focus more on building credible and sustainable institutions and consistent macroeconomic policies. Without these deep reforms, countries risk repeating the crises of the 1980s and 1990s irrespective of debt alleviation.

Andrew Simms begins part II of the book by broadening the analysis of sovereign debt to incorporate ecological concerns. Centuries of consumption by the developed world of the natural resources of the developing world, resources that in many cases were acquired illegally or by force, have produced what Simms describes as an ecological debt of the rich countries to the poor countries. The imbalance in resource consumption helps explain the dramatic divergence in income levels that has occurred since the early twentieth century between rich nations and poor nations. Simms suggests that there is a sustainable equilibrium in the use of the world's natural resources—clean air, fresh water, timber, and petroleum. The wealthy nations of the world have upset that equilibrium at the expense of the poor—taking more than their share of the goods while inflicting the costs of resource depletion and pollution on the poor.

Simms argues that just as the expansion of petroleum-based economic activity contributed to the widening gap between rich and poor, capping emissions of greenhouse gases will contribute to the development of the developing world. By allocating tradable rights to emit greenhouse gases on a per capita basis, a global greenhouse gas trading system will transfer value from those who emit (the wealthy) to those who do not (the poor). Simms's analysis also underscores how the ecological debt expressed in financial terms owed to developing countries easily outweighs their current levels of indebtedness.

In chapter 5, Joseph Hanlon addresses the question that has inspired 10 years of civil society struggle over debt: Why should poor countries be expected to repay the debts imposed upon them by unelected and repressive governments? Who should shoulder the burden of repaying the billions of dollars stolen by the likes of Mobutu, Marcos, and Saddam Hussein? How can creditors expect South Africans to pay for loans taken by the apartheid regime and used to oppress them? Hanlon's focus is on the illegitimacy of debt—what makes a loan improper and therefore void.

Hanlon's argument unfolds in two parts: First, loans to certain borrowers or for certain purposes are prima facie illegitimate. In this category, he puts loans to dictators, odious debt (debt taken with the purpose of repressing the populace), and extortionate loans. Second, certain behavior by lenders can also make a loan illegitimate: usury, money laundering, and gross negligence in lending. When these conditions are met, responsibility for repayment cannot be properly placed on the borrower.

In chapter 6, Chris Jochnick builds on Hanlon's piece by fleshing out the relevant legal principles surrounding sovereign debt. He makes the case that much of the existing sovereign-debt stock is not supported under domestic and international law and could be challenged on various legal grounds. By reference to human rights treaties and UN resolutions, he also describes the obligations of debtor governments to prioritize the welfare of the most vulnerable populations and the corresponding obligations of creditor countries to avoid undermining the broader political and development rights of countries. Jochnick's chapter offers ample arguments to challenge existing debts in a national or international forum and a framework to support the sort of arbitrated debt resolutions described in later chapters.

Former World Bank Chief Economist Joseph Stiglitz takes up the ethics of debt in chapter 7. Long a voice of criticism against the global trading system and policies of the World Bank and IMF, the Nobel Prize–winning economist leaves aside economic theory and in this chapter focuses on the moral obligations of borrowers and lenders. In a world of imperfect information and market failures, ethics must be part of economic decision making.

Stiglitz focuses on three issues: lending behavior, excessive debt, and the role of the global reserve system in fomenting inequality. He argues that where wealthy nations lend to poor nations, asymmetries of power and ability to bear risk arise and should be counterbalanced in debt contracts by removing in some circumstances part of the cost of nonrepayment from the shoulders of the borrower. Similarly, where wealthy lenders permit poor borrowers to take on levels of debt that subsequently prove to be unpayable, or give advice that proves to be detrimental to the borrower, the lender has violated a fiduciary duty to the borrower and should bear part of the cost of nonrepayment. Finally, the global reserve system conspires against poor countries by requiring them to set aside reserves in U.S. dollars, which earn low interest rates, even while they are forced to borrow at high interest rates. This system imposes needless costs on the poor while providing unneeded benefits to the rich.

In chapter 8, Serkan Arslanalp and Peter Blair Henry tackle the central economic question of debt relief: Does it work to promote economic growth? As their chapter indicates, this seemingly straightforward question—often taken for granted by debt campaigners—merits closer attention to ensure that relief bears constructive and sustainable outcomes. The authors conclude that debt relief is highly effective at promoting growth in countries suffering from a "debt overhang," where reducing debt levels will stimulate investment and net resource transfers from abroad, but less effective in countries where infrastructure is weak and where net resource transfers are already positive. These conclusions run contrary to current international priorities. For instance, several countries that would benefit most from debt relief under Henry and Arslanalp's analysis, such as Colombia, Indonesia, and Turkey, are not sufficiently "poor" to qualify for HIPC relief, and those that do qualify would be better served by a greater emphasis on aid than debt relief.

Part III focuses on concrete innovations to alleviate the debt burdens of developing countries. Former Environmental Protection Agency (EPA) Administrator William K. Reilly leads off this section in chapter 9 with an examination of debt-for-nature swaps and their potential to offset sovereign debt. Debt-for-nature swaps originated in the 1980s as a way of preserving natural areas in the developing world while at the same time reducing the external debt of the host country. The win-win nature of this type of transaction created a seemingly infinite set of potential applications, and the U.S. Congress and other national legislatures soon passed legislation enabling billions of dollars of swaps to take place. However, that vast potential was never realized. Legislative mandates were not funded, developing countries became suspicious of swaps as a threat to their sovereignty, and improving debt markets reduced the attractiveness of swap economics. Although swaps are not, as Reilly points out, a panacea for either debt reduction or environmental protection, they offer a concrete tool to promote both ends, and tremendous potential for swaps still exists.

In chapter 10, Seema Jayachandran and Michael Kremer tackle the problem of illegitimate debt from a new angle. Instead of focusing on borrowers, they focus on the role and incentives of creditors who lend to questionable governments for illicit purposes. This approach follows a theme that runs throughout the book: Responsibility for bad loans should lie with lenders as much as borrowers.

Kremer and Jayachandran argue that as long as borrowing countries are obligated to repay odious debts, lenders will have no incentive to avoid bad loans. Furthermore, once a loan is made to an odious regime, no tribunal can be entrusted to label it as such—charges of politics and favoritism will always haunt the tribunal's decisions. The authors propose the establishment of a tribunal that would identify regimes as odious before they borrow money, thereby serving notice to lenders that they run the risk that their loans will be challenged by citizens or a subsequent government of the borrower when the time comes to collect.

Jack Boorman, the former chief policy advisor of the IMF, answers the Fund's critics in chapter 11 with his own ideas for resolving debt crises. Building on Henry and Arslanalp's work, he argues that a narrow focus on debt relief in HIPCs is insufficient (although, unlike Henry and Arslanalp, Boorman argues that the HIPC initiative is working to improve social spending and promote growth) and that the activist community and lenders must focus on broader measures of foreign aid and a fair trading environment. In the end, finding the "right" level of debt relief is impossible and ignores the more important aim of delivering a better life to impoverished people. Boorman goes on to argue for a proposal floated by the IMF for a sovereign debt restructuring mechanism (SDRM) to resolve pending debt crises in developing countries.

Kunibert Raffer, one of the original proponents of an international bankruptcy tribunal, argues in chapter 12 that the IMF's SDRM is misguided in several ways. Most importantly, the SDRM proposal leaves the IMF itself in the position of making two crucial decisions: whether to endorse a stay of payments to creditors, and what amount of debt is "sustainable"—that is, how much debt should be written off. This decision-making capacity creates a conflict of interest, as the IMF itself is almost always a creditor to countries experiencing debt crises. As an alternative to the IMF's SDRM, Raffer proposes a mechanism modeled on Chapter 9 of the U.S. bankruptcy code, which applies to municipalities and resolves some of the knotty problems of dealing with public (as compared with private) insolvency. An approach based on Chapter 9 would rely on ad hoc panels formed by the debtor and creditor committees and therefore would not require that the IMF serve as arbitrator. Treaties adopting the mechanism could also be avoided (though national law in several jurisdictions would need to be changed to void waivers of sovereign immunity in order to protect borrowers from lawsuits by holdout creditors), making implementation faster and more efficient.

In chapter 13, Arturo Porzecanski turns the sovereign bankruptcy argument on its head. Rather than debating the form of the international bankruptcy tribunal, Porzecanski questions the very need for it, arguing that the private market already produces efficient and speedy resolutions to impending crises. Porzecanski notes that private creditors have shown far more flexibility toward debtors than the official creditors such as the Paris Club and IMF, and he criticizes these public creditors for their reluctance to make comparable sacrifices.

Accordingly, Porzecanski's solution is not to create a sovereign bankruptcy tribunal but to empower private creditors to enforce bond contracts—for example, by attaching official foreign reserves held at the U.S. Federal Reserve or Bank for International Settlements—and to force public lenders to participate in restructurings by depriving them of preferred creditor status. Porzecanski argues that these steps will motivate public debtors and official creditors to come to earlier and more efficient resolutions of crises.

In the final chapter, chapter 14, Ann Pettifor describes what is perhaps the most powerful innovation for achieving debt relief for the poor since the mid-1990s: the mobilization of civil societies. The Jubilee 2000 movement was one of the most extraordinary phenomena of the twentieth century—uniting tens of millions of people and spanning nations and continents—all in the name of reducing the burden of developing-country debt. Pettifor's description of the movement's history and analysis of its successes and failures underscores the importance of civil society groups in the debate over debt and their potential role in promoting and implementing solutions.

Part I

Sovereign Debt:
History and Impacts

1

CREDITOR INITIATIVES IN THE 1980S AND 1990S

David Roodman

It is not widely understood outside circles of experts that the term "Third World debt crisis" in fact has referred to two distinct problems in international finance, the second of which is not a crisis. The first problem, a true crisis, broke out suddenly in 1982. Rich-country commercial banks had lent heavily to "middle-income" countries such as Turkey, Mexico, and Brazil—not the poorest of the poor in the community of nations—but global recession and rising interest rates popped the bubble. The debtors could no longer service all their debts and thus could no longer obtain new financing. The result for many of the debtors was years of economic depression and rising poverty. This strain of debt trouble was largely resolved by the early 1990s, though as recent events in Argentina during 2002–2003 demonstrate, it did not completely disappear.

The second kind of debt trouble is not a crisis at all, if by that term one means a problem that threatens to get drastically worse if it is not immediately resolved. This kind primarily involves the poorest of the poor nations, especially those of sub-Saharan Africa. It is perhaps best described as a chronic syndrome. It has spread gradually and arguably worsened to this day. It is different because low-income countries, regarded as risky investments by commercial bankers, have mainly attracted *official* lenders: bilateral agencies, which belong to individual governments' aid agencies, and multilateral lenders, such as the World Bank and the International Monetary Fund (IMF). Whereas commercial lenders followed the classic manic-depressive cycles of private finance, first overrunning countries in their eagerness to lend and then retreating en masse, official lenders stayed on a more even keel. They got into trouble more slowly and have been even slower to end it. The official debt problem gained a public profile in the late 1990s with the Jubilee 2000 campaign for debt cancelation.

Although distinct, the two kinds of debt trouble are historically interconnected. In particular, responses of creditor-country governments to the official debt problem during the 1990s cannot be fully understood without reference to the earlier commercial crisis. Largely in response to the first crisis came the rapid rise of policy-based lending, or "structural adjustment lending," as it is commonly known, whereby the World Bank and IMF made special loans in exchange for borrower promises of economic policy reform. Structural adjustment's failure to pull countries out of the debt trap led to the U.S.-led Brady Plan of 1989, which emphasized writing down old loans over the granting of new ones and proved more effective. Finally, beginning in the late 1980s in response to the debt problems of low-income nations, official creditors made a series of increasingly generous offers to reschedule or reduce official debt, the most recent of which is the enhanced debt initiative for heavily indebted poor countries, or HIPC, program. But the launch of each program in this series has implicitly acknowledged the inadequacy of its predecessor.

One lesson that emerges from this history is that ending debt trouble almost always requires that creditors and debtors strike realistic compromises on repayment. The Brady Plan, for example, successfully fostered compromise. Meanwhile, attempts by creditor-side governments to fix the problem by intervening in borrowers' domestic policy making and political processes have generally not helped. Structural adjustment generally failed to boost borrowers' ability to repay bank loans. The official debt-reduction programs offered compromises but evidently not realistic ones, for official debt trouble persisted.

Among policy makers working today to prevent and solve commercial debt problems, the lessons have not been lost. In 2001, IMF management proposed the creation of a sovereign-debt restructuring mechanism, a sort of bankruptcy court that would in spirit institutionalize the sorts of processes that led to compromises under the Brady Plan. But, as currently conceived, the SDRM would "restructure" debt owed to private lenders only, making it of little use for the poorest countries, which are primarily indebted to official lenders, including the IMF. Indeed, the lessons of the 1980s and 1990s appear to have been mostly lost on those working to end the official debt troubles of the poorest nations— lost not just on creditor institutions such as the U.S. Treasury, the World Bank, and the IMF but on many nongovernmental organizations that have lobbied so effectively for debt cancelation.

The Rise of Policy-Based Lending

Like many major historical developments, the rise of policy-based lending by the World Bank and IMF in the early 1980s had aspects of both the earthquake and the glacier. On the one hand, it appeared to be a novel response to traumatic events. These included the oil price spikes of the 1970s, which were a severe economic shock for oil-importing developing countries, as well as a huge uptick in global interest rates caused by U.S. Federal Reserve Chairman Paul Volcker's war on inflation.

But the rise of adjustment lending also marked the extension of development aid into the new arena of economic policy making. As such, it was a response to long-standing problems and part of an old pattern. Indeed, the history of development aid since President Truman can be seen as a cyclical process in which aid agencies reluctantly, but repeatedly, widen their understanding of what development requires, each time broadening their agendas to match. The pattern can be seen clearly in the history of the World Bank right through to the genesis of policy-based lending.

In its early years, the Bank mainly financed discrete packages of infrastructure such as dams and roads. But it became increasingly apparent that poor countries, unlike postwar Western Europe, needed more than physical infrastructure to progress. Thus, especially under the presidency of Robert McNamara (1968–81), the Bank increasingly lent for projects on the "social" aspects of development, such as education and health (Kapur et al. 1997). And toward the end of his time in office, McNamara appeared to harbor even deeper doubts about the Bank's approach. The focus on projects, from dam building to school building, was missing the mark. Especially in Africa, many failed projects seemed to have been foredoomed by the economic environment in which they operated. Artificially high official exchange rates, for example, made imports cheap and undermined domestic industry. With the passage of time, the failure could no longer be denied. Again, the conception of development assistance had to widen, this time to encompass economic policy.

In 1980, McNamara practically ambushed the Bank's executive board with a proposal to ramp up what had been a relatively rare kind of lending, which would provide direct budgetary support to governments making major economic policy changes (Mosley et al. 1991).[1] Borrowing governments would not need to specify how they would spend or invest the funds. One thing that did not change was the implicit assumption that experts in Washington, D.C., could analyze societies far different from their own well enough to give governments reliable and realistic advice.

Board members greeted the proposal with suspicion. Why should the Bank risk its money in countries whose economic policies had landed them in trouble? Did not the Bank's charter prohibit meddling in the political affairs of client nations, and weren't economic reforms inherently political? If there was no meddling—if the borrowers promised policy reform completely for domestic reasons—then why does the Bank need to demand that the borrowers commit to the reforms in writing and threaten to punish noncompliance by ceasing lending? More basically, why did those countries need money in order to reform their policies? If the Bank did not tie the loans to specific projects, could it trust the borrowers to use the funds well?

McNamara carried the day. These huge, almost frictionless loans would help the Bank expand its mandate and portfolio. They did not require years of planning, environmental impact projections, or follow-up assessments the way a dam did. But many of the board's concerns proved prescient.

The IMF's entry into adjustment lending to developing countries also sprang from old roots. The institution's original mission was to manage the postwar system of fixed exchange rates among Western industrial countries. When a country ran short on reserves of foreign currency, it could borrow more from the IMF rather than desperately selling its own currency below the official rate. Often, the IMF would condition its currency loans on the borrower agreeing to economic reforms meant to end the domestic imbalance that was causing the shortage of foreign currency. But in 1971, as U.S. inflation rose and put downward pressure on the dollar, President Nixon pulled the United States out of the system, leaving it in disarray, rather than take more politically difficult steps to tame inflation. Seeking a new mission, the IMF gradually lent more to poorer countries, especially those hurt by the oil crises. The debt crisis gave the IMF an opening to continue its transformation into a "development" institution.

The year 1982 was thus a sort of appointment with destiny for the two international financial institutions (IFIs). It gave life to a nascent lending approach at the World Bank and gave a whole new purpose to the IMF.

Before Mexico announced in August 1982 that it was on the verge of default, rich-country banks had been cooperative, if increasingly nervous, providers of finance to dozens of poorer nations. Afterward, the climate could not have been more different, as nations from Argentina to Zambia repeatedly came within a hair of defaulting.

Like stock market bubbles, international lending bubbles are a recurring feature of the international capitalist economy. Major international lending crises occurred in the 1820s, 1870s, and 1930s. But the 1980s crisis departed from the historical pattern in one important respect. This time, the major creditors were banks, not bond investors. They numbered in the dozens rather than thousands, and so were much more able to organize themselves and summon public officials to their cause (Suter 1992). When U.S. banks came calling on the Reagan administration for help, the Treasury Department initially greeted the banks' pleas for aid with the hostility of ideological free-marketeers. "You made the loans, you collect them," said one official (Lissakers 1991: 204). But pragmatism and Wall Street's political clout soon triumphed over ideology. The administration pressed Congress into raising the U.S. contribution to the IMF so that it could lend more to countries with big debt-service bills coming due (Makin 1983). In return, as a sort of collateral, the IMF was to demand reforms of these countries' economic policies that the Treasury Department hoped would quickly end the crisis. Thus, once the U.S. government and the IFIs were brought into play, the debtor nations faced a united front. The world's most powerful banks, governments, and multilateral lenders gave them a choice: repudiate their obligations, alienate great powers, and risk losing all ability to borrow for the foreseeable future—or accept the debt burden and try, in the economic term, to "adjust."

Debtor nations almost always chose negotiation over repudiation. When Brazil and Peru unilaterally halted payments in 1987, for example, the commercial banks and the IFIs yielded no ground, and the wayward debtors soon returned to the fold out of desperation for new lending (Lissakers 1991: 202). Brazil's president, José Sarney, assessed the balance of power this way: "[W]e cannot destroy the international system. . . . We can scratch it, but it can destroy us."

Still, the story was more complex than that. In many debtor nations, the political classes that supported the government, such as urban elites, stood to gain from new international loans just as they had from the old ones—yet were able to shift a disproportionate share of the costs of *repaying* those old loans onto others (MacEwan 1986). The loan money had flowed in along channels cut by politics, and so did the repayments flow out—but often along different channels. As the director of UNICEF put it, "It is hardly too brutal an oversimplification to say that the rich got the loans but the poor got the debts" (UNICEF 1989: 11).

The policy reform packages that countries agreed to enact in exchange for the IFI loans were often known as "adjustment," "stabilization," or "austerity" programs. These would function, it was hoped, as the economic equivalent of retraining for the laid-off worker. In practice—and this is a point often overlooked—the pressure to pay debts drove borrowers' economic policies as much as any blueprint drawn up by the IFIs because, like families fallen on hard times, debtor nations had few economic options. To squeeze foreign exchange out of their economies, they had to spend less of it or earn more. The rebalancing had to occur within each government's budget because the debts were contracted by governments through spending cuts or tax hikes. The rebalancing also had to occur within the nation's trade flow through higher export earnings or lower import spending. Thus, typical prescriptions included spending cuts, liberalization of foreign-exchange regulation in order to make imports more expensive and exports more competitive, and tight monetary policies to control inflation.

For most adjusting countries, already reeling from balance-of-payments problems, the full-repayment through austerity strategy succeeded only in prolonging paralysis. Between 1950 and 1980, gross domestic product (GDP) per person had risen 105% in Latin America and 72% in Africa. But between 1980 and 1990, GDP per capita fell 7% on both continents (Maddison 1995: 21–22). In cross-country statistical analysis, Cohen (1997) found that debt problems figured in the slowdown: The more vulnerable to eventual debt trouble a country seemed to be in 1980, judging by indicators such as its ratio of foreign debt to GDP, the less it grew from then on, other factors being equal.

Austerity failed to resolve the debt crisis in part because it was a short-term response to an emergency rather than a long-term strategy for economic development. In countries that practiced austerity, private and public investment usually fell (Killick 1998). Private investors were spooked by doubts about the economic future of debtor nations, and governments preoccupied with meeting their next debt payments cut back on investment in infrastructure, health care, and education (Jayarajah et al. 1996). As debtor economies ate their seed corn, output fell, unemployment climbed, and poverty spread.

Another source of the growth slowdown was falling demand and sagging prices for the exports of debtor nations. In the first half of 1985, for instance, Thailand exported 31% more rice than a year before—and earned 8% less

(George 1998: 61). An index of the "terms of trade" of non–oil-exporting developing countries, which measures how much they could import with the earnings from a given volume of their exports, fell from 100 in 1970 to 76 in 1985 before recovering to around 85 by the late 1990s (IMF 2000: 144–45). Prices fell in part because each nation that tried to bring in more foreign exchange by increasing exports of wheat or tropical timber was competing with dozens of other nations pursuing the same strategy. In addition, rich industrial nations spent the 1980s and 1990s raising import barriers against shirts, sugar, and other exports of developing countries—and subsidizing their own exports of those products. The World Bank estimates that erasing barriers to merchandise exports would raise export earnings of developing countries some $124 billion (U.S.) a year—enough, if it had been accruing since 1982, to repay all the debts.[2] In effect, rich countries have demanded that poor countries repay debts but refused the goods offered as payment (World Bank 2002).

Structural Adjustment

By the mid-1980s, it became clear that austerity was prolonging and deepening most borrowers' problems with debt. As is often the case when institutions encounter failure, the response of major creditor institutions was not to deemphasize the failing approach but to press it harder. With the backing of the U.S. Treasury, the World Bank and the IMF increasingly pressed troubled debtors to make still deeper reforms in exchange for adjustment loans—to make *structural* adjustments. If governments privatized state enterprises, ended subsidies, removed barriers to foreign trade and investment, and generally got out of the way of private enterprise, the IFIs argued, then investors would take risks again, economies would grow, and tax revenues and foreign exchange would flow into government coffers. In essence, structural adjustment sought to bring the economics of Reagan and British Prime Minister Margaret Thatcher to the developing world.

Unfortunately, structural adjustment loans, like the more austerity-oriented loans before them, generally did not work. With respect to core economic policy goals, most of the evidence says that *IFI-backed* adjustment programs have reduced investment, left inflation unchanged, and given at most a modest boost to economic growth and the balance of payments (Killick 1998). During the 1980s and 1990s, the IFIs made adjustment loans to every African nation. But according to a World Bank survey of ten countries, only two—Ghana and Uganda—sustained much commitment to reform (Devarajan et al. 2001). The authorized history of the World Bank published in 1997 concluded: "Perhaps the only argument that will convince the critics of reform [in Africa] that they are wrong will be several cases of definite structural adjustment successes . . . and these have not yet occurred" (Lancaster 1997: 171).

In contrast with austerity programs, which had a certain inexorable logic, structural adjustment stood on weaker theoretical ground. True, countless heavy-handed government interventions were hampering economic development in many countries in the 1970s. Bloated civil services and corrupt leaders drained away revenue. Complex trade and tariff regimes cosseted uncompetitive industries and gave ample opportunity for corruption. But it did not follow that paring government down wholesale would bring economic rebirth—even if it could be done.

Historically, what has mattered most for development is not whether governments intervened in the workings of the economy but the fine details of how they did so. The economies that have grown the fastest since the early 1800s— including those of China, Japan, South Korea, and the United States—saw extensive government involvement in trade and industry (Wade 1994). In an analysis of developing countries' experiences with economic growth since 1975, Harvard economist Dani Rodrik found that two factors best predicted the growth rate of an economy: how much the country invested, and whether the government held the domestic economy steady amidst the turbulence of the global economy. Keeping inflation under control and the currency's exchange rate realistic, major goals of basic austerity plans, mattered. But the openness to foreign trade and investment that *structural* adjustment aimed for did not show up as significant by itself (Rodrik 1999).

Peering deeper, Rodrik found evidence that the key to economic stability was political cohesion. Most governments that stabilized their economies amidst the oil shocks, interest rate gyrations, financial panics, and global recession since the early 1980s had strong mechanisms for reaching political consensus and compromise. Those mechanisms included democracy, as in South Korea and Thailand during the Asian economic crisis of the 1990s, and social programs that made most citizens economically secure, as under the dictatorship of Singapore. Lack of social cohesion, on the other hand, sometimes led countries such as Bolivia to print money and court 50% per month hyperinflation rather than confront politically tougher choices about whose taxes to raise. The paths to high investment were also diverse. In some countries, private entrepreneurs took much of the initiative; in others, they were closely supervised by government planners; in still others, governments did much of the investing themselves. What mattered most was that it happened. "The lesson of history," Rodrik concludes, "is that ultimately all successful countries develop their own brand of national capitalism" (Rodrik 1999: 77–100). When it comes to economic development, one size does not fit all.

Structural adjustment lending faced another layer of problems. Not only was the structural adjustment advice of questionable value, it often went unheeded— or was unneeded. In dozens of case studies, independent economists and political scientists have documented how borrowing governments typically sidestepped the promises they made in adjustment agreements with the World Bank and the IMF, obeyed the letter but not the spirit, or agreed to steps they would have taken anyway (Killick 1998).

The reasons for the historical weakness of conditionality are diverse (see table 1.1) For one, as Rodrik suggests, economic policies in borrower countries were mainly determined by domestic politics. In Zambia, for example, in 1986–87, strikes by government workers and riots over a 120% price increase for staple

TABLE 1.1   Reasons IMF and World Bank pressure for structural adjustment is weaker than it seems

Reason	Examples
Debt trouble	In Bolivia, a debt crisis in the early 1980s led the government to print money, sparking hyperinflation and chaos. In 1985–86, a new administration adopted a harsh stabilization program that raised taxes, laid off state workers, and stopped hyperinflation. Adjustment loans from the IMF and the World Bank came later and thus contributed little to the policy shift (Morales and Sachs 1989).
Domestic politics	In Zambia, in 1986–87, strikes by government workers and riots over a 120% price increase for staple foods forced the government to restore food subsidies and abandon its agreed adjustment program (Killick 1998).
Disasters	In Malawi, in 1986, drought and an influx of 700,000 refugees from civil war in Mozambique necessitated large corn imports and contributed to the government's decision to reverse commitments to end fertilizer and crop subsidies (Harrigan 1991).
Finance	Adjustment lending to Argentina continued through most of the 1980s with little effect except to bolster forces for the status quo with additional funds. Withdrawal after 1988 deepened the economic crisis that soon forced reform (Gunatilaka and Marr 1998).
Geopolitics	In the Philippines, the U.S. government, which viewed the country as an important ally, apparently pressed the IMF and World Bank to keep lending despite low compliance until the final years (1984–86) of the Ferdinand Marcos regime (Mosley 1991; Killick 1998).
Pressure to lend and appear successful	In 1990, the World Bank promised a $100 million (U.S.) loan to support Kenya in ending its rationing of foreign exchange for purchasing imports. The government then resumed rationing. But local Bank officials did not alert the Bank's board for fear that it would not approve the loan (Collier 1999).
Multiple conditions	Among a sample of 13 sub-Saharan African nations, each adjustment agreement in 1999–2000 had an average of 114 policy reform conditions. It is unrealistic for lenders to demand complete compliance with so many conditions. Other surveys have found that countries technically typically comply with 50–60% of conditions (Kapur and Webb 2000: 6; Mosley, Harrigan, and Toye 1991).
Ease of undermining commitments	Starting in 1984, the government of Turkey levied special taxes on imports to support extrabudgetary funds that in turn financed housing and other popular programs. This undermined but did not technically violate loan agreements (Kirkpatrick and Onis 1991).

Source: Worldwatch Institute, Copyright 2001, Worldwatch.org

foods forced the government to restore food subsidies and abandon its structural adjustment program. Bolivia, by contrast, did enact an adjustment program, laying off state workers and raising taxes in 1985–86—but domestic political support for drastic steps to end the hyperinflation drove these changes, not the later pressure from IFIs. Natural and human disasters also hampered compliance. In Malawi, in 1986, drought in the southern half of the country and an influx of

700,000 hungry refugees from war in Mozambique pushed the government into reversing its commitment to end fertilizer and crop subsidies. Then, too, lending millions of dollars to governments uncommitted to reform bolstered forces protecting the status quo.

A natural question is why IFIs, with observers based in or regularly visiting every borrower country, did not spot these deviations from promised reforms and halt lending. But, for their own reasons, the IFIs often found it difficult to say no. Just as car companies exist to make cars, lending institutions exist to lend. Again, no one epitomized the problem more than Robert McNamara in his tenure at the World Bank. Upon assuming the presidency, he vowed to double its lending within five years (Kapur et al. 1997). Thereafter, lending targets sent powerful incentives down the hierarchy for speed and volume in lending, strengthening what a high-profile World Bank report in 1992 called the loan "approval culture" (World Bank 1992a: iii). One World Bank employee described the culture in the 1980s:

> When I worked on Bangladesh we decided at a country program division meeting that the lending program for the next year should be slowed, because Bangladesh could not [use well] any more money. Everyone agreed. Then the division chief spoke. He said he also completely agreed. But if he went to his director and told him the lending should be slowed down, "tomorrow you will have a new division chief." (Wade 1989)

Growing debt troubles have compounded such pressures to lend. Seeking to minimize the appearance of problems, the IMF, World Bank, and regional institutions such as the African Development Bank have often lent still more to countries struggling to service their old loans. Paul Collier, director of the World Bank's Development Research Group, explained: "An aid cutoff is very likely to trigger a suspension of debt service payments by the government. While the net financial impact on the IFIs may well be the same whether they lend money with which they are repaid or suspend lending and are not repaid, the impact on staff careers is liable to be radically different. People do not build careers in financial institutions on default and a lack of loan disbursement" (Collier 1999: 321).

Pressure to lend still seems strong today. At the World Bank, the most publicly self-critical of the multilateral lenders, a 1997 draft internal report warned about the "pressure to lend; fear of offending the client . . . fear that a realistic, and thus more modest, project would be dismissed as too small and inadequate in its impact . . . and more generally, a conviction held by many staff members that the function of the Bank is to help create the conditions for operations to go forward, not to 'sit around and wait' " (Rich 2002). The same year, the environment-focused chapter of the authorized history of the World Bank concluded that "a majority of operational staff, in all probability, still believed there was not a strong . . . case for many of the Bank's [environmental] standards and procedures. Even now some still see them as . . . interfering in the task for which they are most rewarded: getting projects to the Board on time for approval" (Wade 1997: 731).

Then, too, major shareholders, especially the United States, sometimes pressured the IFIs into making loans for political reasons. A survey of 17 countries with well-documented histories of adjustment borrowing from the IMF found that pressure from major shareholders softened the IMF's stance in one-third of the countries, including the Philippines and Sudan, both Cold War allies of the United States (Killick 1995).

The competing pressures over lending decisions are revealed in the pattern of disbursements on adjustment loans. International financial institutions normally disburse adjustment loans in installments to extend their leverage over borrowers. In the 1980s and early 1990s, the World Bank delayed 75% of second installments because borrowers were slipping on agreed reforms. But it eventually granted all but 8%, typically after some face-saving gesture on the part of the borrower (Mosley et al. 1991; Killick 1998). Similarly, the IMF abandoned half of its adjustment loans between 1979 and 1993 after the first installment—but normally then negotiated a new loan with the borrower (Killick 1995).

International financial institutions have not been completely powerless to influence policy. In 1996, for example, the World Bank refused to release the second installment of an adjustment loan to Papua New Guinea because of the government's failure to make agreed anticorruption reforms in the logging industry. The government protested bitterly but gave in after a year and appeared for the time being to be reforming. A World Resources Institute study credits this success to the Bank's desire to be seen fighting for the environment, to a relatively intimate understanding of local circumstances among Bank staff, and to a strong domestic constituency for reform. But such a constellation of circumstances has been rare (Dubash and Filer 2000).

In sum, the second major creditor response to debt trouble in the 1980s and 1990s—structural adjustment lending—failed for two reasons. First, the particular package of policies it promoted, though potentially helpful when done in certain ways and certain contexts, could not realistically have been expected to bring about enough economic progress to get most countries back on top of their debts. Second, the IFIs proved surprisingly unable to change borrower policies anyway. On the evidence from the 1980s and 1990s, IFIs appear to be much better at pushing a country than steering it. Thus, when loans flow to countries that are developing in healthy directions, they can speed progress. But when pressure to lend puts capital in the hands of governments unlikely to use it well, it becomes destructive.

The main, if unintentional, effect of adjustment loans, then—for both austerity and structural adjustment—was to prolong the hope and insistence among creditors that the nations would eventually pay all their debts. This insistence left debtors staggering from one rescheduling agreement to the next. In the end, heroic efforts to maintain the appearance of full repayment did not protect the reputations of debtor nations among investors the way the creditors argued they would. Instead, these efforts stymied economic growth and exacted a price measured in the misery of those least able to defend against them, and they increased the unpayable debts they were meant to diminish.

Neither of the dominant public voices on adjustment have worked very hard to educate the public on the complex realities of structural adjustment lending. For most of the 1980s and 1990s, the IFIs were slow to recognize and publicize their relative lack of influence.[3] Paradoxically, the IFIs' severest critics among nongovernmental organizations (NGOs) also tended to credit the IFIs with more influence than they actually possessed in their eagerness to attack IFIs for perpetuating poverty.

The Brady Plan

Two continents, South America and Africa, were quickly brought low by debt crises starting in the early 1980s. But their fates then diverged—and the reason for the difference lies in the second major creditor response since the 1980s to developing-country debt troubles. By most measures, the crisis that struck in 1982 in Latin America (and in other middle-income nations such as Turkey and the Philippines) came to an end by the mid-1990s. In Latin America and the Caribbean, net transfers on lending (new loan receipts less payments on old loans) turned positive in 1993. Capital flow defined more broadly, to include portfolio and direct investment flows, flipped from $3.4 billion (U.S.) outward in 1990 to $38 billion inward in 1993 (World Bank 2002). Suddenly, foreign exchange was plentiful, and servicing debt was much easier. By mid-2002, only two nations in the region—Argentina and Nicaragua—were not servicing all their foreign debts, down from 17 in 1983. But Africa, the center of the crisis in the low-income nations, remains mired in debt to this day. Twenty-one African states had put servicing of some or all of their debts on hold in 2002—compared with 19 in 1990.[4]

What sent Africa and Latin America on different trajectories? In a word, compromise. Commercial creditors, which dominate lending to Latin America, were quicker to compromise than were official creditors, which dominate lending to Africa. In March 1988, for example, Bolivia's commercial creditors agreed to sell half the country's outstanding foreign commercial claims back to Bolivia for 6 cents on the dollar (Bulow and Rogoff 1990). Commercial creditors, in other words, accepted a 94% loss in exchange for wiping bad loans to one small nation off their books. And some creditors swapped their old bank loans for new bonds with easier repayment terms. For instance, Argentina arranged with banks to replace some of its debts with bonds that had the same face value but an interest rate of just 4% and a 25-year repayment schedule, including a 12-year grace period. In another type of deal, a debt-for-equity swap, Argentina retired $5 billion (U.S.) in debt in 1990 by giving banks its national airline and its phone company (World Bank 1992b: 52–53, 93).

The growing acceptance among banks of such deals allowed the U.S. government to change its position on the debt crisis. In 1988, Treasury Secretary Nicholas Brady publicly described as a failure the outgoing Reagan administration's insistence on full repayment through adjustment:

> [W]e must acknowledge that serious problems and impediments to a successful resolution of the debt crisis remain. . . . Growth has not been sufficient. Nor has

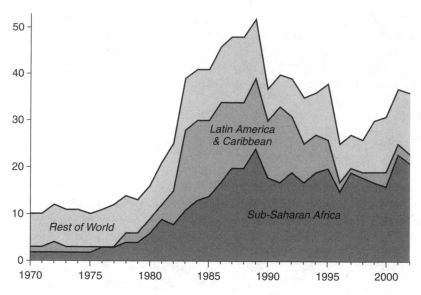

Figure 1.1. Number of countries not servicing all their foreign debts, 1970–2000.
Source: Worldwatch Institute, Copyright 2001, Worldwatch.org

the level of economic policy reform been adequate. Capital flight has drained
resources from debtor nations' economies. . . . Inflation has not been brought under
control. . . . The path towards greater creditworthiness . . . for many debtor countries needs to involve debt reduction. (Lissakers 1991: 227)

The key to resolution, Brady said, was compromise—just as it had been in
every debt crisis since 1820. Under the Brady Plan, announced in early 1989,
each debtor nation gave its commercial lenders a menu of choices. One option
was to lend more money to cover payments coming due. Another was for the
bank to tear up some of its IOUs in exchange for new ones. The new IOUs
could have the same principal as the old ones but a lower interest rate, like
those Argentinean bonds. Or the promised interest payments could stay low for
a few years and then climb. Payments could even be tied to the price of the
country's exports: When export earnings rose, banks would share in the gains,
like stockholders.

One option that was not on the banks' menus was *not* to compromise. If it
had been, then Citibank, for example, might have waited for Deutsche Bank to
strike a deal with Brazil, accept a loss, and help Brazil regain creditworthiness—
at which point Citibank would have demanded full repayment. But Deutsche
Bank and other competitors, of course, would have waited, too. In the ban on
doing nothing lay the genius of the Brady Plan.

Between 1990 and 1994, debtors including Argentina, Brazil, Mexico, Nigeria, and the Philippines struck Brady agreements, in each case ending years
of repeated, crisis-atmosphere negotiations (World Bank 2000). The compromises gave borrowing governments financial breathing room, lifted the atmo-

sphere of uncertainty, brought investment back, and helped rekindle economic growth. As a result, middle-income nations serviced their debts more easily for the rest of the 1990s.

Creditor governments, however, showed less interest in compromise than private bankers. In Venice, in June 1987, leaders of the G7 nations made their first accommodation to the debt troubles in the poorest nations. They agreed to let debtors defer payments on outstanding loans, provided they stuck to structural adjustment agreements with the IMF. At succeeding summits, the G7 gradually offered more. There were the Toronto terms in 1988, the first to allow some outright debt cancelation; the Houston terms in 1990; the Enhanced Toronto or London terms of 1991; the Naples terms of 1994; and the Lyon terms of 1997. The failure of each plan could be measured by the stagnating or worsening indebtedness indicators of the poorest nations.

Creditor governments delayed confronting the official debt crisis in part because they could. They maximized their bargaining power by presenting a solid front, through an informal institution called the Paris Club, while insisting on negotiating with debtors one at a time. "[T]he Paris Club has generally been able to rally its members in a relatively short time along the lines of interpreting reschedulings as extraordinary short-term measures that should not be confused with development efforts" (Suter 1992). Especially after the Cold War ended, most debtors were in no position to push for concessions.

As a result, the politics of debt within rich nations has generally determined how their governments have responded to the official debt problems of the poorest nations. Historically, there was no strong lobby within creditor nations for resolving official debt troubles. But in the late 1990s, the political balance shifted decisively. In 1996, British Christian aid groups launched one of the most successfully organized international movements ever: the Jubilee 2000 campaign. By the end of 2000, when Jubilee 2000 shut itself down, more than 100 organizations belonged, ranging from small nongovernmental groups in Uganda, to dozens of local, church-based chapters, to heavyweights such as Oxfam.[5] They demanded that creditors cancel debt immediately and that debtors use the savings to fight poverty. The campaign gained clout from the 24 million signatures on its petitions and from endorsements from Pope John Paul II, the Dalai Lama, and U2 lead singer Bono. And it drew strength from the Bible's book of Leviticus, which records God's laws for ancient Israel. Leviticus 25: declared that every fiftieth year was to be a year of Jubilee, in which creditors forgave debtors and farmers reclaimed land they had sold off to survive a bad year. Such redistribution was intended to prevent extreme inequalities from arising to tear the fabric of Israelite society.

Jubilee 2000 scored a major victory at the G7 summit in 1999, where official creditors announced the enhanced HIPC initiative. The initiative, which is administered by the IMF and the World Bank, represents an artful political compromise among the opponents and proponents of quick cancelation and multilateral lending agencies as well. The initiative bows to Jubilee's demand by promising that bilateral and multilateral creditors alike will write off substantially more debt than before—up to 45%, on average, for 42 qualifying nations.[6]

It also requires each debtor to first design a poverty reduction strategy paper (PRSP) in consultation with civil society groups, such as NGOs and churches, and then to implement the strategy with savings from debt cancelation. But by requiring structural adjustment, the HIPC initiative accommodates those skeptical about writing blank checks to dictators. And it helps the multilateral creditors by partially reimbursing them (through an HIPC trust fund) for canceling debt. Finally, it attempts to head off criticism of official lenders by casting the write-offs as a one-time act of generosity rather than an unavoidable consequence of ongoing problems. In addition, Canada, Italy, the United Kingdom, the United States, and other countries individually offered to write off all their loans to poor debtors, which could bring the total reduction to 55%. Most of these offers piggyback on the HIPC initiative: To take advantage of them, countries must first qualify for the initiative.

The Enhanced HIPC Initiative: The Bankruptcy Perspective

Only time will tell if the enhanced HIPC initiative, which represents the third major creditor response to developing-country debt trouble, will succeed in ending that trouble in the poorest nations. But the lessons from the first two responses strongly suggest it will not.

One observation is essential for evaluating the HIPC program. Most HIPCs are, to the extent that states can be, bankrupt. They cannot realistically be expected to pay back more than a fraction of their external debts. As recently as the late 1990s, commercial debts of Benin and Rwanda traded at 10 cents on the U.S. dollar in secondary markets. Honduras's commercial debt has gone for 25 cents on the dollar.[7] Private investors, in other words, do not expect these nations to repay most of their debts. The U.S. government estimated that $346 million of the $3.8 billion owed it by HIPCs at the end of 1998 was collectable, or 9% (GAO 2000: 128). Cohen (2000) has drawn on the experience of middle-income debtors in the 1980s to project how much poor countries will ultimately pay on their loans from both commercial and public lenders. His results should be interpreted carefully because they are based on an extrapolation from the experience of countries with predominantly commercial rather than official debt problems. That said, they suggest that the HIPCs together can repay $45.9 billion (U.S.), which is 22% of the face value of the loans (28% of present value).[8] Country by country, the results also suggest that even after going through the HIPC program, most of the countries will still owe significantly more than they can ultimately pay (see table 1.2). Put another way, about 90% of the debt to be written off under HIPC would never have been repaid anyway.

The notion that most HIPCs owe much more than they can repay is straightforward. Yet it has radical implications for the two dominant interpretations of the debt problem, those emanating from official creditors on the one hand and NGOs in the Jubilee network on the other. To the extent that HIPCs are effectively bankrupt, it follows that they are not servicing their debts. Thus, if they *appear* to be servicing their debts, that is in large part because they are simul-

TABLE 1.2 Value of debts: paper and actual, 1999

	(present value, in million U.S. $)		
Country	On paper	Estimated collectable[a]	Remaining after enhanced HIPC program[b]
Benin	1,067	586	973
Bolivia	4,808	1,077	2,333
Mozambique	2,173	408	886
Uganda	2,388	535	1,157
Zambia	4,548	795	1,715
All 42 HIPCs	161,175	49,560	88,006

[a]Using methodology of Cohen (2000).
[b]Based on a debt/exports target of 150% using exports of 1999.

taneously receiving new money from official lenders in the form of loans or grants in a phenomenon known as defensive lending (or granting). As discussed earlier, defensive lending may serve the interests of lending institutions and their individual employees better than a cutoff of new lending, even though the net financial transfer may be about the same. Birdsall et al. (2002) found that in 1977–87, among countries with high debts to multilateral lenders, paying more in debt service had almost no effect on receipts of loans and grants. But in 1988–98, as the number of high–multilateral-debt countries greatly expanded, almost the exact opposite occurred. Every dollar of debt service due led to 94 cents of additional loans or grants being given. In other words, at the margin, official donors covered essentially all the debt service paid by high–multilateral-debt countries.

In fact, 24 of the 42 HIPCs received more in new loans than they spent servicing old ones during 1998–2000. Adding in grants, every HIPC received more from official agencies than it sent to them (World Bank 2002) (see figure 1.2).

In lobbying the parliaments of rich countries to contribute to the HIPC trust fund, multilateral development banks and many NGOs have argued that the money is needed to pay for debt relief. But it costs almost nothing to cancel loans most of which would never have been repaid anyway. It is rather a matter of honest accounting. By the same token, to the extent that low-income debtors are not truly servicing their foreign debts, debt payments are not coming at the cost of domestic health and education spending. Debt is not killing 19,000 children a day as the Jubilee campaign asserted. By the same token, canceling uncollectable debt *in itself* will not free up more money to spend on health and education or other priorities. To see why, consider a simple example. Before entering the HIPC program, a borrower is spending $400 million (U.S.) a year servicing debts to official lenders overseas. But it is receiving even more—$500 million a year—which probably reflects defensive lending and granting. Then,

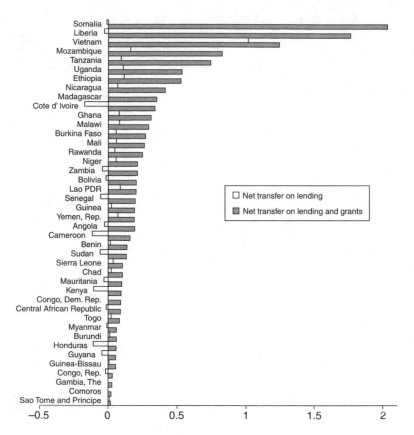

Figure 1.2. HIPCs: Average annual net official transfers, 1998–2000 (billion $).

under HIPC, enough of its debts are written off to reduce its annual debt service by $200 million, to $200 million. But its receipts of grants and loans simultaneously drop by the same amount, to $300 million. As before, it is receiving $100 million net from donors. The cloud of uncertainty created by heavy debt has been reduced, but no funding has been freed up for social services (see figure 1.3).

There is one important caveat to this line of argument. Under the HIPC program, a trust fund channels new aid from rich-country governments to multilateral lenders, who can be expected to relend it to poor countries. To the extent that donors are not paying for their contributions to the trust fund by cutting other forms of aid—to the extent the contributions are truly additional—aid receipts in poor countries will go up. These receipts, however, will take the form of loans and will thus contribute once more to the build-up of debt (see the third panel of figure 1.3). Thus, even if the HIPC program succeeds in reducing countries' debts to the "sustainable" maximum of 150% of their annual

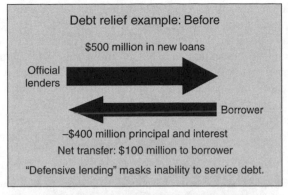

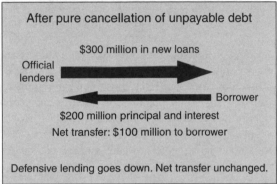

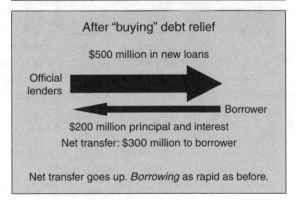

Figure 1.3. Net resource transfers: Before and after debt relief.

export earnings, their debts will soon rise again, surpassing the officially sustainable level.[9]

Moreover, the new lending will occur without appreciable reform of creditor institutions that would give hope that history will not repeat itself. When governments of developing countries bail out insolvent private banks, economists working for lending agencies worry about the "moral hazard" this creates by effectively rewarding and encouraging bad lending decisions. Similarly, the trust fund partially insulates multilateral lenders from past mistakes and thus may help entrench the management that led to those mistakes. Similarly, casting HIPC as an act of generosity rather than reconciliation to the reality of bad debts insulates lenders from what could be healthy public scrutiny of past mistakes.

The HIPC initiative *appears* to reflect the lessons of history on the weakness of structural adjustment conditionality. It requires debtor governments to work with nongovernmental groups on plans to fight poverty with savings from debt relief, known as poverty reduction strategy papers. This is in a way a welcome note of humility. Through the PRSP condition, lenders are tacitly admitting that they and borrowing governments do not hold a monopoly on wisdom about fighting poverty, and that domestic political ownership is essential if envisioned reforms are to be carried out. By supporting domestic voices calling for reforms to benefit the poor, the PRSP requirement could make a subtle contribution to the political and economic development of borrowing nations over the long term.

But from another point of view, the lessons on the weakness of conditionality appear to have gone unheeded. The HIPC program still requires debtors to stick to a standard structural adjustment plan—for three to six years to obtain permanent debt reduction (to reach the "completion point"). According to NGOs polled by the European Network on Debt and Development (EURODAD), most local IMF representatives still seemed to care more about structural adjustment than poverty reduction strategies (EURODAD 2000). Debtor governments are taking the cue, emphasizing measures such as privatization of state companies in their economic plans.

Moreover, requiring PRSPs is arguably the most ambitious use of conditionality yet. It extends the instrument beneath economic policy into the deeper firmament of the political process. A consultation process raises questions akin to those confronted by drafters of a constitution. Who should participate? Churches? NGOs based in the capital? Elected leaders of certain villages? What is a legitimate process for selecting participants? Once selected, should participants have a veto, a vote, or just a voice? For officials on the debtor side, who must design the processes, these questions are among the most politically charged they could ask. For officials on the creditor side, who must judge the process, the questions are hard to answer with confidence. A report by the U.S. General Accounting Office gives a sense of the tensions:

> [I]n 1997 the government of Bolivia conducted a "national dialogue" to involve civil society in its effort to build support for its new economic and social priorities. Although government officials considered that effort to have been quite worthwhile, some nongovernmental organizations and donors . . . disagreed. They told us the dialogue consisted of a 1-day meeting in which the government selected whom to invite, involved little regional participation, little background information, and used the meeting to present its views. One nongovernmental organization representative characterized this effort as having been more a "regional monologue than a national dialogue." (GAO 2000: 123)

The HIPC initiative has spurred the government of Bolivia to organize a second, more inclusive consultation that may prove more worthy of the PRSP label.

It would be hard to design debt-cancelation conditions more likely to engender domestic political opposition and more difficult to enforce. Debtors uncommitted to poverty reduction—or less responsive to pressure from civil society—may be putting on disingenuous PRSP shows in order to obtain debt relief. On the other hand, debtors that are committed to helping the poor will probably owe their commitment much more to their own history and leadership than to outside pressure.

In sum, the HIPC program, although a step forward, does not adequately take into account the lessons from other attempts by creditors in the 1980s and 1990s to respond to debt trouble in the developing world. It does not strike realistic compromises on repayment in the spirit of the Brady Plan. It relies too much on conditionality, including structural adjustment conditions, to put borrowers on a sustainable borrowing path.

Ad hoc responses such as the HIPC initiative are most useful if they evolve into more systematic, permanent approaches. National bankruptcy codes, for example, embody centuries of experimentation and refinement of just this sort. Indeed, what is ultimately needed is an international sovereign bankruptcy process, something like the sovereign debt restructuring mechanism proposed by the IMF deputy director in 2001. This process, however, would need a mandate to cancel official debt, including debt owed to the IMF, along with commercial debt (see chapters 11–13).

A sovereign bankruptcy system, established under international treaty, could systematically and speedily allocate losses among the parties (Raffer 1993). All countries would be eligible to seek its protection. The panel could estimate how much debt would never be repaid and cancel it immediately and unconditionally, without imposing conditions for structural adjustment or poverty reduction. In the case of HIPCs, the amount canceled might be as much as 80–95% of the present value of the debt. Just as in a commercial bankruptcy, such cancelations would be acts not of charity but of realism and efficiency. In the short term, quick resolution would end the stagnation that has characterized the HIPC debt problem. In the long run, the possibility of borrower bankruptcy might lead official lenders to lend more cautiously, which could provide a healthy antidote to pressures to lend, and perhaps encourage a shift toward grantmaking. In turn, the fear of losing access to cheap credit would give recipients incentives not to abuse bankruptcy protection.

Notes

1. In the mid-1980s, World Bank President James Wolfensohn initiated another round in this cycle. Part of the failure of policy-based lending could be laid at the doorstep of poor governance in borrowing countries. The Bank would therefore attempt to improve that governance. Thus the Bank's agenda expanded from policy to political process.

2. This incorporates an estimate of the dynamic benefits of trade liberalization (rising exports leading to industrial development and thus more export capacity). It is expressed in 1997 dollars (U.S.) but is a projection for the year 2015.

3. At the World Bank, the official line changed with the publication of its report *Assessing Aid in 1997* (World Bank 1997), which argued aid had not influenced borrowers' policies but that aid to countries with "good" policies had made a difference. Thus, the key to making aid work was not in choosing the right conditions for loans but in choosing the right countries. (The underlying evidence for this change of perspective has proved weak; see Easterly et al. 2003.) In 2001, under a new director, the IMF embarked on a review of conditionality, which initially focused on the relatively narrow question of whether loan agreements contained too many conditions.

4. Figures include defaults, consolidation periods agreed to with the London or Paris Clubs of private and public creditors (during which no payments are made on some debt), and instances of countries going into "nonaccrual" status with the World Bank or "overdue" status with the IMF. Five defaults—Bulgaria's in 1932, China's in 1939, Czechoslovakia's in 1960, East Germany's in 1949, and Russia's in 1918—are treated as having terminated at the end of 1989, when the organization representing holders of these nations' bonds, the London-based Corporation of Foreign Bondholders, dissolved. Figures are based on Suter (1992) and the author's own compilations.

5. Several successor organizations continue, including Jubilee Research and Jubilee Movement International.

6. Author's estimate, based on debt and export levels in present-value terms in World Bank (2000: 144–6) and a debt/exports target of 150%, and assuming that all 42 eligible countries participate.

7. Debt prices from John Garrett, senior researcher, Jubilee 2000 coalition, London, e-mail message to author, 15 August 2000.

8. Figures are author's estimates, based on methodology of Cohen (2000) and updated data.

9. Of course, countries' export earnings could rise in tandem, keeping the debt/exports ratio flat. But the fact that the export earnings of most HIPCs depend on commodities, whose prices are volatile and arguably falling over time, does not allow us to be sanguine about this possibility.

References

Birdsall, N., Claessens, S., and Diwan, I. 2002. Policy Selectivity Foregone: Debt and Donor Behavior in Africa. Working Paper 17. Washington, DC: Center for Global Development.

Bulow, J., and Rogoff, K. 1990. Cleaning Up Third World Debt without Getting Taken to the Cleaners. *Journal of Economic Perspectives* 4, 1 (Winter): 31–42.

Cohen, D. 1997. Growth and External Debt: A New Perspective on the African and Latin American Tragedies. Paper No. 9715. Paris: Ecole Normale Supérieure, Centre d'Etudes Prospectives d'Economie Mathématique Appliquées à la Planification (July).

———. 2000. The HIPC Initiative: True and False Promises. Working Paper. Paris: Organisation for Economic Co-operation and Development.

Collier, P. 1999. Learning from Failure: The International Financial Institutions as Agencies of Restraint in Africa. In *The Self-Restraining State,* ed. A. Schedler, L. Diamond, and M. F. Puttner, pp. 313–30. Boulder, CO: Lynn Rienner.

Devarajan, S., Dollar, D., and Holmgren, T., eds. 2001. *Aid and Reform in Africa: Lessons from Ten Case Studies*. Washington, DC: World Bank.

Dubash, N. K., and Filer, C. 2000. Papua New Guinea. In *The Right Conditions: The World Bank, Structural Adjustment, and Forest Policy Reform*, ed. F. J. Seymour and N. K. Dubash, pp. 29–57. Washington, DC: World Resources Institute.

Easterly, W., Levine, R., and Roodman, D. 2003. New Data, New Doubts: Revisiting "Aid, Policies, and Growth." Working Paper 26. Washington, DC: Center for Global Development (March).

European Network on Debt and Development (EURODAD). 2000. *Poverty Reduction Strategies: What Have We Learned So Far?* (draft). Brussels: EURODAD (23 September).

George, S. 1998. *A Fate Worse than Debt: The World Financial Crisis and the Poor*. New York: Grove Press.

Gunatilaka, R., and Marr, A. 1998. Conditionality and Adjustment in South-east Asia and Latin America. In *Aid and the Political Economy of Policy Change*, ed. T. Killick, pp. 53–84. London: Routledge.

Harrigan, J. 1991. Malawi. In *Aid and Power: The World Bank and Policy-Based Lending*, vol. 2, ed. P. Mosley, J. Harrigan, and J. Toye, pp. 166, 201–69. London: Routledge.

International Monetary Fund (IMF). 2000. *International Financial Statistics Yearbook 2000*. Washington, DC: International Monetary Fund.

Jayarajah, C., Branson, W., and Sen, B. 1996. *Social Dimensions of Adjustment: World Bank Experience, 1980–93*. Washington, DC: World Bank.

Kapur, D., and Webb, R. 2000. *Governance-Related Conditionalities of the International Finance Institutions*, G–24 Discussion Series, no. 6. Cambridge, MA: Harvard University, Center for International Development.

Kapur, D., Lewis, J. P., and Webb, R., eds. 1997. *The World Bank: Its First Half Century*, vol. 1. Washington, DC: Brookings Institution Press.

Killick, T. 1995. *IMF Programmes in Developing Countries: Design and Impact*. London: Routledge.

———. 1998. *Aid and the Political Economy of Policy Change*. London: Routledge.

Kirkpatrick, C., and Onis, Z. 1991. Turkey. In *Aid and Power: The World Bank and Policy-Based Lending*, vol. 2, ed. P. Mosley, J. Harrigan, and J. Toye, pp. 9–38. London: Routledge.

Lancaster, C. 1997. The World Bank in Africa since 1980: The Politics of Structural Adjustment Lending. In *The World Bank: Its First Half Century*, vol. 2, ed. D. Kapur, J. P. Lewis, and R. Webb, pp. 161–99. Washington, DC: Brookings Institution Press.

Lissakers, K. 1991. *Banks, Borrowers, and the Establishment: A Revisionist Account of the International Debt Crisis*, New York: Basic Books.

MacEwan, A. 1986. Latin America: Why Not Default? *Monthly Review* 38, no. 4 (September): 1–13.

Maddison, A. 1995. *Monitoring the World Economy, 1820–1992*, Paris: Organisation for Economic Co-operation and Development.

Makin, J. H. 1983. *The Global Debt Crisis: America's Growing Involvement*, New York: Basic Books.

Morales, J. A., and Sachs, J. D. 1989. Bolivia's Economic Crisis. In *Developing Country Debt and the World Economy*, ed. J. D. Sachs, pp. 57–80. Chicago: University of Chicago Press.

Mosley, P. 1991. The Philippines. In *Aid and Power: The World Bank and Policy-Based*

    Lending, vol. 2, ed. P. Mosley, J. Harrigan, and J. Toye, pp. 39–71. London: Rout-
    ledge.
Mosley, P., Harrigan, J., and Toye, J., eds. 1991. *Aid and Power: The World Bank and
    Policy-Based Lending,* vol. 1. London: Routledge.
Raffer, K. 1993. What's Good for the United States Must Be Good for the World: Ad-
    vocating an International Chapter 9 Insolvency. In *From Cancún to Vienna: Inter-
    national Development in a New World,* ed. B. Kreisky, pp. 64–74. Vienna: Bruno
    Kreisky Forum for International Dialogue.
Rich, B. 2002. The Smile on a Child's Face: The World Bank under James Wolfensohn.
    In *Reinventing the World Bank,* ed. J. R. Pincus and J. A. Winters, pp. 26–53. Ithaca,
    NY: Cornell University Press.
Rodrik, D. 1999. *The New Global Economy and Developing Countries: Making Openness
    Work,* Policy Essay No. 24. Washington, DC: Overseas Development Council.
Suter, C. 1992. *Debt Cycles in the World-Economy: Foreign Loans, Financial Crises,
    and Debt Settlements, 1820–1990,* Boulder, CO: Westview Press.
United Nations Children's Fund (UNICEF). 1989. *Children in Jeopardy: The Challenge
    of Freeing Poor Nations from the Shackles of Debt,* New York: UNICEF.
U.S. General Accounting Office (GAO). 2000. *Developing Countries: Debt Relief Initia-
    tive for Poor Countries Faces Challenges.* Washington, DC: U.S. Government Print-
    ing Office.
Wade, R. 1989. Unpacking the World Bank: Lending versus Leverage. Mimeo. Wash-
    ington, DC, March 1989, cited in P. Mosley, J. Harrigan, and J. Toye, eds., *Aid and
    Power: The World Bank and Policy-Based Lending,* vol. 1. London: Routledge, 1991.
————. 1994. Selective Industrial Policies in East Asia: Is The East Asian Miracle
    Right? In *Miracle or Design? Lessons from the East Asian Experience,* ed. A. Fish-
    low, C. Gwin, S. Haggard, D. Rodrik, and R. Wade. Policy Essay No. 11. pp. 55–
    80. Washington, DC: Overseas Development Council.
————. 1997. Greening the Bank: The Struggle over the Environment. In *The World
    Bank: Its First Half Century,* vol. 2, ed. D. Kapur, J. P. Lewis, and R. Webb,
    pp. 611–34. Washington, DC: Brookings Institution Press.
World Bank. 1992a. Effective Implementation: Key to Development Impact. Working
    Paper R92-195. Washington, DC: World Bank.
————. 1992b. *World Debt Tables 1992–93: External Finance for Developing Countries,*
    vol. 1. Washington, DC: World Bank.
————. 2000. *Global Development Finance 2000,* vol. 1. Washington, DC: World Bank.
————. 2002. *Global Development Finance* (electronic database). Washington, DC:
    World Bank.

2

PLAYING GAMES WITH AFRICAN LIVES: THE G7 DEBT RELIEF STRATEGY AND THE POLITICS OF INDIFFERENCE

Fantu Cheru

Introduction

Since the 1980s, the international financial institutions (IFIs) and Western creditor governments have engaged in a self-deceptive and destructive game of managing the Third World debt problem from afar and forcing unpopular economic policies down the throats of powerless countries in the belief that the bitter medicine of macroeconomic adjustment would ultimately put those countries on a path to prosperity and freedom from debt. Two decades later, however, many poor countries are in worse condition than when they started implementing structural adjustment programs mandated by the IMF and World Bank. Structural adjustment programs have failed to create a framework either for sustained economic recovery or for enabling the poor to benefit from market reforms. The debt "hangover" has had a crippling effect on the achievement of human-development targets. This is particularly pronounced in sub-Saharan Africa, which has undergone two decades of adjustment without making a dent in the extreme level of human deprivation (Mkandawire and Soludo 1999).

This chapter examines the politics of policy reform in low-income Africa and specifically the double standard applied by the creditor countries in dealing with the debts of middle-income Latin American and low-income African countries. Whereas the Latin American debt was promptly dealt with by Western creditors because of the risk it posed to the stability of the Western banking system, equal attention was never given to the debt burden of the poorest African countries, whose debts were largely owed to the multilateral financial institutions. Finally, the chapter examines the adequacy of the heavily indebted poor countries

(HIPC) initiative, which was introduced in 1996 to address the problem of debt owed by low-income countries to the multilateral development banks. Although 26 countries have benefited thus far from HIPC debt relief, an analysis by the IMF and the World Bank concluded that *the majority of countries will find themselves in worse condition after the "completion" point than when they entered the HIPC process.* The net present value (NPV) of the debt-to-exports ratio for the majority of HIPC countries could be above the 150% threshold at their completion points (IMF/World Bank 2002b). There is clear evidence that the initiative is not working and that a fundamentally different approach is needed to deal with poor countries' debt once and for all.

African Debt: Mortgaging the Future

Africa's burden of foreign debt represents the single largest obstacle to the continent's development. Although measurable in dollar terms, the debt burden takes its toll on human beings with a brutality that is difficult to capture in words. For the majority of poor people in Africa, continued debt repayment means increasingly inadequate diets, insufficient income to feed and educate children, and mounting susceptibility to diseases. As long as African countries are forced to spend almost $15 billion (U.S.) per year repaying debts to G8 governments and international financial institutions, they will be unable to address their urgent domestic needs. The constant outward flow of desperately needed resources undermines poverty-reduction initiatives and cripples efforts to cope with the devastating impact of the HIV/AIDS crisis. Without freeing the continent from the shackles of debt, it would be impossible to stem the spread of the pandemic on the continent (Cheru 2002).[1]

At the beginning of 1999, the total foreign debt owed by developing countries was $2 trillion (U.S.).[2] The regional distribution of this debt was as follows: $792 billion for Latin America; $340 billion for Africa (of which $175 billion was owed by sub-Saharan Africa); and $972 billion for Asia (United Nations 2000: 276, 277). Yet, by most conventional indicators, such as the ratio of debt to gross national product (GNP), sub-Saharan Africa's debt was the most burdensome at 133% of its GNP, compared with 41.4% for Latin America and 28.2% for Asia. In terms of the ratio of external debt to exports, the figures are striking: 202% for Latin America; 340% for sub-Saharan Africa; and 121% for Asia (United Nations 2000: 279). In short, Africa is considerably more "debt-stressed" than Latin America.

There is another important difference between Latin American and African debt. Whereas most of Latin America's debt is owed to commercial banks, a large proportion of African debt is owed to official donors. For low-income countries (defined by the World Bank as those with per capita GNP below $785 U.S.), multilateral debt increased by some 544% between 1980 and 1997, from $24.1 billion to $155 billion, as credit from other sources dried up and repayments mounted. Multilateral debt constitutes 33% of the long-term debt burden of the most impoverished countries (United Nations 1998: 167). For middle-income countries, the corresponding percentage is 15%. Neither the IMF nor the World Bank is permitted, under existing rules, to reschedule or write off debt, and repayment to both must be made in full.

Officials from the IMF, the World Bank, and the Group of Seven (G7) industrialized nations consistently maintain the position that these debts can and must be repaid. To remedy the problem, they have advised developing countries to increase their exports, reduce their imports, and implement a set of policy measures called structural adjustment programs (SAP) under the watchful eyes of the IMF. They claimed that under these conditions and assuming higher growth rates and stable interest rates worldwide, Third World countries would eventually be able to work their way out of debt.

In return for agreeing to implement structural adjustment programs, the debts of many of these countries have been rescheduled repeatedly. Between 1986 and 1996, for example, 178 debt-restructuring agreements were concluded with official creditors of the Paris Club, and 55 separate debt-restructuring agreements had been reached with commercial banks in the London Club. Of the 178 agreements with official creditors, 106 were with sub-Saharan African governments (United Nations 1997: 172). Nevertheless, these measures have done little to ease the pressure of the debt burden. For example, about 40% of the long-term nonconcessional debt African countries owed to the Paris Club at the end of 1988 represented interest capitalized by Club rescheduling. Rescheduling is merely an "accounting fiction" and does little to ease the volume of debt that countries owe to official creditors. On the contrary, developing countries continue to pay out more cach year in debt service than they actually receive in official development assistance.

The Roots of Indebted Development

There are many reasons why African countries got themselves into debt that they cannot honor. It would be wrong to put all blame solely on either the debtor governments or on creditor nations and institutions. It is safe to say from the outset that the policies pursued by both creditors and debtors are responsible for accentuating the economic and social crisis in Africa and that both must share the burden of adjustment equally.

The widespread economic stagnation that Africa has experienced since the 1970s cannot be understood in isolation from the export-led growth development strategy consistently encouraged by both multilateral and bilateral donors since the early 1950s (Cheru 1989; Jamal 1993). Because development was assumed to be synonymous with Westernization and urbanization, newly independent countries enthusiastically embarked on "imitative" development strategies that emphasized both export promotion of primary products and large-scale import-substitution industries. With revenues from export agriculture barely able to finance needed imports, African countries were urged to accept foreign loans to finance large-scale infrastructure projects on the theory that these investments would help to kick-start their economies and help them to "take off" on their own toward industrialization and development. Higher levels of GNP growth, it was said, would generate funds needed to repay the loans.

On the contrary, the economies of the majority of African countries did not take off as a result of pursuing these strategies. The overemphasis on primary export trade merely reinforced the inherited colonial division of labor, further condemning these countries to be suppliers of raw materials to industrialized nations while importing finished goods at much higher prices. Persistent declines in commodity prices did not help. Many countries faced mounting competition from substitutes such as synthetics for cotton, aluminum for copper, and corn syrup for sugar. Discriminatory tariffs continued to grow, whereas market access to African products remained limited. Neither commodity-price stabilization agreements nor assistance in diversifying agricultural export bases has been forthcoming (Brown and Tiffen 1992). To the extent that the industrialized countries have prevented debtor nations from earning their way out of debt, they must take some responsibility themselves for the Third World's inability to repay loans.

Two successive oil price hikes by the OPEC countries further aggravated the economic stagnation in the 1970s. Unable to keep their economies productive because of mounting oil bills, many countries turned to Western commercial banks and the multilateral institutions for more loans. But when the U.S. Federal Reserve Bank adopted a tight monetary policy in 1979, real interest rates rose to historically high levels. For debtor countries, this not only made new borrowing more expensive but also unexpectedly increased the amount of interest they owed on their existing loans because much of this commercial borrowing was originally contracted with floating interest rates. This was particularly true for the Latin American countries that had borrowed heavily from commercial banks. It was in this environment of a credit squeeze that the African countries became increasingly dependent on IMF and World Bank lending. As will be shown later, this dependence on the multilateral institutions has had a tremendous impact on the capacity of African countries to manage their economies independently.

Indebtedness was also aggravated by poor economic governance at the national level as corrupt and unaccountable political elites, often supported by Western powers, let loose their predatory instincts and indulged in corruption, abuse of office, and repression. Ill-conceived projects, fiscal imprudence, and capital flight subsequently increased many countries' external debt burdens. The excesses of many corrupt leaders, however, did not raise eyebrows as long as these puppet regimes faithfully served the foreign policies of Western powers. The cruel irony is that the burden of paying for the extravagant mistakes of powerful local elites and their external supporters falls on the shoulders of the poor, who are forced to tighten their belts and eat less.

Enter the IMF: He Who Controls the Purse Strings
Calls the Tune

The growing importance of the IMF and the World Bank as creditors has made debt management less flexible. As more and more Third World countries ran into greater difficulties servicing their huge loans, pressure to adopt structural adjustment grew as a wide range of bilateral and multilateral donors insisted upon economic reform as a condition for the disbursement of funds and for rescheduling the debt. By the end of 1985, 12 of the 15 debtors designated as top-priority debtors—including Argentina, Mexico, and the Philippines—had submitted to structural adjustment programs (Cavanagh et al. 1985). Over the next seven years, structural adjustment loans (SALs) proliferated as the economies of more and more Third World countries came under the surveillance and control of the World Bank and the IMF. Cooperation between the two institutions was brought to a higher level with the establishment in 1988 of the structural adjustment facility (SAF) to closely coordinate both institutions' surveillance and enforcement activities.

The basic philosophy of structural adjustment has been to persuade indebted countries to "export their way out of the crisis" through closer integration into world markets while devoting less attention to the expansion of public expenditures to boost production for domestic needs. The IMF calls this "demand management." It is meant to ensure that more of debtor nations' resources will be used to produce exports to be sold for dollars that can then be used to pay debts. Among the conditions typically required by the IMF and the World Bank are the following (Kahn 1990; Mosley et al. 1991):

- Deep reduction or elimination of subsidies and price controls, which distort internal prices for a number of goods and services;
- Drastic reduction of trade and exchange controls designed to protect the local economy from foreign competition;
- High interest rates to fight inflation, promote savings, and allocate investment capital to the highest bidders;
- Privatization of state-owned firms;
- Reduction of the role of the state not only in the economy but also in the provision of social services such as health, education, and social security;
- Indiscriminate export promotion through devaluation of the currency.

These policies are uniformly applied to all debtor countries requesting assistance from the IMF regardless of the special circumstances of each country experiencing balance-of-payments difficulties. Since the 1980s, from Argentina to Ghana, state intervention in the economy has been drastically curtailed, protectionist barriers to Northern imports have been largely eliminated, restrictions on foreign investment have been lifted, and, through export-first policies, internal economies have been more tightly integrated into the capitalist world market.

The countries of sub-Saharan Africa have largely been turned into an IMF/World Bank "macroeconomic guinea pig" because their poor credit ratings make them largely dependent on resources from the multilateral institutions. Out of the total of 47 countries in the region, 30 were implementing adjustment programs in 1999 that were jointly administered by the World Bank and the IMF. Whereas the number of IMF standby arrangements declined from a high of 132 in the 1981–85 period to 49 in 1996-98, the number of enhanced structural adjustment facilities (ESAFs) grew from 18 in 1986–90 to a record high of 99 in 1991–95 and 96 in the 1996–98 period (IMF 1998: 87). A very high proportion of ESAFs were with the countries of sub-Saharan Africa. Because most of these countries have very weak political structures, an IMF-World Bank condominium has been imposed over them under the guise of providing aid. As a result, these countries have ceded important parts of their sovereignty to the IMF and the World Bank (Mkandawire and Soludo 1999; Cheru 1989).

Although it is generally true that some indebted African countries have witnessed varying degrees of growth following reform, there are few countries where macroeconomic stability and policy-induced growth have been consistent over the medium term (Killick 1991; Mkandawire and Soludo 1999). Demand-management policies have had a regressive impact by reducing the amount of resources available to purchase necessary imports, leading to severe import strangulation, depriving industry and agriculture of needed input. Moreover, as indebted countries flooded the world market with their coffee, cocoa, and other goods, this created a glut in the market and a precipitous decline in their earnings. Instead of graduating from debt, indiscriminate market reform of liberalization and deregulation has taken these countries in the wrong direction (Cheru 1989; UNECA 1991; Cornia et al. 1993). Investment in the productive sectors of the economy has dwindled as resources have been shifted to service the mounting external debt.

More importantly, economic adjustment has been achieved on the back of the poor. Debt-servicing requirements have diverted funds from the promotion and protection of human rights, as defined in the principal human rights treaties. Consequently, living standards for the majority of Africans have declined (Weissman 1990). Increasing malnutrition, declining school enrollments, and rising unemployment and poverty threaten the social fabric of highly indebted poor countries (Cornia et al. 1987). Increasing globalization and trade, which has pushed many poor countries to the margins of the world economy and compelled an overreliance on unsustainable raw materials exports, compounds this situation (Chossudovsky 1997). Reform has focused on satisfying the demands of external creditors for servicing debt and has not adequately accounted for the domestic requirements of human-centered growth and development.

The key weakness in IFIs' approach to economic reform has been the failure to recognize that structural adjustment at the domestic level is meaningless without a corresponding adjustment at the global level. Efforts to reform economies at the national level have often been derailed by market failures at the global level. Much more effort by the international community will be required to establish a more propitious trading and financial climate within which debtor nations can hope to increase their exports and attract various forms of financing needed to achieve positive momentum in their economic development. In order for trade to generate sustainable growth, however, there must be a more equitable trading relationship between rich countries and African countries. Specifically, ensuring fair prices for commodities and market access to these products are of dominant importance. This requires structural changes in the field of primary commodity trade by giving the least developed countries better access to Northern markets, encouraging more processing of their commodities before export, and extending the preferential treatment now accorded them.

Indebtedness and the Human Crisis

The World Bank and the IMF have single-handedly managed the Third World debt crisis since the 1980s without enough regard for the social and economic costs of macroeconomic adjustment. The dramatic situations of heavily indebted countries affected by war, natural disasters, and the HIV/AIDS pandemic have not been given the special attention they deserve. In the social sector, debt servicing and the adjustment policies pushed to free up foreign exchange needed to service the debt have worsened social welfare (Kanji 1995; Onimode 1989; Cheru 1999). The cuts mandated by adjustment have been indiscriminate, thereby jeopardizing the following fundamental human rights:

- *The right to food:* There is convincing evidence demonstrating that nutritional levels decrease among poor segments of the population as a result of the removal of food subsidies. Growing unemployment has a similar result. The effect of switching agricultural production, primarily from food crops for local consumption to coffee, tobacco, or cotton destined for export markets, has resulted in a drastic decline in food production, reduced nutritional levels, and increased malnutrition (Mukherjee 1994; Ziegler 2001).
- *The right to education:* Article 26 of the Universal Declaration of Human Rights declares that all people have the right to education. The Convention of the Rights of the Child has also established the right to early development and education. Thanks to extraordinary efforts during the 1960s and 1970s, the percentage of children completing at least four years of primary education reached 50% or more in almost all developing countries. But since the 1980s, increasing debt and consequent implementation of structural adjustment programs has led many governments to freeze or cut educational spending (Oxfam 1999; Tomasevski 1995). Primary schooling has often suffered disproportionately, and there was significant slippage in sub-Saharan Africa. The percentage of 6–11-year-olds enrolled in school dropped from a high of 55% in 1979 to 45% in 1995 (UNESCO 1996; Oxfam 1999).
- *The right to health:* Health is one of the fundamental human rights embodied in Article 25 of the 1948 Universal Declaration of Human Rights. The goal of "Health for All by the Year 2000" agreed upon in the Alma Alta Declaration has been severely undermined by cutbacks in government health budgets as social and development objectives have

been superseded by financial imperatives (Cornia et al. 1987; WHO 2001). The imposition of "user fees" for primary health care drove large numbers of people away from public health services, contributing to increased rates of sexually transmitted diseases. Moreover, cutbacks in the public sector helped send health professionals to the private sector or abroad and reduced investments in health-care delivery systems (Turshnet 1994).

In the face of widespread public criticism, however, the World Bank and the IMF insist that structural adjustment programs not only are working but are also a necessary element of long-term transformation. In early 1994, the Bank released a progress report on Africa, *Adjustment in Africa: Reform, Results and the Road Ahead*, to defend its failed policy of structural adjustment (World Bank 1994). By manipulating selective data from cross-country analyses, and without revealing the fact that the Bank's own economists objected to the report's conclusion, the Bank claimed that African countries that implemented structural adjustment programs in the 1980s experienced greater positive growth than those that did not. Two years earlier, a draft World Bank study stated, "World Bank adjustment lending has not significantly affected growth and has contributed to a statistically significant drop in investment ratios" (World Bank 1992: 37). Of the six countries the Bank put forward as adjustment "successes"—Ghana, Tanzania, The Gambia, Burkina Faso, Nigeria, and Zimbabwe—four had deteriorating rates of investment and two had negative GDP growth rates during their respective adjustment periods.

A similar verdict was delivered on the ineffectiveness of the IMF's enhanced structural adjustment facility (ESAF) in a report prepared by a team of external evaluators hired by the IMF's executive board in 1996 (Botchwey et al. 1998). The evaluation team concluded that although ESAF-supported economic reforms generally have positive effects on growth and income distribution, they also entail temporary costs for certain segments of the population.

The inflexibility of the IMF and the World Bank on macroeconomic conditionalities put undue pressure on countries where high HIV/AIDS prevalence is wiping out decades of development (UNAIDS/World Bank 2001). In addition, debt servicing often absorbs well over one-quarter of African countries' limited government revenues, crowding out critical public investment in human development. Throughout sub-Saharan Africa, health systems are collapsing for lack of medicines, schools have no books, and universities suffer from a debilitating lack of library and laboratory facilities. Even the so-called African "success" cases, such as Ghana and Uganda, are basically being held afloat for demonstration purposes by continuing aid inflows.

Creditor Strategy: A Decade of Complacency

The indifference of Western creditor governments to the plight of poor people in low-income indebted countries was clearly evident in the piecemeal approach adopted by the G7 governments since 1987. Successive debt-relief initiatives introduced by the G7 governments with great fanfare have done little more than apply ill-conceived, short-term palliatives to what is arguably the most intractable obstacle to Africa's recovery.[3] The G7 debt-reduction initiatives were set and reset arbitrarily rather than on the basis of a serious assessment of the needs of each country.

The reason for this arbitrary approach is not difficult to figure out. For 25 years, the guiding principle of official debt relief has been to do the minimum necessary to avert default but never enough to solve the debt crisis. A mixture of debt relief and repeated rescheduling operations has so far prevented extensive default on Africa's debt. Indeed, between 1987 and 1996, there were 166 debt-restructuring agreements with official creditors in the Paris Club, of which 96 cases involved African countries (United Nations 1998: 172). Although these debt-restructuring initiatives helped to reduce some debt, their overall impact on reducing the debt burden of poor countries was negligible, as these proposals gave considerable latitude to participating creditor countries to take the strategy that was least costly to them. The HIPC initiative, though presented as a major break from past practices, is guided by the same logic of damage control.

A good illustration of this point is the "Toronto terms" introduced during the G7 Toronto meeting in 1989. The creditor nations agreed on a "menu" of options for rescheduling nonconcessional debt. These included the following options for creditors:

1. Cancel 33% of debt service covered by the agreement and reschedule the rest with a 14-year maturity and 8-year grace period;
2. Reduce interest rates by 3.5 percentage points or 50%, whichever is less, and reschedule the debt with a 14-year maturity and 8-year grace period;
3. Extend the grace period to 14 years and the maturity to 25 years. In addition, aid debt will be rescheduled over 25 years with a 14-year grace period at existing concessional interest rates.

Options 1 and 2 involved an immediate cost to creditor governments and immediate relief to the debtor. Option 3 merely increased debt stock and future debt service as deferred interest payments were capitalized and added to the total debt stock.

The less-than-generous options provided by the G7 governments to the poorest countries in Africa stand in stark contrast with the treatment of the massive debts owed by the Latin American debtors to commercial banks. Both the 1985 Baker Plan and the 1989 Brady Plan represented swift reactions to the threat posed to the Western banking system by the magnitude of debts owed by Latin American borrowers.[4] Both plans tried in general to use an aggressive strategy, employing measures to induce commercial banks to rewrite existing contracts to exchange debt either for secured liquid assets on better terms or for cash. For example, the Brady Plan made it possible to replace a portion of outstanding debt with "Brady bonds" having a lower face value and a longer repayment schedule (Browne 1999; Cavanagh et al. 1985).

Finally, the various G7 proposals (i.e., Toronto, Trinidad, and Naples terms) gave paltry attention to the debt owed by low-income African countries to multilateral development banks. For most of the world's impoverished countries, multilateral debt looms larger than other debts because the G7 industrialized countries have given the IMF and the World Bank the status of "preferred creditors." For many African countries, debt servicing to the IMF and the World Bank accounts for 36% of total debt-service payments. Because of the preferred creditor status of these two institutions, payments of multilateral debt take priority over private and bilateral debt. Borrowing governments have special incentives to stay current with their multilateral debts because they do not want to jeopardize their access to more concessional forms of finance needed to support recovery.

The HIPC Initiative: Old Wine in a New Bottle?

In October 1996, as a result of many years of persistent campaigning by a global coalition of NGOs and civil society organizations, the IMF and World Bank finally conceded the need to address the issue of poor-country debt owed to them and they approved the HIPC initiative. The ostensible aim of the program is to make the debt burden of the poorest and most indebted countries "sustainable." The IMF and the World Bank initially identified 41 countries as possible candidates for debt relief under the HIPC initiative. In total, they owed $221 billion (U.S.) in 1998, about $61 billion of which (roughly 26% of the total debt stock) was owed to the multilateral financial institutions (GAO 1998: 123–28; United Nations 1998: 167).

Once a country is deemed eligible, it must demonstrate a commitment to "sound economic policies"—the IFIs' usual euphemism for SAPs—to receive debt relief.[5] Under the original HIPC program, a country could not obtain benefits until it completed six consecutive years of implementation of the Fund's ESAF. The first stage entails a rescheduling of debt-servicing obligations to Paris Club countries on Naples terms. At the end of that period, the debtor may be accorded up to a two-thirds reduction of debt. At this point, a decision can be made on whether the second stage is needed. Eligibility criteria for the second stage of the initiatives, which could reduce debt-servicing obligations up to 80% (13 percentage points beyond that accorded under Naples terms), is much higher, and relief is granted on a case-by-case basis.

By 1999, however, the limitations of the HIPC initiative's ability to lighten the debt burden of poor countries became clear. By the spring of 1999, only three countries had become eligible for actual debt relief: Uganda and Bolivia, in April and September 1998, respectively, and Mozambique in mid-1999. Although eight others—Mali, Cote d'Ivoire, Benin, Honduras, Senegal, Tanzania, Guyana, and Burkina Faso—had reached their "decision point" and had assistance committed to them by the end of 1999, they represented only a small proportion of the total initially targeted (IMF 1998: 66). The stringent qualifi-

TABLE 2.1   HIPC's changing criteria

	HIPC-1	HIPC-2
Debt sustainability ratios		
Debt/exports	200–250%	150%
Debt/revenues	280%	250%
GDP-related ratios		
Exports/GDP	40%	30%
Revenues/GDP	20%	15%
Time until actual relief	6 years	Uncertain

Sources: IMF, World Bank.

cation criteria (see table 2.1) simply excluded many deserving indebted countries from requesting debt relief.

Moreover, the original HIPC initiative simply did not take into account human development and poverty-eradication issues in the debt-sustainability analysis. Nor did the initiative take into account the special circumstances of many poor countries that are confronted with a wide-scale humanitarian crisis caused by the effects of war and genocide (for example, Sierra Leone and Rwanda), natural disasters (for example, Hurricane Mitch in Honduras and Nicaragua), and health emergencies such as the HIV/AIDS pandemic in Africa (Nyamugasira 1999; Cheru and Figueredo 2000). These disasters are wiping out decades of development advances.

The Enhanced HIPC Initiative

Barely two years had passed since the introduction of the HIPC initiative when the IMF and the World Bank conceded in the spring of 1999 that the HIPC initiative had major shortcomings and agreed that there was a need for more substantive steps to address the debt problem of low-income countries. Reacting to this, the G7 leaders announced from Cologne in June 1999 a major debt-reduction initiative aimed at improving the HIPC initiative. A total of $90 billion (U.S.) was promised for 33 countries, with the cost to creditors (net present value) at $27 billion (World Bank 1999; Oxfam and UNICEF 1999: 15). Shortly thereafter, the original HIPC initiative was revamped to provide three key enhancements:

1. *Deeper and broader relief:* Debt sustainability thresholds were lowered from 250% in the original framework to 150%, thus providing more debt relief (table 2.2). Also, more countries became eligible for debt relief as a result of the relaxation of the stringent qualification criteria.
2. *Faster relief:* A number of creditors began to provide interim debt relief immediately so that decision-point countries could reach the completion point faster; Britain, Norway, Sweden, and Australia agreed to

TABLE 2.2   Total debt stock reduction under HIPC I (millions of U.S. dollars)

Country	Total nominal debt relief	Reduction in debt stock (NPV terms)	Total debt relief (NPV terms)
Uganda	650	20%	347
Bolivia	760	13%	448
Burkina Faso	200	14%	115
Guyana	410	25%	256
Cote d'Ivoire	800	6%	345
Mozambique	3,700	57%	1,700
Mali	250	10%	128

Source: *HIPC Initiative Consultation Meeting: Background Materials,* IMF/World Bank, March 1999. Updates on Guyana and Mozambique from IMF press releases dated 14 May 1999 and 30 June 1999, respectively.

cancel 100% of their bilateral debts, and Canada announced that it would apply a moratorium on debt repayments from 11 countries in Africa and Latin America.

3. *A Stronger link between debt relief and poverty reduction*: The new version of HIPC seeks to ensure that debt relief will effectively reduce poverty. Countries wishing to apply for debt relief are required to prepare a poverty reduction strategy paper (PRSP). The PRSPs are to be country-driven; prepared and developed transparently with the broad participation of civil society, key donors, and other relevant international financial institutions; and linked clearly with agreed international development goals. The PRSP, which would be updated regularly, would in essence become the basic framework that would be used to guide World Bank/IMF lending operations to poor countries in the future.

One significant aspect of the enhanced HIPC initiative is the decision to place poverty reduction at the heart of the initiative. Countries start out initially by preparing an interim poverty reduction strategy paper (I-PRSP). The I-PRSP is intended as a road map to preparing a full PRSP and as a bridge between the long-term PRSP objectives and a country's short-term needs for financing and debt relief. The I-PRSP paves the way for the country to reach its "decision point," which is followed by an interim support (or a loan) to the government from the IMF's poverty reduction and growth facility, formerly called the ESAF (Cheru 2000). Thereafter, countries are expected to formulate a full PRSP in consultation with all societal actors. The full PRSP must clearly show the links between macroeconomic policies and agreed international social development goals to be reached by 2015.[6]

Eligibility for debt relief is conditioned upon "good performance" in the implementation of an IMF program for a period of three years. Having reached the "decision point" after the first three years of good economic performance, each country must then demonstrate that its debt servicing is unsustainable.[7] If the country finally qualifies for relief after reaching this "decision point," its debt servicing is brought down to what is deemed, within the terms of the initiative, to be a sustainable level, but only after reaching the "completion point," or after a further three-year waiting period. So far, only eight countries have completed the process: Uganda, Bolivia, Burkina Faso, Guyana, Mauritania, Tanzania, Mali, and Mozambique.[8] This less-than-generous arrangement still leaves the country deflecting a sizable portion of its scarce foreign-exchange earnings into debt servicing for an indefinite period of time.

Although the emphasis on strengthening the link between debt relief and poverty reduction represents a tremendous step forward in the tortured history of debt relief for poor countries, the enhanced HIPC, like its predecessor, is caught up in a complex web of excessive and stringent IMF and World Bank policy prescriptions, or conditions. A study by the UN Economic Commission for Africa (UNECA) concluded that progress in aligning donor procedures to support the implementation of poverty-reduction strategies in Africa has not lived up to expectations: Donor conditions have not decreased, reporting requirements have not been harmonized, and donor funding remains unpredictable (UNECA 2003). Moreover, the envisioned debt relief has been neither sufficiently deep nor sufficiently broad; nor has debt relief been delivered at the pace required to address the pressing needs of many African countries.

The Limitations of the HIPC Initiative

As of July 2002, 26 countries benefited from debt relief under the enhanced HIPC initiative, of which seven have reached the completion point. The seven include Bolivia, Guyana, Burkina Faso, Mauritania, Mozambique, Tanzania, and Uganda. These seven have received debt relief amounting to $7.5 billion (U.S.) in NPV terms (equivalent to $13 billion in nominal terms). The remaining 20 (19) countries received interim relief when they reached decision points in the amount of $17 billion in NPV terms (or $27 billion in nominal terms). Twelve additional countries with substantial arrears problems that are in need of significant relief are yet to be considered, as these countries are mostly conflict-affected. To provide the opportunity for these countries to qualify for HIPC relief, it is proposed to extend the sunset clause of the initiative by another two years to the end of 2004 (IMF/World Bank 2002a).

The $24.5 billion (U.S.) of debt cancelation delivered so far is no small change by any stretch of the imagination, but it is not enough. Debt relief is making a real difference to the lives of ordinary people. Two-thirds of resources released are being spent on health and education, with most of the remainder being used for HIV/AIDS, water supplies, roads, and governance reforms. For example, the Ugandan government has disbursed resources released from debt relief to its districts to improve education. School management committees monitor expenditures, the quality of education, and student test results. In concrete terms, the program to provide free primary education has in a short period of time doubled the school enrolment rate (Cheru 2001). In Mozambique, resources released through debt relief have been channeled into various areas, all vital to sustaining development. The budgets for health, education, agriculture, infrastructure, and employment training have all benefited.

Despite evidence that debt relief can save lives, neither the original HIPC initiative nor the "enhanced" version introduced in 1999 has succeeded in resolving Africa's debt crisis. The envisioned debt relief has been neither sufficiently deep nor sufficiently broad (Cheru 2000). The first 26 countries to qualify for HIPC are still spending more on debt servicing than on health care. In a surprisingly candid admission, both the World Bank and the IMF released two documents in time for the spring 2002 meeting that concluded that the HIPC initiative is failing (IMF/World Bank 2002a and 2002b), stating:

- Over half of the HIPCs are spending more than 15% of their government revenue on debt servicing. The medium- to long-term projections of debt-service requirements for a large number of HIPCs are alarming.
- Of the five countries already at the completion point, at least two of them—Uganda and Burkina Faso—do not have sustainable levels of debt according to the HIPC criteria. This will bring to 13 the number of countries expected to face unsustainable debt burdens at the completion point. In the case of Uganda, this is the third time that the country has exceeded its debt sustainability after reaching completion points, mainly because of the collapse in coffee prices.
- In one case, Burkina Faso, the joint board of the IMF/World Bank approved raising assistance to bring that country's NPV debt to 150% of exports at the completion point. Although this was considered an exceptional measure by the IFIs, other countries that had gone through the completion point and still show NPV of debt-to-export ratios in excess of the sustainability threshold might be granted increased assistance.
- Of the 20 countries that are currently between the decision point and completion point under the Initiative, at least 8–10 (60%) will have annual debt-service payments due in 2003–05 that will be higher than their annual debt-service payments in 1998–2000. These countries include Benin, Chad, Ethiopia, The Gambia, Guinea-Bissau, Malawi, Niger, Rwanda, Senegal, and Zambia (IMF/World Bank 2002b: 25). Thirteen of the 20 countries had their PRGF program suspended because of a failure to stay on track with IMF programs. Suspension delays debt cancelation and denies countries interim service relief. Among the countries in this group was Ghana, once the darling of the IMF.
- There have even been delays in providing interim debt-service relief for some countries that are entitled to this relief and are "on track" with IMF programs. The HIPC initiative appears to be working only for 7 to 10 countries out of the 42 included within the initiative. Part of the reason for the delay in granting relief has to do with the inadequacy of the HIPC trust fund. It is currently estimated that the financing required to support debt relief for the 34 HIPCs that have already reached their

decision points will fully exhaust the resources mobilized to date and will leave a potential funding gap of up to $800 million (U.S.) (IMF/World Bank 2002a: 17). In this context, in June 2002, the G8 members agreed to fund their share of the shortfall, recognizing that it will be up to $1 billion.[9]

One of the principal factors explaining the failure of the HIPC initiative has to do with the unrealistic projections of debt sustainability, which is calculated by comparing total debt in NPV terms to a country's total exports. If a country can pay its debt from its export earnings without going broke, then it is assumed to have "sustainable" debt. When the total stock of debt is more than one and one-half times the value of exports, the country is deemed to have an "unsustainable" level of debt.

Unfortunately, the optimistic export projections that the World Bank and the IMF use to determine sustainability have not materialized. For example, for the first 24 HIPCs to reach their decision points, the average growth in exports for 2001 was projected to be 11.6%. This figure bears little resemblance to the historical performance of the HIPC countries. Since 1965, annual export growth for low-income countries has been less than one-third of this level. It therefore comes as no surprise that the actual export growth for these 24 countries during 2001 was less than half the World Bank's projected level at 5.1% (IMF and World Bank 2002b: 8). For several countries that had a worsened NPV of debt-to-export ratio in 2001, the majority of the deterioration in the NPV of debt-to-export ratio was the result of *lower* exports (IMF and World Bank, 2002a: 24). A similar conclusion was made in an independent evaluation undertaken by the U.S. General Accounting Office (GAO). The GAO report, which analyzed debt sustainability for 10 African countries, found that only 2 of the 10 countries would have sustainable debt levels if these countries' exports were to grow at rates consistent with their historical levels (GAO 2002: 6).

Much of the shortfall in exports has been caused by dramatic decreases in commodity prices over 2000–01, particularly for coffee and cotton, which fell by 60% and 10%, respectively. As a result of this shortfall, the average ratio of debt to exports in 2001 for 24 HIPC countries is now estimated to have been a staggering 280%, almost twice the level deemed "sustainable" (see table 2.3 by the World Bank and the IMF. Even the four countries that have already passed the completion point are estimated to have an NPV of debt-to-export ratio of 156% (IMF/World Bank 2002a: 10).

Jeffrey Sachs argues that debt reduction for the HIPCs should not be based on arbitrary criteria such as a 150% debt-to-exports ratio but rather on a systematic assessment of each country's needs for debt reduction and increased foreign assistance measured against explicit development objectives (Sachs 2002). Sachs argues that the correct starting point for assessing needs should be the targets enshrined in the Millennium Development Goals (MDGs), a set of eight major goals and 18 intermediate targets endorsed by all UN members in September 2000.

TABLE 2.3   Debt sustainability ratio (NPV/Exports) for selected HIPCs (after additional bilateral debt forgiveness)

	Decision point projection	Spring 2002 projections	Updated projections
Benin	138	148–154	158–170
Chad	188	188–219	188–224
Ethiopia	149	164–186	137–159
The Gambia	153	162–177	162–174
Guinea-Bissau	107	147–152	147–152
Malawi	156	158–165	165–166
Niger	164	144–148	159–167
Rwanda	185	161–171	180–198
Senegal	112	157–158	158–159
Zambia	106	151–154	152–154
Cameroon	101	99–112	95–113
Ghana	82	—	82–83
Guinea	123	139–141	135–140
Guyana	57	68–76	69–77
Honduras	74	90–91	91–92
Madagascar	101	75–81	76–83
Mali	143	139–140	128–130
Nicaragua	93	108–117	108–117
Sao Tome and Principe	139	124–140	132–143
Sierra Leone	139	—	139–150

Source: IMF, *Heavily Indebted Poor Countries Initiative: Status of Implementation*, 21 September 2002, p. 10, Table 4.

A serious commitment to addressing Africa's development challenges must begin by releasing the continent from debt bondage. Many of the HIPCs currently service their debts at the cost of widespread malnutrition, premature death, excessive morbidity, and reduced prospects for economic growth. If the resources devoted to debt service were freed up and successfully redirected toward basic human needs, there could be significant improvements in human welfare. A 2001 study indicated that both the World Bank and the IMF hold sufficient wealth on their own balance sheets to absorb the full cost of multilateral debt cancelation from their internal resources. An audit of these institutions by two independent accounting firms in Britain revealed that the World Bank and the IMF could write off all of the debts of the world's poorest countries from their own assets without negatively impacting their credit rating or their ability to function (Drop the Debt 2001). Unfortunately, the World Bank and the IMF continue to maintain the position that outright debt cancelation is a financial impossibility because it would critically undermine their future operations, and such an action could create a moral hazard and encourage other debtor countries not to honor their commitments to them.

Conclusions

The HIPC initiative has failed to resolve Africa's debt crisis. Instead, it has left many developing countries committing scarce resources to debt servicing instead of meeting the needs of their people. The reason for the failure of the initiative is that it is designed by creditors and controlled by creditors. Creditors have the power to define who gets what, when, and how. Even by its own measure, the HIPC initiative is not reducing debt to levels described by the World Bank as "sustainable." As shown in table 2.1, the majority of countries will find themselves in worse condition after the completion point than when they first entered the process. Moreover, the HIPC initiative obfuscates the illegitimacy of most of this debt. Tinkering with the HIPC initiative is a shell game. Tying debt relief to conditions determined by creditors undermines African priorities and initiatives and affords creditors an inordinate degree of control over the running of African countries. Preservation of that influence and control is a far more important factor in the G8 approach to debt policy than recovery of the funds loaned.

Debt relief alone is not going to place desperate African countries on a sound economic footing to enable them to effectively address the debilitating effect of poverty and the HIV/AIDS pandemic. Adequate and predictable funding from the international community is critical to expanding treatment and prevention programs over the long term. During the UN Special Session on HIV/AIDS in summer 2001, UN Secretary-General Kofi Annan proposed the establishment of a global HIV/AIDS trust fund of $7–10 billion (U.S.) a year to assist in the struggle against HIV/AIDS worldwide. So far, the response from the international community has been very disappointing when compared with the international response against terrorism following the tragic events of September 11, 2001, that killed innocent citizens in New York and Washington, DC. The indifference toward African lives must be challenged and exposed if we are to create a just world order where human rights and human dignity take precedence over corporate rights and creditors' greed.

If the richest creditor nations and institutions are serious about confronting the worst plague in human history, they must stop the charade, cancel Africa's debt, and remove the major economic obstacle to African efforts to fight AIDS (Booker and Minter 2001; Dakar Manifesto 2000).

Notes

1. Booker, S., Forgive the Debt to the Dying Millions, *Los Angeles Times,* 24 June 2001: M.5.

2. According to Article 22 of the Universal Declaration of Human Rights, every one is "entitled to realization through national efforts and international cooperation, of the economic, social and cultural rights indispensable for his dignity." In poor indebted countries, this condition often is not fulfilled.

3. These included the "Naples terms" which were designed to provide 67% debt stock

reduction, and the "Trinidad terms" of reducing debt stock by two-thirds instead of the 50% provided for under the "enhanced Toronto terms."

4. Named after the architects of the plans, U.S. Treasury Secretary James Baker and Nicholas Brady.

5. Sustainability is defined as the ability "to meet current and future external debt service obligations in full without recourse to debt relief, rescheduling of debt or the accumulation of arrears, and without unduly compromising growth."

6. The MDGs are quantified goals for poverty alleviation, reduction of hunger, reduction of disease burden, and other targets, mostly for the year 2015.

7. The enhanced HIPC initiative stipulates that, in order to qualify for relief, a country must have a debt-to-exports ratio of 150% and debt-to-export ratio of 250% or more combined with tax-to-GDP and exports-to-GDP ratios of at least 15% and 30%, respectively.

8. Statement by the Group of Eight (G8) countries in Birmingham, UK, on African debt (www.birmingham.g8summit.gov.uk).

9. See The Kananaskis Summit Chair's summary, "The 2002 Summit," Kananaskis, Canada (www.g8.gc.ca/kan_docs/chairsumary-e.asp).

References

Booker, S., and Minter, W. 2001. Global Apartheid. *The Nation* (9 July: 11–17).

Botchwey, K., Collier, P., Gunning, J. W., and Hamada, K. 1998. *Report of the Group of Independent Persons Appointed to Conduct an Evaluation of the Enhanced Structural Adjustment Facility (ESAF)*. Washington, DC: IMF (draft), 1998.

Brown, M., and Tiffen, P. 1992. *Short Changed: Africa and World Trade*. London: Pluto Press.

Browne, S. 1999. *Beyond Aid: From Patronage to Partnership*. London: Ashgate.

Cavanagh, J., et al. 1985. *From Debt to Development: Alternatives to the International Debt Crisis*. Washington, DC: Institute for Policy Studies.

Cheru, F. 1989. *The Silent Revolution in Africa: Debt, Development and Democracy*. London: Zed Press.

———. 1999. *Effects of Structural Adjustment Policies on the Full Enjoyment of Human Rights*. UN Commission on Human Rights. E/CN.4/1999/50. Geneva: United Nations.

———. 2000. Debt Relief and Social Investment: Linking the HIPC Initiative to the HIV/AIDS Epidemic in Africa: The Case of Zambia. *Review of African Political Economy*, Vol. 27, No. 86: 519–35.

———. 2001. *The PRSP Process in Uganda: What Is The Secret of Its Success?* Addis Ababa: UN Economic Commission for Africa (November).

———. 2002. Debt, Adjustment and the Politics of Effective Response to HIV/AIDS in Africa. *Third World Quarterly*, Vol. 23, No. 2: 299–312.

Cheru, F., and Figueredo, R. 2000. *Debt Relief and Social Investment: Linking HIPC to the HIV/AIDS Epidemic in Africa and Post-Hurricane Mitch Reconstruction in Honduras and Nicaragua*. E/CN.4/2000/51. Geneva: United Nations Commission on Human Rights (14 January).

Chossudovsky, M. 1997. *The Globalization of Poverty: Impacts of IMF and World Bank Reforms*. Penang: Third World Network.

Cornia, G. A., Jolly, R., and Stewart, F. 1987 *Adjustment with a Human Face: Protecting the Vulnerable and Promoting Growth*. New York: Oxford University Press.

————. 1993. *Africa's Recovery in the 1990s: From Stagnation and Adjustment to Human Development.* New York: UNICEF.

Dakar Manifesto. 2000. *Africa: From Resistance to Alternatives.* Report issued by the December 2000 gathering in Dakar of representatives of organizations campaigning for cancelation of Africa's debt.

Drop the Debt. 2001. *Reality Check: The Need for Deeper Debt Cancellation and the Fight Against HIV/AIDS.* Report incorporating independent audits by accountants Chantrey Vellacott DFK and Subhrendu Chatterji. London (10 April).

International Monetary Fund (IMF). 1998. *Annual Report 1998.* Washington, DC: IMF.

International Monetary Fund (IMF)/World Bank. 2002a. *Heavily Indebted Poor Countries Initiative: Status of Implementation.* Washington, DC: IMF/World Bank (21 September).

————. 2002b. *The Enhanced HIPC Initiative and the Achievement of Long-term External Debt Sustainability.* Washington, DC: IMF/World Bank (15 April).

Jamal, V. 1993. Surplus Extraction and the African Agrarian Crisis in a Historical Perspective. In *Economic Crisis and Third World Agriculture,* ed. A. Singh and H. Tabatabi, pp. 65–91. London: Cambridge University Press.

Kahn, M. 1990. *The Macro-economic Effects of Fund-Supported Adjustment Programs,* IMF Staff Paper 37: 2.

Kanji, N. 1995. Gender, poverty and economic adjustment in Harare, Zimbabwe. *Environment and Urbanization,* Vol. 7, No. 1, pp. 37–56.

Killick, T. 1991. Problems and Limitations of Adjustment Policies. Working Paper No. 36. London: Overseas Development Institute.

Mkandawire, T., and Soludo, C. 1999. *Our Continent, Our Future: African Perspectives on Structural Adjustment.* Trenton, NJ: Africa World Press.

Mosley, P., Harrigan, J., and Toye, J. 1991. *Aid and Power: The World Bank and Policy-based Lending.* London: Macmillan.

Mukherjee, A. 1994. *Structural Adjustment Programs and Food Security.* London: Aldershot.

Nyamugasira, W. 1999. Rwanda and the Impact of Debt Relief on the Poor: Reconciliation Can't Wait; Children Headed Households Can't Wait. An NGO Input to the HIPC Review Seminar, Addis Ababa. (29 July).

Onimode, B. 1989. *The IMF, The World Bank and The African Debt: The Social and Political Impact.* London: Zed Press.

Oxfam. 1999. *Education Now: Break the Cycle of Poverty.* Oxford: Oxfam-UK.

Oxfam and UNICEF. 1999. Debt Relief and Poverty Reduction: Meeting the Challenge. Report Submitted for HIPC Review Seminar, Addis Ababa (29 July).

Sachs, J. 2002. *Resolving the Debt Crisis of Low-Income Countries.* Brookings Papers on Economic Activity, No. 1. Washington, DC: Brookings Institution.

Tomasevski, K. 1995. The Influence of the World Bank and IMF on Economic and Social Rights. *Nordic Journal of International Law,* Vol. 64, pp. 385–95.

Turshnet, M. 1994. The Impact of Economic Reforms on Women's Health and Health Care in Sub-Saharan Africa. In *Women in the Age of Economic Transformation,* ed. N. Aslanbegui, S. Pressmant, and G. Summerfield, pp. 77–93. London: Routledge.

UNAIDS/World Bank. 2001. *AIDS, Poverty Reduction and Debt Relief.* Geneva: UNAIDS.

UN Economic Commission for Africa (UNECA). 1991. *Africa's Alternative Framework to Structural Adjustment and Transformation.* Addis Ababa: UNECA.

————. 2003. *Report of the Second Meeting of the Africa Learning Group on The Poverty Reduction Strategy Papers (PRSP-LG)*. Addis Ababa: UNECA, 31 May.

United Nations. 1997. *World Economic and Social Survey 1997.* New York: United Nations.

————. 1998. *World Economic and Social Survey 1998.* New York: United Nations.

————. 2000. *World Economic and Social Survey 2000.* New York: United Nations.

United Nations Educational, Scientific, and Cultural Organization (UNESCO). 1996. *Trends and Projections of Enrollment, 1960–2025.* Paris: UNESCO.

U.S. General Accounting Office (GAO). 1998. *Status of the Heavily Indebted Poor Countries Debt Relief Initiative.* Washington, DC: GAO.

————. 2002. *Switching Some Multilateral Loans to Grants Lessens Poor Country Debt Burdens.* Report to Congressional Requesters. Washington, DC: GAO.

Weissman, S. R. 1990. Structural Adjustment in Africa: Insights from the Experience of Ghana and Senegal. *World Development,* Vol. 18, No. 12, pp. 1624–34.

World Bank. 1992. *Adjustment Lending and Economic Performance in Sub-Saharan Africa in the 1980s: A Comparison with Other Low-Income Countries.* Washington, DC: World Bank.

————. 1994. *Adjustment in Africa: Reform, Results, and the Road Ahead.* Washington, DC: World Bank.

————. 1999. Heavily Indebted Poor Countries (HIPC) Initiative: Strengthening the Link between Debt Relief and Poverty Reduction. Working Paper IDA/SecM99-45 (26 August). Washington, DC: World Bank.

World Health Organization (WHO). 2001. *Macroeconomics and Health: Investing in Health for Economic Development,* Report of the Commission on Macroeconomics and Health. Geneva: WHO.

Ziegler, J. 2001. *Economic, Social and Cultural Rights: The Right to Food.* UN Commission on Human Rights, E/CN.4/2001/53. Geneva: United Nations.

3

SOVEREIGN DEBT AND THE DEBT CRISIS IN EMERGING COUNTRIES: THE EXPERIENCE OF THE 1990S

Daniel Marx
Jose Echague
Guido Sandleris

Introduction

The decades since the 1970s have witnessed a significant increase in financial capital mobility on a global scale. This process has been connected with two main factors. First, technological innovations facilitated access and dissemination of information and lowered transaction costs. Accompanying this process, all major industrialized countries and a significant number of emerging economies liberalized their capital accounts. The growth in international capital flows clearly outpaced the rate of expansion of other relevant indicators of the world economy, such as world trade and GDP. Between 1970 and 2000, cross-border capital flows—measured in constant U.S. dollars—averaged an annual growth rate of 5.2%, whereas the average annual growth rates for world trade and world GDP were 2.6% and 2.3%, respectively. Flows to emerging countries were a part of this phenomenon.

However, the Mexican, Asian, and Russian financial crises have taken their toll on the speed of this process. Although overall capital flows have still been growing, there has been a sharp contraction in lending to emerging economies since then. Even more importantly, the crises fueled the debate on international capital flows and balance-of-payment crises by making clear that the new structure of financial markets created opportunities but also serious challenges.

Since 1998, a series of sovereign debt crises in the developing world reminded everybody that although increased external financing can enhance economic growth and welfare by financing investment projects or allowing the government to smooth out economic shocks, it might also make countries more vulnerable to costly debt crises. In effect, the defaults of Russia, Ukraine, Pakistan, Ecuador, and Argentina renewed the debate on emerging countries economic policies and raised several questions regarding the current architecture of the world financial system, particularly in relation to sovereign credit markets.

Policy choices in some emerging countries without a doubt bear an important share of the responsibility for their debt crises. Many such crises could have been avoided, or their scope made more limited, had some of these countries developed a better institutional framework and/or pursued a more defined growth strategy adapted to challenging global competitive circumstances and/or followed more prudent fiscal policies in the "good years."

At a more global level, the financial crises of the 1990s suggest that international financial institutions (IFIs) are not necessarily well-prepared to deal with the challenges of this new globalized capitalism, where capital flows and financial markets have reached a large scale and demonstrated significant volatility. Several questions follow naturally: Have the world financial markets changed so much as to render obsolete the IMF and World Bank, masterminded at the end of World War II? Do we need to update their mandates further or set up completely new institutions? In addition to these more general questions, there are some issues specifically related to sovereign debt markets such as: Is a sovereign bankruptcy procedure necessary, and how should it work? Should the introduction of explicit contingent clauses in sovereign bonds be encouraged? How can we strengthen credit institutions to foster growth as opposed to creating high-risk options where countries tend to narrow their policy choices?

The objective of this chapter is to analyze the main problems of the current global sovereign debt markets—particularly in relation to emerging countries—and present some policy recommendations. In the next section, we describe the evolution of sovereign debt markets during the 1990s. We then focus on the emerging countries' debt crises of the late 1990s and their resolution. Finally, drawing from the analysis of the previous sections, we argue that there is room for significant improvements in the architecture of sovereign debt markets but also that emerging countries have much to do in terms of unilateral reforms that could improve their well-being.

International Sovereign Debt Markets in the 1990s

Market Structure

One important characteristic of sovereign debt instruments is that, unlike corporate debt, it is very difficult to enforce contracts.[1] Lenders cannot take control of a country or seize a significant amount of its assets in the event of a default, which tends to restrict the supply of credit to sovereigns. On the other side, underdeveloped domestic financial markets and the short horizon of government policy makers may lead governments in emerging countries to rely too much on cross-border borrowings and to assume excessive risks. The tension between these two factors is clear, and the result is that governments in emerging countries usually seem to be "credit starved" when facing perceived political uncertainties and pressing expenditure demands, and they tend to rely on potentially risky and high-cost short-term foreign debt. This makes emerging countries prone to suffer painful debt crises.

In fact, sovereign borrowing in relatively weak institutional environments has been characterized by recurrent cycles of booms, busts, and subsequent crises.[2] More often than not, debt crises are accompanied by balance-of-payments and banking crises.[3]

The resolution of the widespread debt crisis of the 1980s initiated a new period of international credit market expansion for developing countries. In effect, the exchange of nontradable bank loans for publicly tradable bonds that began in the late 1980s created the basis for a new market for sovereign borrowers. Subsequently, direct bond issuance replaced commercial bank loans as the preponderant form of government financing in emerging countries. The commercial banks that had been the main source of financing in the previous expansive cycle of international lending to developing countries faced tougher regulations and credit committees who were reluctant to risk repeating their previous unpleasant experience in emerging markets.

Under these conditions, when compared with the available funds from commercial banks, bonded debt had the following advantages:

- It provided relatively better term structure, as it offered long-term financing that commercial banks simply could not entertain because of their own liability structure. Institutional investors—particularly domestic and international pension funds and insurance companies—were trying to get fixed-rate long-term assets.
- Fixed rates were also attractive to borrowers because they reduced vulnerability to monetary market fluctuations.
- The liquidity of the instruments gave the advantage of reduced intermediation costs. A given size would also give participants a certain depth that would reduce transaction costs in the secondary market, which would also be reflected in more attractive initial offering terms.

The most striking characteristic of the international sovereign debt market in the 1990s was the variety of players involved. In addition to the long-term institutional purchasers of securities, in the shorter end of the maturity structure there were mainly domestic investors, including retail investors, mutual funds, and banks seeking liquid instruments as reserves, and certain foreign high-yield funds looking for higher returns. The end of the decade saw the incorporation of so-called crossover buyers and, to a lesser extent, hedge funds that were also seeking fixed income with the prospect of capital gains from credit-rating upgrades. Finally, some governments placed sovereign bonds in retail markets abroad. This was facilitated by the sharp reductions in interest rates in the United States and the European Union, which made emerging debt yields an attractive alternative for some retail investors. As a result, there are now numerous holders of sovereign debt covering a very wide geographic distribution and varying in size and sophistication from retail to institutional investors.

Another important characteristic of debt markets in the 1990s was that, directly or indirectly, reports given by credit-rating agencies became highly important for many investors. This resulted from the fact that many institutional investors were required by mandate to invest only in debt instruments of a certain rating, or because they even had to comply with regulatory requirements that referred to those ratings.

These factors, combined with the mixed track record of local-currency financings and certain disadvantages of applicable domestic law, explained why domestic and foreign investors had strong preferences for instruments denominated in a foreign currency. Borrowers also felt at that time that domestic-currency financings were less attractive: In many cases, the purchasing power of the domestic currency was relatively weak, interest rates were higher, and maturities were shorter.

In general, holders of emerging countries' sovereign debt instruments represented a broad range of investors who relied in a significant manner on the ability of borrowers to improve credit quality. Their motivation was portfolio-driven (i.e., they tended to optimize investment considerations as opposed to other trade-offs, such as business to be generated with the borrower or geopolitical influence).

Evolution of Flows and Spreads

The evolution of international credit markets for sovereign borrowers from emerging countries during the 1990s went through three clearly differentiated periods, as illustrated in table 3.1 and figure 3.1 The first, between 1991 and 1994, was characterized by low international interest rates and market-oriented reforms in emerging countries, and it resulted in a period of large inflows and falling sovereign spreads. The second phase, between 1995 and 1998, started when the Mexican crisis temporarily interrupted the trend of the previous years. However, flows to emerging markets quickly resumed after the resolution of the crisis. Furthermore, although sovereign spreads rose sharply with the Mexican crisis, they reached record lows in the months prior to the Asian crisis in late 1997. Finally, the Asian and Russian crises inaugurated a period characterized by increased systemic risk and reduced flows to emerging markets compared with previous years.

The Idyllic Years (1991–1994)

During the first half of the 1990s, a favorable international environment coupled with the implementation of market-oriented policy reforms in emerging countries and normalized debtor–creditor relationships generated large net capital inflows to emerging countries. A significant portion of these went to the private sector—during those first years of the decade, public-sector financing requirements were not very significant. High economic growth, fiscal adjustment, and one-time revenues from privatization processes improved fiscal accounts, while the debt restructuring of the 1980s had reduced amounts coming due in the initial stages.

At the aggregate level, the inflow of capital relaxed the external financial constraints that these economies often faced in the 1980s. Growth was fueled

TABLE 3.1 Net capital flows to emerging markets, 1990–2000 (Current Billions of $US)

	1990	1991	1992	1993	1994	1995	1996	1997	1998	1999	2000	Total
Emerging markets												
Total private capital inflows (net)	47.5	123.8	158.8	190.9	152.8	193.3	212.2	149.1	64.1	68.3	118.3	1479.1
Bank loans and other debt (net)	11.9	55.7	40.7	19.8	-35.5	55.3	16.3	-57.6	-103.8	-71.8	-50.2	-119.2
Portfolio investment	17.3	36.9	64.3	102.0	105.6	41.3	80.9	66.8	36.7	21.6	40.2	613.6
Foreign direct investment	18.3	31.2	53.8	69.1	82.7	96.7	115.0	139.9	131.2	118.5	128.3	984.7
Net official flows	16.0	35.9	23.1	19.0	8.6	28.9	-18.3	24.3	43.5	9.4	-2.2	188.2
Change in reserve assets	66.2	75.1	31.5	83.9	90.9	123.1	101.1	59.2	58.3	51.1	76.2	816.6
Current account balance	-27.1	-79.0	-69.7	-107.3	-69.7	-96.1	-92.6	-91.8	-53.6	-24.8	-45.3	-757.0
Asia Pacific												
Total private capital inflows (net)	19.6	34.2	57.3	66.4	66.4	95.1	100.5	3.2	-55.3	-29.5	-3.3	354.6
Bank loans and other debt (net)	13.0	18.4	3.3	11.7	11.7	34.4	32.8	-60.3	-89.9	-62.8	-43.5	-131.2
Portfolio investment	-2.7	1.4	21.0	9.4	9.4	10.9	12.6	0.9	-15.4	-8.3	-2.9	36.3
Foreign direct investment	9.3	14.4	33.0	45.3	45.3	49.8	55.1	62.6	50.0	41.6	43.1	449.5
Net official flows	8.4	10.9	10.3	8.5	10.5	6.7	-0.5	30.0	27.5	-0.4	2.3	114.2
Change in reserve assets	47.4	45.9	6.9	43.0	78.3	47.7	61.4	23.5	63.3	42.2	47.3	506.9
Current account balance	1.7	4.5	3.6	-13.3	-3.8	-36.3	-37.5	5.6	101.7	75.5	55.8	157.5
Latin America												
Total private capital inflows (net)	13.7	24.0	55.9	62.5	47.5	38.3	82.0	87.2	68.9	47.1	62.7	589.8
Bank loans and other debt (net)	-10.5	-2.0	11.7	-10.6	-38.2	10.6	2.7	-3.1	-18.1	-7.7	-4.0	-69.2
Portfolio investment	17.5	14.7	30.3	61.1	60.8	1.7	40.0	39.7	33.0	12.0	23.6	334.4
Foreign direct investment	6.7	11.3	13.9	12.0	24.9	26.0	39.3	50.6	54.0	42.8	43.1	324.6
Net official flows	1.8	2.7	-1.7	0.7	-3.4	21.1	-14.1	-8.4	4.1	4.8	-0.1	7.5
Change in reserve assets	14.7	18.0	23.0	20.2	-4.3	24.8	26.2	13.5	-9.9	-6.7	4.1	123.6
Current account balance	-1.0	-16.9	-34.5	-45.7	-50.9	-35.9	-39.0	-65.1	-89.5	-56.5	-56.5	-491.5

(continued)

TABLE 3.1 (Continued)

	1990	1991	1992	1993	1994	1995	1996	1997	1998	1999	2000	Total
Africa												
Total private capital inflows (net)	4.4	8.9	6.9	8.7	4.9	6.9	7.6	16.3	10.3	11.7	18.2	104.8
Bank loans and other debt (net)	4.7	8.4	5.8	5.8	0.7	1.2	2.3	5.8	0.0	0.9	4.8	40.4
Portfolio investment	-1.5	-1.5	-0.6	1.0	0.8	1.5	-0.2	2.9	3.5	2.4	4.7	13.0
Foreign direct investment	1.2	2.0	1.7	1.9	3.4	4.2	5.5	7.6	6.8	8.4	8.7	51.4
Net official flows	7.1	9.1	12.1	8.3	13.5	11.7	-0.2	-4.7	2.2	4.8	-3.5	60.4
Change in reserve assets	4.6	3.7	-2.8	1.6	4.6	1.9	5.5	3.8	-1.5	1.4	8.2	31.0
Current account balance	-9.0	-7.4	-10.4	-11.0	-11.8	-16.4	-5.7	-6.1	-18.1	-18.8	-15.2	-129.9
Middle East												
Total private capital inflows (net)	9.9	73.0	31.0	27.2	17.8	5.0	-3.1	7.1	22.6	17.4	11.0	218.9
Bank loans and other debt (net)	5.8	50.8	19.6	5.9	2.6	-6.1	-8.5	1.8	9.6	7.1	-4.7	83.9
Portfolio investment	3.5	21.9	11.3	18.1	12.1	8.3	3.7	2.8	10.8	6.5	6.2	105.2
Foreign direct investment	0.6	0.3	0.1	3.2	3.1	2.8	1.7	2.5	2.2	3.8	9.5	29.8
Net official flows	-1.8	3.9	-1.2	2.2	-1.5	-1.5	-1.1	-0.8	-1.1	-1.7	-2.0	-6.6
Change in reserve assets	-2.9	6.0	0.7	4.6	2.5	7.7	5.1	11.8	2.4	6.8	5.1	49.8
Current account balance	3.4	-64.2	-25.5	-24.6	-10.8	-3.9	8.7	6.4	-25.0	-8.9	-9.2	-153.6
Europe												
Total private capital inflows (net)	-0.1	-16.3	7.7	26.1	16.2	48.0	25.2	35.3	17.6	21.6	29.7	211.0
Bank loans and other debt (net)	-1.1	-19.9	0.3	7.0	-12.3	15.2	-13.0	-1.8	-5.4	-9.3	-2.8	-43.1
Portfolio investment	0.5	0.4	2.3	12.4	22.5	18.9	24.8	20.5	4.8	9.0	8.6	124.7
Foreign direct investment	0.5	3.2	5.1	6.7	6.0	13.9	13.4	16.6	18.2	21.9	23.9	129.4
Net official flows	0.5	9.3	3.6	-0.7	-10.5	-9.1	-2.4	8.2	10.8	1.9	1.1	12.7
Change in reserve assets	2.4	1.5	3.7	14.5	9.8	41.0	2.9	6.6	4.0	7.4	11.5	105.3
Current account balance	-22.2	5.0	-2.9	-12.7	7.6	-3.6	-19.1	-32.6	-22.7	-16.1	-20.2	-139.5

Source: Dobson and Hufbauer (2001).

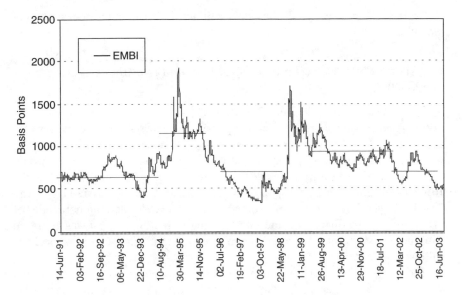

Figure 3.1. EMBI global stripped spread. Source: J.P. Morgan.

by a fast recovery in domestic demand. A significant portion of inflows was in fact repatriation of monies that had left during the previous decade. Increased current account deficits reflected these inflows. The expectation was that inflows would continue, and at some point future export growth would make them un-necessary. Real exchange-rate appreciation was common, while aggregate real incomes rose and credit spreads shrank.

The Mexican Crisis: Is There a "Deep Pockets" International Lender of Last Resort? (1995–1998)

Mexico's crisis of December 1994 abruptly interrupted the initial idyllic period of credit market expansion. However, the massive rescue package assembled by IFIs and G7 governments stabilized the economy and restored confidence in Mexico among market participants, who were also given the impression that international sovereign credit markets were close to having a lender of last resort.

International lending to emerging countries quickly recovered after the crisis, and sovereign spreads that had shot up in the wake of the Mexican crisis came down quickly to near precrisis levels. Three main factors contributed to these results. First, the intervention of the U.S. Treasury, the IMF, and other major institutions left international investors with the impression that there was an international lender of last resort, and this contributed to a reduction in perceived systemic risk. At the same time, investors believed that domestic policy reforms in other emerging countries were not derailed by the Mexican crisis. Finally, and at a more general level, investors' risk appetite was still high. High returns in the U.S. equity markets left investors willing to take more chances with their wealth.

No, There Is Not: Hell (Debt Crisis) or Heaven (Investment Grade) (1998–2002)

The Southeast Asian (1997) and Russian (1998) crises made clear that this new period of international credit market expansion for emerging countries was also subject to sudden stops in capital flows. Agents became aware that the negative effects of these sudden stops on the performance of emerging economies would last longer than previously expected.[4] Even more important was the fact that the IFIs and G7 governments' response to the crises in Southeast Asia (1997) and Russia (1998) showed that there was no "deep pockets" international lender of last resort. Furthermore, the idea of "too-big-to-fail" countries was removed from investors' expectations after Russia's default, as no gigantic rescue package followed the crisis.

These crises and their resolution generated a very significant change in the way international financial markets operated. They affected in important ways investors' perceptions and behavior. First, the perceived risk of investments in emerging countries increased, with negative consequences for financial conditions in emerging countries. Growth rates in most emerging countries were reduced considerably during this period. There were concerns about payoffs of many reforms undertaken in the previous years. Moreover, some developed countries during those years achieved substantial gains in productivity, whereas emerging countries were showing signals of reform fatigue and losing competitiveness in relative terms.

After many years of high-risk exposure in both developed and emerging debt and equity markets, it also appears that investors' appetite for new and increased risk was starting to fade. Emerging countries' bonds as an asset class have been increasingly correlated with the evolution of high-yield debt markets of developed economies (in both the U.S. dollar and euro areas) (see figure 3.2). Clearly, this connection does not come from the fact that those asset classes have similar fundamentals or are exposed to the same fundamental shocks. The only "real" connection between these asset classes is that they were beginning to share a common investor base (usually institutional investment funds with a mandate for investing in asset classes within a given credit rating). A consequence of this connection is the possibility that the performance of sovereign bonds could be affected by shocks to these other high-yield markets.

The change in investors' perceptions of the emerging markets' risk triggered by the Southeast Asian and Russian crises, and the IFIs and G7 policy responses that followed, contributed to a strong contraction in capital flows and lending to emerging countries during the period. Sovereign spreads shot up in the aftermath of the Russian crisis and have remained well above precrisis levels (see figure 3.1). Investors became more wary and selective. Two main factors drove this process. First was the change in investors' perceptions regarding the availability of financing from IFIs in the event of a crisis. Second, the economic

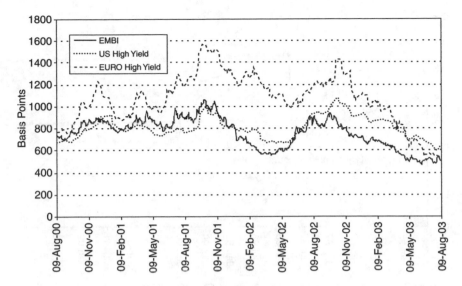

Figure 3.2. EMBI global composite and U.S. and EURO high-yield stripped spread. Source: J.P. Morgan.

outlook started to differ considerably across emerging countries: Countries displayed different prospects of achieving integration with the developed world and had experienced varied degrees of success in the implementation of reforms during the prior decade.

The direct result of these factors was that the correlation of sovereign spreads across emerging countries dropped from their 1997–98 peaks (see figure 3.3).

The combination of higher perceived risk in emerging-market credit and reduced appetite for risk among global investors resulted in a polarization of emerging countries. Countries with strong fundamentals were rewarded with a sharp reduction in credit spreads and in some cases the achievement of an investment-grade credit rating. Those with weaker fundamentals (in political and economic terms) started to lose the confidence of investors and with it market access. For this set of countries, spreads increased and default or some form of restructuring became more likely.

This first group includes Mexico and most Eastern European countries. Those countries ended up reducing their relative borrowing costs from 1998 levels. Convergence with perceived stronger economic areas stands out as the single most important factor that these successful economies had in common. However, specific policies were required to take advantage of greater opportunities derived from integration into those areas, and most of these countries undertook them.

The countries in the second group were characterized in general by weak institutions coupled with a dismal economic performance and failure to integrate successfully with the rest of the world. Table 3.2 shows the main macroeconomic indicators of those countries in the second group that have experienced default

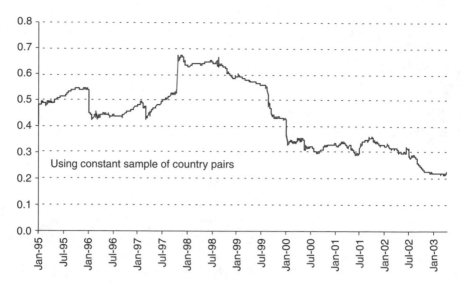

Figure 3.3. Average 12m correlation between EMBIG countries.

between 1998–2003. All defaulter countries share poor economic performances in the periods before default. In countries that combined default with a run on local banks, sharp decreases in reserves also occurred. A significant common factor among all the defaulter countries is the existence of a political crisis or high political instability: Presidential resignations occurred in Argentina, Ecuador, and Pakistan, and prime ministers were replaced in Russia and Ukraine.

Debt Crises in Retrospect

Anatomy of Recent Debt Crises: 1998–2003

Increased systemic risk and worsened financial conditions for certain emerging countries characterized the period since 1998. This new environment that began with the Southeast Asian and Russian crises triggered a number of currency and debt crises in the developing world.

Brazil devalued its currency in 1999, significantly reducing the real value of its domestic liabilities. In 2000, Ecuador, Turkey, Ukraine, and Pakistan defaulted on their liabilities outright. At the end of 2001, Argentina devalued its currency—abandoning the hard peg it had for 10 years—and defaulted on its sovereign liabilities to the private sector in the middle of a bank crisis. Uruguay in 2002–2003 achieved a voluntary restructuring of its debt, avoiding default, and was able to weather a bank run thanks to an international rescue package. All of these countries either defaulted, were forced to reprofile their domestic and/or external liabilities, or significantly reduced the real value of their liabilities denominated in domestic currency through devaluations.

TABLE 3.2   Main macroeconomic indicators of defaulting countries

	Previous semesters				Default period	Next semesters	
	T−4	*T−3*	*T−2*	*T−1*		*T+1*	*T+2*
Reserves (% Change)							
Argentina	−10.3	−13.0	−19.7	−30.1			
Ecuador	−7.0	2.7	−4.7	0.5	−51.8	16.2	30.7
Pakistan	37.5	−10.4	−13.5	40.8	−8.1	−4.7	19.3
Russia	0.9	45.0	−34.9	−26.1	86.7	13.3	26.2
Ukraine	−14.0	−52.3	54.1	3.5	−9.8	8.7	44.0
Output (% Change)							
Argentina	−0.4	−1.9	−0.2	−10.7			
Ecuador	2.7	0.2	−0.1	−7.2	2.1	5.0	
Pakistan	−0.1		2.6		2.7	5.6	
Russia	−1.1	−1.4	−3.8	−0.9	5.1	3.2	
Ukraine	−5.1	−1.2	−5.3	−1.2	−0.1	18.6	
Fiscal surplus (% of GDP)							
Argentina	−3.5	−1.7	−3.1	−3.8			
Ecuador	−3.5	0.7	−0.1	0.3	1.0	−2.1	−1.3
Pakistan	−7.8		−6.4		−6.9	−5.9	
Russia	−6.4	−7.3	−5.0	−6.0	−0.7	1.6	3.4
Ukraine	−5.2	0.3	−1.2	−1.6	2.8	0.8	2.0
Current Account (% of GDP)							
Argentina	−4.6	−3.4	−3.0	−3.0			
Ecuador	−0.6	−2.9	7.9	10.6	18.1	16.6	15.4
Pakistan	−3.1		−3.9		−1.6	−0.2	
Russia	2.9	1.8	−0.6	−2.9	13.7	16.6	15.4
Ukraine	−1.2	−0.2	2.3	0.8	−0.7	2.6	1.0

Source: Sturzenegger (2002).

Whereas the debt crisis of the 1980s was triggered by a series of adverse external shocks (including a significant tightening of monetary policy in the United States) that affected most developing countries simultaneously, more recent crises, starting with the Russian crisis, have so far been of a more selective nature (see figure 3.4).

In broad terms, these latest crises seem to be driven by investors' perception of deterioration in a particular sovereign borrower's willingness and/or ability to service debt, or, in other words, a contraction of creditworthiness. Sovereign investors who detect a negative change in a country's sovereign credit profile reduce their positions, selling out or collecting at maturity, or adopting short positions in the credit. Lack of confidence might also spread to holders of non-government securities, who fear that corporate issuers could be affected by a crisis in the government.

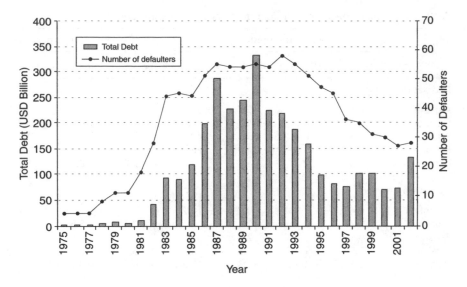

Figure 3.4. Evolution of sovereign defaults. Source: Beers and Chambers (2002).

This behavior by investors generates capital outflows and pressure on foreign reserves, the exchange rate, and asset prices. A weakening of domestic institutions caused by deteriorating finances would further justify capital outflows. Moreover, a depreciation of the domestic currency would not likely be fully reflected in domestic prices, so foreign-currency–denominated debt service in terms of government revenues would increase, worsening the government's balance sheet.[5]

Note that the positive potential effect of a currency devaluation on the tradable sector—which might mitigate the adverse impact on the sovereign balance sheet through a higher level of economic activity—would be limited by the lack of financing for the private sector.[6] Firms in emerging countries in distress are usually strongly credit-constrained because of the lack of external financing and the underdevelopment of domestic financial markets. As a result, governments cannot rely on currency devaluations to spur economic activity (and tax revenue) because firms are unlikely to be able to take advantage of the improved terms of trade because of limited financing.

Once this situation unravels, the government is usually between a "rock and a hard place." In order to regenerate confidence, markets demand new policy initiatives that are often costly in both economic and political terms.[7]

Moreover, the use of traditional macroeconomic policy instruments is very constrained in this type of situation. The use of an expansive fiscal policy to jump-start the economy could further compromise government solvency. Furthermore, given the lack of external and domestic financing at this point, a fiscal expansion often requires printing money to finance it. However, such a response puts additional pressure on the exchange rate as well as triggering inflation, especially given the inflationary history of these countries.

A fiscal tightening, on the other hand, might succeed, although its implementation in such an environment is likely to be extremely costly in economic terms, as tax increases and spending cuts would likely deepen the recession. Repetitive fiscal-tightening exercises could then be required to counterbalance the negative effect on revenues of the deepening recession. Accompanying a restrictive fiscal policy with a rise in interest rates would not help much either. Higher interest rates usually fail to attract capital when sovereign spreads are already at very high levels, and they would only further damage domestic firms' balance sheets.

So, the introduction of reforms (fiscal adjustment or other reforms) that could help regain credibility in this context is very costly and politically difficult. However, failure to undertake these "required" reforms means confirming investors' original lack of confidence. In this case, the situation would only deteriorate further, and ultimately complete loss of market access would force the government to seek a "voluntary" debt rescheduling and, if this fails, to unilaterally default on its debts.

In some instances, recognizing the high political and economic costs associated with defaults and breaches of contracts, certain governments have gone to great lengths to avoid them. Others took a different path, seeking political benefits from declaring default and then blaming others for their economy's dismal performance. There are few, however, that succeeded in addressing the fundamental issues driving the crisis of confidence by implementing policies that would reduce the relative debt burden (with or without restructuring) over time in a credible manner with necessary political support.

High risks are associated with the failure to address fundamental economic problems. Defaulting further undermines the performance of the private sector, particularly those areas that are more exposed to economic hardship (usually lower income classes), but not defaulting means accepting high rollover costs and increasing the exposure of the domestic financial system to sudden changes in macroeconomic variables such as interest rates and trade flows.

Debt Crisis Resolutions: Yesterday versus Today

In 1982, Mexico declared a unilateral moratorium on external debt services following a widespread bank-lending slowdown caused by a series of external shocks, particularly a significant tightening of monetary policy in the United States. The debt crisis quickly consumed several other countries, mainly from Latin America. Sovereign and private-sector defaults ballooned.

During the 1980s, there were many attempts to find a comprehensive solution to the debt problem. However, its resolution turned out to be more complex than generally anticipated. The initial approach consisted of requiring banks to extend new financing through maturity extension and some additional lending with the purpose of enabling borrowers to remain current on their obligations. This scheme was usually called the "new money approach." In practice, this mechanism suffered major drawbacks as some banks increasingly adopted free-rider behavior, by which they collected payments from countries in difficulty but did not agree to extend additional credit. This flaw in the incentive scheme increasingly complicated resolution of the problem.

Another issue that delayed the process was the systemic-risk implications that sovereign defaults produced. Relatively good commercial credits were affected by increased sovereign risk factors—private-sector borrowers with sound fundamentals had to face severely increased financing costs. Economic activity suffered as a consequence. At the same time, several creditor countries wanted to avoid the negative consequences on the international financial system that would have resulted from marking loans to market (or constituting adequate provisions), which would have impaired the solvency of many banks from developed countries, particularly the United States. These losses were ultimately cushioned to a big extent by drops in market interest rates.

By the late 1980s, a new, comprehensive approach to debt resolution had been implemented. Debtor countries agreed to pursue a series of economic reforms (mainly of a structural and fiscal nature) aimed at laying sound growth foundations, while creditor banks agreed to more lasting debt relief. Various existing bank claims were exchanged for newly issued public bonds of reduced face value (principal or interest) but with partial, solid guarantees acquired by debtors in conjunction with long-term financing provided by IFIs and government agencies of developed countries.

This approach was attractive for both debtors and creditors, allowing the former to regularize their situation, reprofiling and reducing their debt obligations, and allowing the latter to receive a liquid and easily traded asset. Evidence of the success of this new approach emerged from the fact that the market price of the new instruments ended up being higher than the old impaired claims. This resolution restored faith among market participants that the difficulties preventing certain countries from paying were being overcome. Furthermore, it kick-started the market for emerging countries' government bonds, which subsequently became the main form of financing during the 1990s.

Sovereign credit markets changed substantially in the 1990s in comparison with the 1980s. Probably the most striking fact is the change in the composition of creditor groups. The resolution of a debt crisis now requires dealing with a very large number—tens of thousands—of bondholders scattered around the globe (including residents of emerging countries). This more diverse and atomistic investor base is coupled with debt instruments issued in many countries under different legislation and in different currencies.

In the 1980s, on the other hand, it was possible to deal with creditors in a more direct fashion. Investors were a more homogeneous group, and their number was much smaller (in the hundreds). They were generally foreign banks, with a much closer relationship with their regulators, who could help to coordinate the process if necessary.

The volume of claims involved in workout situations has also increased dramatically since 1998.[8] The aggregate amount of the so-called Brady bonds issued in the aftermath of the 1980s crisis by all countries is only 1.5 times the amount to be restructured by Argentina in 2004. Table 3.3 summarizes the main differ-

TABLE 3.3   More recent crises compared with those of the 1980s

	1980s	Recent crises
Debtor	Both public and private sectors	Mainly public or Quasi public sector ([a])
Creditors	Commercial banks	Holders of securities
Number	Limited (in 00's)	Large (000's)
Geographical distribution	Foreign	Both local and foreign
Amounts involved	Brady bonds = $160 billion (U.S.)	Large multiple
First approach to resolution	New money	Exchange (+/− voluntary)
Complication	Free riders	Holdouts
Final resolution	Exchange w/ guarantees and haircut	Forced exchange, TBD

[a]Including banks on some occasions.

ences in creditor base and resolution approaches between debt crises of the 1980s and more recent crises.

Debt workouts between 1998 and 2005 have been characterized by comprehensive exchanges of certain securities defined by debtor countries as eligible debt. In some instances, the diagnosis was that the crisis was driven by transitory external events and therefore temporary relief was required, meaning extension of the maturities of that debt. In other cases, where the crisis was perceived as structural, a more profound change of economic policy became an implicit condition preceding the restructuring. The exchange offer was proposed to all holders of that debt class. High participation rates were required to make the exchange effective. Table 3.4 displays important aspects of the major debt workouts since 1998.

Given the larger investor base, the diversity of debt instruments, and the larger amounts involved, a surprising fact is that the length of time taken to resolve more recent sovereign debt workouts has been much shorter than in the 1980s (see table 3.5 Furthermore, after resolution, sovereign spreads have often improved rapidly.

Lessons from Debt Crises Since the 1990s

Sovereign defaults have created a number of lessons in relation both to economic policy making in emerging countries and more general systemic issues that refer to the international financial architecture, including the functioning of the IFIs.

Domestic Policy Considerations

The political context of a given country, its institutions and macro policies, and the influence of external events interact and explain particular economic per-

TABLE 3.4   Main indicators of sovereign debt workouts: 1998–2004

	Russia	Ukraine	Ecuador	Pakistan	Uruguay	Argentina[a]
# Old bonds involved	3	5	5	3	66	152
# New bonds issued	2	2	2	1	31	?
Amount restructured (in millions $U.S.)	31,600	2,600	6,600	610	4,900	100,000
# of legislations involved	1	3	2	1	6	8
Exchange participation rate	98%	95%	97%	95%	92%	
Minimum threshold to perform the exchange	Yes	Yes	Yes	Yes	Yes	
Up-front payments	0.8%	8.5%	15.2%	0.0%	Selective	
# of months between default and closing	18	3	10	2	0	
Official debt/ total debt	45%	75%	50%	88%	45%	18%
Face value reduction	36%	0%	32%	0%	0%	
Maturity extension	Yes	Yes	Yes	Yes	Yes	
Coupon reduction	No	Yes	No	Yes	No	

[a]estimates
Source: Authors.

formances. A detailed analysis of domestic macro policies in emerging countries is well beyond the scope of this chapter. The focus here will be on just a few particularly relevant issues.

Institutional Arrangements

As is well-known, institutions are crucial in the development process, and emerging countries have a lot to do in this regard. Enforcement of contracts in some emerging countries is frequently seen as weak or "imperfect," thus raising uncertainties that translate into higher risk premiums for the affected countries.

TABLE 3.5   Default and resumption of access

	Average number of years until resumption
1980s	5.4
1990s	0.9

Source: Gelos, et al. (2003).
Note: Data cover the period 1980–99, including only countries that regained access during that period. Access is defined as issuance of a public or publicly guaranteed bond or syndicated loan (Source: Bondware, Loanware). Year of default is defined as the year in which the sovereign defaulted on foreign-currency debt according to Standard & Poor's (Source: Beers and Bhatia, 1999).

Contradictory, changing, and superfluous regulations are not uncommon. Judicial and regulatory authority often lacks independence from the political process.

Improvements in these areas take significant effort and time, and undertaking them is politically unappealing because benefits take a long time to emerge, whereas costs are borne up front. Nevertheless, well-defined rights and obligations, their enforcement, and transparency are associated with significant improvements in asset allocation and overall productivity. Proper regulatory and supervisory bodies have an important effect on agents' behavior and could diminish or eliminate some market imperfections.

Although reforms could have positive aggregate results, they usually have distributional effects, with winners and losers. An important challenge is posed by sequencing reforms and finding alternatives for those that are displaced. This challenge becomes even more relevant when deep reforms with deep effects on employment patterns are implemented over a short period of time. Changes that in some countries occurred over a generation were in others implemented over a few short years, without the cushion provided by time. A way of reducing the associated distributional costs of reforms is through opening alternative opportunities that could absorb resources.

Macro Consistency: The Choice of the Exchange-Rate Regime

One meaningful pervasive feature of economic policy making in emerging countries, where institutions are relatively weak, is the variation in credibility that authorities face. Sometimes, economic policy making in these countries seems like a constant fight to regain, maintain, or increase credibility.

The choice of exchange-rate regime is usually related to this feature. Lack of credibility in domestic institutions, inflationary history, and a certain international consensus led many emerging countries to choose a fixed or quasi-fixed exchange-rate regime as an "external anchor" as part of their stabilization plans in the early 1990s, therefore foregoing the use of monetary policy.[9] More recently, the pendulum has moved and the international consensus has shifted to a flexible exchange rate coupled with some form of inflation targeting, an appropriate policy combination for coping with current levels of capital mobility.

Note, however, that emerging countries often have limited instruments with which to manage liquidity pressures generated by capital inflows even under floating exchange-rate arrangements. Monetary policy tools are undermined by weak fiscal fundamentals or significant changes in demand for domestic currency or high debt ratios. Under these conditions, monetary tools are simply insufficient to cope with the flows involved. This effect is reinforced by the fact that in many emerging countries domestic financial markets are fairly underdeveloped. In such cases, external and domestic equilibria are in tension.

What the experience of the 1990s demonstrates is that the importance of the choice of exchange-rate regime is overrated. What really matters is the development of strong institutions and an underlying sound macroeconomic policy that enables growth. No exchange-rate regime can be successful in the absence of these factors. Moreover, the relative performance of different exchange-rate regimes would not vary so much in the presence of consistent and credible fiscal, financial, and monetary policies and institutions. As Calvo and Mishkin (2003: 1) put it: "[L]ess attention should be focused on the general question whether a floating or a fixed exchange rate is preferable, and more on these deeper institutional arrangements. A focus on institutional reforms rather than on the exchange rate regime may encourage emerging market countries to be healthier and less prone to the crises that we have seen in recent years."

In many of the countries that suffered debt crises since the 1980s, this focus was lacking or incomplete. Not only were institutional reforms not deep enough, but in many cases the underlying macroeconomic policies were inconsistent. For example, although debt denominated in foreign currency attracted both foreign and domestic investors, positive net borrowings from abroad expand domestic demand, which is not the case with positive net domestic borrowings. Fiscal policies should counterbalance those effects, and yet net foreign borrowing is often undertaken in order to finance expansionary fiscal policies—a procyclical approach that tends to accentuate the boom–bust economic cycle of emerging countries.

Regional Integration as a Strategy

One factor that several successful emerging countries share is the implementation of a regional integration strategy with a broader and more developed economic area. In effect, integration produces the result of improving growth opportunities through access to larger markets, significant economies of scale, better asset allocation, and resulting productivity gains. Integration can also provide access to greater depth and diversity of financial instruments and a more reliable institutional framework. Furthermore, creating deeper markets for goods, services, and financial products that function in an integrated fashion seems to provide strong incentives to reduce the divergence of economic policies and increase their predictability.

These elements contribute to strong capital inflows (with a significant proportion of Foreign Direct Investment) to countries seen as benefiting from integration. Although in the short term these flows can be destabilizing, over time, integration seems to reduce vulnerability and volatility in a significant manner. For mature economies, over time, integration also expands possibilities, adds flexibility, and increases security. The process that resulted in the creation and expansion of the European Union is one case that illustrates these points.

International Sovereign Debt Markets

Advantages of Uniform Regulations in International Standards

Increased capital mobility strengthens the case for stronger regulatory and supervisory functions that complement each other across jurisdictions. Convergence in standards among national regulators would not only result in lower processing costs of market information but also more uniform and smoother functioning of markets.

However, many international regulatory bodies are structured under multilateral soft-law agreements with a vague definition of their scope and power. Political factors are mainly responsible for this situation: Countries are reluctant to cede power over their domestic systems to international bodies. Although the core objectives—protection of investors; ensuring that markets are fair, efficient, and transparent; and the reduction of systemic risk—are shared ones, practical shortcomings arise when different traditions, regulatory structures, and policy rules need to be assembled. Regulation heterogeneity allows for "regulation arbitrages" that have the effect of diminishing the effectiveness of domestic regulations and increasing systemic risk.

There is still significant work to be done on the areas of convergence that would yield very encouraging results.[10] International cooperation should be strengthened in order to not only achieve specific goals (harmonization of standards, regulation of current nonregulated markets and financial institutions, transparency improvements, efficient surveillance performed by qualified professionals, etc.) but also to ensure democracy within international regulatory institutions. Otherwise, the reputation of these institutions, a key factor in their success, risks being undermined.

Resolution Mechanisms

Because of the diversity of contractual arrangements in different markets, there is not currently a coherent way of resolving problems in international debt workouts. A well-known example relates to collective-action clauses to modify bond indentures: Whereas English and Japanese laws allow collective-action clauses without the need for unanimity, American and German laws do not. It is hotly debated whether the lack of a sovereign bankruptcy procedure across jurisdictions increases the difficulty of achieving timely resolution of sovereign defaults.

It is true that this heterogeneity of legislation did not prevent the resolution, in relatively limited timeframes, of crises that occurred during the 1990s. However, limited holdout strategies since then have proved to be successful, complicating the prospects for future workouts.

In the current context, international sovereign debt markets should move on to a new generation of contracts that include supermajority rules to resolve conflicts involving a broad array of securities from the same issuer. In dealing with the transition problem between the current generation of contracts and the new contractual arrangements, codes of conduct with international recognition promise a short-term solution.

The Role of the IMF and other IFIs

As noted during the 1990s, crises in emerging countries seem to have been focused around issues of sovereign creditworthiness. Although the IMF has a mandate to act on balance-of-payments crises, it does not have a clear-cut mandate to deal with sovereign debt crises. Furthermore, its financial resources are clearly insufficient to deal with them. This becomes clear when the evolution of IMF capital is compared with almost any measure of international capital flows or cross border lending since the 1970s. For example, between 1970 and 2000, cross-border capital flows measured in constant U.S. dollars grew at a yearly average rate of 5.2%, whereas the IMF's capital grew by 1.3% (see figure 3.5).

The IMF position regarding sovereign defaults was not consistent during the period of 1995–2005, probably reflecting the changing approach of some of the major shareholders to the matter and the lack of a clear-cut mandate in this regard. Following the Mexican crisis of 1994–95, the IMF's actions resembled those of an international lender of last resort. In contrast, its approach was much more cautious during other more recent debt crises, where the IMF viewed default as the only "viable" alternative and encouraged a more active private-sector role in the resolution. Moreover, as many defaulting countries had significant outstanding debts with the IMF, it became reluctant to contribute new capital.

Although many IMF policy recommendations prior to and during the crises of the 1990s were debatable at best, one often overlooked area in which the IMF could have performed better was in communicating to different stakeholders its policy regarding lending possibilities and sovereign defaults. Since the 1990s, the IMF has adopted unclear and inconsistent policies that made its intentions hard to predict. As a result, stakeholders made assessments that then proved to be wrong. Investors misinterpreted the systemic implications of IMF's actions and their impact on particular countries. In turn, this also allowed governments from emerging countries to postpone necessary reforms or adopt risky or inconsistent policy mixes—taking advantage of relaxed market discipline.

In many cases, when a change in IMF policy became evident, investors reassessed the risk in their portfolios and rebalanced them. Countries that had pursued inconsistent policies suffered drastic changes in capital flows and lending

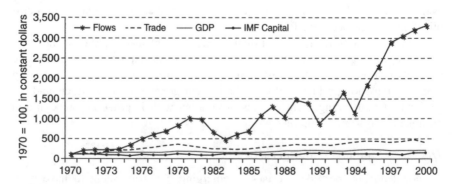

Figure 3.5. Evolution of some relevant indicators of the world economy. Source: IMF and WTO.

conditions. By this time, it was usually too late or too costly to undertake the domestic policy reforms that should have been taken years before. The indecision of the IMF and some of its major shareholders on how to respond to sovereign debt crises aggravated some of them and, even worse, in some instances contributed to the conditions for the crises' occurrence. This happened obviously with the complicity of some shortsighted emerging country governments.

It is therefore natural to ask how the IMF should act in the future to reduce systemic risk and prevent sovereign debt crises. The conventional wisdom is that the IMF's treatment of sovereign debt problems should be contingent on whether the problems are temporary liquidity problems or more structural solvency-related ones. In other words, the response to a debt crisis should depend on whether the crisis is fundamentally driven or just the result of poor coordination of expectations ("sunspots").[11] When the crisis is not fundamentally driven, all of the standard theoretical arguments in favor of a lender of last resort would apply. However, the IMF cannot and should not put together large packages of financial assistance to solve a sovereign debt problem that is structural. Such packages merely bail out private creditors of those sovereign borrowers. Fostering a strong private-sector involvement in the resolution of fundamentally driven crises is extremely important, as it provides the correct incentives to investors for a more responsible assessment of risks, which will ultimately prevent crises.

This approach will reduce the incidence of crises but will not eliminate them altogether. Even when investors assess risks responsibly and governments pursue responsible policies, bad outcomes occur and will still cause crises. So, another relevant question is how the IMF should respond once a debt crisis has already occurred.

The crucial issue after a crisis develops is how the government can regain credibility and investors' confidence. Restoring confidence in the government improves the chances of a successful debt restructuring and with it the possibility of regaining market access. One device that the IMF has employed in the past with disastrous results is the "short leash" approach to economic policy making, which features very frequent (quarterly) reviews of economic performance and policy initiatives. This approach does not rebuild credibility. Quite the opposite, it creates recurrent uncertainty and with it the sensation of a "debt overhang"— as if the debt carried large quarterly amortizations in the short term. In fact, past experience shows that a crucial element of successful debt restructurings such as the Brady Plan was the long maturity of the new arrangements.

We believe that the IMF should have a leading role in resolving sovereign debt crises. However, the IMF should broaden its approach from its current narrow reliance on macroeconomic tools, as many important policy reforms are structural and institutional in nature. The IMF should increase its coordination with other IFIs that are specialized in these areas. Increased transparency, better communication, and a broader approach to crisis solving would make the IMF more effective in its role as stabilizer of the international financial system.

Conclusion

Debt crises and their resolutions have generated many lessons and left unanswered even more questions. A globalized world with high capital mobility creates significant opportunities for emerging countries but also engenders important challenges. Notable success stories as well as painful failures have resulted.

In order to analyze possible improvements in the functioning of international debt markets and find some policy lessons from debt crises of the 1990s, this chapter began by reviewing the evolution and structure of international debt markets during this period.

We argued that these crises had more of a "sovereign credit" nature than the typical balance-of-payments crisis of previous years. The crises in emerging countries between 1998 and 2003 (starting with the Russian crisis) seem to have been driven by investors' perception of deterioration in a particular sovereign borrower's willingness and/or ability to service debt. Regardless of whether this perception was fundamentally based, breaking the "confidence trap" usually required difficult, costly reforms, as the standard macroeconomic policy response usually was not enough. When societies were unable or unwilling to undertake these reforms, a debt crisis would follow.

Resolution of debt crises since the 1990s has been ad hoc, usually including comprehensive exchanges of certain securities defined by debtor countries as eligible debt. The diversity and large number of current debt holders, probably the main feature of sovereign debt markets in the 1990s, coupled with debt instruments issued in many international markets under different legislation and currencies, creates problems of comparability and approaches to the resolution of crises. Given these problems, it is encouraging that most exchanges were completed fairly quickly. However, this may not be true in the future. Among other factors, the success of past "holdout" strategies could make future resolutions more complicated.

Without diminishing the importance of reforms that countries could undertake to improve their economic welfare, we believe that there is room for significant improvements in the functioning of sovereign debt markets in terms of a better architecture. A convergence of international standards and regulations, and incorporating some features in sovereign debt contracts, such as supermajority rules to resolve conflicts involving a broad array of securities from the same issuer, could contribute to reduced systemic risk. This could be enhanced by a redefinition of and clearer communication by IFIs, particularly the IMF policies regarding debt crises, as their performance in the 1990s contributed to creating the conditions for some elements of the 1990s debt crisis. However, the final responsibility for preventing such crises lies with the governments of emerging countries. Deep institutional reforms, consistent macroeconomic policies, and adequate growth strategies could do much to prevent future crises. Proper economic integration processes are very useful because they not only advance opportunities for participants but also create a more stable common framework that reduces perceived risk.

The issues mentioned are not intended to exhaust the debate but rather enrich it with some thoughts drawn from the experience of the 1990s. The objective should be to reduce some of the idiosyncratic and systemic risk that feeds on itself and sometimes turns into a significant constraint to development.

Acknowledgments Chapter 3 written with the collaboration of Juan Bruno.

Notes

1. Why do countries repay? Why would a government ever repay its debts with private creditors and particularly foreign ones? Several researchers consider this question crucial for understanding international debt markets, and they have been trying to answer it since at least the 1980s. This question arises as a result of difficulties surrounding enforceability of sovereign debt contracts. In effect, if the legal framework does not make defaults costly, then sovereign borrowers have fewer incentives to repay, and therefore lenders would have few incentives to provide money. However, lenders do extend credit to governments, and governments usually do repay their debts, even those owed to foreign creditors. So the most essential task of the sovereign-borrowing literature is to identify governments' incentives to repay. That is, the central theoretical issue has not been why governments default but rather why they usually choose not to default given the weak legal framework. The literature on sovereign borrowing has historically focused on two main explanations: reputation and sanctions. The first emphasizes the role played by the borrower's reputation. The idea, first modeled by Eaton and Gersowitz (1981), is that repayment may hold the carrot of a good reputation for the borrower (usually implying the ability to borrow again). That is, the reputation literature emphasizes the costs of being excluded from credit markets in the event of a default. However, Bulow and Rogoff (1989), in a seminal paper, argued that if governments had access to a sufficiently rich set of assets after defaulting, then reputation for repayment alone could not explain why governments repay. Based on this result, they suggest that, instead of reputation for repayment, it is the threat of direct sanctions (usually trade-related) that compels governments to repay.

More recently, Cole and Kehoe (1997) and Sandleris (2003) argued that there are other costs of defaulting beyond those of potential sanctions or exclusion from credit markets. Cole and Kehoe argue that a default may be costly in terms of affecting a country's reputation beyond the borrower/lender relationship (which they call reputation spillovers). Sandleris extends this idea to emphasize the role of the information that defaults convey as one of the reasons why governments repay. He argues that a default could be a signal to the private sector (resident and nonresident) about the state of the economy and future tax rates or government spending, and as a result could negatively affect private-sector investment decisions.

Although this debate may be academic, it is clear that defaults often have severe short-term consequences for economic performance on top of the other noneconomic implications for those that are under the sovereign umbrella. Different views on why governments repay would have very different implications in terms of policy recommendations regarding the architecture of international debt markets.

2. Lindert and Morton (1989) review the history of foreign lending to sovereign debtors, finding that generalized debt crises occurred recurrently after periods of credit expansions. They found such episodes in the 1820s, 1870s, 1890s, 1930s, and 1980s.

3. See Reinhart (2002) for a detailed analysis of this relation.

4. See Calvo et al. (2002) for a detailed analysis of this issue.

5. This would be the result unless a large enough share of government revenues were linked to foreign currency. An example of such a situation would be Venezuela, where a large proportion of government revenues are related to oil exports, and therefore the balance sheet and fiscal accounts could improve following a depreciation.

6. Furthermore, this positive effect could potentially be outweighed by the negative effects of a depreciation on firms with currency mismatches between revenues (in local currency) and liabilities (in foreign currency).

7. Had the government introduced these policy actions at an earlier stage, before the change in investors' perceptions, maybe investors' expectations would not have turned so negative. A typical example of the policy actions we have in mind would be more responsible fiscal management during the "idyllic times."

8. Workout situations include both outright defaults and voluntary restructuring.

9. It is clear that countries cannot simultaneously maintain fixed exchange-rate parities, an open capital account, and a domestic-oriented monetary policy. So, choosing an optimal combination among the three is what Obstfeld and Taylor (1998) called the open-economy trilemma.

10. The creation of institutions such as the International Organization of Securities Commissions (IOSCO), comprising securities markets regulatory bodies from more than 90 countries, is a good example.

11. We acknowledge that applying this policy recommendation requires being able to clearly distinguish whether the problem is structural or temporary, and this is often not easy to do ex ante.

References

Beers, D. T., and Bhatia, A. 1999. *Sovereign Defaults: Hiatus in 1999?* New York: Standard and Poors Credit Week, December.

Beers, D. T., and Chambers, J. 2002. *Sovereign Defaults: Moving Higher Again in 2003?* New York: Standard & Poors.

Bulow, J., and Rogoff, K. 1989. Sovereign Debt: Is to Forgive to Forget? *American Economic Review,* Vol. 79 (June): 43–50.

Calvo, G., Izquierdo, A., and Talvi, E. 2002. Sudden Stops, the Real Exchange Rate and Fiscal Sustainability: Argentina's Lessons. Background Paper presented at the seminar "The Resurgence of Macro Crises: Causes and Implications for Latin America." Washington, DC: Inter-American Development Bank.

Calvo, G., and Mishkin, F. 2003. The Mirage of Exchange Rate Regimes for Emerging Market Countries. Forthcoming: *Journal of Economic Perspectives,* Vol. 17 (4): 99–118.

Cole, H., and Kehoe, P. 1997. Reviving Reputation Models of International Debt. *Federal Reserve Bank of Minneapolis Quarterly Review,* Vol. 21, No. 1 (Winter): 21–30.

Dobson, W., and Hufbauer, G. 2001. *World Capital Markets: Challenge to the G-10.* Washington, DC: Institute for International Economics.

Eaton, J., and Gersowitz, M. 1981. Debt with Potential Repudiation: Theoretical and Empirical Analysis. *Review of Economic Studies,* Vol. 48: 289–309.

Gelos, G., Sahay, R., and Sandleris, G. 2003. Sovereign Borrowing: What Determines Market Access. IMF Working Paper. Washington, DC: IMF.

Lindert, P., and Morton, P. 1989. How Sovereign Debt Has Worked. In *Developing Coun-*

try Debt and Economic Performance, vol. 1, ed. J. D. Sachs, pp. 39–106. Chicago and London: University of Chicago Press.

Obstfeld, M., and Taylor, A. 1998. The Great Depression as a Watershed: International Capital Mobility over the Long Run. In *The Defining Moment: The Great Depression and the American Economy in the Twentieth Century,* ed. M.D. Bord, C. Goldin, and E. White, pp. 353–402. Chicago: University of Chicago Press.

Reinhart, C. 2002. Default, Currency Crises and Sovereign Credit Ratings. National Bureau of Economic Research. Working Paper 8738. Washington, DC: National Bureau of Economic Research.

Sandleris, G. 2003. Sovereign Borrowing: Neither Reputation Nor Economic Sanctions. Unpublished manuscript.

Sturzenegger, F. 2002. *Default Episodes in the 90's: Factbook and Preliminary Lessons.* Washington, DC: World Bank.

Part II

Sovereign Debt: Law and Ethics

4

ECOLOGICAL DEBT—THE ECONOMIC POSSIBILITIES FOR OUR GRANDCHILDREN

Andrew Simms

Over his shoulder I saw a star fall. It was me.

Falling Angels, *Tracy Chevalier*

Introduction

Centuries of global economic development have witnessed two striking phenomena: first, a huge expansion in the size of the global economy; and second, a dramatic divergence in the way that wealth is distributed.

Both wealth creation and appropriation have been based, significantly, on the exploitation of natural resources. From the early days of globally ambitious European empires, the gold and silver of Latin America kept Europe economically afloat and financed its adventures. Then, for more than the last century, the black gold of humanity's fossil fuel inheritance has driven the expansion and divergence of the global economy.

Now, the fact that the rich are taking more than their fair, and sustainable, share of a finite resource base has an extra, potentially catastrophic dimension. Observed climate change and increased scientific understanding of environmental limits, coupled with new international commitments to poverty reduction, mean that the enormous ecological debt run up by the rich takes on a new geopolitical importance.

The fact of ecological debt in an age of climate change moves the balance of power in international relations. Using ecological debt as both analytical framework and political argument, it is possible to imagine a paradigm shift from centuries of global economic expansion and divergence to one of contraction and convergence (Meyer 2000). In other words, to imagine the architecture necessary for the global economy to work within natural limits and equitably distribute its benefits. It has become a logic necessary for our collective survival.

Expansion and Divergence: For Richer, for Poorer

> The modern age opened, I think, with the accumulation of capital which began in the sixteenth century. I believe that this was initially due to the . . . treasure of gold and silver which Spain brought from the New World into the Old. (Keynes 1931)

Although he would not have thought in these terms, John Maynard Keynes made the point that the modern age was triggered by the Old World running up an enormous ecological debt with the New World. In the name of the struggle against inadequate labels inherited from the language of our forefathers, it should be pointed out that, in terms of deep historical human migration patterns, the New World was often just as old, as it were, as the Old.

For reasons that will become obvious in the context of climate change, Keynes's view of the magic of compound interest is a useful, if underrated, warning, "From that time until today the power of accumulation by compound interest . . . over two hundred years is such as to stagger the imagination."

Writing in 1931, Keynes points out that Francis Drake, the pirate-turned "Knight of the Realm," robbed the Spanish robbers in 1580 using his ship the *Golden Hind*, to remarkable and lasting effect. Out of the share of the spoils taken by Queen Elizabeth, she was able to pay off England's foreign debt, balance the country's budget, and have left over a substantial £40,000 sum in hand. The queen invested in the Levant Company, whose profits gave birth to the East India Company and, to simplify the story, the British Empire. Keynes took an envelope and did a few sums. That £40,000 cash in hand, invested at 3.25% compound interest, subsequently equaled the total value of England's foreign investments at various times up to the point of Keynes's writing. By then, in 1930, £1 brought home by Drake would have been worth £100,000. At the time of writing, that original single pound would have turned into £1,032,701.[1]

Also, today the ironically named "positive environmental feedbacks" that are likely to accelerate climate change have become the compound interest of ecological debt. And, lest we in the already industrialized North think that we have escaped with our earlier expropriation of natural wealth of the southern hemisphere, we haven't. It has been noticed.

Guaicaipuro Cuautemoc, a Latin American Indian chief, in a letter to "all European governments," asked for his continent's money back: "Paper after paper, receipt after receipt, signature after signature show that between 1503 and 1660 alone, 18.5 thousand kgs of gold and 16 million kgs of silver were shipped in San Lucar de Barrameda from America" (Cuautemoc 1997).

The gold and silver, Cuautemoc concluded, must be considered as the first of several "friendly loans" granted by America for Europe's development. Any other way of seeing "such fabulous capital exports" would "presuppose acts of war." It was, according to Cuautemoc, a "Marshalltezuma Plan to guarantee the reconstruction of a barbarian Europe." To repay in weight of gold and silver, now popular again in these deflationary times, and using the "European formula" of compound interest would require an amount whose weight "fully exceeds that of the planet earth" (Cuautemoc 1997).

However, any shame, apology, or display of remorse on the part of the "borrowers" seems still to be missing. On the contrary, the Old World and their descendants are prepared to go to court to claim and keep their stolen property. Early in 2003, news emerged of a French galleon, the *Notre Dame de Deliverance*, once in service to the King of Spain. It had sunk in a storm off the Florida Keys on 1 February 1755.[2] It had sailed from Havana loaded with "treasure" dug from the mines of Peru, Colombia, and Mexico and was heading back to fill the vaults of the Spanish king Charles III. Seventeen chests of gold bullion, over 15,000 gold doubloons, one million "pieces of eight," 24 kg of silver and more silver ore, 153 gold snuff boxes, and countless more items of silver, diamond jewelery, and precious stones were sitting at the bottom of the sea. In deep sea limbo, the wealth estimated to be worth $2 billion (U.S.) was long lost to both the land of its original owners and the "Old World" plunderers.

Media interest, however, was aroused not by further historical evidence of systematic colonial theft but by claims and counterclaims for the sunken cargo. The U.S.-based Sub Sea Research Company claimed to have located the wreck and was seeking salvage rights. But the Spanish government was "almost certain" to claim the *Deliverance* under a treaty of 1902 it has with the United States. The French, too, as owners of the ship, were thought to have a chance at a claim. The countries not even mentioned in the haggle over the "treasure" were those countries from whom the wealth was taken. It shows, perhaps, how deeply we have internalized and accepted the "natural logic" of history's negative redistribution of wealth between continents to our, Northern, advantage and how invisible are the real ecological and economic debts that have paid for the unequal world we live in today.

These observations are more than historical point scoring. According to John Kenneth Galbraith (1975), "Discovery and conquest set in motion a vast flow of precious metal from America to Europe." Prices rose in Europe in response to the increase in supply of "the hardest of hard money." A combination of high prices and low wages freed up enormous amounts of capital for investment. These prices, notes Galbraith, rather than the tales of the conquistadors, "were the message to most Europeans that America was discovered." Some view that the influx of gold and silver "per se" gave birth to European capitalism. Galbraith prefers to emphasize that the consequences of the lustrous metals, rather than the metals themselves, were more important.

Temples in America were looted of precious objects, but it was the rape of the earth, principally for silver, that was most significant. Mines in Mexico and Peru were principally important. Most of the action was over by 1630, with the richest ores already exploited. But just under a century and a half of wealth extraction had been enough to refloat some of the Old World's great powers, previously made almost bankrupt by constant warring. Max Weber estimated that 70% of Spain's and two-thirds of other European nations' earnings from this time went to finance war, which also meant, of course, more colonial conquests (Galbraith 1975).

What happened between Europe and Central and South America in the sixteenth and seventeenth centuries, in terms of the way that it opened up enduring gaps of wealth and well-being between continents, was, rather than being historically isolated, the start of what a criminal psychologist might today call "repeat offending behavior."

"If the history of British rule in India were to be condensed into a single fact, it is this: there was no increase in India's per capita income from 1757 to 1947," observes Michael Davis (2002) in *Late Victorian Holocausts: El Nino Famines and the Making of the Third World*. In Britain, on the other hand, per capita incomes rose 14% between 1700 and 1760, 34% between 1760 and 1820, and 100% between 1820 and 1870 (Baldwin et al. 1998).

In a period of time during which the British Empire expanded to become, for a time, the dominant global power, India, its jewel in the imperial crown, experienced "no economic development at all in the usual sense of the term," according to Davis (2002). In the last 50 years of the nineteenth century, when the empire was at its peak, income in India dropped by an estimated 50%. From 1872 to 1921, the average Indian's life expectancy fell by one-fifth.

Britain reengineered India's economy toward cash crops for export. Opium, cotton, and wheat all pushed out the farming of crops for local consumption. Grain exports went up from 3 to 10 million tons between 1875 and 1900. These were also years that included the "worst famines in Indian history." Forests were felled to build a railroad infrastructure vital for the new, crude, extractive economy. Cash, too, was a major export, as the Empire's merciless demands continued to bleed the country for taxes, even during times of famine. And famines there were aplenty (Davis 2002).

British rule was not without its internal critics. Lieutenant Colonel Osborne commented in 1879 that to the great mass of people, the English official was hard, mechanical, and enigmatic, "a piece of machinery possessing the powers to kill and tax and imprison" (Davis 2002).

As the new economy dismantled established coping mechanisms, dispossessed large segments of the population, and took away many of their customary rights, the population became much more vulnerable to natural, climatic disasters. Their increased exposure to a harsh climate walked hand in hand with increased integration into the world markets and a "dramatic deterioration in their terms of trade" (Davis 2002).

Explaining how the global economy expanded and diverged in this period shows both why millions more died in climate-related disasters such as famines than was humanly avoidable and describes much of the "origins of modern global inequality" (Davis 2002). It shows also why it is still the case that, without radical changes, the poor majority of the world stands to suffer disproportionately in the face of currently inevitable global warming.

There were few differences in wealth among the major civilizations of the eighteenth century (see table 4.1). Research by Paul Bairoch (1995) led him to

TABLE 4.1   Shares of world GDP (percent)

	1700	1820	1890	1952
China	23.1	32.4	13.2	5.2
India	22.6	15.7	11	3.8
Europe	23.3	26.6	40.3	29.7

Source: Maddison (1998).

conclude that "It is very likely that, in the middle of the eighteenth century, the average standard of living in Europe was a little bit lower than that of the rest of the world." Pomeranz reaches the same conclusion in his comparison of China and Europe (Pomeranz 2002).

As with India, China's slide from world economic prominence was helped by a major shove from Britain's gunboat economic diplomacy, notably around their forced incorporation into the opium trade with British India. But both former (and perhaps future) world powers, China and India, gave up their positions only slowly and grudgingly up until 1850. The fact that they appeared to stand still and then slide back had less to do with the natural indigenous dynamism of European capitalism and the liberating power of the free market than the fact that their competition was "forcibly dismantled by war, invasion, opium and (in the case of Britain) a Lancashire-imposed system of one-way tariffs" (Davis 2002). Davis (2002) points out that even if account is taken of internal cultural and political factors, from the end of the eighteenth century, "every serious attempt by a non-Western society to move over into a fast lane of development or to regulate its terms of trade was met by a military as well as an economic response from London or a competing imperial capital."

So much for Asia and Central and South America. Africa's turn was coming. For centuries, the Old World—in this case Europe—had been taking slaves from the Older World—Africa. If they survived transit, and millions did not, they were put to work on colonial plantations producing sugar, tea, and tobacco around the world. In 1695, Bristol sugar merchant John Carey described slavery as "the best Traffik the Kingdom hath . . . as it doth occasionally give so vast an Imployment to our People both by Sea and Land" (Davis 2002). A member of Parliament argued that the abolition of slavery would be "ruinous to the colonies and commerce of the country" (Reindorp and Simms 1997).

Here is another kind of debt still waiting to be settled, one that demands more than embarrassed apologies from Western world leaders as they visit the old slave ports of the west coast of Africa. Slavery remains an unsettled historical account that, like ecological debt in the form of global warming, is heading for the courts.

But, apart from the slave trade, until the mid-1870s, Africa was, for Europeans, still largely unexplored. Then, between 1876 and 1912, according to Thomas Pakenham, the scramble for Africa was complete (Pakenham 1991). Five European nations—Britain, Germany, Italy, Portugal, and France—had sliced up Africa "like a cake" (Pakenham 1991) and swallowed the pieces. It was an experience that the continent still suffers from today. Africa is home to the majority of the world's least developed countries and is still tyrannized by conflicts directly related to the old, imperial power play.

Many of the half-myths that drew the Spanish to America also stirred the European imaginations in Africa. Once again, according to Pakenham (1991), "there were dreams of El Dorado, of diamond mines and goldfields criss-crossing the Sahara." In the Congo, for example, the French imagined a cornucopia of natural resources: ivory, rubber, maize, copper, palm nuts, and lead. The salivation was inspired by reports from a British explorer, Lt. Cameron, in January 1876. He had been in Central Africa and reported that, "The interior is mostly a magnificent and healthy country of unspeakable richness" (Pakenham 1991). Of course, it was not to stay that way for long. King Leopold II of Belgium's subsequent reign of terror and pursuit of riches in the Congo remains, even today, a murderous, suppurating historical sore. Rubber from the Congo made millions for Leopold. In the late 1890s, over 1,000 tonnes (U.K.) per year were exported.

Demand was high because in Europe Mr. Dunlop had invented the pneumatic tire to soothe the vibrating behinds of the traveling public. At home in Brussels, Leopold spent some of his proceeds on building a fabulous baroque palace, which he turned into a museum of Central Africa. Together with promises of social reform, the story seemed dream-fulfilling, benign, and adventurous—except that, for the indigenous people, the rubber trade was a genuine nightmare.

Leopold, cousin of Britain's Queen Victoria, wasn't just "enjoying a slice of this magnificent African cake" (Pakenham 1991) (his words); he was also cooking the books. The Congo rubber trade was based on murderous forced labor. Edmond Morel, a Quaker-influenced reformer who at first held conventional, supportive views of colonialism, found the trade to be "legalized robbery enforced by violence." Shocked at his discoveries in Leopold's private fiefdom, he observed, "It must be bad enough to stumble upon a murder. I had stumbled upon a secret society of murderers with a King for a croniman." It transpired that whole populations were being set impossible targets to collect rubber. Workers were "encouraged" by the sight of their friends and family being summarily shot for underperforming. To save on bullets, they were made to stand in a line and a single bullet shot through them. Others had ears and hands cut off. Pakenham records that soldiers collected them by the "basket load" to prove they were not wasting ammunition. Farms were abandoned to collect rubber, leading to widespread hunger and starvation (Pakenham 1991).

Some might dismiss the story of Leopold's Congo as an aberration. But tales from the textile wars between Britain and India also record the severing of thumbs to debilitate Indian textile workers. Henry Stanley, of Dr. Livingstone fame, earlier boasted that during his expeditions of 1876–77 he had "hurled himself down the Congo like a hurricane, shooting down terrified natives left and right" (Pakenham 1991). The year that Leopold's atrocities became the subject of serious public debate, the same production method was beginning to earn profits in French Congo. Meanwhile, Germany was preoccupied with the extermination of the Herero people in South-west Africa (modern Namibia). In 1867, the discovery by an African shepherd of diamonds on the veld was to transform South Africa and the British involvement in it. Again, the legacy lived on with well-known and depressing consequences.

The United Nations Conference on Trade and Development (UNCTAD), the UN specialist body on trade, regularly shows in its *World Investment Reports* that more than a century after the start of the colonial era the major focus of the small amount of foreign direct investment going into Africa is still to extract its minerals and other natural resources—oil from Nigeria and Angola, diamonds still, and even a rare metal needed for the manufacture of mobile phones. When Joseph Conrad wrote *Heart of Darkness*, says the writer Sven Lindqvist (1998), the dark heart he was describing was not that of Africa the continent but the souls of its European conquerors.

There is another ecological tale to tell about the history of colonialism and the divergence between nations. The story is told by Alfred Crosby (1993) in his book *Ecological Imperialism: The Biological Expansion of Europe, 900–1900*. It is about how the conquering nations took with them plants, animals, and diseases that, as much as any of their weapons or religion, directly and inadvertently displaced the people that they found in the lands they took. Then, of course, there is also the small matter of profits made from the plants they found in situ and put to their own use—coffee, tea, opium, cocoa, rubber, coca, tobacco, and potatoes, to name a few, most continuing to be staples of modern Western life. Imagine what the wealth of the majority, Southern world would have been today if they had been able to apply modern, broad-based patent protection to their natural resources.

All of these commodities are important, and the way that their modern markets are still controlled (it would be more honest to say "fixed") goes a long way toward explaining why the gap between rich and poor has persistently grown. The ecological debt of climate change soon emerges, however, as the biggest, most life-threatening, and most urgent to address of all the ecological debts.

The consequence of this history emerges in simple statistics from the UN Human Development Report (UNDR) (see table 4.2). Income gaps between people living in the richest fifth of countries and those living in the poorest fifth have steadily diverged.

The problem is that orthodox neo-liberal theory predicted that the opposite of this divergence should happen. "Convergence," noted the World Bank's *1995 World Development Report,* "is a notion dear to economists, who like its close fit with theory, and is abhorred by populists in rich countries, who see it as a threat to their incomes. Past experience, however, supports neither the hopes of the former nor the fears of the latter." It goes on to observe that "Overall, divergence, not convergence, has been the rule" (World Bank 1996).

During the last two to three decades, an intense debate has been raging about the precise effects on overall poverty, and the gaps between rich and poor, of

TABLE 4.2   Ratio of richest to poorest fifth
of countries

Year	Ratio
1820	3:1
1870	7:1
1913	11:1
1960	30:1
1990	60:1
1997	74:1

Source: United Nations Human Development Report
(1999).

the accelerated (if partial) unmanaged movement of money, goods, and services around the world. A key attack on the critics of economic globalization is that they are wrong to say that the global gap between rich and poor is growing.

Critics make the case that if you measure income not by U.S. dollars (the nearest thing we have to a truly global currency) but by purchasing power parity (PPP), which takes into account the different local costs of living, actually the gap between rich and poor countries is closing and therefore globalization must be working. But this argument is fundamentally flawed for several reasons.

First, dollars are an important measure in their own right, especially where economic globalization is concerned. Whenever poor countries engage with the global economy, they have to use dollars: to pay the service on their foreign debts, to conduct international trade, and, notably, to buy oil to run their domestic economies if they are energy importers.

Second, the percentage of the population in the least developed countries (LDCs) living on less than $2 (U.S.) per day has remained effectively static since the early 1970s—while the wealth of the already industrialized countries has grown hugely—but the actual number of such poor people has more than doubled from around 211 million to 449 million. Their average daily consumption also marginally fell.

Writing in the New Economics Foundation's (2003) *Real World Economic Outlook* (RWEO), Robert Wade of the London School of Economics concludes that there is overwhelming evidence for the rise in global inequality. Comparing several different methodologies for measuring income inequality based on both market exchange rates and PPP, he states that "The strong conclusion is that world inequality has risen. . . . A rising share of the world's income is going to those at the top. Moreover the absolute size of the income gap between countries is widening rapidly."

Comparing the incomes of the richest 10% of the world's population with the middle 10%, and the middle 10% with the poorest 10% global income distribution has become much more unequal since the 1980s.

Yet there is another story still that suggests the situation is even worse, and it underlines how inequalities within countries have worsened as a mirror of the situation between nations. This story concerns assets. According to the RWEO, since the 1970s there has been an explosion in financial assets, such as equity shares, which have been mostly captured by an already wealthy global minority.

In the United States, for example, since 1983 almost all of the increase in wealth has accrued to the richest 10% of the population. Also, crucially, almost all of the increase in debt since 1983 has accrued to the poorest 90% of the population, whereas very little has accrued to the richest 10% (New Economics Foundation 2003).

In the United Kingdom, the bottom 50% of the population now owns only 1% of the wealth, whereas in 1976 they owned 12% (New Economics Foundation 2003). Our economic system's incentive structure, instead of "trickle down," is causing a "flood up" of resources from the poor to the rich. So, as finance outstrips the real economy, and when we include assets as well as income in the equation, the gap between rich and poor is even bigger.

The tale of ecological debt in the modern age began with gold and silver. The story moves rapidly to the black stuff of fossil fuels.

Ecological Debt

"All life depends on plants" is the motto of the Royal Botanical Gardens at Kew in London. Although the economy is obviously a subset of the environment, the alarming resilience of the opposite notion means that this simple point requires tedious repetition. It is very easy to forget that, apart from the plants that give us drugs to heal, food to stay alive, and industrial chemicals and materials with which to make things, the global economy is still more than four-fifths dependent on fossil fuels derived from plants for energy.

Even mainstream debates among environmental economists about natural capital still appear as an exotic fringe in the dominant "real" economics discourse of city prices and exchange rates. It is still surprising how directly, and yet invisibly, the fates of our natural resources are interwoven with the self-absorbed human economy. For example, by peculiar coincidence, the financial loss to Africa because of its declining terms of trade on primary commodities— plant products and mining production—between 1980 and 1992 was around $350 billion (U.S.) and it has been much more since then. This figure was nearly the same as the amount of unpayable debt held by the group of heavily indebted poor countries, mostly in Africa, that the Jubilee 2000 debt-relief campaign mobilized to get written off.

Another example would be the direct link between land and income distributions. Numerous studies have found a direct link between unequal distribution of land and the income gap between rich and poor (Beer and Boswell 2002).

But what, exactly, is ecological debt? Ecological debt is a different way of understanding economic relations. It grounds economies in the real world of natural resources upon which they ultimately depend. The idea of ecological debt has several historical roots, some already alluded to, and various expressions. It is not a new concept. In the nineteenth century, observers of the British

Empire noted that "all parts of the world are ransacked for the Englishman's table." It was, after all, hard to miss.

In the 1960s, Georg Borgstrom shone a light on the "ghost acres" that countries such as Britain depended on in other lands to feed their people. Britain required an even larger area of land overseas to meet domestic demand than it had under cultivation at home. In the late 1980s, inquiries into equity and geographical carrying capacity introduced the language of "environmental space." At the start of the 1990s, the Canadian geographer William Rees began talking about "ecological footprints."

The answers these new analytical tools produced were simple. Rich people, and big cities, took up a lot of space—they needed many "distant elsewheres" for their survival and growth. Taking more than their fair or sustainable share if everyone's needs were to be met, they were running up ecological debts. At this point, under the shadow of a financial debt crisis that had lasted at least a decade, South American researchers and academics such as those at the Instituto de Ecologia Politica in Chile pointed to the exploitation of their countries' natural resources and began to speak about ecological debt. It was a different way of describing something that indigenous people had been legitimately sore about for centuries.

Ecological debts can be very broadly defined. They include pollution, "theft," and disproportionate use of finite resources in the environment. Ecuador is now home to a campaign to reclaim its eco-debts. The international Jubilee debt-relief campaign embraced ecological debt as a concept following a report by the British aid agency Christian Aid and work by The New Economics Foundation think tank (Simms, Meyer, and Robins 1999). Environmental group Friends of the Earth campaigns on the issue.

The discussion is about how and why countries and people become impoverished and enriched, and at the expense of what and whom. The crucial question in a global economy resting shakily on foundations of financial debt and reliant on the unsustainable use of natural resources is, "Who owes who?" And what should be done about it?

Who Owes Who?

Industrialized countries still prosecute highly indebted developing countries to pay off their foreign financial debts, at great cost to the millions who subsequently go without vital health and education services. But industrialized countries are now responsible for the much larger debt to the global community mentioned briefly earlier. The prospect of global warming introduces a level of environmental determinism that takes political debate beyond a contest over preferred options for the organization of society and the daily haggle over budgets between different government departments—a few dollars more for health and education or all to the military and tax cuts for the rich. Instead, it moves into the theatre of mutual survival, or not, as the case may be. Put another way, if we don't get this debate right, we've had it.

Rich countries' reckless use of fossil fuels has created climate change. But it is poor people in poor countries, in particular, that suffer first and worst from both extreme weather conditions related to climate change and from the struggle to clear unpayable, and often illegitimate, conventional foreign debts.

Using natural resource accounts, it can be seen that it is very poor countries who finance development in the rich world in several ways and not the other way around. They concede their environmental space and the economic opportunities it represents, and bear the environmental costs of development in rich countries through direct physical and environmental damage and through the ill-afforded cost of adapting to problems such as global warming. Social upheaval generates still further costs yet to be accounted for.

In many cases, the payment of orthodox external debt can lead to further pressure on natural resources, especially where the prevailing policy paradigm emphasizes export-led development strategies in the context of economies that are highly dependent on primary commodities.

Just as the silver and gold of America were the midwife and full breast at the birth of Western capitalism, and the systematic expropriation of natural resources from beyond its borders fed it through childhood, so the discovery of oil in the second half of the nineteenth century was the intoxicating liquid food that marked its passage from adolescence into adulthood.

And So to the Black Stuff

It has been fashionable since the 1990s to point to an increasingly "weightless economy." The information age, the triumph of services over displaced manufacturing, and the old "new economy" were supposed to reduce our dependence on raw materials. But where one of the *most* raw materials, carbon from fossil fuels, is concerned, economies all around the world, even the most advanced ones, just keep getting heavier.

Virtual shopping via the Internet heralded the anticipated weightless economy. In the United States, fuel economy in cars at the end of the millenium hit its lowest level in 20 years as technical improvements went into performance rather than fuel efficiency. There was virtually no air freight before 1950; now, by way of illustration, the equivalent of one tonne (U.K.) of goods travels 100 billion kilometers by plane each year (Kumar, Robins, Simms 2000).

They may not have known it at the time, but the early industrializing nations were as successful in their disproportionate occupation of the atmosphere with carbon emissions as they were in their military occupation of the terrestrial world. Up until around the time of the Second World War, they had managed this atmospheric occupation largely through exploiting their own fossil fuel reserves. However, beginning around 1950, another form of divergence occurred as these nations became more and more dependent on energy imports. For so-called less developed countries, the experience was a mirror image. At about the same time, they began to produce more than they consumed (Podobnik 2002).

Using a "World Energy Gini Coefficient," Bruce Podobnik (2002) shows that over the second half of the 1900s, with the exception of one decade, global inequality in energy consumption continued to increase in line with a long historical trend. By 1998, the wealthiest fifth of the world's population were consuming 68% of commercial energy and the poorest fifth 2%. But the peaks and troughs of inequality paint an even more extreme picture.

A decade after the UN Framework Convention on Climate Change (UNFCCC) was signed, countries from the United States to Australia, Canada, and Europe are pumping out more carbon dioxide per person than they were at the time of the 1992 Earth Summit. To put that into perspective, beginning from the stroke of the new year until they sit down to their evening meal on January 2, a U.S. family will already have used, per person, the equivalent in fossil fuels that a family in Tanzania will depend on for the whole year.

Even with technological advances in energy efficiency and the creeping introduction of renewable energy sources, there is still an incredibly close correlation between crude measures of economic wealth and the consumption of fossil fuels. Rich people simply pump more greenhouse gases into the atmosphere. Unfortunately, until renewable energy goes mainstream, access to economic opportunity and access to fossil fuels remain more or less the same thing. It is a very big problem. This means that there is no more fundamental issue than the distribution of wealth in a carbon-constrained world economy.

Estimates vary, but some scientists suggest that to stop dangerous climate change from becoming irreversible will require 60–90% cuts in greenhouse gas emissions by the middle of this century. Understandably, however, the less developed countries that make up a majority of the world believe they have the same right to material wealth that the citizens of rich countries take for granted.

Without a radical change in how we manage the global commons of the atmosphere, that means one of three things:

1. There has to be a massive reduction in rich-country emissions that goes far beyond the scope of the current international agreement, the Kyoto Protocol, to give poor countries the environmental space to develop.
2. Or, poor countries are to be simply denied the carbon-rich development path followed by industrialized countries, an instruction that, to a degree, they can simply and understandably ignore.
3. Or, finally, the third option is that the engine of conventional development keeps running on carbon, and there is climatic chaos. In this case, radical or, perhaps, logical change suddenly becomes an attractive option.

It's easy to forget how relatively new this predicament is. The global economy's oil addiction is little more than a century old. After early discoveries in Oil Creek in Titusville, Pennsylvania, in the United States in the late 1850s, it took John D. Rockefeller until 1870 to form the Standard Oil Company of Ohio.

No other single event bound the fate of economies as tightly to the fate of the environment and world politics. Where Britain was concerned, says Anthony Sampson (1975), oil was, from the beginning, associated with "national survival and diplomacy, and oil soon seemed part of the empire itself." The firm Royal Dutch that later merged with, and assumed control of, the British firm Shell had "origins belonging to the world of Conrad." The Anglo-Persian Oil Company, which from its start enjoyed the special protection of the British government, later became Anglo-Iranian before changing again to become British Petroleum, or BP.

During its early years, Sampson notes, BP "had a captive production, and a captive market, protected by the army in order to supply the navy." In an echo of Drake's gold and silver and his relationship with Elizabeth I, in the early 1920s BP was making handsome profits "from which the Treasury collected its half" and from which Churchill boasted of the financial rewards the government received. Perhaps predictably, BP was resented by foreign, especially colonial, countries "as an arm of government."

In 1928, the greatest "carveup" in oil history, known as the "Red Line Agreement," divided up the oil resources of what was considered the former Ottoman Empire in the Middle East by granting hugely one-sided concessions to British and American oil companies. At a meeting in Ostend in Belgium, oil entrepreneur Calouste Gulbenkian literally took a red pencil and drew a line around Saudi Arabia, Iraq, Jordan, Syria, and Turkey, at a stroke changing more than just their destinies. For example, no participation was allowed in the oil concession by the government of Iraq, which had wanted a minor role in partnership to exploit its own oil. It became a source of lasting bitterness and is still referred to by Iraqis today in the context of the current U.S. and British occupation.

Unbalanced concessions between oil companies and host-country governments, grossly in favor of the companies, were a particular feature of the late days of empire. Unsurprisingly, the companies fell victim during the subsequent waves of national independence movements. In 1969, Libya supplied one-quarter of Western Europe's oil and used its position to break the companies' steel grip, emboldening OPEC for the great standoffs with their old masters in the 1970s.

With geopolitical shock waves that still live with us, from Libya in North Africa to the almost permanent battleground of Angola and to mighty Nigeria, oil has been, and remains, the color of struggle, conflict, and debt between rich and poor and between the North and South. In 2002, Nigeria was producing around two million barrels of oil a day. Crude oil accounted for 80% of government revenue and 90% of foreign-exchange earnings. The approximate $11 billion (U.S.) earnings from oil sales, if shared equally, would give each Nigerian about 27 cents a day. But Nigeria racked up financial debts of $5.6 billion at market rates under its military dictators. Just servicing its debts in 1999 and 2000 cost Nigeria $1.4 billion each year. Several mainstream banks, including Barclays, HSBC, and Merrill Lynch, were censured by U.K. regulators for flouting anti–money-laundering rules in relation to accounts linked to Nigerian dictator Sani Abacha. Abacha stole an estimated $4 billion from his country. Other parts of Nigeria's debts are made up of foreign-funded projects that have failed because of their dependence on foreign inputs, equipment, and technical support.

Nigeria, however, still has to keep paying with the revenue from its oil. At the same time, the cost of environmental degradation in Nigeria, much of it in the oil-producing Niger Delta, which has been a long-time playground for the likes of Shell, Mobil, and Chevron, has been put at $5.1 billion (U.S.). By early 1998, around 14,000 compensation claims for oil-related damages had been made by groups, individuals, and communities in Nigerian courts (Owusu 2001). Harder to value are the ethnic tensions exacerbated in the oil areas.

The world has now been divided again by a conflict in Iraq with multiple causes, among them the control of oil. And in South America, the United States has been happy to undermine the government of Venezuela with fears over the price of oil a likely motivation.

Were he writing today with the benefit of hindsight and the knowledge of global warming, Sampson might have used a different title: *"The Great Oil Companies and the World They Broke."*

Almost all of humankind's fossil-fuel emissions of carbon dioxide, the main contributor to global warming, have happened since the early 1900s. Coal dominated first, followed by oil. The use of natural gas took off in the 1970s. All along there has been an almost exact correlation between greenhouse gas emissions and levels of economic activity—they rise and fall together.

It is possible to see the changes in the life of a single family. James Marriott has spent years looking at the oil industry and its impact on our lives. He worked

---

The Journey of Oil

Abraham Ringe works on a hydroscope—a vast liquid clock that arguably is one of *the* determinants of the rhythm of the United Kingdom. Abraham works for BP at Kinneil, he's a throughput analyst on the Forties pipeline system. Essentially what he does, from a portacabin on the edge of a vast refinery and chemicals plant, is to make predictions as to how much crude oil will be coming down the Forties pipeline tomorrow, next week, next year, and so on. He's a futurologist who gives a picture as to the credit-worthiness of BP, and for that matter the United Kingdom.

The Forties pipeline is one of the two great pipeline systems in the U.K. sector of the North Sea. It gathers the oil and gas output of 46 offshore fields and transports it over 300 miles across the sea bed and under the soil to the gas separation plant at Kinneil. About 40% of the United Kingdom's daily oil production passes through this pipe; every 24 hours, $30 million (U.S.) of hydrocarbons moves along its length—nearly $11 billion in a year, a discernable slice of the United Kingdom's GDP. As I stated, Abraham works on a hydroscope, a water clock that runs roughly as follows:

- Thirty minutes for oil and gas to rise 10,000 feet from the Lower Palaeocene sandstone layer (created 67 million years ago) of the geological strata underneath the North Sea.
- Forty-eight hours for the oil and gas to pass down the Forties pipeline to Kinneil.

- Two hours to separate the oil from the gas at the Kinneil separation plant.
- Two hours for the crude oil to travel the 15 miles to the loading terminal at Hound Point.
- Seventeen hours to load the crude oil onto a 300,000 tonne (U.K.) tanker at Hound Point in the Firth of Forth.
- Twenty-four hours for a tanker to sail to the Coryton refinery on the Thames Estuary in Essex.
- One hundred twenty hours for the crude to be refined into aviation fuel, among other products.
- Nine hours for this aviation fuel to pass by pipeline to the fuel depot at Heathrow.
- Fifteen minutes for a 747 to refuel its tanks at Terminal 3.
- Thirty minutes for the 747, bound for New York, to take off and, above the Irish Sea, achieve a speed of 555 miles per hour and an altitude of 31,000 feet.

This hydroscope takes under 10 days to run its course—for liquid to move from 10,000 feet below sea level to 31,000 feet above sea level, for a liquid hydrocarbon to turn into a carbon dioxide gas; for something laid down 67 million years ago to melt into air.

This material is taken from a collaborative performance between James Marriott of Platform and the author, Andrew Simms, at the United Kingdom's first conference on ecological debt, held at the Institute of Contemporary Arts, London, in the summer of 2001. Abraham Ringe is a pseudonym.

out that his great grandfather was the first in their family to smell petrol. James was the first to travel in a car before he was born, and his own parents are the first generation to spend their pensions on international air travel. Because of climate change, they also may be the last.

Aubrey Meyer of the London-based Global Commons Institute, who has challenged complacency in government, business, and campaign groups for many years, likens the growth of emissions and concentration levels of carbon dioxide to watching an explosion in slow motion.

In particular, the sections of the global economy that have grown rapidly are also those that most depend on fossil fuel, such as transport and international trade. In the postwar period, trade has grown much faster than production. Between 1950 and the mid-1990s, while total world output grew by a factor of 5, exports went up by over 14 times (Kumar et al. 2000).

According to astrophysicist Alberto di Fazio, we are now returning carbon to the atmosphere one million times faster than natural processes removed it during the youth of the planet to create a habitable climate. And, worse, we are doing it through economic processes that are socially divisive—increasing risk and instability—and undermining the basic security needed for sustainable livelihoods and stable communities. Even the ultraconservative former head of the IMF, Michel Camdessus, recognized that "poverty is the ultimate threat to stability in a globalising world. . . . The widening gaps between rich and poor within nations, and the gulf between the affluent and the most impoverished nations, are morally outrageous, economically wasteful, and potentially socially explosive."

By making a few assumptions about what levels of equitable global per capita carbon emissions are sustainable, it is possible to indicate where, by over- or underconsuming, people are running up ecological—or, more specifically, "carbon"—debts and credits.

Figure 4.1 compares two groups of countries, the G7 nations, usually the creditors, and the group of highly indebted poor countries, or HIPC nations. It reverses the traditional roles. In ecological or carbon terms, it shows that, per person, the HIPCs are in credit and the G7 is in debt.

The New Economics Foundation's 2003 *Real World Economic Outlook* showed that in 1995, based on IPCC assumptions, to stabilize atmospheric greenhouse gas concentrations at a safe level implied a global equal per capita entitlement of about 0.43 tons (U.S.) of carbon. Typical U.S. per capita carbon use in 1995 was 5.3 tons (Engleman 1998).

The U.K. government estimates that the damage cost of carbon emissions related to how they disturb the climate (but not including their much larger economic value) is in the range of $56 to $223 (U.S.) per tons of carbon. That

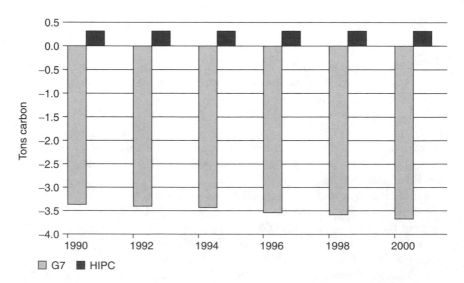

Figure 4.1. Carbon debts of the G7 nations compared with the carbon credits of the heavily indebted poor countries (HIPCs). Source: CDIAC, UNFCCC, IPCC, GCI.

means that just to account for the damage cost of their unsustainable carbon use, each U.S. citizen would have been liable to pay between $273 and $1,086 each year for the privilege of polluting more than their fair share (DTI 2003). Nationally, for the United States alone, at 2002/03 prices, that implied a bill of between $73 billion and $290 billion, money that could be channeled to invest in sustainable development and the Millennium Development Goals for reducing global poverty. An assessment of the value of the G7 countries' economic output, built on the foundations of unsustainable per capita carbon use at around the same time as the calculations just presented, put the figure in 1994 prices at between $13 and $15 trillion (Simms, Meyer, Robins 1999).

Tuvalu

For many years the most interesting thing to happen to the Pacific island state of Tuvalu was the sale of its Internet domain name, .TV, for $50 million (U.S.) (£35 million). But, just as Tuvalu trades in its virtual domain, it is about to lose its real one. As sea levels rise and extreme weather conditions worsen, appeals have gone out from the authorities in Tuvalu to the governments of New Zealand and Australia to help plan for the long-term relocation of Tuvalu's population as the island sinks beneath the sea. Tuvalu is paying for the rich world's experiment with the global atmosphere. At that price, you could say that it has become the world's most significant creditor nation. Although a land of no mobile phones and one radio station, Tuvalu is going down in history. The archipelago may be home to only around 10,000 people, but on other islands seven million more are threatened. In Bangladesh alone, another 20 million people could become environmental refugees. The price of ecological debt is being paid by people living in environmentally vulnerable places and by people who play the least role in creating global warming. The damage to human life is very unevenly distributed, with poor people in poor countries suffering first and worst.

The economic costs of global warming are rising dramatically. The number of major climate-related and flood disasters quadrupled during the 1990s compared with the 1960s, while resulting economic losses increased eightfold over the same period. If that trend continues, we will by about 2065 be facing the bizarre situation where the cost of natural disasters driven by global warming will overtake the value of the gross world product. It is time, as they say, to try something different. It is important for the global economy to stage a rapid, managed retreat from its fossil fuel addiction because there is no other way to get off the hook from impending climate chaos.

Contraction and Convergence

It is unlikely that everyone in the world will ever use identical amounts of fossil fuels. However, it is highly likely, says the RWEO, that any deal to manage the global commons of the atmosphere will have to be based on the principle that, in a carbon-constrained world, everyone should have equal entitlements to their share of the atmosphere's ability to safely absorb pollution.

Such an agreement implies that those people and nations that take the economic benefits by polluting more than their fair share will have to somehow pay compensation to the "underpolluters" by purchasing their spare entitlements. Otherwise, they run up a huge ecological debt (Greenhill and Simms 2002).

The process necessary is to cap total emissions, progressively reduce them, and equally share entitlements to emit. If a target is set for an acceptable concentration of greenhouse gases in the atmosphere and an "emissions budget" set to meet it, it becomes possible to work out for every year from now until the target is met everybody's logical and equal share of the atmosphere's ability to soak up our waste emissions.

To do this, a formula is used such that, in an agreed timeframe, entitlements to emit are predistributed in a pattern of international convergence so that, globally, shares become equal per capita. This procedure—unavoidable if chaos is to be prevented—was given the term "contraction and convergence" by the London-based Global Commons Institute (Meyer 2000). It is opposite to the dynamic that has characterized the global economy up to now.

In essence, it says that the world has a "carbon cake" strictly limited in size—beyond certain dimensions it rapidly becomes poisonous for everyone—and that the only way to begin negotiations on how to cut the cake is to start with the principle that we all have equal access rights. What we do with them is another matter.

How Contraction and Convergence Reconciles the Ecological Debt of Climate Change

Under a plan proposed by Meyer (2000), all countries collectively agree on a target for a stable atmospheric concentration of carbon dioxide in the atmosphere. A "global emissions budget" is then calculated that is derived from the target atmospheric concentration figure. The target is reviewed annually so that it can be revised with new scientific findings. Once the "contraction budget" has been chosen, the next question is how to distribute the entitlements within it between countries. Under contraction and convergence, the allocations of emissions entitlements among countries would converge by a specific date. By that year, entitlements would be allocated in proportion to the national population in a specified baseline year. Full emissions trading is a design feature of the concept. Contraction and Convergence would reduce the complexity of climate negotiations to two simple variables that would need to be agreed upon: the target atmospheric concentration of CO_2 and the date at which entitlements would converge at equal per capita allocations.

The approach offers the best chance of solving a great, and immensely destructive, international paradox. Less developed countries stand to be hit first and worst by global warming. The New Economics Foundation's report *The End of Development? Global Warming, Disasters and the Great Reversal of Human Progress* makes the case that all the internationally agreed targets for reducing poverty to emerge out of the 1990s decade-long series of UN conferences—collectively known as the Millennium Development Goals—will be tragically undermined by climate change (Simms and Walter 2002). Yet developing countries have been reluctant to play along with the climate negotiations as conducted to date. They see no reason—if rich countries have had a free ride on the Earth's finite fossil fuel resources for the whole of their development—that they should jeopardize their own development through accepting any perceived restraints on their economic activity. But contraction and convergence deals with this seemingly inescapable trap.

Developing countries have consistently refused to take part in a framework that preallocates the property rights to a finite carbon budget in a manifestly inequitable way—so-called grandfathering—in which the starting point is one where countries "inherit" their historical emission levels. That approach creates, in effect, a carbon aristocracy.

By specifying a set date for convergence at equal per capita rights, the contraction and convergence approach would give developing countries surplus emission allocations that they could then sell to countries that need extra permits—most of them developed countries. The revenue flow from the sale of surplus permits would give developing countries an income flow from climate change policy, which would encourage participation, and would also create an added incentive to invest in clean technologies. Less developed countries also stand to benefit more the sooner such an agreement is made because, as time passes, the cuts needed to prevent runaway global warming get bigger and so tradable emissions get fewer. And, in the interim, it means that rich over-polluting countries are abusing the global commons of the atmosphere without having to pay.

Contraction and Convergence and the United States

Interestingly, contraction and convergence would also fit with the stated position of the otherwise recalcitrant United States. In his statements on climate change, President George W. Bush has set out specific criteria for what sort of treaty the United States would be willing to support. These include a truly global deal that includes emission targets (or, from another perspective, entitlements) for developing countries and the need for a science-based approach. Contraction and convergence, with its global participation design and formal greenhouse gas concentration target, is exactly such an approach. Contraction and convergence is also fully consistent with the famous 1997 Byrd–Hagel U.S. Senate resolution that stipulated that the United States would not be a signatory to any treaty that did not include developing countries.

Contraction and Convergence has enormous, and from a development perspective very positive, consequences in that it can liberate resources to finance development. But, as action to combat global warming is delayed, emissions grow, and populations rise, the sustainable size of a carbon cake slice will get smaller and smaller. In other words, the sooner we act, the better.

But, the notion that there are limits, however unpredictable and flexible, within which we must work is still difficult for many to grasp. This can be demonstrated by how easily even senior civil servants can completely misunderstand the challenge. Take a graph from the U.K. government's environment department, DEFRA, reproduced in the RWEO (figure 4.2). Without an overlong explanation, it's enough to say that their projection for cutting emissions to "stabilize" greenhouse gases at a certain level shows that by around 2070 there will be no fossil fuels at all for countries outside the First World club—not a barrel of oil, heap of coal, or canister of gas to burn. How they explain that logic to India, China, Brazil, or Ethiopia will make for an interesting ministerial meeting. They have shown the necessary contraction but not the convergence. Yet the two must occur together.

There are several subtly differing, equity-based proposals for global frameworks to tackle climate change that could supersede the Kyoto Protocol when the Protocol's first phase has run its course in 2012. They are assessed in Evans (2002). Only contraction and convergence, however, passes the tests for both environmental integrity—working within secure environmental limits—and political feasibility, offering real entitlements to less developed countries.

It is all very well making abstract theoretical arguments, but is there any chance at all that the advanced industrial economies could possibly make the kind of resource cuts necessary to fit into such a model? History suggests the answer is yes.

War economies provide an approximate analogy (Simms 2001). All the major industrialized countries have relatively recent experience of them. They can generate senses of extended responsibility, purpose, and focus. They always involve the complete regearing of the economy. The enemy here, of course, is

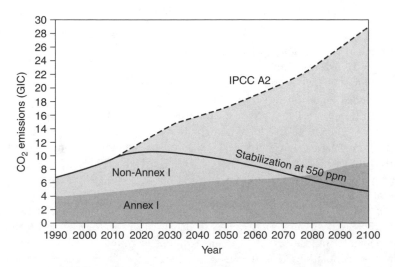

Figure 4.2. Projected global emissions under one business-as-usual scenario and a possible pathway to stabilization at 550 ppm.

a hostile climate, not another country. The victims of climate change could also be greater in number than in any war.

Resource efficiency was a major focus for British people during the Second World War. In the six years beginning in 1938, there was a 95% cut in private vehicle use. Public transport increased significantly. Consumption of all goods and services fell 16% in a similar period. A change in diet meant that although people were eating less, they were eating better. Life expectancy for people away from the bombs and bullets increased and infant mortality fell. For some, less really was more.

Behavior changed partly in response to a massive government information campaign, itself amplified through media as far-ranging as *Good Housekeeping* and *Feeding Cats and Dogs in Wartime*. It changed because people clearly understood the nature of the threat. New patterns of behavior became self-policing. Profligacy with food, material, or fuel was seen as antisocial. Rationing was a fact and parameters were set by government, but without public support the country would have been ungovernable.

But is this asking too much of people in rich countries? Poor countries with conventional foreign debts, and lacking the systems of social support that the North enjoys, have lived with badly designed "structural adjustment programs" for decades. These are imposed in the name of the economic discipline necessary to make debt repayments. To tackle the ecological debt of global warming, rich countries could now run the equivalent of environmental war economies, working within the framework of "sustainability adjustment programs."

In 1943, Hugh Dalton, president of the U.K. Board of Trade, said, "There can be no equality of sacrifice in this war. Some must lose their lives and limbs, others only the turn-ups on their trousers." Today, in Bangladesh some 20 million people are threatened by homelessness caused by flooding in order that we can drive sport-utility vehicles.

At the time of the first OPEC crisis, a U.S. congressional declaration of purpose to shape domestic policy called for "positive and effective action" to protect "general welfare . . . conserve scarce energy supplies" and "ensure fair and efficient distribution." Applied more generally, there is a sentiment absolutely in line with contraction and convergence and a way of reconciling the ecological debt crisis.

But it is possible that neither the contraction and convergence framework nor the approach of an environmental war economy will succeed alone without reform of our monetary system to reconnect the abstract world of finance to the physical world of natural resources. Coming full circle, there once was a link between the money supply and gold and silver. Their availability was, to a degree, a limiting factor on what economies did.

If trade in emissions permits were to be conducted in U.S. dollars, for example, there would still be a built-in bias in favor of the dominant "hard currency" countries. The United States could further exploit its position as the key currency holder and print money to meet its needs. This would mean that it could escape pressure to reform and entrench existing imbalances in the world economy.

The point is not to reduce the amount of energy that people use per se but to reduce the amount used that comes from fossil fuels.

A proposal for how this could be done comes from Richard Douthwaite (1999). He says spare emissions permits from underconsuming countries in the contraction and convergence framework could be traded in a special currency, the "EBCU" (energy-backed currency unit). The EBCU issue to governments would be a one-time event on the same per capita basis as the emission permits. Spare permits under a given ceiling would be made available upon payment in EBCUs.

Thereafter, when "spent," the EBCUs are withdrawn from circulation, and used permits are destroyed. This strictly controls the volume of spare emissions permits or "special emissions rights" in the market. Such an approach creates a parallel monetary system and incentives to ease the managed withdrawal from a fossil fuel economy. The complexity of implementation is reduced by the fact that, according to Douthwaite (1999), "80 percent of the fossil carbon that ends up as man-made CO_2 in the earth's atmosphere comes from only 122 producers of carbon-based fuels."

Conclusion

So what are the economic possibilities for our grandchildren? When Keynes asked that question in 1931, the prognosis seemed miserable. Reckless speculation on shares had led to spectacular stock market crashes. A long depression had begun. But Keynes was optimistic. He saw in the long-term growth of capital—remember Drake's pound—and dramatic advances in technical efficiency a great prize looming within one hundred years of his writing.

Keynes considered the end of what he called "the economic problem" in sight. "The struggle for subsistence," meeting those needs that are absolute and not preferential, characterized not just the human race but the whole "biological kingdom." All that had to be avoided were "important wars" and important increases in population. Keynes could not have known the immensity of the conflicts to come nor the precise dynamics of population growth. But to balance that, he could not have known of the coming breathtaking technological acceleration. It is fair to say then that, on his terms, it is still the case that the economic problem is not, or does not have to be, *the permanent problem of the human race.* But Keynes was also writing in ignorance of global warming. His sense that deep economic trends bade well for human society faces a tougher obstacle today.

That other eminent voice, the Intergovernmental Panel on Climate Change, also likes to look one hundred years into the future. Its scenarios for global temperature increase and sea level rise imply enormous upheaval in all cases. In moderate to bad scenarios, they suggest pressures that could actually lead to the opposite of Keynes's optimism—a great reversal of human progress. It is not merely a prognosis for countries least able to adapt. In the summer of 2002, the German election was affected by extreme flooding across Europe. In August

2003, high government officials in France resigned after a heat wave left an estimated 15,000 more dead than the seasonal average. Direct causal relationships cannot be proven in the French case, but climate change will lead to further similar extreme weather events. To hold climatic instability at its current level implies cuts in carbon emissions that no government privately believes are possible.

Nauru is a remote South Pacific island. Guns, booze, and venereal disease signaled its earliest encounters with the development brought by progressive Europeans. Then, in 1899, progress really took off when a visitor, Albert Ellis, saw a lump of high-grade phosphate being used as a doorstop. The whole interior of the island was made of it. Over the following century, the island was almost entirely dug out, leaving the indigenous population clinging to a rim of land around the island's edge and almost entirely dependent on imports for their needs (McDaniel and Gowdy 2000). When environmental limits are transgressed on an island, it's just possible, notwithstanding restrictive immigration laws, that people can move. When the limits are crossed on an island in space, the problems presented are a little more difficult, regardless of immigration laws.

How will a growing, increasingly unequal world population fit into the shrinking environmental space of the carbon economy? In the rich world, we know the answer, even if we are unprepared to accept the consequences. We have to use less—much less—of the stuff that comes from burning fossil fuels. The academics who studied the history of Nauru boiled it down to the basics in their conclusion:

> In the long run, a lavish existence—whose attributes include big cars and vans for transportation; goods originating thousands of miles away; large homes, second homes, yachts, and recreational vehicles; and resort-style vacations in faraway places—has huge environmental effects that result in a much smaller carrying capacity for and area than a lifestyle with a quite different consumption pattern that includes travel by bicycle and mass transit; a diet of locally grown grains, fruits, vegetables and other foods; simple but adequate homes; and local vacations. (McDaniel and Gowdy 2000)

This may seem obvious. But how many of us who have the luxury of being able to make the choice are actually prepared to take it in a world of looming atmospheric chaos and with a global economy hopelessly addicted to fossil fuels? What does the future hold in a world rife with widening inequality and the conflict, unhappiness, and instability that it ushers in? Not much, unless we have the imagination and logic to begin a process of reversing several hundred years of economic history and finding a way to reconcile life-threatening ecological debts.

A great problem remains the profession of economics. Economic historian Robert Heilbroner characterized the early nineteenth century as a world that was "not only harsh and cruel but that rationalised its cruelty under the guise of economic law." The laws dressed in the costume of natural forces and could be no more defied than the law of gravity. With choking irony, it is still the case today that immature economic assumptions about the use of natural resources are usurping a natural order that took millions of years to establish. Keynes called on economists to think of themselves humbly, on a "level with dentists." Now would be a good moment for them to get back into the dentist's chair.

Importantly, just because we need to contract those parts of the economy that rely on the exploitation of nonrenewable natural resources does not mean that other, beneficial parts of the economy cannot expand.

We can expand the informal, social economy, for example, and recognize the often unpaid work of childcarers. In an increasingly bland and uniform retail economy, dominated by a handful of brands and chains, we can expand diversity by encouraging micro and small business. We can expand human well-being with an economics that redefines wealth and that measures and takes account of the losses to social and environmental welfare that occur in the current system.

Local currencies and time banks can be used to bring marginalized people back into making useful social contributions such as in the care economy—productive employment otherwise defined. They can create new economic space in the vacuums left by orthodox "free" markets in poor communities and housing estates around the world. There can be expanding economies based upon a cycle of economic reuse, recycling, and innovation rather than one of throughput and waste of materials.

Keynes saw the wealthy classes of his day as the "advance guard . . . spying out the promised land" of a world liberated from striving for its basic needs. Based on his observation, he looked forward with dread. The wealthy had "failed disastrously" to put their freedom from want to good use. Ironically, this could be a message of hope. If better distributed, there is already enough wealth to meet the basic needs of all. All we would then need to do is follow Keynes's advice to free ourselves from the ephemeral satisfactions of conspicuous consumption and become those people who "can keep alive, and cultivate into a fuller perfection, the art of life itself and . . . not sell themselves for the means of life."

But now, if we look over each other's shoulders, we can see a star falling. It is ours. The brief ascendance of modern human civilization is set to fall. We have been a highly unlikely species in the universal scheme of things and, therefore, you would think, worth doing everything to protect. But unless we can stop global warming, based on the best evidence currently available, little else will shortly matter. Because of the stake at play—a habitable planet—all other economic concerns, however important, become secondary.

Acknowledgments A book about ecological debt that expands on this chapter will appear in 2006. With apologies to J. M. Keynes, *Economic Possibilities for Our Grandchildren* (1931) for the title of this chapter.

Notes

1. That original £40,000 appreciating at 3.25% would today be worth around £30,000,000,000.

2. *Guardian.* 2003. US battle for $2 Billion Undersea Treasure. 7 January 2003.

References

Bairoch, P. 1995. *Economics and World History.* Chicago: University of Chicago Press.

Baldwin, R., Martin, P., and Ottaviano, G. 1998. Global Income Divergence, Trade and Industrialisation: The Geography of Growth Take-Offs. Available online at: http://ssrn.com/abstract=92169.

Beer, L., and Boswell, T. 2002. The Resilience of Dependency Effects in Explaining Income Inequality in the Global Economy: A Cross-National Analysis, 1975–1995. *Journal of World Systems Research,* 3 (Winter).

Crosby, A. W. 1993. *Ecological Imperialism: The Biological Expansion of Europe, 900–1900.* Cambridge: Cambridge University Press.

Cuautemoc, G. 1997. The Real Foreign Debt. *Resurgence* (September/October).

Davis, M. 2002. *Late Victorian Holocausts: El Nino Famines and the Making of the Third World.* London: Verso Books.

Douthwaite, R. 1999. *The Ecology of Money.* London: Green Books.

DTI. 2003. *Energy White Paper: Our Energy Future—Creating A Low Carbon Economy.* London: DTI.

Engleman, R. 1998. *Profiles in Carbon: An Update on Population, Consumption and Carbon Dioxide Emissions.* Washington, DC: Population Action International.

Evans, A. 2002. *Fresh Air? Options for the Future Architecture of International Climate Change Policy.* London: New Economics Foundation.

Galbraith, J. K. 1975. *Money: Whence It Came, Where It Went.* New York: Houghton Mifflin.

Greenhill, R., and Simms, A. 2002. *Balancing the Other Budget: Proposals for Solving the Greater Debt Crisis.* London: New Economics Foundation.

Keynes, J. M. 1931. *Economic Possibilities for Our Grandchildren.* Cambridge: Cambridge University Press.

Kumar, R., Simms, A., and Robins, N. 2000. *Collision Course: Free Trade's Free Ride on the Global Climate.* London: New Economics Foundation.

Lindqvist, S. 1998. *Exterminate All the Brutes.* London: Granta.

Maddison, A. 1998. *Chinese Economic Performance in the Long Run.* Washington, DC: Brookings Institution Press.

McDaniel, C. N., and Gowdy, J. M. 2000. *Paradise for Sale: A Parable of Nature.* Berkeley: University of California Press.

Meyer, A. 2000. *Contraction and Convergence: The Global Solution to Climate Change.* Totnes, Devon: Green Books for the Schumacher Society.

Owusu, K. 2001. *Drops of Oil in a Sea of Poverty: The Case for a New Debt Deal for Nigeria.* London: New Economics Foundation and Jubilee Plus.

Pakenham, T. 1991. *The Scramble for Africa.* New York: Random House.

Pettifor, A. (ed.) 2003. *Real World Economic Outlook: The Legacy of Globalisation, Debt and Deflation.* London: New Economics Foundation and Palgrave.

Podobnik, B. 2002. Global Energy Inequalities: Exploring the Long-Term Implications. *Journal of World Systems Research,* 3 (Winter).

Pomeranz, K. 2002. *The Great Divergance: China, Europe and the Making of the Modern Economy.* Princeton: Princeton University.

Reindorp, J., and Simms, A. 1997. *The New Abolitionists: Slavery in History and the Modern Slavery Of Poor Country Debt.* London: Christian Aid.

Sampson, A. 1975. *The Seven Sisters: The Great Oil Companies and the World They Made.* London: Hodder and Stoughton.

Simms, A. 2001. *An Environmental War Economy: The Lessons of Ecological Debt and Global Warming.* London: New Economics Foundation.

Simms, A., Meyer, A., and Robins, N. 1999. *Who Owes Who? Climate Change, Debt, Equity and Survival.* London: Christian Aid.

Simms, A., and Walter, J. 2002. *The End of Development? Climate Change, Disasters and the Great Reversal of Human Progress.* London: New Economics Foundation and Bangladesh Centre for Advanced Studies.

United Nations. 1999. *UN Human Development Report.* New York: United Nations.

World Bank. 1996. *World Development Report 1995.* Washington, DC: World Bank.

5

DEFINING "ILLEGITIMATE DEBT": WHEN CREDITORS SHOULD BE LIABLE FOR IMPROPER LOANS

Joseph Hanlon

Introduction

"Certainly the people of Iraq shouldn't be saddled with those debts incurred through the regime of the dictator who is now gone," said U.S. Treasury Secretary John Snow in April 2003.[1] The U.S. financier George Soros agreed: "I personally would be very happy to see the old creditors of Iraq not getting paid. That would send a signal to the financial markets that it's dangerous to deal with oppressive regimes."[2] This echoes a view taken by the United States a century earlier when it occupied Cuba and refused to pay Cuba's debts because they had been "imposed upon the people of Cuba without their consent and by force of arms. . . . The creditors, from the beginning, took the chances of the investment" (Adams 1991: 164).

Campaigners have argued that the concept should be applied not only to countries where the U.S. military has imposed "regime change" and overthrown dictators opposed to it but also to dictators supported by the United States, such as Mobutu Sese Seko in Zaire (now the Congo). Campaign groups in the South have gone further and argued that a substantial part of poor-country debt is "illegitimate" and that, in Snow's terms, the people of those countries "shouldn't be saddled with those debts."

International lenders have made improper loans that would not have been acceptable under domestic law on the assumption that the international community would enforce repayment. Lenders should be made liable for their bad lending, both on the grounds that the people of poor countries should not be forced to repay loans that the lenders should never have made and also on grounds of "moral hazard"—that lenders will only learn to exercise the required caution and prudence if they are penalized for past negligence and if, in Soros's terms, financial markets learn that it is dangerous to make illegitimate loans.

"Illegitimate" has no formal meaning in law, and in this chapter national legislation and practice with respect to debt and insolvency is applied to the international situation in combination with the few existing international doctrines such as odious debt. We will argue that a loan is "illegitimate" if it would be against national law; is unfair, improper, or objectionable; or infringes public policy. We separate the loans themselves from the conditions attached to those loans so that a loan can be legitimate but the conditions, for example usurious interest rates, can be illegitimate. Second, we distinguish between loans and conditions that are "unacceptable" and those that are "inappropriate." We consider a loan or condition to be "unacceptable" if it is obviously improper. We consider a loan or condition to be "inappropriate" if it would be acceptable in some circumstances but not those in which it was made.

Examples of these four categories are given. Odious loans to dictators such as Mobutu or Saddam Hussein are examples of unacceptable loans. Usury and requirements to violate national law are unacceptable conditions. Loans to a poor country for consumption could be argued to be inappropriate loans on the grounds that it was imprudent to lend to a country that had no chance of repaying the loan. Conditions imposed by the IMF could be argued to be inappropriate if they created an economic environment that made it impossible to repay the loan. Also considered are the problems of fungibility of money and of "loan laundering"—using new loans to pay off old loans.

Finally, it is important to distinguish three related issues that are often confused:

- The international Jubilee 2000 campaign called for the cancelation of "unpayable debt," which is determined by the ability of the debtor to repay and is akin to the processes involved in personal bankruptcy or corporate insolvency. This is often referred to as "debt relief" and carries a charity consciousness in that the rich North is showing beneficence to the poor South. Thus, it often comes with conditions imposed on the poor South. As with Victorian charity, it is limited to the "deserving poor." Issues of unpayability have been dealt with elsewhere (Hanlon 2000). A rights-based approach, using the 2015 Millenium Development Goals, requires that $600 billion (U.S.) of debt be canceled according to our study (Hanlon 2000). That paper also looks at historic precedents of debt cancelation (e.g., Peru, Germany, Indonesia) that took into account how much money the countries needed to spend before paying debt service. Following these precedents would mean that at least $1 trillion in debt would be canceled—about 40% of developing-country debt.
- Southern campaigners are increasingly arguing that the Northern industrialized countries owe debts to the South for damages done by colonialism, the slave trade, global warming, and other depredations. These

counterclaims are discussed in an appendix to this chapter but are un-
related to loans taken by developing countries.

• Illegitimate debt, which is the subject of this chapter, must be distin-
guished from both unpayable debt and counterclaims. Legitimacy is entirely an issue of whether a lender should have made the loan. No financial institution should have lent money to Mobutu, and it is the loans
themselves that are illegitimate; they are solely the liability of the creditor and should not be repaid, independent of the quality of the Congo
government and whether or not it "deserves" debt "relief."

The issue for this chapter is debts that *should not* be repaid rather than debts
that *cannot* be repaid. Unpayability puts the spotlight on the debtor and its
inability to pay. Illegitimacy puts the spotlight on the creditor and argues that
the loan was improper and should be declared null and void and not be repaid,
even if the borrower could do so.

Debts That Are "Null" Need Not Be Repaid

Background

As the debt crisis grew in the 1980s, voices in the developing countries began
to argue that at least some of the debt was illegitimate and should not be repaid.
But it was not until the end of the century and the growth of the Jubilee movement that there were strong demands from activists and civil society in the South
to cancel or repudiate "illegitimate debt."

Jubilee 2000 declared that "All illegitimate debt, in accordance with the Doctrine of Odious Debt, and debts resulting from failed development projects
should be cancelled" (Jubilee 2000 Consensus Statement). Jubilee South goes
much further and argues that "debt steals resources from meeting people's most
basic needs" (Jubilee South 2001). It cites high interest rates, which mean that
new loans are only used to repay old loans, thereby increasing indebtedness.
Jubilee South goes on to argue that loans were given to support the apartheid
in South Africa and other dictatorships, that loans fueled corruption, and that
loans for dams and mining projects "resulted in intense environmental and social
damage" (Jubilee South 2001). It argues that the World Bank and International
Monetary Fund use indebtedness to impose conditions "designed in the interest
of the elites in the North and further impoverish the poor" and "For these reasons, we argue that the purported debt of the South to the North is illegitimate"
(Jubilee South 2001).

Other campaign groups argue that debt is also illegitimate where it has funded
capital flight, where it has been linked to bad policy advice and bad projects,
and where private loans have been converted to public debt under duress in
order to bail out lenders.[3]

One common aspect of the campaigns against "illegitimate debt" is the view
in the South that lenders no longer shoulder a fair proportion of the liability and

responsibility for the loan and that the World Bank and IMF are enforcing repayment independent of whether the loan should be repaid.

The term "illegitimate debt" seems not to have been used in any law or court ruling until an Argentine federal judge in 2000 ruled that debt contracted during the period of the military dictatorship (1976–1983) was illegitimate. Patricia Adams, a specialist in odious debt, noted that "the implications of this ruling extend beyond Argentina and send a clear message to the citizens of all the highly indebted countries that international creditors were responsible for ensuring that the money loaned was used for the interests and needs of the state" (Gaona 2001). When Michael Kremer and Seema Jayachandran (see chapter 10, this volume) presented a paper to an IMF conference in March 2002, it was probably the first time the term "illegitimate debt" had been used by the international financial institutions (Kremer and Jayachandran 2002).

In all legal and social systems, there are certain debts that are not expected to be repaid either because the debt itself is improper or because of the hardship that would be caused by repaying the debts. Furthermore, it is always accepted that the lender takes a certain risk that the loan will not be repaid—it is up to the lender to exercise prudence and to determine whether the borrower will be able to repay and to charge an appropriately higher interest rate (the risk premium) on more doubtful loans.

There is relatively little case law on illegitimacy in the context of international debts but substantial law and tradition nationally. In what follows, we largely draw on national law, especially that of bankruptcy and insolvency, because this legislation defines most clearly what loans are invalid and what limits can be placed on creditors. Bankruptcy administrators or trustees look into the background of debts and are expected to exclude as void debts that involve fraud, undue pressure or victimization, or usury, or that arise out of an illegal act. In Britain and Australia, gambling debts cannot be enforced (Rose 1990; Gregory 1992).

The term "illegitimate debt" seems almost never to have been used in legislation or court judgments. The Merriam-Webster Collegiate Dictionary (2004) defines "illegitimate" as "not sanctioned by law; illegal." This is only partly helpful because the *Oxford Companion to Law* notes that "illegal" is "a very general term for what is contrary to law, with no precise meaning or consequence" (Walker 1980). But it goes on to note that the term "illegal contract" is "sometimes extended to cover contracts which are objectionable and void as being contrary to public policy." Similarly, *Words and Phrases Legally Defined* (Hay 2001) points out that "illegal" actually means more than "unlawful" and also means that it "infringes some public policy." Thus, a court could determine that "a contract is void or unenforceable for public policy reasons" (Hay 2001).

Thus, an "illegitimate debt" is one that satisfies one of the following conditions: (1) It is against the law or not sanctioned by law; (2) is unfair, improper, or objectionable; or (3) infringes some public policy. In terms of creditor misconduct, only two specific terms have been defined, odious debt and "extortionate" debt.

Examples of Illegitimacy in the Courts

Odious Debt

When the United States seized Cuba from Spain in 1898, Spain demanded that the United States pay Cuba's debts. The United States refused on the grounds that the debt had been "imposed upon the people of Cuba without their consent and by force of arms." Furthermore, the United States argued that, in such circumstances, "the creditors, from the beginning, took the chances of the investment. The very pledge of the national credit, while it demonstrates on the one hand the national character of the debt, on the other hand proclaims the notorious risk that attended the debt in its origin, and has attended it ever since" (Adams 1991: 164). In the century since, the United States has never revised its view that Cuban debt was not the liability of the new government, and in 2003 this concept was raised again with respect to Iraq.

Three decades after the United States said Cuba's debts should not be repaid, Alexander Sack, an expert on the obligations of successor governments, formalized this into the doctrine of odious debt. He wrote:

> If a despotic power incurs a debt not for the needs or in the interest of the state, but to strengthen its despotic regime, to repress the population that fights against it, etc., this debt is odious to the population of all the state. This debt is not an obligation for the nation; it is a regime's debt, a personal debt of the power that has incurred it, consequently it falls with fall of this power. . . . The creditors have committed a hostile act with regards to the people; they can't therefore expect that a nation freed from a despotic power assume the "odious" debts which are the personal debts of that power.[4]

Sack makes four points that we will apply later:

1. A condition of legitimacy of a loan is that it is "employed for the needs and in the interests of the state."
2. Odious debts fall with the regime and are not owed by successors.
3. Debts can be considered odious if they are used for personal rather than state purposes.
4. Creditors commit a hostile act when they make an odious loan.

The concept of odious debt was further recognized by the British House of Commons International Development Committee in 1998 when it wrote that:

> [T]he bulk of Rwanda's external debt was incurred by the genocidal regime which preceded the current administration. . . . Some argue that loans were used by the genocidal regime to purchase weapons and that the current administration and, ultimately, the people of Rwanda, should not have to repay these "odious" debts. . . . We further recommend that the [UK] government urge all bilateral creditors, in particular France, to cancel the debt incurred by the previous regime. (House of Commons 1997: 11, 57)

Loans to Dictators

There has been little in international law in this area, except for a landmark arbitration ruling in 1923 by U.S. Supreme Court Chief Justice Taft. A Costa Rican dictator, Frederico Tinoco, was overthrown, and the new government refused to repay loans made by the Royal Bank of Canada to the Tinoco government. Taft ruled that the payments were made by the bank to Tinoco himself and that the case of the Royal Bank depends

> upon the good faith of the bank in the payment of money for the real use of the Costa Rican government under the Tinoco regime. It must make out its case of actual furnishing of money to the government for its legitimate use. It has not done so. The bank knew that this money was to be used by the retiring president, F. Tinoco, for this personal support. . . . The Royal Bank of Canada cannot be deemed to have proved that the payments were made for legitimate governmental use. Its claim must fail. (Adams 1991:168)

Extortionate Debt

In this context, Britain's Consumer Credit Act of 1974 sets an important benchmark that we will try to apply more broadly. That law says that "a credit bargain is extortionate if it (a) requires the debtor . . . to make payments . . . which are grossly exorbitant, or (b) otherwise grossly contravenes ordinary principles of fair dealing."[5] This definition is extremely broad, and the courts have wide powers to cancel the debts or change the terms. Perhaps most remarkably, if a debtor alleges that a credit bargain is extortionate, the burden of proof lies on the creditor to prove that the bargain is *not* extortionate (Harding 1995). The court is expected to take into account the borrower's "age, experience, business capacity and state of health," the degree to which the borrower was under "financial pressure and the nature of that pressure," and "any other relevant consideration." British courts have, for example, ruled that a loan could be considered "extortionate" when the borrower had no choice in their financial circumstances but to accept the terms of the loan, and have also found that failing to assess the creditworthiness of the potential debtor contravenes ordinary principles of fair dealing (Guest and Lloyd 2000).

Important Issues

Next, we grapple with three difficult concepts where national law and moral philosophy provide less obvious guidance—usury, successor loans, and fungibility.

Usury

Usury, or the lending of money at exorbitant interest rates, has been opposed for millennia. Most countries consider loans at usurious interest rates to be illegal and thus illegitimate. But there are wide variations in rulings as to what interest rates are acceptable. In Britain and elsewhere, variable or floating interest rates have been ruled to be acceptable (Guest and Lloyd 2000).

A central factor in the present loan crisis was the huge increase in real interest rates at the end of the 1970s. In the mid-1970s, international loans had a *negative* real interest rate—that is, interest rates were less than inflation and so a borrower actually had to repay less than they borrowed. The borrowers thought these floating-rate loans were cheap but became trapped when real rates were pushed up to 12% in the early 1980s[6] (Cardoso and Dornbusch 1989).

Between 1980 and 1984, interest payments by the low- and middle-income countries nearly doubled, and by 1984 there was a net flow of $10 billion (U.S.) per year toward the North. Table 5.1 shows the impact of the interest rate increase.

Argentina is one of the more extreme cases. All of its debt was at variable interest rates, and its interest payments jumped from $1.3 billion (U.S.) in 1980 to $3.3 billion in 1984 and $4.4 billion in 1985. That was a jump from 12% of export earnings to 43% of export earnings. Is 43% of income a usurious interest rate?

International loans are denominated in hard currency, typically U.S. dollars, British pounds, or German marks.[7] Most poor countries devalue, which makes the loans much more expensive in real terms. Between 1986 and 1990, Mozambique's debt in dollars increased from $3.3 billion to $4.7 billion, but its debt in meticais increased from 132 billion to 4,465 billion meticais. Officially, most of the loans were concessional, and the dollar interest rate was only 2%. But the metical interest rate was 123%. This is a story repeated across the world.

Countries pay their foreign debts from export earnings (and remittances). Since the debt crisis, most commodity prices have fallen and terms of trade have deteriorated badly. By the end of 2001, non-energy commodity prices averaged 44% of their 1980 value and 76% of their 1990 value. In other words, the value of the commodities that countries use to pay has been falling at nearly 4% per year for more than two decades.[8] This needs to be added to any interest rates. In table 5.2, we look at the effect of falling commodity prices.

What this means is that Ghana, whose main export is cocoa and was officially paying an interest rate of only 3% in the 1980s, was actually paying over 10%

TABLE 5.1   Impact of higher interest rates, in millions of dollars (U.S.)

US$ million	Middle-income countries		Low-income countries	
	1980	1984	1980	1984
New borrowing	84,645	67,155	20,613	24,049
Less				
Interest payments	27,817	45,507	4,324	7,325
Principal repayments	37,393	37,831	5,493	9,949
Net flow on debt	19,435	−16,183	10,796	6,775

Source: World Bank, *World Debt Tables 1991–92.*

TABLE 5.2   Imputed interest rates for exports of four agricultural commodities

	Price per tonne, U.S. $			Tonnes to pay U.S. $1 million			Annual "interest"	
	1980	1990	2000	1980	1990	2000	1980–90	1990–2000
Cocoa	2604	1267	906	384	789	1104	7.5%	3.4%
Coffee	3243	1182	913	308	846	1095	10.6%	2.6%
Sugar	632	277	180	1582	3610	5556	8.6%	4.4%
Cotton	2062	1819	1302	485	550	768	1.3%	3.4%

Annual "interest" = % increase in commodity volume to keep same payment levels.
Source of average prices: World Bank.

because of the falling price of cocoa. Suddenly, World Bank "concessional" interest rates do not look so good. Similarly, Rwanda's debt was almost entirely from multilateral creditors and its official interest rate in the 1980s was only 1.5%, but in terms of coffee exports, it was paying 12%. (Ghana and Rwanda had little variable-rate debt, so they were not affected by interest rate fluctuations.)

Successor Loans and Loan Laundering

The Brady Plan at the end of the 1980s started a trend to replace loans given during the loan-pushing era of the 1970s with new bonds guaranteed by governments. During the 1990s, most developing-country loans were refinanced in one way or another, with the original loans being paid off or replaced by new loans or bonds. One example is South Korea, which reached agreement in 1998 with a group of 13 leading international banks to extend the maturities on $24 billion (U.S.) in short-term loans to local banks. "Under the plan, announced in New York City, banks can exchange debt due in 1998 for loans maturing in one to three years. In a major victory for lenders, Seoul will guarantee the new loans . . . which will be publicly traded," wrote the *Japan Economic Institute Report* in an article headlined "South Korean Debt Rollover Boon to Japanese Banks" (Altbach 1998). United States "Secretary of the Treasury Robert Rubin had put pressure on both Seoul and international banks by not releasing any of the money the United States had promised to South Korea as part of the International Monetary Fund–led rescue package until the loan rescheduling talks were completed," the magazine noted.

This report illustrates three key points:

1. Bad loans on which Korean banks might have defaulted were replaced by new bonds that can be publicly traded and sold by the original Japanese, German, and U.S. banks. Thus, the banks that made the original bad loans will not retain the bonds issued to replace those loans.
2. A bad private debt is being replaced by a new government-guaranteed debt.

3. The deal was made under heavy pressure from the IMF and the U.S. Treasury.

In this chapter, we argue strongly that lenders must be held liable for their negligence, misconduct, and poor judgment. But international policy in the 1980s and 1990s was just the opposite—that lenders should be bailed out and not be held responsible. In part, this was because of a genuine fear in the early 1980s that banks had made so many bad and corrupt loans that the banking system would collapse if they were held liable. Thus, whereas loan-pushing in the 1920s led to default in the 1930s, loan-pushing in the 1970s simply led to new lending. Just as we talk of money laundering, perhaps we should also talk of "loan laundering," whereby corrupt, negligent, or foolish loans were washed and converted into new, good loans.

But this presents a serious problem for any attempt to declare loans illegitimate and force the corrupt lenders to take the hit, because the thief has fled. Are these successor loans illegitimate?

Where a loan is simply rolled over or the same institution simply grants another loan to pay back the first, as is done by the World Bank and IMF, then it is clear that any original illegitimacy carries forward. If the lender was guilty of misconduct in the first instance, then its responsibility continues.

Similarly, where publicly traded bonds are used to refinance an illegitimate debt, the buyers of such bonds should have known of the risk that these bonds would be declared illegitimate, and they accepted the risk. In other words, the illegitimacy carries forward—even if the original loan has been formally paid off, its successor loan or bond is, in practice, the same illegitimate loan. And a bank that sells a bond for an illegitimate debt has the same responsibility as a dealer who knowingly sells a stolen car.

That leads us to the following definitions of what we will call an "illegitimate successor loan":

1. If an institution replaces, rolls over, or pays off an illegitimate debt with a new loan, then the new loan is an illegitimate successor loan.
2. If a bond or new loan is issued for the sole or main purpose of paying off an illegitimate debt, then this is an illegitimate successor loan and the creditor has taken the risk.
3. A government guarantee of an illegitimate successor loan does not make the loan any less illegitimate. Furthermore, it strengthens the illegitimacy if international financial pressure has forced the government to accept responsibility for a private debt.

Fungibility

Something is "fungible" if it is interchangeable. The word has been used increasingly to apply to money, and in particular to aid or loan funds for poor countries. Aid or a loan can be supplied for a specific beneficial purpose—rural credit or an electricity supply line for poor people—but the aid or loan releases funds that the government would have used for the rural credit or the electricity line, and those funds can be used for another purpose, such as to buy arms or to put in a foreign bank account. When the apartheid regime in South Africa became desperately short of foreign exchange because of sanctions in the 1980s, it perfected the technique of floating bond issues for seemingly acceptable projects such as expansions of the electricity grid. Many of these projects did not need foreign currency and could have been built using local currency, but the bond issues meant that South Africa obtained scarce U.S. dollars despite sanctions (Samson et al. 1997).

We therefore argue that because of fungibility, all loans to odious regimes and dictators can be classed as odious, even if the ostensible purpose was permissible. As with the original Cuban debt that started the discussion, the debt was taken by the regime and not by the country.

Therefore, we are forced to conclude that fungibility means that either all loans to a government are illegitimate, probably due to odiousness, or to be illegitimate, an individual loan must be clearly linked to an illegitimate purpose or conduct.

Capital flight is an example of fungibility. Half of the money lent to the Argentine military dictatorship during the 1980s remained abroad, often with the knowledge of the lending banks because the money remained in the original account or was transferred to another account in the same city or country. Clearly, these loans were not being used to the benefit of the country and must be seen as illegitimate.

Where Lender Misbehavior Makes Loans Illegitimate

The years since the 1970s have seen a massive increase in developing-country debt—from $73 billion (U.S.) in 1970 to $610 billion in 1980, $1,458 billion in 1990, and $2,492 billion in 2000. But since 1982 much of this has simply been refinancing. From 1984 through 1989, there was a net flow of more than $100 billion from the poor South to the rich North.[9] In the early 1990s, there was again a flow of money south. But since 1998 the flow has been to the North again; in the three years 1999–2001, debt repayments by all developing countries were $282 billion more than new loans and all grant aid.

The international financial community portrays lending as necessary and good. But since 1999 developing countries have been paying more than $260 million (U.S.) per day net to the industrialized countries because of that lending, and it seems that the benefits to many poor countries have been less than claimed. We argue here that lender misconduct has been substantial.

Usury—Latin America and the Debt Treadmill

Latin America's debt crisis is rooted in the increases in global interest rates in the 1970s. Since 1982, Latin America and the Caribbean have received no new long-term loan funding and paid $236 billion (U.S.) to their creditors—this is net and means that debt service (interest payments and principal repayments) going out of Latin America and the Caribbean has exceeded new loans coming in by $236 billion. This is shown in table 5.3 Over nearly two decades, in only one year, 1998, was there a significant inflow of new money—and that money went out again the next year. Yet the total debt has more than tripled, from $209 billion to $660 billion. During this same period, Latin America and the Caribbean have made an incredible $612 billion in interest payments—but the debt continues to increase.

How does this happen? In the 1970s, when banks were anxious to lend, they provided enough new money to repay old loans and have money left for development projects. In 1975, for example, Latin America and the Caribbean made

TABLE 5.3   Latin America and the Caribbean long-term debt, billions of dollars (U.S.)

Year	Total debt	Interest	Net transfer
1977	100	6	11
1978	127	8	13
1979	148	13	11
1980	187	18	6
1981	209	22	16
1982	237	27	2
1983	286	26	−10
1984	316	29	−16
1985	331	32	−21
1986	360	26	−20
1987	385	30	−19
1988	364	29	−25
1989	377	29	−22
1990	380	29	−9
1991	387	23	−11
1992	398	22	−9
1993	426	24	3
1994	456	22	−4
1995	497	30	5
1996	527	30	9
1997	557	34	2
1998	648	37	29
1999	673	43	−24
2000	662	46	−57
2001	660	44	−38
Total			
1977–2001		679	−180
1982–2001		612	−236

Notes: (1) This is for long-term debt (LDOD in World Bank code), excluding IMF loans, for Latin America and the Caribbean.

(2) Interest is interest on long-term debt (LINT) plus, for the period 1985–94, changes in interest arrears (treated as short-term debt) and capitalized interest.

(3) Net transfers equals new loans plus grant aid, minus loan capital repayments and loan interest payments. A negative transfer indicates that poor countries made loan repayments larger than the combined flow of aid and new loans.

Source: World Bank.

$7 billion (U.S.) in principal repayments and $5 billion in interest payments—
$12 billion in total debt service. The region was then provided $18 billion in
new loans, which covered all the payments to the banks and left the region with
$6 billion to spend. However, interest rates began to rise, from 5% on average
in 1970 to 10% in 1979 and 13% in 1982. At first, the banks continued to lend
to cover the payments—in 1981 Latin America was lent an incredible $61 bil-
lion, of which $45 billion immediately went back to the banks as repayments,
but it still left Latin America with $16 billion to spend. The crunch came in
1982, when the banks stopped lending; since 1983, Latin America was paying
more in debt service than it received in new loans, and this has continued to the
present day.

Interest payments were vastly more than the amount that was actually being
repaid to the creditors. Not only did Latin America stop repaying the principal,
it could not even keep up with the new higher interest payments. So each year
the unpaid interest was added to the loan, and the next year interest was charged
on the unpaid interest, and that, too, was added to the loan, and interest was
charged on the interest on the interest—and so it went, as Latin America ran
on its debt treadmill. Is this usury or extortionate? We calculate that if interest
rates had remained at their 1970 levels, an average of 5%, and the remaining
money had been used for capital repayments, the present long-term debt as of
2001 would be only $233 billion—the level before the 1982 debt crisis.

Lending to Oppressive Regimes: Argentina

As well as being in the headlines in 2002–2003, Argentina is an example of
most of the issues related to illegitimate debt: odious debt, corrupt debt, successor loans, nationalization of debt, and policy advice. Argentina is perhaps
most important, however, because it is the only country in which a national
court has ruled some of the foreign debt to be illegal and illegitimate (Olmos
1995; Pettifor et al. 2001).

In a coup on 24 March 1976, a military junta seized power in Argentina, and
it was only overthrown on 10 December 1983, after its failure to win the Mal-
vinas (Falklands) War against Britain. In those seven years, the military junta
and its allies in right-wing militias killed at least 20,000 people, and during the
same period, foreign debt rose from $8 billion to $46 billion (U.S.), most of it
owed to banks.

Even before the end of the dictatorship, Alejandro Olmos began an investigation of that debt. In 1982, he filed a criminal accusation against the former
minister of economy and other officers of the regime regarding the illegal origin
of the Argentinean external debt. Olmos found that soon after the military took
power, it began clandestine borrowing, particularly from U.S. and British banks,
in ways that violated Argentine law. State-owned companies were forced to take
foreign loans and hand the money over to the central bank; the state oil company
Yacimientos Petroliferos Fiscales took $6 billion (U.S.) in loans during that
period. Mario Caffiero, an Argentinean member of Parliament, told a seminar

in London that the World Bank calculated that half of the debt of the military regime was for capital flight.[10]

In 1982, over the opposition of the then finance minister, the central bank guaranteed the loans, effectively nationalizing them. These debts were then rolled over and refinanced several times, most recently with new bonds issued in the early 1990s.

After 18 years of a complicated procedure, Federal Judge Dr. Jorge Ballesteros finally ruled on 13 July 2000 that the debt contracted during the 1976–83 dictatorship was illegal and illegitimate. He found that the increase in private and public foreign debt between 1976 and 1982 was "excessive, harmful and with absolutely no justification from an economic, financial or administrative point of view." The debt was contracted under the regime without parliamentary control as required by the national constitution.[11]

Ballesteros also looked at the IMF and World Bank, stating that:

> The exact co-responsibility and eventual guilt of the international financial institutions (particularly the IMF and the World Bank) must be established, as well as that of the creditors, because during the whole period under examination (1976 to 1982) many technical missions sent by the IMF visited our country. . . . The conclusion is that the creditor banks, the IMF and the World Bank acted with imprudence themselves. (Ballesteros 2000)

Thus, the federal judge has established many of the conditions for the illegitimacy of this debt. He has ruled that it was taken by the regime, not the country, and he has ruled that the IMF and World Bank acted imprudently.

Continued reschedulings pushed the debt up from $46 billion to $65 billion (U.S.) by the early 1990s, but as we have shown, this is really just the same debt that Dr. Ballesteros has ruled to be illegitimate.

More than $500 billion (U.S.), 20% of all developing-country debt, can be attributed to dictators in 23 different countries (see table 5.4). Most were backed by the United States and the West, although Mengistu Haile Mariam was backed by the Soviet Union and Siad Barre gained support from both East and West at different time. In the terms set out by Alexander Sack, these are all odious debts that are personal debts of those dictators and their regimes and in Sack's words "fall with the fall of this power."

Successor Debt: South Africa

When Nelson Mandela walked out of prison in 1990, the international banks handed him a bill for $21 billion (U.S.). In effect, the bankers told Mandela: "In 1985 we told the white government that we understood that they had financial problems and that it was expensive to keep you in jail and attack the neighbouring states. So we told P. W. Botha that he could defer payments on his debt. But now that you are out of jail and South Africa has majority rule, it is time for you to pay the cost of keeping you in jail."

And Mandela was told by the international community to pay up because if

TABLE 5.4   Debts that can be attributed to dictators, in billions of dollars (U.S.)

Indonesia	Suharto	126
Brazil	military	100
Argentina	military	65
Philippines	Marcos	40
Syria	Assad	22
South Africa	apartheid	22
Pakistan	military	19
Sudan	Nimeiry/al-Mahdi	17
Thailand	military	14
Nigeria	Buhari/Abacha	14
Chile	Pinochet	13
Zaire/Congo	Mobutu	13
Algeria	military	5
Iran	Shah	5
Kenya	Moi	4
Ethiopia	Mariam	4
Bolivia	military	3
Somalia	Siad Barre	2
Paraguay	Stroessner	2
Malawi	Banda	2
El Salvador	military	1
Liberia	Doe	1
Haiti	Duvalier	1

Source: Updated from Joseph Hanlon 1998, "Dictators and debt."

he didn't there would be no foreign investment. So he did. In 1997, South Africa paid an incredible $6.5 billion (U.S.) in debt service—more than four times what the banks demanded of the apartheid state. Nevertheless, South Africa did not attract foreign investment.

Because of apartheid, South Africa was forced to leave the British Commonwealth in 1961. In 1973, the United Nations began to describe apartheid as a crime against humanity, and in 1977 it imposed a mandatory arms embargo on South Africa. In 1982, two lawyers from the First National Bank of Chicago wrote an article in the *University of Illinois Law Review* in which they warned their employers and other banks of "the consequences of a change of sovereignty for loan agreements" in countries like South Africa (Foorman and Jehle 1982: 21). They noted that "if the debt of the predecessor is deemed to be 'odious', i.e. the debt proceeds are used against the interests of the populace, then the debt may not be chargeable to the successor," and stressed that the use of funds as described in loan documents was often too general to ensure adequately that such loans benefited the people. The banks did not listen, however, and debt jumped from $16.9 billion (U.S.) in 1980 to $24.3 billion by the end of 1984.[12] With apartheid officially a crime against humanity, there is no question that the apartheid state satisfied Alexander Sack's description of "a despotic state [which] incurs a debt not for the needs or in the interests of the state, but to strengthen its despotic regime" (Adams 1991: 165).

Protest was growing inside South Africa. On 20 July 1985, a state of emergency was proclaimed, and on 1 September, South Africa defaulted and stopped paying its creditors. Negotiations with the banks continued over two years. Archbishop Desmond Tutu called on the banks not to reschedule the debts and instead confiscate South African assets abroad (Hanlon 1998). In fact, the banks not only made a deal but gave the apartheid state a very soft ride. In four years, South Africa had to repay only $4.8 billion (U.S.) of capital—$1.2 billion per year.

Except for a small amount of new lending ($1.5 billion) in the first two years of majority rule, there has been little change in the total volume of South African debt. This suggests that at least long-term debt is simply being rolled over. However, principal repayments exceed the amount of long-term debt inherited from the apartheid era, which suggests that much of the original debt has been paid off and refinanced. Therefore, it seems likely that South Africa's current indebtedness is almost entirely successor debt. This debt is illegitimate because the current loans obviously refinanced apartheid debt, which is odious debt.

Gross Negligence in Lending: Zaire/Congo

With U.S. support, General Joseph Mobutu took power in the Congo in 1965, and he became one of the world's most corrupt dictators. In 1978, the IMF appointed its own man, Irwin Blumenthal, to a key post in the central bank of Zaire. He resigned in less than a year, writing a memo that said that "the corruptive system in Zaire with all its wicked manifestations" is so serious that there is "no (repeat no) prospect for Zaire's creditors to get their money back" (Lissakers 1992). When Blumenthal wrote his report, Zaire's debt was $4.6 billion (U.S.). By the time Mobutu was overthrown and died in 1998, the debt was $12.9 billion (World Bank 2000). For once, the private sector saw that they had no chance of getting their money back and stopped lending in 1981. But shortly after the Blumenthal memo, the IMF granted Zaire the largest loan it had ever given an African country; over the next decade, it gave Mobutu $700 million, most of which has never been repaid. The World Bank was hardly involved in Zaire when Blumenthal wrote his memo, but in the next 15 years it lent $2 billion to Zaire—and was still giving new money to Mobutu as late as 1993. Western governments were the biggest lenders and continued to pour in new money until 1990—even though Zaire had virtually stopped repaying its debts in 1982. There is perhaps no clearer example of odious debt. Money was poured into Zaire when the lenders had already been told there was "no (repeat no) prospect" of being repaid.

Lending to Self-Enriching Regimes: The Philippines

By the time the Philippine dictator Ferdinand Marcos was finally overthrown in 1986 and had fled into exile with his wife, Imelda, he had an estimated $5–13 billion (U.S.) stashed away in foreign banks.[13] Up to one-third of the Philippines' foreign debts had passed into his very large pockets. The largest single debt of the Philippines is the Bataan nuclear power station. Completed in 1984 at a cost of $2.3 billion, it was never used because it was built on an earthquake fault at the foot of a volcano. "Filipinos have not benefited from a single watt of electricity," said the national treasurer, Leonor Briones. "It's a terrible burden which never fails to elicit feelings of rage, anger and frustration in me. We're talking of money that should have gone to basic services like schools and hospitals." The nuclear power station was financed by the U.S. export credit agency Ex-Im Bank, Union Bank of Switzerland (which is accused of holding some of the Marcos billions), Bank of Tokyo, and Mitsui and Company, all of whom are still being repaid. The Philippines still pays $170,000 per day for the power station, and the debt will not be repaid until 2018. The nuclear power station was built by the U.S. multinational Westinghouse in spite of a much lower bid by General Electric that was favored by a technical committee. Marcos overruled his own advisers, and Westinghouse later admitted that it paid a commission to a Marcos associate, which the *New York Times* estimated at $80 million. Much of the construction was done by companies in which Marcos had an interest. Bribes were paid in Switzerland (Adams 1991: 157–167; George 1988: 18–19).

Failed Projects: Tanzania, Nigeria, and Indonesia

Tanzania owes the World Bank more than $575 million (U.S.) for 26 failed agricultural projects, according to the Tanzania Coalition on Debt and Development. In Nigeria, at least 61 development projects, financed by more than $5 billion in foreign loans, have either failed or never opened, according to a government commission (*Post Express* 1999). Dam projects all over the world have been unsuccessful. In Indonesia, the dictator Suharto moved millions of Javanese people to populate other islands as part of the "transmigration" program. Despite complaints about the human rights and environmental problems, the program was funded, in part, by nearly $1 billion in World Bank loans (Hancock 1985: 133). Many of the migrants were put on marginal land where they could not survive, so the World Bank had to put in more money to try to support them (Caufield 1997).

In this context, the United Nations Institute for Training and Research *Debt and Financial Management (Legal Aspects) Training Package* has some useful views:

> Developing countries rely on external expertise because they lack the technical know-how and assistance to plan infrastructure policies and to implement projects. Consequently, developing countries should not bear the burden of . . . bad planning and bad implementation performed by external sources. . . . [C]omparative law studies indicate that modern civil and commercial law has broadened contractual obligations in complex business transactions beyond the strict delivery of goods . . . to include dissemination of professional information, exchange of motivated opinions, discovery of special risks, and instructions and consultations, especially if one party is less knowledgeable than the other and therefore must trust the

other's superior skills. Neglecting these accessory obligations may be considered a breach of contract . . . and should be all the more applicable if the lender is an official donor with the statutory obligation to finance and assist in the execution of development projects. (UNITAR 2004)

A Definition with Some Examples

For 30 years, creditors have been making international loans that would never have been acceptable under national laws precisely because they felt that no one would ever bring them to account for improper lending and that repayment would be enforced no matter how gross the misconduct by the lenders. So far, this has indeed been the case.

In the absence of any definition in law, we have tried to define "illegitimate debt" in terms of national law and practice and in terms of the few phrases such as odious debt, extortionate debt, and usury that have entered the legal language. We propose the following definition: "Illegitimate debt" is debt that the borrower cannot be required to repay because the original loan or conditions attached to that loan infringed the law or public policy, or because they were unfair, improper, or otherwise objectionable.

We note the need for a fair and independent adjudication process to consider claims of illegitimacy, and we distinguish between the liability of creditors for illegitimate loans and protection of debtors who took legitimate loans that are now unpayable. Illegitimate debts are those that should not be paid, but unpayable debts are those that cannot be paid.

Four Categories

In terms of creditor liability and responsibility, we propose to make two distinctions—between the real purpose of the loan and the conditions attached to it, and between "unacceptable" and "inappropriate" loans and conditions. An illegitimate condition makes the entire loan illegitimate, even if the purpose or use of the loan is acceptable and proper. Furthermore, a loan or condition is "unacceptable" if it is manifestly, or prima facie, null and should not be repaid because the original loan violated lending rules in national laws, involved obvious misconduct by the lender, or in the words of the British Consumer Credit Act "grossly contravenes ordinary principles of fair dealing." In contrast, a loan or condition is "inappropriate" where it might be acceptable in other circumstances but where it is not acceptable for the borrower in question. The lender failed to apply prudence and due diligence, and gave a loan that was inappropriate for the circumstances.

1. Unacceptable loans would include loans that were odious, were given to known corrupt officials, and were for obviously bad projects. Examples include:
   - Odious debts, such as those of the apartheid state in South Africa, and loans to dictators such as Mobutu in Zaire, Duvalier in Haiti,

Suharto in Indonesia, and the military in Argentina, which were clearly not in the interests of the people of those countries. They are loans taken by the regime and not the state.
- Loans that involve corruption and kickbacks.
- Loans directly linked to capital flight, as happened in Argentina and Brazil in the 1990s.
- Loans for manifestly bad projects, such as the Bataan nuclear power station in the Philippines, and for environmentally damaging projects, especially ones such as dam projects and Indonesian "transmigration," which would not be funded now.
- Successor loans that are explicitly renewals, exchanges, or rollovers of loans that are independently unacceptable.
- Private loans taken over by the state, nationalized, or guaranteed, and where the lender should have accepted the cost of making a bad loan to a private enterprise.

2. Unacceptable conditions would include usurious interest rates and policy demands that violate national laws. Examples include:
- Usury, including the very high interest rates of the 1980s imposed on floating-rate loans. In assessing usury, interest rates can be calculated in the currency in which the loan is denominated or in the prices of the main export commodities.
- Conditions that are illegal under national law, such as the requirement for repayment of Brazilian debt before the audit required by the constitution.
- Conditions that violate public policy, such as cuts in health or education spending or the imposition of poverty wages on civil servants, especially where later statements by the international financial institutions admitted that such conditions were incorrect or unduly harsh.
- Conditions that ultimately increase the cost of the debt, such as dollar convertibility in Argentina, even if they are accepted by the elected government.
- Requiring the government to nationalize or guarantee unacceptable or inappropriate loans made to the private sector.

3. Inappropriate loans are consumption loans and loans given where grants would have been more correct. Examples include:
- Consumption loans made to poor countries that have no chance of repaying without imposing unacceptable privation on their people. These are loans that should have been grants and, as a result of policy changes in the 1990s, often are now grants.
- Loans to formally elected governments that had become dictatorial and were no longer using the funds in the interest of the people, such as Robert Mugabe in Zimbabwe and Alberto Fujimori in Peru.

4. Inappropriate conditions are linked to unsuitable policies. Examples include:
- Restrictions that are inappropriate to the circumstances, such as limits on post-disaster reconstruction.

Conclusion

National bankruptcy and insolvency procedures always involve a court or arbitrator as a neutral party between debtor and creditors. The claims and justifications on an alleged extortionate debt are debated before a judge. Nothing like that exists in international lending, and campaigners have long called for some sort of fair, neutral, independent international body. Within our definitions, such a mechanism would be needed to decide on issues of acceptability and appropriateness. The need for an international debt body has been raised by IMF First Deputy Managing Director Anne Krueger, who called for a formal sovereign debt restructuring mechanism (SDRM) analogous to domestic insolvency regimes such as the U.S. bankruptcy court (Krueger 2001). Eventually, the U.S. Treasury vetoed the idea, but the need has not disappeared, as U.S. attempts to cancel Iraq's debt show.

Critics of debt cancelation often raise the same issue that was raised in the nineteenth century by opponents of the then new concept of bankruptcy. If debts could be canceled, they argued, then lenders would be afraid to lend, and there would be a capital shortage. There are two contradictory responses. First, one of the goals of creating the concept of illegitimate debt is precisely to force lenders to reduce their lending where lending is unlikely to produce positive economic and social effects in the borrowing country. But, second, history has demonstrated that bankruptcy protection and the possibility of debt cancelation do not deter lending. Most Western countries have, since at least the 1970s, employed bankruptcy regimes that force creditors to cancel debts of borrowers who cannot repay their loans. Yet notwithstanding this restriction on the rights of creditors, the availability of credit in these countries has exploded over the same time period.

The concept of "illegitimate debt" is important because it puts the liability for bad and imprudent lending back where it belongs, with the lender. The concept of illegitimacy is also important as a contribution to ending blaming the victims because it makes clear that much of the blame for the debt crisis belongs to politically driven and imprudent actions by the creditors rather than corruption and incompetence by the borrowers. The issue of moral hazard is important here because creditors made illegitimate loans to developing countries because they assumed that the IMF and World Bank would enforce repayment, no matter how odious or dubious the loan. If lenders are not disciplined now, then they will know that they can make totally outrageous loans with no risk. If discipline is to be reintroduced to the international capital markets, then this moral hazard must be eliminated and lenders must be penalized for past bad lending.

Appendix: Setting Off Other Claims

Over a four-year period, Jubilee 2000 took the arcane concept of poor-country debt and turned it into a hot political issue. It put the concept of "unpayability" on the international agenda and forced the G7 and the IMF and World Bank to take action to cancel some debt (albeit not a lot). More recently, the Jubilee movement worldwide has taken up the issue of "illegitimate debt" that should be canceled because the lender granted it improperly, and this chapter has tried to define that concept. Campaigners in the South have tabled a third and equally important issue—counterclaims of debts owed *to* the South. This issue is only beginning to be raised internationally, and we use this appendix to highlight the three kinds of counterclaims that are relevant.

First are claims against lenders. Creditors who made odious loans "have committed a hostile act with regards to the people," noted Alexander Sack (Adams 1991). Thus, when banks and international financial institutions lent to Congo's Mobutu or the apartheid government in South Africa, they were not simply making bad loans but also helping to oppress the people of those countries; the government of the Congo should be able to claim compensation for the damage done to the country by the massive lending that helped to keep Mobutu in power. Claims for social and environmental damage are being made against the World Bank for dam projects it funded. Dollar convertibility in Argentina was a manifestly foolish and unworkable policy from the start, and it is arguable that the IMF should be required to compensate Argentina for the harm done.

The second type of counterclaim involves capital flight. "Bringing back even a fraction of the $130 billion or so in Latin flight capital would take care of the region's debt servicing problems for years to come," wrote Karin Lissakers in 1986 (George 1988: 19–21), and she actually suggested using the flight capital to pay the debts. She is a former U.S. State Department official who later became the U.S. executive director of the IMF, so she wrote with some authority.

Third, it is argued that the rich North has a debt to the South, historically for the slave trade and colonialism, and more recently for the damage done by Cold War proxy wars and environmental depredations.

It is important not to confuse calls for economic justice with definitions of illegitimacy. In this chapter, we have tried to set out a clear definition of illegitimacy that is in keeping with national law and practice and with commonly accepted judgments of morality and debt. But any settlement of debts must go beyond simply the cancelations of illegitimate debt and must take into account countervailing claims.

Acknowledgments This chapter is based on a Working Paper first published by the Development Policy and Practice research group of the Open University, Milton Keynes, England. The research was funded by Norwegian Church Aid.

Notes

1. Snow, J. 2003. Interviewed on *Your World with Neil Cavuto,* Fox News, 11 April 2003. Transcript available online at: www.foxnews.com/printer_friendly_story/0,3566,83939,00.html.

2. Soros, G. 2003. Quote from Reuters, 13 May 2003. Available online at: http://onebusiness.nzoom.com/onebusiness_detail/0,1245,189671-3-168,00.html.

3. This chapter draws on three serious attempts within the Jubilee debt cancelation movement to define "illegitimate debt"—by Latin American and Caribbean Jubilee 2000 in the Tegucigalpa Declaration agreed on 27 January 1999 (online at: www.ceji-iocj .org/English/international/TegucigalpaDeclaration(Ja99).htm), by the Canadian Ecumenical Jubilee Initiative at a policy forum 15–16 November 2000 in Toronto ("Illegitimate Debt: Definitions and Strategies for Repudiation and Cancellation," 15–16 November 2000, online at: www.ceji-iocj.org/English/debt//IlligitimateFull(Dec00).htm), and by AFRODAD, the Zimbabwe-based African Forum and Network on Debt and Development, in a policy brief in early 2002 ("Fair and Transparent Arbitration Mechanism on Debt," Policy Brief No. 1/2002).

4. Translated from the French by Patricia Adams and quoted in Adams, *Odious Debt*, 1991, p. 165.

5. Section 138 of the Consumer Credit Act of 1974. Identical language is used in Section 343 of the Insolvency Act of 1986 to define "extortionate credit transactions."

6. In the mid-1970s, world inflation averaged 11.4%, whereas LIBOR, the London Interbank Offer Rate, was only 8%, meaning that real interest rates were −3.4%. By contrast, real interest rates for 1981–84 exceeded 12%.

7. In the pre-euro era.

8. The decline averaged 5.5% a year in the 1980s and 2.4% a year in the 1990s.

9. Net flow equals new loans plus grant aid minus loan capital repayments and loan interest payments. A negative flow means poor countries are making loan repayments larger than the combined flow of aid and new loans. Figures are from the World Bank.

10. Author's notes from remarks of Mario Caffiero at a seminar organized by the New Economics Foundation, London, 15 January 2002.

11. Case No. 14, 467, Buenos Aires Federal Economic Criminal Court No. 2. "Olmos, Alejandro versus/Various Former Government Officers," 14 July 2000. Excerpts from the case are available at http://listas_ecuanex.net.ec/pipermail/alai-amlatina/2000q3/000111.html.

12. Data note: The World Bank's data, even for a particular country and particular year, can vary substantially from one report to the next. We have tried to put together our data series using six World Bank reports: *World Debt Tables* for 1983–84, 1986–87, and 1991–92, and its renamed successor *Global Development Finance* for 1997, 2001, and 2002, using the most recent data in all cases. (All are published by the World Bank, Washington, DC.)

13. In 1986, the new president, Corazon Aquino, created the Presidential Commission on Good Government. Its chairman, Jovito Salonga, later estimated the loot at around $5 billion to $10 billion (U.S.). Later, former Solicitor General Francisco Chavez published a full-page ad in three Manila newspapers claiming that the Marcoses had $13.4 billion deposited in Switzerland.

References

Adams, P. 1991. *Odious Debt*. London: Earthscan.

Altbach, E. 1998. South Korean Debt Rollover Boon to Japanese Banks, *Japan Economic Institute Report* (6 February). Available online at: www.jei.org/Archive/JEIR98/9805w4.html.

Ballesteros, J. 2000. Olmos, Alejandro versus/Various Former Government Officers (14 July). Case No. 14, 467, Buenos Aires Federal Economic Criminal Court No. 2.

Available onlline at: http://listas_ecuanex.net.ec/pipermail/alai-amlatina/2000q3/000111.html.

Cardoso, E., and Dornbusch, R. 1989. Brazilian Debt Crises: Past and Present. In *The International Debt Crisis in Historical Perspective,* ed. B. Eichengreen and P. Lindert, pp. 106–39. Cambridge, MA: MIT Press.

Caufield, C. 1997. *Masters of Illusion: The World Bank and the Poverty of Nations.* New York: Henry Holt and Co.

Foorman, J., and Jehle, M. 1982. "Effects of State and Government Succession on Commercial Bank Loans to Foreign Sovereign Borrowers." 1 *University of Illinois Law Review* 9.

Gaona, A. 2001. The Illegal Foreign Debt: The Value and Likelihood of a Legal Ruling. Paper presented at Jubilee 2000 Conference, Bamako, Mali, April 21–23.

George, S. 1988. *A Fate Worse than Debt.* London: Penguin.

Gregory, R. 1992. *Bankruptcy of Individuals.* Bicester: CCH Editions.

Guest, A., and Lloyd, M. 2000. *Encyclopedia of Consumer Credit Law.* (Supplement). London: Sweet and Maxwell.

Hancock, G. 1985. *Lords of Poverty.* London: Macmillan.

Hanlon, J. 1998a. *Paying for Apartheid Twice.* London: Action for Southern Africa and World Development Movement.

Hanlon, J. 1998b. *Dictators and Debt.* London: Jubilee 2000.

Hanlon, J. 2000. How Much Debt Must Be Cancelled? *Journal of International Development* 12: 877.

Harding, G. 1995. *Consumer Credit and Consumer Hire Law: A Practical Guide.* London: Sweet and Maxwell.

Hay, D., ed. 2001. *Words and Phrases Legally Defined* (Supplement). London: Butterworths.

House of Commons. 1997–1998. International Development Committee 3rd Report. Debt Relief.

Jubilee 2000. Consensus Statement of the Jubilee 2000 International Conference, Okinawa, 21 July 2000.

Jubilee South. 2001. We Don't Owe You, You Owe Us—Statement of Jubilee South Africa and Jubilee South, Durban, South Africa (August).

Kremer, M., and Jayachandran, S. 2002. Odious Debt. Paper presented to the Conference on Macroeconomic Policies and Poverty Reduction, International Monetary Fund, Washington, DC. Available online at: www.imf.org/external/NP/Res/seminars/2002/poverty/index.htm.

Krueger, A. 2001. Speech given to the National Economists' Club, Washington, DC, 26 November 2001. Available online at: www.imf.org/external/np/speeches/2001/112601.htm.

Lissakers, K. 1992. *Banks, Borrowers and the Establishment.* New York: Basic Books.

Olmos, A. 1995. *Todo Lo Que Usted Quiso Saber Sobre La Deuda Externa y Siempre Se Lo Ocultaron.* Buenos Aires: Editorial de los Argentinos.

Ovenden, K., and Cole, T. 1989. *Apartheid and International Finance.* London: Penguin Books.

Pettifor, A., Cisneros, L., and Gaona, A. 2001. *It Takes Two to Tango.* London: New Economics Foundation.

Post Express (Nigeria). 25 November 1999.

Rose, D. 1990. *Australian Bankruptcy Law.* Sydney: The Law Book Company.

Samson, M., Macquene, K., van Niekerk, I., and Ngqungwana, T. 1997. *South Africa's Apartheid Debt.* Cape Town: South African Institute for Financial Policy Options.

Walker, D. 1980. *The Oxford Companion to Law.* New York: Oxford University Press.
The Commonwealth Intergovernmental Group of Officials. 1989. *Banking on Apartheid.* London: James Currey.
United Nations Institute for Training and Research (UNITAR). 2004. "Debt and Financial Management (Legal Aspects) Training Package." New York: United Nations. Available at: www.unitar.org/dtm/Resource_Center/TrainingPackage/LegalAspects.htm.
World Bank. 2000. *World Debt Tables.* Washington, DC: World Bank.
———. 2002. *Global Development Finance.* Washington, DC: World Bank.

6

THE LEGAL CASE FOR DEBT REPUDIATION

Chris Jochnick

Introduction

Sovereign debt is not only the most urgent economic issue facing many countries but perhaps the leading cause of human rights violations in the developing world. Debt servicing deprives governments of as much as half of their annual budgets, eliminating vital social services, undermining democratic processes, and condemning the poorest populations to a vicious cycle of impoverishment. Civil society campaigns and debtor governments have invoked economic and moral arguments to challenge sovereign debt but have largely neglected the law.[1] This chapter outlines a series of legal arguments challenging the legitimacy of debt and underscoring the obligations of creditors and Northern governments to make amends.

The widely held assumption that all sovereign debt is legal (and thereby legitimate) obscures the inequities and burden of debt and helps shield creditors from greater accountability. In an integrated and increasingly rule-bound world, law conditions both creditor and debtor expectations and sets the limits of the reasonable and possible. Debts that might have been repudiated or subject to military intervention in the past[2] are today bounded by legal regimes and negotiated under specific guidelines. The international legal principle of *pacta sunt servanda*—"every treaty in force is binding and must be complied with"—sets the ground rule: Legal debts must be serviced, no matter how burdensome, questionable, or counterproductive.

There is an urgent need to reconsider the legal case for existing sovereign debt. This chapter briefly describes the tremendous social and economic costs of overindebtedness and the role of Northern creditors and governments in fomenting debt problems. The chapter then sets forth legal arguments for debt repudiation and/or relief along three lines: (1) the heightened responsibilities of creditors and Northern governments; (2) violations of human rights, and (3) the illegitimacy of debt. The arguments are based on well-established principles of domestic and international law that are applicable to domestic proceedings and particularly relevant to any future international insolvency mechanism. More generally, the arguments should serve to challenge popular or political under-standings of the legal sanctity of debt, thereby creating space and support for more ambitious solutions to debt crises.

Background

The human cost of debt and the responsibility of creditors and Northern gov-ernments for debt crises have formed the backbone of ethical and political ar-guments for debt relief and repudiation. These issues are also relevant to legal arguments questioning the validity of debt based on the excessive burden of indebtedness and the "dirty hands" of creditors.[3] The role of Northern govern-ments in creating the conditions for overindebtedness also supports legal argu-ments for corresponding obligations of these governments to redress debt-related problems.

The Human Impact of Debt

In the late 1980s, French President Mitterand called the debt crisis the greatest threat facing mankind. Ten years later, British Chancellor of the Exchequer Gordon Brown declared debt to be "the greatest single cause of poverty and injustice across the earth and potentially one of the greatest threats to peace" (Hanlon and Garrett 1999: 2). Debt servicing robs developing countries of be-tween one-quarter and one-half of their national budgets, depriving them of funds for basic services and economic development. As a consequence, debt has a dramatic impact on the health, education, nutrition, and employment of hun-dreds of millions of people, as well as undermining political stability, the en-vironment, and long-term development among the poorest countries.

The United Nations has estimated that seven million children die every year as a direct result of the debt crisis, or 19,000 per day. Tens of millions more are deprived of primary education, clean water, sanitation, and vaccinations, and are unnecessarily exposed to a range of infectious diseases. The poorest and most highly indebted countries (HIPCs) account for two-thirds of all AIDS vic-tims and have an average life expectancy of 51 years. The immediate benefits of debt relief underscore the flip side of the crisis. International organizations estimate that debt relief put to good use could immediately reduce the toll of malaria by 400,000 fewer deaths per year and ensure universal primary educa-tion in sub-Saharan Africa. Limited debt relief quickly succeeded in doubling primary school enrollment in Uganda and causing half a million children to be vaccinated in Mozambique.[4]

Debt payments now outweigh international aid by a factor of almost ten to one and make it impossible for developing countries to tackle pressing crises, including AIDS, refugees, and natural disasters. Having sacrificed a generation of children, sold or destroyed much of their natural resources, and undermined their economic potential to service debts, the long-term prospect for these countries is desperate.

In addition to the economic and social costs, the debt burden also undermines democratic processes and the capacity of governments to meet the basic needs of their populations. Debt servicing opens the door to foreign influence and intervention in fundamental development decisions. The political, economic, and legal pressure exerted by creditors on debtor governments has, according to the UN Secretary General, "led to the erosion of national sovereignty and domestic control [and shifted] the initiative in formulating economic policies . . . from the national authorities to international sources" (Turk 1995: para. 23).

Despite various creditor initiatives, these problems, in most cases, are only getting worse. In 1980, the debt stock of the 41 HIPC countries stood at $412 billion (U.S.). By 2000, it had grown to $543 billion, accompanied by increasing debt payments (an increase of 25% between 1996 and 1999). Between 1981 and 1997, developing countries paid almost $3 trillion in interest and principal payments and received less than half of that in new loans. In 1999 alone, developing countries borrowed $246 billion while paying back $349 billion just in interest on old loans, resulting in a net transfer of $103 billion from South to North.[5]

Creditor Responsibility for Debt Problems

Creditor countries and banks share much of the blame for the overindebtedness of countries, having played a critical role in both the international economy and the local processes that created the crisis. At the global level, much of the debt problem can be attributed to three factors, each strongly influenced by creditor country and bank actions: (1) irresponsible bank lending in the 1970s prompted by the need to recycle OPEC deposits and a lack of regulatory oversight;[6] (2) a dramatic increase in interest rates, prompted by U.S. monetary policies; and (3) a fall in commodity prices and terms of trade, driven in large measure by the protectionism of Northern countries and the short-sighted export policies imposed by the multilateral banks.

At the local level, debt crises have been exacerbated by the mismanagement of loans, including corruption, capital flight, military spending, and wasteful development projects. The creditors played a secondary but still vital role in these processes, at best ignoring and more commonly encouraging and facilitating them.[7]

By the same token, Northern governments and banks facilitated the transfer of national wealth out of the developing countries by corrupt governments. (Capital flight alone accounts for 60–100% of the developing countries' original debt.)[8] European countries until recently granted tax deductions for the cost of bribery, and the multilateral banks were long reluctant to acknowledge the corruption of debtor governments (Hawley 2000; Wesberry 1998). It is estimated that 20% of the developing countries' debt went to dictators (see Hanlon, chapter

5, this volume). Having helped produce a debt crisis, the multinational banks then reaped benefits from it, with soaring profits in the first years of the crisis. The chairman of the U.S. Federal Reserve, Paul Volcker, commented in 1983: "We're all being induced to close our eyes to loose banking practices. If there were a God in heaven, the banks would not profit from the current crisis."[9]

Bankers had reason to lend irresponsibly to governments even in the face of obvious corruption and negative long-term impacts.[10] As *The Economist* aptly described the dynamic:

> The banker, hungry for assets, with an eye for the league tables that will rank his bank according to balance-sheet size, not profitability. The export credit agencies doling out cheap loans to foreign buyers of their country's produce . . . The borrowing countries for whom foreign credits are the easy route to status-boosting high-technology projects and to investment without the need for domestic savings. Who among this cast of characters is going to say no to a loan proposal? The situation is made worse by the fact that the banker probably has a job-life expectancy of about three years before he moves on to other tasks. The job-life of the finance minister in the borrowing country is probably shorter still. It will not be they who have to pick up the pieces when the bicycle finally crashes.[11]

In the past, most "insolvent" countries would have repudiated their debts or arrived at permanent solutions with creditors rather than incur prolonged periods of suffering. Sovereign debt has been a source of conflict between countries dating back to antiquity, and renegotiations and default are legion. Debt crises have followed a regular pattern since the 1800s, with overindebtedness leading to widespread defaults in the 1820s, 1870s, 1890s, and 1930s.[12] The current debt problems of developing countries have been prolonged by creditors and Northern governments eager to avoid formal defaults. Rather than writing off bad loans, debts have been rescheduled and recycled through secondary markets, resulting in a permanent state of economic crisis for debtor countries, a steady flow of resources from South to North, and an ever stronger political-economic influence of creditor governments over the policies of developing countries.

Creditor Obligations

Under international and domestic law, Northern governments and creditors may have special obligations to debtor countries that would be relevant in determining the validity of existing debts and appropriate redress. These heightened obligations are based on evolving legal principles relating to inequities in the global economic order, power imbalances between creditors and debtors, and past and continuing harms suffered by debtor countries. They are relevant in determining the legitimacy of existing debt and appropriate measures to resolve and redress overindebtedness.

Just Economic Order

Multilateral institutions are premised on the notion of a common bond and shared responsibilities among participating countries. These bonds and responsibilities are evident and elaborated in numerous international treaties, most prominently the UN Charter. In the post-colonial era, the United Nations and regional bodies have recognized enhanced responsibilities for the richest countries to ensure a just economic order and provide special consideration and treatment for developing countries.

The United Nations was founded on the principle that countries are capable of and legally responsible for creating adequate conditions for peace and justice in the world. This obligation is clearly stated in the UN Charter, which declares that "All Members pledge themselves to take joint and separate action [to promote]: higher standards of living, full employment, and conditions of economic and social progress and development; and solutions of international economic, social, health, and related problems" (arts. 55, 56). The principle was reaffirmed in the UN Millennium Declaration: "We recognize that, in addition to our separate responsibilities to our individual societies, we have a collective responsibility to uphold the principles of human dignity, equality and equity at the global level. As leaders we have a duty therefore to all the world's people, especially the most vulnerable" (art. 2).

The obligation to establish a just economic order has since been reaffirmed through human rights treaties and declarations. The Universal Declaration of Human Rights stipulates that "Everyone is entitled to a social and international order in which the rights and freedoms set forth in this Declaration can be fully realized" (art. 28). Under the International Covenant on Economic, Social and Cultural Rights (ICESCR), each State party "undertakes to take steps, individually and through international assistance and co-operation . . . with a view to achieving progressively the full realization of the rights recognized in the present Covenant" (art. 2.1) and "to take appropriate steps [through] international co-operation . . . to ensure" the right to an adequate living standard for all populations (art. 11.1). The UN body responsible for overseeing the ICESCR has underscored these obligations on multiple occasions: "The Committee wishes to emphasize that in accordance with Articles 55 and 56 of the Charter of the United Nations, with well-established principles of international law, and with the provisions of the Covenant itself, international cooperation for development and thus for the realization of economic, social and cultural rights is an obligation of all States" (UNCESCR 1990B: art. 14).

More recent UN declarations and resolutions have addressed global economic and political inequities. The UN Declaration on the Right to Development holds that "States have the duty to cooperate with each other in ensuring development and eliminating obstacles to development," and "States should . . . promote a new international economic order based on sovereign equality, interdependence, mutual interest and cooperation among all States, as well as to encourage the observance and realization of human rights" (art. 3.3). The Charter of Economic Rights and Duties of States similarly declares that "every State should cooperate with the efforts of developing countries to accelerate their economic and social development by providing favorable external conditions and by extending active assistance to them, consistent with their development needs and objectives, with strict respect for the sovereign equality of States and free of any conditions derogating from their sovereignty" (art. 17).[13] The Millennium Declaration similarly reinforces the international commitment "to address the special needs of the least developed countries" (art. 15).

Since the 1950s, the world has grown increasingly integrated, and the impacts and responsibilities of the international community over local affairs have grown in turn. The faltering international commitments to a New International Economic Order of the 1970s have been strengthened by a series of international resolutions flowing from the UN-sponsored world conferences of the 1990s. By their presence and influence over the final resolutions of these conferences, Northern governments have explicitly recognized their obligations to the developing world, in particular those relating to commercial relations, international assistance, and debt relief. The UN Millennium Declaration brings many of these pledges together, including the commitment

> To adopt, preferably by the time of that Conference, a policy of duty- and quota-free access for essentially all exports from the least developed countries; To implement the enhanced programme of debt relief for the heavily indebted poor countries without further delay and to agree to cancel all official bilateral debts of those countries in return for their making demonstrable commitments to poverty reduction; and To grant more generous development assistance, especially to countries that are genuinely making an effort to apply their resources to poverty reduction. (art. 15)

These declarations are further strengthened by the interpretations and resolutions of UN bodies. The UN Commission on Human Rights, its subcommission, and various UN special experts have repeatedly underscored the international community's obligation to address the debt issue as one of mutual responsibility. As the UN Committee on Economic, Social and Cultural Rights has stated: "[I]nternational measures to deal with the debt crisis should take full account of the need to protect economic, social and cultural rights through international cooperation. In many situations, this might point to the need for major debt relief initiatives" (UNCESCR 1990a: art. 9).

Reparations and State Responsibility

Under evolving principles of international law and particularly human rights law, Northern countries may be responsible for making amends for past and continuing harms to the developing world that should also be considered in the context of debt negotiations. States are accountable for harms to other states and may be obliged to make financial and other reparations. This basic legal principle is evident in the work of various UN bodies and has been strengthened by the establishment of various international tribunals, domestic jurisprudence, and government decisions to accept broader responsibility for past abuses.[14]

Many of the most serious crimes against populations have yet to be accounted for, but international and domestic laws are increasingly cognizant of the need to recognize and redress these harms. Much of the developing world is owed reparations from Northern (and former colonial) countries for mass extermination, slavery, looting, and environmental degradation.[15] Calculating reparations and assigning appropriate blame for these crimes is almost impossible, but rough estimates of damages provide sums far exceeding current debt levels from the developing countries.

The law of state responsibility as the precursor to human rights law established the principle that states are responsible for injuries to citizens of other countries and that "every internationally wrongful act by a State gives rise to international responsibility."[16] Subsequent human rights treaties have reinforced this principle by obliging governments to make economic and political amends for violations of human rights.[17]

The UN Human Rights Commission has elaborated an initial set of guidelines for reparations for victims of "gross violations of human rights" that include the following principles: (1) "Reparation may be claimed individually and where appropriate collectively, by the direct victims, the immediate family, dependents or other persons or groups of persons connected with the direct victims"; and (2) "Statutes of limitations shall not apply in respect of periods during which no effective remedies exist for violations of human rights and humanitarian law."[18] These principles find support in the establishment of international criminal courts and the Security Council resolutions holding Iraq liable for various crimes against Kuwait, including environmental damage and the depletion of natural resources.

The violations of human rights and international law committed by Northern creditor states against developing countries include: slavery, mass murder, destruction of indigenous cultures, depletion of natural resources, and environmental degradation. All of these crimes warrant reparations under international law, particularly those of more recent origin with ties to current states and populations. As the Charter on Economic Rights and Duties of States declares:

> It is the right and duty of all States, individually and collectively, to eliminate colonialism, apartheid, racial discrimination, neo-colonialism and all forms of foreign aggression, occupation and domination, and the economic and social consequences thereof, as a prerequisite for development. States which practice such coercive policies are economically responsible to the countries, territories and peoples affected for the restitution and full compensation for the exploitation and depletion of, and damages to, the natural and all other resources of those countries, territories and peoples.

Domestic courts accepting slave-labor lawsuits relating to World War II have affirmed that there is no statute of limitations on war crimes or crimes against humanity, opening the door to a wide range of possible reparations cases dealing directly with debtor-creditor nations.

It is next to impossible to quantify such harms; however, conservative estimates suggest that the magnitude of potential reparations would dwarf current developing-country debts. Using reparations by Germany to victims of the Holocaust as a basis, one author calculates the debt owed to Latin America and Africa by colonial powers for the tens of millions of people killed at over $2 trillion (U.S.)[19] Another author estimates that the silver taken by the Spanish from the Andean region between 1545 and 1803 would be worth well over $100 billion at today's prices.[20] These estimates are only intended to provide some perspective on current levels of indebtedness between and among these same countries.

Additional legal claims can be made for the so-called ecological debt (see Simms, chapter 4, this volume) consisting of the historic looting and destruction of natural resources, the appropriation of genetic resources and traditional knowledge,[21] and the ongoing imbalances in the use and/or destruction of the environment. Given the widespread recognition that consumption is outpacing the Earth's limits, the richer countries are clearly taking an undue toll on poorer countries. International law recognizes the human right to a healthy environment and state liability for environmental destruction at home and abroad.[22] For purposes of illustration (1) according to the UNDP, the 20% of the world's population living in the highest income countries consume 58% of all energy used by humans, whereas the poorest 20% use less than 4% (UNDP 1998: 2) and (2) experts quantify the G8 carbon debt to developing countries (based on harmful levels of carbon dioxide emissions) at as much as $155 billion/yr (GRIAN 2005).

The Northern countries are unlikely to ever make full reparations on their historic colonial and ecological debts, but as a matter of legal responsibility, these past abuses should be recognized in the context of current debt negotiations. Debt cancelation would provide a simple and concrete mechanism to make at least partial reparations for past harms. Moreover, the present and future imbalances in environmental use and destruction should definitely be factored into debt negotiations, as is contemplated to a limited extent by debt-for-nature swaps and the Kyoto Protocol.

Fiduciary-like Duties of Creditors

The responsibilities under international law to create a just order and take special measures for developing countries are strengthened by fiduciary principles of particular relevance to the debtor–creditor relation. Common law systems have provided an increasing range of protections for borrowers based on their particular vulnerability, their trust in and dependence upon lenders, and the imbalance of power between the two. These same principles should inform the level of obligations of creditor states under international law, which has contemplated fiduciary obligations in cases of weakened states and vulnerable populations.[23] Under a fiduciary standard, creditors, whether states, multilateral institutions, or private banks, would assume part of the legal responsibility for irresponsible loans or unjust loans based on their relation with the debtor and the terms of the loans.

Fiduciary relations have long been contemplated in common-law systems, going back as far as sixteenth-century England. In the mid-1800s, Lord Chelmsford provided the following authoritative definition of these relations:

> Whenever two persons stand in such a relation that, while it continues, confidence is necessarily reposed by one, and the influence which naturally grows out of that confidence is possessed by the other, and this confidence is abused, or the influence

is exerted to obtain an advantage at the expense of the confiding party, the person so availing himself of his position will not be permitted to retain the advantage.[24]

Common-law courts have found fiduciary relations in a wide range of contexts and have established the principle that fiduciaries should be held to a higher standard of good faith in their commercial dealings and must avoid conflicts of interest.

U.S. Courts have increasingly recognized fiduciary or quasi-fiduciary relations between private lenders and borrowers[25] and have established a range of rights for borrowers and corresponding liability for lenders based on the following factors: a power imbalance between the parties, the closeness of the relationship, and the particular vulnerability of debtors. As one court explains, a creditor–debtor relationship "can become a fiduciary relationship if the borrower reposes a faith, confidence, and trust in the bank which results in dominion, control or influence over the borrower's affairs."[26] One of the most influential U.S. federal courts, the 9th Circuit Court of Appeals, decided in favor of a plaintiff debtor who sued his bank for bad advice, recognizing a fiduciary relationship based on the plaintiff's: (1) perception of a close relationship to the loan officer, (2) implicit reliance on the bank's advice, and (3) sharing of confidential financial information with the bank.[27]

The dependency and inequality of resources and influence that characterize the relationship between many developing countries and an institution such as the IMF or multinational bank syndicates arguably meet the criteria defining a fiduciary relationship under common law. As one banker describes the process of lending to developing countries: "The loans resulted from the exploitation of nation states in a context of systematic poverty and inequality, and the bankers had multiple roles in this structural situation: they were (i) lenders, (ii) internal funders, and (iii) partners of the multinational corporations which in turn helped organize and benefit from the dualistic economy, with its hierarchical profile of production and consumption" (Lothian 1995). Such a relationship should heighten creditor responsibility for the problems created by irresponsible lending and strengthen debtor claims that loans are illegitimate or otherwise legally unenforceable.

The Northern countries have a responsibility both for their bilateral loans and for the actions of multilateral banks under their influence. Although private banks are primarily responsible for their irresponsible loans, Northern governments play an additional role by their lack of effective oversight of such lending.[28] Northern countries are also responsible for their influence on international economic policies and processes that have often made sovereign debt impossible to service, including protectionist measures against developing-country exports, increased interest rates, and short-sighted structural adjustments imposed upon the South.

A comprehensive study by the UN special expert on sovereign debt describes these processes in detail, underscoring creditor responsibilities:

Poor advice from multilateral institutions and the self-interest-based nature of Western bilateral donors, and the structure of the global economy have badly affected developing countries . . . Persistent decline in commodity prices despite rapid expansion in production, resulting from policies of adjustment, . . . Discriminatory tariffs continue to grow while market access for third world products remains limited . . . Therefore, to the extent that the industrialized countries have prevented debtor nations from earning their way out of debt, they themselves must take some responsibility for the third world's inability to repay loans. (Cheru 1999: para. 17)

Human Rights and Debt

Sovereign debt has broad implications for human rights and has been a subject of investigations and resolutions from UN bodies since the 1970s. The primary concern of these bodies has been the impact of debt on the welfare of the poorest populations and on the overall economies of developing countries. Financial limitations resulting from overindebtedness and conditions imposed by creditors have also raised concerns about self-determination and political freedoms.

Under international law, human rights predominate over conflicting obligations, including debt servicing. The UN Charter and the primary human rights treaties put respect and promotion of human rights at the top of the international legal framework. Those rights included in the Universal Declaration of Human Rights are considered part of customary law, binding all governments, and supersede conflicting treaty provisions.[29] The United Nations and regional bodies responsible for monitoring human rights make clear that human rights and the right to development have priority over debt-related obligations and that negotiations and economic adjustment measures must take human rights into account.

The human rights obligations relevant to debt are rooted in the Universal Declaration of Human Rights (UDHR), the International Covenant on Economic, Social and Cultural Rights (ICESCR), and more recent UN General Assembly resolutions on the right to development and self-determination. These instruments have been interpreted and strengthened by the resolutions and commentary of UN human rights bodies and international jurists, offering an authoritative body of international jurisprudence in support of the following four principles relevant to debt: (1) basic needs must be prioritized over debt servicing; (2) development decisions must be participatory and accountable; (3) countries must be free to determine their political and economic systems; and (4) the circumstances surrounding the accumulation of debt combined with unsustainable levels may invalidate much existing debt.

Priority of Basic Needs

The UDHR, the ICESCR, and additional treaties on the rights of women, children, workers, minorities, and others establish basic needs as a legal priority for development. The UN Committee on Economic, Social and Cultural Rights has underscored the supremacy of basic needs on many occasions:

[The Covenant] imposes an obligation to move as expeditiously and effectively as possible towards . . . the realization of economic, social and cultural rights . . . [A]

State party in which any significant number of individuals is deprived of essential foodstuffs, of essential primary health care, of basic shelter and housing, or of the most basic forms of education is, prima facie, failing to discharge its obligations under the Covenant. (UNCESCR 1990b)

The Inter-American Commission on Human Rights (IACHR) has likewise declared that "The essence of the legal obligation incurred by a government is to ensure the economic and social aspirations of its people, by assigning priority to the basic health, nutritional and educational necessities. The prioritization of the "right to survival" and basic necessities is a natural out-growth of the right to personal security" (IACHR 1982: 322).

A number of UN bodies have investigated and reported on the threat posed to human rights by debt and structural adjustment programs. Their combined commentary strongly supports the principle that human rights and needs are a government's first priority. The United Nations Commission on Human Rights (UNCHR)—the most authoritative international body dealing with debt and human rights—has stated that: "Any foreign debt strategy must be designed not to hamper the steady improvement of conditions guaranteeing the enjoyment of human rights and must be intended, *inter alia*, to ensure that debtor developing countries achieve an adequate growth level to meet their social and economic needs and their development requirements" (UNCHR 1989: art. 21). In a more recent resolution, the Commission "*Affirms* that the exercise of the basic rights of the people of debtor countries to food, housing, clothing, employment, education, health services and a healthy environment cannot be subordinated to the implementation of structural adjustment policies, growth programs and economic reforms arising from the debt" (UNCHR 2001: art. 7).

Participatory and Accountable Decision Making

Only a small group of economically powerful countries determines, formulates and imposes economic policy guidelines, including those related to foreign debt and structural adjustment policies, on the developing countries. . . . Agreements concluded between the IMF and debtor countries are conducted without any consultation with the population that ultimately bears the brunt of the agreement. (UN SG 1995: para. 92)

Human rights are based on the principles of empowerment, participation, and accountability. At one time, these principles were seen as irrelevant or antagonistic to economic growth and development, but today the importance of participatory and accountable decision making has been echoed by virtually every relevant international body, and "good governance" directives are a key element of multilateral lending. Given the impact of debt on a country's development and welfare policies, human rights law requires that debt negotiations and related policies ensure participation, transparency, and accountability.

Civil and political rights and ESCR together oblige governments to establish open and accountable decision-making processes. The UN Declaration on the Right to Development underscores the primacy of participation in development decisions in its first article: "The right to development is an inalienable human right by virtue of which every human person and all peoples are entitled to participate in, contribute to, and enjoy economic, social, cultural and political development, in which all human rights and fundamental freedoms can be fully realized" (art. 1). The Limburg Principles—one of the most authoritative documents on ESCR—likewise states: "A concerted national effort to invoke the full participation of all sectors of society is, therefore, indispensable to . . . realizing economic, social, and cultural rights. Popular participation is required at all stages, including the formulation, application and review of national policies" (art. 11).

Accountability goes to the core of human rights—it is the implicit goal of all human rights instruments. Treaties impose specific reporting requirements aimed at "facilitat[ing] public scrutiny of government policies . . . and encourag[ing] the involvement of the various economic, social and cultural sectors in society in the formulation, implementation and review of the relevant policies" (UNCESCR 1989: art. 5). The UN Committee on Economic, Social and Cultural Rights emphasizes that "the raison d'etre of the Covenant . . . is to establish clear obligations for the States parties" and notes that any steps backward in terms of human welfare "need to be fully justified by reference to the totality of the rights provided for in the Covenant" (UNCESCR 1990b: art. 9). Civil and political rights treaties impose more specific obligations with regard to fulfilling all rights (including ESCR), meaning, at a minimum, transparent decision making and recourse for policies that violate rights.

These principles are summarized in a report on debt by the UN secretary general:

> States should ensure greater transparency in negotiations and agreements between States and international financial and aid institutions. This must include the publication and widest possible dissemination of proposed and final agreements concerning financial aid, debt repayment and monetary policy. The public must be given an appropriate opportunity to provide their own views prior to final decisions being made, with plan modifications remaining a possibility at any time. (UN SG 1995: para. 91)

The history of loans, particularly to nondemocratic governments, and the current nature of debt negotiations allows for neither participation nor accountability.[30] As Joseph Stiglitz, the former chief economist of the World Bank from 1997 to 2000, states:

> The IMF likes to go about its business without outsiders asking too many questions. In theory, the fund supports democratic institutions in the nations it assists. In practice, it undermines the democratic process by imposing policies. . . . [A]ll the power in the negotiations is on one side—the IMF's—and the fund rarely allows sufficient time for broad consensus-building or even widespread consultations with either parliaments or civil society. Sometimes the IMF dispenses with one pretense of openness altogether and negotiates secret covenants. (Stiglitz 2000)

Self-Determination

> What I find most objectionable about this [HIPC] initiative and most of the other debt reduction initiatives, is that they are being used as the whip to enforce unquestioning acceptance of the economic orthodoxy, the so-called Washington consensus. . . . The choice which we are left with under HIPC is thus to either abandon all independent and rational thinking in economic policy making or wallow in the quagmire of unsustainable debt.
>
> —Ethiopian Prime Minister Meles Zenawi[31]

The right of self-determination is considered the source and base for all other human rights. It was a basic principle undergirding the establishment of the United Nations (UN Charter: arts. 1, 55, 56) and appears in the first article of the two central human rights conventions: "All peoples have the right of self-determination. By virtue of that right they freely determine their political status and freely pursue their economic, social and cultural development" (International Covenant and Civil and Political Rights and ICESCR: art. 2.1). Although the right of self-determination was originally linked to decolonization and the legal recognition of new states, it has come to include the right of populations and governments to control their political, economic, and cultural development.

In a series of resolutions, the UN General Assembly has elaborated the basic components of this right, including: (1) the right "of all peoples freely to pursue their economic, social and cultural development" (UNGA 1970); (2) the right of every state to "choose its economic system . . . without outside interference, coercion or threat in any form whatsoever" (UNGA 1974: Art 1); and (3) that "economic and financial agreements between the developed and the developing countries must be based on the principle of equality and of the right of peoples and nations to self-determination" (UNGA 1962 preamble).

Based on the world conferences on human rights and development and on the many international treaties and declarations, the UN secretary general has extracted the following principles relating to self-determination and debt:

> Every country has the sovereign right freely to dispose of its natural resources in the interest of the economic development and well-being of its own people; any external, political or economic measures or pressures brought to bear on the exercise of this right is a flagrant violation of the principles of self-determination of peoples and non-intervention, as set forth in the Charter of the United Nations. . . . No State may use or encourage the use of economic, political or any other type of measures to coerce another State in order to obtain from it the subordination of the exercise of its sovereign rights and to secure from it advantages of any kind. Such measures include economic pressure designed to influence the policy of another country or to obtain control of essential sectors of its national economy. . . . The provision of economic and technical assistance, loans and increased foreign investment must not be subject to conditions which conflict with the interests of the recipient States. (UN SG 1996: paras. 165, 173)

Beyond nonintervention, self-determination requires that countries have the economic and political capacity to manage their economies and government and provide basic public services—education, health, civil service, and political development. The right to self-determination entitles governments to the necessary flexibility to find solutions to the debt problem without sacrificing either sustainable development or the basic needs of their populations.

Debt servicing that infringes upon a government's ability to carry out basic sovereign functions and conditions imposed by creditors that go to the heart of sovereign prerogatives undermine the right of self-determination. The UN special expert on debt has described these arguable violations in his reports:

> The countries of sub-Saharan Africa, with their poor credit rating, have largely been turned into IMF "macroeconomic guinea pigs" since they depend largely on resources from the multilateral institutions. . . . Since most of these countries have very weak political structures, an IMF-World Bank condominium has been imposed over them under the guise of providing aid. As a result, these countries have pretty much ceded their sovereignty to the IMF and the World Bank. (Cheru 1999: para. 30)[32]

Illegitimate and Voidable Debts

Much existing sovereign debt is illegitimate, and debt contracts could arguably be voided or reformed on various legal grounds. Debts may be voided for (1) the manner in which they were contracted (under duress or through fraud) or (2) the conditions and purposes of the loans (unconscionability, usury, odious debts). Other debt contracts may be reformed or voided based on mistaken presumptions, a change in circumstances, or the impracticability of paying. All of these arguments find support in international and domestic legal systems, and some of them, as general principles, are explicitly recognized in loan agreements. They are only briefly described here to suggest the various contract-based arguments that may be marshaled against debt.

Odious Debt

Much developing-country debt was incurred by governments with questionable claims to legitimate authority and was often used to repress the civilian population or was stolen through official corruption, presumably with the lenders' knowledge. The current governments of Iraq, South Africa, Rwanda, and Nigeria, for instance, are burdened by predecessor debts used for the most perfidious purposes. There is a long-standing body of international law supporting the principle that such debts are invalid for having been contracted against the interests of the population.

There are various legal doctrines supporting the basic principle that debts imposed on a community without its consent and contrary to its true interests need not be repaid. The "burden and benefit" doctrine (populations should not be burdened by debts from which they did not benefit) holds that "Whether the new sovereign should accept the obligations incurred by its predecessor [will depend on] the beneficial or detrimental connection of particular debts with the area concerned" (Hyde 1945: 413). An original and oft-cited treatise on successor debts explains their legality in the following terms:

If a despotic power incurs a debt not for the needs or in the interest of the State, but to strengthen its despotic regime, to repress the population . . . , this debt is odious. . . . This debt is not an obligation of the nation; it is a regime's debt, a personal debt of the power that has incurred it. The reason these "odious" debts cannot be considered to encumber the territory of the State is that such debts do not fulfill one of the conditions that determine the legality of the debts of the State—[they] must be employed for the needs and in the interests of the State. . . . The creditors have committed a hostile act with regard to the people; they can't therefore expect that a nation freed from a despotic power assume the "odious" debts, which are personal debts of that power.[33]

The doctrine of "odious debt" is consistent with the historic practice of repudiating debts linked to subjugation, to wars against the successor states, or to former colonial governments. As the Soviet government declared upon overthrowing the Tsarist regime: "Governments and systems that spring from revolution are not bound to respect the obligations of fallen governments. . . . The French Convention for which France declares herself to be the legitimate successor proclaimed that the 'sovereignty of peoples is not bound by the treaties of tyrants.' "[34] The original 13 U.S. states similarly refused to honor British debts, and the United States and Great Britain refused to assume any legal obligations for the debts of annexed territories (O'Connel 1967). The Vienna Convention on the Succession of States in Respect of State Property, Archives and Debts lends further support to these principles by affirming that recently independent states are under no obligation to assume the debts of their predecessors.[35]

The doctrines of "benefit and burden" and odious debt have proved broad enough to cover successor states as well as successor governments. When the United States wrested control over Cuba from Spain in 1898, it refused to honor Cuba's debts, arguing that they were invalid not for belonging to a prior regime but for having been "imposed upon the people of Cuba without their consent and by force of arms." By the same logic, when Germany annexed Austria in 1938 and refused to honor its debts, the United States insisted on repayment because the loans "were made in time of peace, for constructive works and the relief of human suffering."[36]

In one of the few such cases to reach international arbitration, Chief Justice Taft of the U.S. Supreme Court held that loans to the president of Costa Rica need not be honored by the successor government: "The case of the Royal Bank depends not on the mere form of the transaction but upon the good faith of the bank in the payment of money for the real use of the Costa Rican Government under the Tinoco regime. It must make out its case of actual furnishing of money to the government for its legitimate use. It has not done so."[37]

International precedents and the commentary of jurists establish two basic criteria for defining a debt as odious: first, that the purpose of the loan was not legitimate or in the interests of the population, and second, that the creditor was aware of or indifferent to those illegitimate purposes.[38] Under that general definition, a large part of the debt of developing countries is arguably "odious" and thereby invalid, including much of the debt contracted by dictators or corrupt governments, which can be shown to have propped up these governments and served their personal illegitimate interests in opposition to democracy and human rights.

As one former official of the World Bank reports in her extensive study of odious debts:

> When government officials treat state investments as vehicles for political favors, graft, and capital flight, and are prepared to turn a blind eye to the technical and economic viability of such projects, foreign bank loans become grease in wheels that turn against state interests. Foreign bankers who fail to recognize or to act upon pricing irregularities, slipshod loans, and suspect contracts soon become parties to hostile acts against a populace. (Adams 1991: 170)

According to a more recent investigation, at least 20% of all debt acquired by developing countries up until 1996 was contracted by military dictators; this percentage rises to 56% in Brazil, 42% in Argentina, and 98% in Indonesia (Hanlon, chapter 5, this volume; Hanlon 2000). This debt helped maintain antidemocratic governments, facilitating their abuses and irresponsible investments and strengthening their resistance to democratic forces. Beyond these dictatorships, the actual amount of loans that served the interests of populations is far smaller and should be relevant to an odious debt analysis. Branford and Kucinski (1990: 130) have calculated that between 1976 and 1981, Latin America received $273 billion (U.S.) in loans. Of this amount, 92% was returned directly to international banks—62% as debt servicing, 21% in capital flight, and 9% in the establishment of foreign reserves. Only 8% was invested in Latin America, and only a fraction of that went toward constructive development projects or other items that might arguably have served the interests of the population.

Unconscionability/Usury

It is well-established in domestic legal systems that grossly unfair or "unconscionable" contracts may be voided. Courts of equity were established for the very purpose of ensuring such fairness: "[T]he exclusion of a plaintiff from the peculiar favors of courts of equity results equally where his conduct has been unconscionable by reason of a bad motive or where the result . . . will be unconscionable either in the benefit to himself or the injury to others."[39] U.S and European courts have broad latitude to strike down contracts considered unconscionable and have established unconscionability in cases paralleling sovereign debt contracts, including loans with oppressive conditions and interest rates.[40]

The leading case from the U.S. federal courts describes as unconscionable an "absence of meaningful choice on the part of one of the parties together with contract terms which are unreasonably favorable to the other party. . . . In many cases the meaningfulness of the choice is negated by a gross inequality of bargaining power."[41] Commonwealth courts have arrived at similar definitions: "[I]f two persons . . . stand in such a relation to each other that one can take an undue advantage of the other . . . [and] one party has taken undue advantage of the other . . . a transaction resting upon such an unconscionable dealing will not be allowed to stand."[42]

Although a single unreasonable provision will sometimes suffice, courts are more likely to find a contract unconscionable where both procedural and substantive abuses exist.[43] In those cases, courts will apply a less stringent standard: "Usually . . . the bargain is infected with something more than substantive unfairness. It is typically mixed with an absence of bargaining ability that does not fall to the level of incapacity or with an abuse of the bargaining process that does not rise to the level of misrepresentation, duress, or undue influence" (Farnsworth 1990: 321). As one court explains:

> The procedural aspect [can be] manifested by . . . an inequality in bargaining power resulting in no meaningful choice for the weaker party. . . . "Substantive" unconscionability, on the other hand, refers to an overly harsh allocation of risks or costs which is not justified by the circumstances under which the contract was made. . . . [T]here is a sliding scale relationship between the two concepts; the greater the degree of substantive unconscionability, the less the degree of procedural unconscionability that is required to annul the contract or clause.[44]

In extreme cases, courts have determined a contract unconscionable based on price alone: "Indeed, no other provision of an agreement more intimately touches upon the question unconscionability than does the term regarding price."[45] Courts have likewise found loan agreements unconscionable based on interest rates. As a leading U.S. federal court declared: "[W]e believe we may look to cases finding unconscionability on the basis of gross price disparity as analogous authority. In essence, the interest rate is the "price" of the money lent; at some point the price becomes so extreme that it is unconscionable."[46]

Unconscionability based on interest rates has been traditionally regulated through usury laws, common to all legal systems and going back thousands of years.[47] As one expert notes:

> Societies have recognized throughout recorded history that people burdened with excessive debt are prime candidates for exploitation; civil and religious leaders in all parts of the world have assumed that laws regulating the taking of interest were necessary. Most usury prohibitions are grounded in deep ethical and religious condemnations of the exploitation of the weak, of socially destabilizing concentrations of wealth, and of the accumulation of money or wealth without an investment of labor. (Glaeser and Scheinkman 1998)

The interest rates paid by developing countries for their loans, particularly to private banks, and the fact that in many cases these rates were unilaterally raised by a factor of as much as four, offer powerful grounds for usury arguments (Espeche 1989). Those rates coupled with the conditions surrounding debt negotiations, the imbalance of power between a small developing country and bank syndicates and the Paris Club, and the lack of viable options offer additional grounds for claims of unconscionability. Sylvester (1992: 302) states: "It is easily arguable that the predatory behavior of the banks, coupled with the grossly inferior bargaining power and absence of meaningful choice for the debtor nations, constitutes procedural unconscionability. Moreover, the impact of the massive and exponentially expanding burden of repayment on the already abominable living conditions in most sub-Saharan debtor countries would seem to constitute substantive unconscionability."

Impracticability, Changed Circumstances, and Mutual Mistake

All legal systems recognize the need to reform or annul contracts when mistaken assumptions or supervening events make them unreasonably burdensome on one of the parties. These legal excuses are common to international law and supported by the Vienna Convention on the Law of Treaties (Vienna Convention). Their applicability to the current debt crisis has been touched on by a range of commentators and finds strong support under both common law and international-law interpretations.[48]

The doctrine of impracticability or frustration allows a court to annul or reform a contract in the event of unexpected conditions that impose an "excessive and unreasonable cost"[49] on one of the parties. This doctrine arose around cases in which performance was made physically impossible by an intervening event, but common-law courts have significantly expanded its scope under the term "impracticability." Contract law in the United States holds that "a party's performance is made impracticable without his fault by the occurrence of an event the non-occurrence of which was a basic assumption on which the contract was made" (Restatement (Second) of Contracts: Sec. 261) and provides the following guidance for determining what is "impracticable": "Increased cost alone does not excuse performance unless the rise in cost is due to some unforeseen contingency which alters the essential nature of the performance. . . . But a severe shortage of raw materials . . . or shutdown of a major source of supply or the like, which either causes a marked increase in costs or altogether prevents . . . performance" would constitute impracticability (U.C.C. 2-615, com. 4). In the context of debt agreements, it is important to underscore that impracticability does not require impossibility and is measured by reference to the parties' expectations.[50]

The related doctrine of *Rebus sic stanibus* or change in circumstances offers a similar defense, with an even broader standard for burden. The full Latin term, *Contractus qui habent tractum succesivum et dependetiam de futurum, rebus sic stantibus intelligentur,* may be translated as "contracts which require a successive fulfillment in the long term are subject to the condition that the circumstances do not change."[51] An authoritative definition states: "[A] tacit condition, said to attach to all treaties, that they shall cease to be obligatory so soon as the state of facts and conditions upon which they were founded has substantially changed."[52] Scholars trace the roots of rebus sic stanibus as far back as Greek and Roman law, and it has been employed throughout history to revoke treaties (Fenwick 1965).

The Vienna Convention requires that the change in circumstances be unforeseen and: (1) the existence of those circumstances constituted an essential basis of the consent of the parties to be bound by the treaty; and (2) the effect of the change is to radically transform the extent of obligations still to be performed under the treaty (art. 62). Based on a thorough review of the doctrine's use in international arbitration, one author describes the rule to lie with

> whether the unforeseen event has upset the original balance of mutual perform-
> ances or the "economy" of the agreement in an excessive manner, going beyond
> the risk of the contract. The performance of the obligation would then impose
> upon one party an "intolerable burden" or an "unreasonable sacrifice" which is
> not contemplated in the treaty and, therefore, not to be expected of the party.
> (Vamvoukos 1985: 194)

The third defense of mutual mistake overlaps with impracticability and rebus but is even more flexible in terms of burden. Where a change of circumstances concerns itself with "good contracts going bad," mutual mistake looks at whether the contract was flawed to begin with, and the two doctrines overlap where the mistake involves a false assumption about the future, as is the case with sovereign debt.

In the 1600s, the father of international law, Hugo Grotius, elaborated the principle in the following terms: "[I]f a promise has been based on a certain presumption about a fact that does not come to pass, by the law of nature it does not carry force because the person did not consent to the promise except under a certain condition that, in fact, did not exist" (Grotius 1925: 2). Three centuries later, the Vienna Convention on the Law of Treaties codified the principle under international law: "A State may invoke an error in a treaty as invalidating its consent to be bound by the treaty if the error relates to a fact or situation which was assumed by that State to exist at the time when the treaty was concluded and formed an essential basis of its consent to be bound by the treaty" (art. 48.1). Under U.S. law, "where a mistake of both parties at the time a contract was made as to a basic assumption on which the contract was made has a material effect on the agreed exchange of performances, the contract is voidable by the adversely affected party" (Restatement (second) of contracts: 152). Courts have found mutual mistake when the error was sufficient to have influenced the making of the contract and subsequently caused a significant change in the agreed upon exchange (Calamari and Perillo 1987).

One influential case from the U.S. federal courts helps define these various defenses. The case involved a long-term contract for the provision of aluminum in which the parties worked out a price formula for the production costs but over the course of the contract the actual costs to the producer, ALCOA, were significantly higher than expected. ALCOA was still making a profit (though less than expected) when it filed the case, asking a court to reform the contract on the basis of mutual mistake and impracticability. The court declared that "relief can only follow if the mistake was mutual, if it related to a basic assumption underlying the contract, and if it caused a severe imbalance in the agreed exchange." Using that standard, it found that the production costs were a basic assumption and that the rise in price (and expected losses of $60 million for ALCOA) was sufficient to reform the contract.[53] The court also considered that the additional costs (even though viable for ALCOA) would have made the contract impracticable. Finally, in response to the argument that parties assume a certain risk of change, the court explained that: "The proper question is not simply whether the parties to a contract were conscious of uncertainty with respect to a vital fact, but whether they believed that uncertainty was effectively limited within a designated range so that they would deem outcomes beyond that range to be highly unlikely."[54]

These three defenses—impracticability, rebus, and mutual mistake—raise serious questions about the legitimacy of much existing debt. The doctrine of impracticability alone would suffice in many cases based on the level of hardship imposed on debtor countries by factors unforeseen and outside of their control. The fact that the creditor countries had a hand in impeding performance on the loan agreements (e.g., through interest rate hikes and trade measures) should preclude them from demanding compliance (Haile-Mariam 1990). The mere fact that so many loan agreements have been in de facto default since 1982 and the many creditor initiatives to renegotiate debts offer testament to the impracticability, indeed impossibility, of complying with the original contracts.

Beyond that, many of these contracts may be voidable under a lesser standard of impracticability based on the mutually mistaken assumptions upon which they were made and by the subsequent change in circumstances. Many of the original loans were premised on two false assumptions. First, it was assumed that interest rates would remain within a certain traditional range when in fact they rose by a multiple of more than 4 and in real terms from -1 to 9% between 1978 and 1982 (World Bank 1990: 15). Based on this interest rate change, between 1983 and 1991, debtor countries paid $209 billion (U.S.) more in repayment than in new loans, but their total debt only doubled. Second, it was assumed that commodity prices—the primary source of exchange for developing-country debtors—would remain relatively unchanged when in fact they dropped precipitously (Haile-Mariam 1990).

These assumptions went to the heart of the loans and were shared as much by the multilateral banks promoting export policies from the developing countries as by the private banks trusting in repayment and the creditor and debtor nations. The fact that virtually every developing country had to reschedule its debts in the 1980s underscores how widely shared the mistaken assumptions of the 1970s were and how extreme were the unforeseen changes. The original loan agreements may be challenged under either mutual mistake or rebus.

Conclusion

Although future resolutions of overindebtedness in the developing world will continue to hinge largely on political and economic factors, legal arguments are likely to play an increasingly important role. The narrow presumption that debtors are legally bound to service even unjust and overly burdensome debts poses an unwarranted obstacle to fair and sustainable solutions. This presumption should be challenged with contractual arguments aimed at bringing a fuller range of considerations to the table and with fiduciary and human rights principles that refocus attention on the joint culpability of creditors and the rights of third-party victims. These counterarguments are unlikely to win the day on their own, but they should serve to bolster negotiating positions and help to frame eventual resolutions.

Notes

1. In those rare cases that have gone to court, debtor governments have largely defended themselves on procedural and jurisdictional grounds (sovereign immunity, comity, and state action) but have rarely challenged the actual legitimacy of the debts. See Wälde (1987).

2. See Drago (1907) and Lothian (1995).

3. These arguments are complicated by the fact that much debt has been recycled and is now held by private investors (arguably "holders in due course") with no ties to the original creditors and thus not implicated by any original improprieties. This issue merits more substantive consideration than is possible here. See Khalfan et al. (2003), Eggert (2002), and Power (1996).

4. Evidence of the positive development impacts of debt relief has been provided by a number of organizations working on these issues, including UNICEF, Oxfam, and Jubilee 2000. See, for example, Greenhill (2002).

5. World Bank figures cited in Hanlon (2000).

6. Branford and Kucinski (1990) and Lissakers (1991).

7. Throughout the mid-1970s, the U.S. money center banks as a group derived almost 50% of their earnings from overseas activities. For some banks, overseas operations accounted for as much as 70% of earnings (Reisner 1982: 4). See Darity and Horn (1988).

8. The U.S. Federal Reserve Bank estimated that $84 billion (U.S.) was sent out of Mexico, Chile, Venezuela, Argentina, and Brazil between 1974 and 1982, one-third of the total new debt contracted by these countries during that period. Cited in Cheru (1999).

9. Cited in Lissakers (1991: 206).

10. See the review of relevant literature and discussion of motives in Khalfan et al. (2003).

11. "There Must Be Another Way," *The Economist*, 20 March 1982.

12. Between 1820 and 1986, investigators report over 80 cases of unilateral default (Lindert and Morton 1989). Northern governments are well-represented in these defaults—for example, the United States' original colonies defaulted on their debts, and all the European governments (except Finland) defaulted on World War I loans (Wood 1986).

13. The Charter also obliges States to "cooperate in facilitating more rational and equitable international economic relations and in encouraging structural changes in the context of a balanced economy in harmony with the needs and interests of all countries, especially developing countries" (art. 8).

14. Examples include British Prime Minister John Major seeking reparations from Japan for prisoners of war; Australian Aborigines demanding an apology and compensation from the Australian government; Queen Elizabeth apologizing to the native Maoris for England's role in enslaving them; a Chicago city ordinance pushing for reparations for slavery; two U.S. Congressional bills seeking an apology and reparations for slavery; and Kenya's independence war veterans demanding 60 billion pounds sterling from the British government as compensation claims for colonial brutalities against them.

15. The Amsterdam Appeal for the Cancellation of African Debt asserts: "In the specific case of sub-Saharan Africa, an irrefutable historical argument in favour of un-

conditional cancellation [of the financial debt] is that what is owed to Western 'lenders' is only a tiny portion of what the Europeans have stolen [from Africa] since the 15th century. Slavery robbed the continent of 60 to 100 million inhabitants to transport them to the Americas."

16. International Law Commission, Draft Articles on Responsibility of States for Internationally Wrongful Acts, in Report of the International Law Commission on the Work of Its Fifty-third Session, UN GAOR, 56th Sess., Supp. No. 10, at 43, UN Doc. A/56/10 (2001), available at: www.un.org/law/ilc (art. 1).

17. Relevant UN-sponsored resolutions include those relating to indigenous peoples, victims of human rights violations, forced evictions, and environmental destruction.

18. Revised set of basic principles and guidelines on the right to reparation for victims of gross violations of human rights and humanitarian law prepared by Mr. Theo van Boven pursuant to Sub-commission decision 1995/117 E/CN.4/Sub.2/1996/17, 24 May 1996.

19. Cited in "Ecological Debt: South Tells North 'Time to Pay Up' " *Economic Justice Report* XI/3. Toronto: Ecumenical Coalition for Economic Justice (September 2000).

20. The cost of Britain's exploitation of Zimbabwe between 1896 and 1996 is calculated at $38 billion (U.S.), more than nine times Zimbabwe's sovereign debt (*National Catholic Reporter,* 22 January 1999).

21. It is estimated that medicinal plants and microbials from the South contribute at least $30 billion (U.S.) a year to the North's pharmaceutical industry (Ecumenical Coalition for Economic Justice, supra note 19).

22. See, for example, the Rio Declaration (princ. 13) and Stockholm Declaration (princ. 22).

23. The United Nations has established fiduciary obligations under the trustee and mandate systems and rules relating to occupying states, among others. Under these regimes, states are held to a higher level of responsibility and must take affirmative steps to ensure the welfare of populations of other states.

24. *Tate v. Williamson,* 2 Ch. 55, 61 (1866).

25. One legal scholar's review of recent U.S. court decisions concludes that: "The booming field of lender liability has virtually revolutionized the conventional relationship between borrowers and lenders. . . . [T]he claim that lenders owe a duty to act in good faith and are liable for its breach has received the majority of attention and acceptance by both scholars and judges" (Hunt 1994; see also Phillips 2000).

26. *Garrett v. Bankwest, Inc.,* 459 N.W.2d 833, 838 (S.D. 1990).

27. *Barrett v. Bank of America,* 183 Cal. App. 3d 1362 (1986). The court stated that a bank-depositor relationship is at least quasi-fiduciary, though in a later decision it reconsidered this term and instead derived lender obligations from the duty of good faith dealings. *Copesky v. Superior Court,* 280 Cal. Rptr. 338, 348 (Cal. Ct. App. 1991).

28. The Banking Committee of the U.S. House of Representatives concluded that "the lending banks had been imprudent and the regulators had been almost criminally lax and complacent" (cited in Sylvester 1992: 265).

29. The Vienna Convention on the Law of Treaties invalidates a treaty that conflicts with a "peremptory norm" of international law—among them core human rights and arguably including all rights contained in the Universal Declaration of Human Rights (art. 53).

30. "[A]ccording to insider Stiglitz, the Bank's 'investigation' involves little more than close inspection of five-star hotels. It concludes with a meeting with a begging finance minister, who is handed a 'restructuring agreement' pre-drafted for 'voluntary' signature. Stiglitz has two concerns about the IMF/World Bank plans. First, he says,

because the plans are devised in secrecy and driven by an absolutist ideology, never open for discourse or dissent, they 'undermine democracy.' Second, they don't work. Under the guiding hand of IMF structural 'assistance' Africa's income dropped by 23%." See Gregory Palast, "How Crises, Failures, and Suffering Finally drove a Presidential Adviser to the Wrong Side of the Barricades," *The Observer*, 29 April 2001.

31. Declaration to the Conference of African Ministers, 6 May 1999, quoted in Hanlon and Garrett (1999: 28).

32. See also Lissakers (1991: 198–204).

33. Alexander Nahum Sack, Les Effets des Transformations des Etats sur leurs Dettes Publicques et Autres Obligations financieres (p. 159), cited in Adams (1991: 165).

34. "The Foreign Debt Policy of Soviet Russia," *Foreign Policy Association Information Service*, 24 November 1926, at p. 25 cited in Foorman and Jehle (1982: 20).

35. I.L.M. p. 306 UN Document A/CONF.117/14 of 7 April 1983.

36. Hackworth. 1940. "Effects of the Change of Sovereignty" 1 *Digest of International Law* 545, cited in Hoeflich (1982: 63).

37. Cited in Adams (1991: 168).

38. See Hanlon (chapter 5, this volume) and Jayachandran and Kremer (chapter 10 this volume). See also Khalfan et al. (2003).

39. *Larsheid v. Hashek Mf. Co.*, 142 Wis. 172 (1910). S. M. Waddams's review of Commonwealth contract jurisprudence summarizes unconscionability with the comment that "[T]he decline of the highly individualistic view of society that prevailed in the late nineteenth century has been accompanied by a greater willingness of courts and legislatures to grant relief from disadvantageous contracts" (Waddams 1993: 437).

40. See, for example, *Carboni v. Arrospide*, 2 Cal. Rptr. 2d 845, 848 (Cal. App. 1st Dist. 1991). See also Waddams (1993).

41. *Williams v. Walker-Thomas Furniture Co.*, 350 F.2d 445, 448–49 (D.C. Cir. 1965).

42. *Black v. Wilcox* (1976), 70 D.L.R. (3d) 192 (Ontario Court of Appeal), cited in Waddams (1993: 511).

43. "Some courts have indicated that a sliding scale applies—for example, a contract with extraordinarily oppressive substantive terms will require less in the way of procedural unconscionability" (*American Software, Inc. v. Ali*, 46 Cal. App. 4th 1356).

44. *Carboni v. Arrospide*, 2 Cal. Rptr. 2d 845, 848 (Cal. App. 1st Dist. 1991).

45. *Jones v. Star Credit Corp*, 298 N.Y.S. 2d 264 (finding sale price of house unconscionable in and of itself). *Perdue v. Crocker Natl. Bank*, 38 Cal. 3d 913 (1985) (referring to a bank's $6 charge on bounced checks, the court declared "it is clear that the price term, like any other term . . . may be unconscionable").

46. *Carboni v. Arrospide*, 2 Cal. Rptr. 2d 845 (Cal. App. 1st Dist. 1991).

47. Usury laws go back to the Code of Hammurabi in 3000 B.C. and to the Old Testament. In 1545, England established its usury laws, which served as models for the American colonies. Today, in the United States, the "fixed" control of usury has been generally replaced by the more "variable" standard of unconscionability, partly because of the high interest rates and deregulation push of the 1970s and 1980s.

48. The fact that unpayable and/or voidable debts are commonly renegotiated as a matter of political expediency has precluded the need to raise these arguments in court, which helps explain the lack of legal precedents.

49. "A thing is impossible in legal contemplation when it is not practicable; and a thing is impracticable when it can only be done at excessive and unreasonable cost." *Mineral Park Land Co. v. Howard*, 172 P. 458, 460 (1916).

50. The "focus of the impracticability analysis is upon the nature of the agreement

and the expectations of the parties, not [their] size and financial ability." *Alimenta v. Cargill, Inc.*, 861 F.2nd 650 (11th Cir. 1988).

51. Quoted in Bederman (1988).

52. Black 1990: 1267.

53. *Aluminum Company of America v. Essex Group*, 499 F. Supp. 53, 64 (W.D. Pa. 1980).

54. *Aluminum Company of America v. Essex Group*, 499 F. Supp. 53, 70 (W.D. Pa. 1980).

References

Adams, P. 1991. *Odious Debt.* London: Earthscan.

Bederman, D. 1988. "The 1871 London Declaration, Rebus Sic Stantibus and a Primitivist View of the Law of Nations." 82 *American Journal of International Law* 1.

Black, H. 1990. *Black's Law Dictionary.* 6th ed. St. Paul, Minn: West Publishing Company.

Branford, S., and Kucinski, B. 1990. *The Debt Squads: The US, the Banks, and Latin America.* London: Zed Books Ltd.

Calamari, J. and Perillo, J. 1987. *The Law of Contracts.* St. Paul, Minn.: West Publishing Company.

Cheru, F. 1999. "Effects of Structural Adjustment Policies on the Full Enjoyment of Human Rights: Report by the Independent Expert." E/CN.4/1999/50. New York: United Nations.

Darity, W., and Horn, B. 1988. *The Loan Pushers.* Cambridge: Ballanger.

Drago, L. 1907. "State Loans in Their Relation to International Policy." 1 *American Journal of International Law* 692.

Eggert, K. 2002. "Held Up in Due Course: Codification and the Victory of Form Over Intent in Negotiable Instrument Law." 35 *Creighton Law Review* 363.

Espeche, M. A. 1989. "Unlawfulness of Unilateral Increases in Sovereign Debt Interest Rates." XV Congress IHLADI (unpublished paper).

Farnsworth, A. 1990. *Farnsworth on Contracts.* 2d ed. Boston: Little, Brown.

Fenwick, C. 1965. *International Law.* 4th ed. New York: Appleton-Century-Crofts.

Foorman, J., and Jehle, M. 1982. "Effects of State and Government Succession on Commercial Bank Loans to Foreign Sovereign Borrowers." 1 *University of Illinois Law Review* 9.

Glaeser, E., and Scheinkman, J. 1998. "Neither a Borrower Nor a Lender Be: An Economic Analysis of Interest Restrictions and Usury Laws." 41 *Journal of Law and Economics* 1.

Greenhill, R. 2002. *The Unbreakable Link—Debt Relief and the Millennium Development Goals.* London: Jubilee Research/New Economics Foundation.

Greenhouse Ireland Action Network (GRAN). 2005. Press release and charts. 4 July 2005. Available online at: www.grain.ie/Policy/G8%20charts%20and;%20graphs.htm.

Grotius, Hugo. 1925. *De Jure Belli ac Pacis Libri Tres, II.XI.VI.* (Kelsey, F. trans.). London: Oxford.

Haile-Mariam, Y. 1990. "Legal and Other Justifications for Writing-off the Debts of the Poor Third World Countries: The Case of Africa South of the Sahara." 20 *Journal of World Trade Law.*

Hanlon, J. 2000. *How Much Debt Must Be Cancelled.* London: Jubilee 2000 Coalition.

Hanlon, J., and Garret, J. 1999. *Crumbs of Comfort.* London: Jubilee 2000 Coalition.

Hawley, S. 2000. *Exporting Corruption: Privatisation, Multinationals and Bribery.* London: The Corner House.

Hoeflich, M. H. 1982. "Through a Glass Darkly: Reflections upon the History of the International Law of Public Debt in Connection with State Succession." 1 *University of Illinois Law Review* 9.

Hunt, C. J. 1994. "The Price of Trust: An Examination of Fiduciary Duty and the Lender–Borrower Relationship." 29 *Wake Forest Law Review* 719.

Hyde, C. 1945. *International Law Chiefly as Interpreted and Applied by the United States.* Boston: Little, Brown and Company.

Inter-American Commission on Human Rights (IACHR). 1982. *Ten Years of Activities.* Washington, DC: Organization of American States.

Khalfan, A., King, J., and Thomas, B. 2003. Advancing the Odious Debt Doctrine. Working Paper. Montreal: CISDL.

"Limburg Principles on the Implementation of the International Covenant on Economic, Social and Cultural Rights." 1987. 9 *Human Rights Quarterly* 122.

Lindert, P., and P. Morton. 1989. How Sovereign Debt Has Worked. In *Developing Country Debt and Economic Performance, Vol. 1, The International Financial System,* ed. J. Sachs. Chicago: University of Chicago Press.

Lissakers, K. 1991. *Banks, Borrowers and the Establishment.* New York: Basic Books.

Lothian, T. 1995. "The Criticism of the Third-World Debt and the Revision of Legal Doctrine." 13 *Wisconsin International Law Journal* 421.

O'Connel, D. P. 1967. *State Succession in Municipal Law and International Law.* Cambridge: Cambridge University Press.

Phillips, R. 2000. "Lender Liability—Banks As Fact-Sensitive Fiduciaries." 340 Ark. 518, 10 S.W.3d 885.

Power, P. 1996. "Annual Survey Issue: International Insolvencies: Note: Sovereign Debt: The Rise of the Secondary Market and Its Implications for Future Restructuring," 64 *Fordham Law Review* 2701.

Reisner, R. 1982. "Default by Foreign Sovereign Debtors: An Introductory Perspective." 1 *University of Illinois Law Review* 1.

Restatement of the Law of Contracts. 1981. Washington, DC: American Law Institute.

Stiglitz, J. "What I Learned at the World Economic Crisis: The Insider." *The New Republic,* April 2000.

Sylvester, J. 1992. "Impracticability, Mutual Mistake and Related Contractual Bases for Equitably Adjusting the External Debt of Sub-Saharan Africa." 13 *Northwest Journal of International Law and Business* 258.

Turk, D. 1995. "Preliminary Set of Basic Policy Guidelines on Structural Adjustment Programmes and Economic, Social and Cultural Rights." E/CN.4/Sub.2/1995/10.

UN Committee on Economic, Social and Cultural Rights (UNCESCR). 1989. General Comment No. 1: Reporting by State Parties. Geneva: United Nations.

———. 1990a. General Comment No. 2: International Technical Assistance Matters. Geneva: United Nations.

———. 1990b. General Comment No. 3: The Nature of States Parties' Obligations. Geneva: United Nations.

UN General Assembly (UNGA). 1970. Resolution 2625: "The Declaration on Principles of International Law Concerning Friendly Relations and Cooperation among States in Accordance with the Charter of the United Nations." New York: United Nations.

———. 1962. "UNGA Resolution 1803: Permanent Sovereignty over Natural Resources." New York: United Nations.

————. 1974. "UNGA Resolution 3281: Charter of Economic Rights and Duties of States." New York: United Nations.

————. 1986. "UNGA Resolution 41/28: Declaration on the Right to Development." New York: United Nations.

United Nations Commission on Human Rights (UNCHR). 1989. Final Resolutions. Geneva: United Nations.

————. 2001. Final Resolutions. Geneva: United Nations.

United Nations Development Program. 1998. Human Development Report. New York: Oxford University Press.

United Nations Secretary General (UN SG). 1995. "Preliminary Set of Basic Policy Guidelines on Structural Adjustment Programmes and Economic, Social and Cultural Rights." E/CN.4/1995/25, 16 January 1995. New York: United Nations.

————. 1997. "Ways and Means to Carry out a Political Dialogue between Creditor and Debtor Countries in the United Nations System, Based on the Principle of Shared Responsibility." E/CN.4/1996/22, 5 February 1996. New York: United Nations.

Vamvoukos, A. 1985. *Termination of Treaties in International Law: The Doctrine of Stanibus Sic Rebus and Desuetude.* Oxford: Clarendon Press.

Vienna Convention on Succession of States in Respect of State Property, Archives and Debts, at I.L.M. p. 306, UN Document A/CONF.117/14 of 7 April 1983.

Vienna Convention on the Law of Treaties, UN Doc A/Conf 39/28, UKTS 58 (1980), 8 ILM 679. Vienna: United Nations.

Waddams, S. M. 1993. *The Law of Contracts,* 3rd ed. Toronto: Canada Law Book.

Wälde, T. 1987. The Sanctity of Debt and Insolvent Country Defenses of Debtors in International Loan Agreements. In *Judicial Enforcement of International Debt,* ed. D. Sassoon and D. Bradlow, pp. 119–45. Washington, DC: International Law Institute.

Wesberry, J. 1998. "International Financial Institutions Face the Corruption Eruption." 18 *Northwestern Journal of International Law and Business* 498.

Wood, P. 1986. *Law and Practice of International Finance.* New York: Clark Boardman Company, Ltd.

World Bank. 1990. *World Development Report 1990.* Washington, DC: World Bank.

7

ETHICS, MARKET AND GOVERNMENT FAILURE, AND GLOBALIZATION: PERSPECTIVES ON DEBT AND FINANCE

J. E. Stiglitz

This chapter looks at certain ethical aspects of the way that globalization has proceeded during the 1990s. It argues that in the way that they have sought to shape globalization, the advanced industrial countries and some of the multilateral institutions that they control can be viewed as having violated some basic ethical norms. Elsewhere, I have argued for the reform of the institutions and policies that have governed globalization and that these institutions and policies, although they may have served the interests of the advanced industrial countries or at least special interests within those countries, have not served well the interests of the developing world and especially the poor within those countries (Stiglitz 2002). Unless there are serious reforms in governance, the legitimacy of the institutions will be undermined; unless there are serious reforms in practices, there may well be a backlash.

Although there are strong forces pushing globalization forward—in particular, the lowering of transportation and communication costs—the forward march of globalization is by no means inevitable. After World War I, there were marked reductions in capital and trade flows (relative to the size of GDP). Today, within the developed world, there is a growing awareness of some of the darker sides of globalization, as terrorism, too, can move more easily across borders. But the developing countries have long experienced many of the other darker sides of globalization.

Here, however, the subject of globalization is approached from the perspective of practical ethics (Stiglitz 2000). The particular aspect of practical ethics upon which this chapter focuses is *social justice*. It begins from the ethical premise that "all men are created equal" and accordingly takes it as fundamental that perspectives concerning social justice should be nationally and ethnically blind as much as they should be blind to gender and color (Rawls 1999). Globalization, in short, should extend not only to economics but to views on social justice and solidarity. This chapter will not adopt Rawls's argument that social justice requires exclusive focus on the welfare of the worst-off individual (in any country) (Rawls 1999). Instead, the basis of the chapter's argument is that social justice prohibits advanced industrial countries from benefiting at the expense of poorer countries: At the very least, negative redistributions should be viewed as ethically wrong.

Some economists have questioned whether ethics has much or anything to do with economics. After all, Adam Smith's basic insight was that individuals, in pursuing their own self-interest, were actually pursuing the general interest. Economics, of course, had its limitations: It could not solve all problems. It was not intended to solve issues of social justice, only those of efficiency. It was the responsibility of government, and political processes, to address the distributive issues. And these were matters about which economists had little to say—they could only point out the consequences of different policies.

However, when there are market failures, individuals in the pursuit of their own interests may not further general interests. There can be real conflicts of interest. These have been brought out forcefully in the literature on asymmetric information, where agents may not take actions that are in the best interests of those for whom they are supposed to be acting. They can violate their fiduciary trust.

There is a fine line between ordinary incentive problems and broader ethical issues. We typically do not say a worker who does not give his all for his employer is unethical; we are as likely to blame the employer for failing to provide adequate incentive structures. But we are likely to say that a worker who steals from his employer is acting in an unethical manner. We do not say that the problem is only that the employer has failed to give the right incentive structure. But between these two extremes there are many subtle shades of gray. In the United States, corporate, accounting, and banking scandals—in each of which individuals acted in ways that reflected their own interests and that were, for the most part, totally legal—raised serious ethical issues. Chief Executive Officers and other executives deliberately took advantage of their positions of trust to enrich themselves at the expense of those they were supposed to serve (Stiglitz 2003a).

These are market failures. There were also public failures. The government not only failed to address the problems posed by the conflicts of interest and the misleading accounting—even after public attention had been drawn to these problems—but with the repeal of the Glass-Steagall Act the scope for these conflicts of interest was even expanded. Rather than correcting the market failures, actions by the government exacerbated them.

At what point do actions cross over the line so that they not only contribute to economic inefficiency but can be considered unethical? Those who commit self-enriching acts almost always come forward with arguments for why what they did was in the public interest. For example, the elimination of the restrictions designed to prevent conflicts of interest are described as allowing for more market flexibility, enabling the market to respond better to the ever-changing landscape. Likewise, the intellectual property rights that deprived so many in the developing countries access to life-saving drugs are described as necessary to ensure that there is a steady supply of new drugs to meet the health care needs of the world. These arguments often have a grain of truth in them, and those who put them forward may even believe them. But they have only a grain of truth.[1]

In any case, it is in areas where markets fail—where, for instance, there are information asymmetries and imperfections of competition, where the informed and powerful can take advantage of the uninformed and weak—that self-enriching behavior is most likely to cross the line into unethical behavior. And it is in these arenas that ethical discourse may have the most important impact; by calling attention to these problems, it may be possible to limit the scope of such behavior and to enact policies and reform institutions so that they are less likely to occur.

As a final preliminary remark, I note that there are some circumstances in which a chain of actions together leads to a particular result. This "package" of actions might be considered unethical if great harm is done to the poor, even though none of the individual actions would themselves have resulted in the dire consequences. I would argue that if there is a reasonable probability that the adverse consequences follow from any individual action—that is, that if the other actions that are part of the package are likely to occur, and therefore that the dire results are reasonably foreseeable—then the individual actions themselves can and should be viewed as unethical. (This is reflected in legal doctrine where, for instance, someone who has supplied a gun in a murder is guilty as an accomplice to the crime even if the gun supplier did not know the murderer's intention.)

This chapter considers these ethical issues in the context of global finance. It focuses on three central issues: first, the design of debt contracts between developed and less developed countries and other aspects of lending behavior; second, the consequences of excessive debt; and finally, broader issues associated with the global reserve system. It discusses three types of ethical problems: (1) where markets (or international institutions) take advantage of their "power" and the weaknesses of the developing country to pursue their own interests at the expense or risk of those in the developing countries; (2) where international financial institutions provide advice that works to the disadvantage of the developing countries; and (3) where the market, and especially the international financial institutions, have not done as much as they could for the well-being of the developed countries (a sin of omission rather than a sin of commission) (Stiglitz 2003b).[2]

Lending Behavior

In most religions, there has long been strong ethical guidance regarding lending behavior, almost surely reflecting the imbalance of economic power between lenders and borrowers. This imbalance of power has the potential to give rise to abuse, with the lender taking advantage of the needs of the borrower. There are thus proscriptions against usury, and the Old Testament tradition of Jubilee (Lev. 25) focused on the importance of debt forgiveness, of giving those who have become indebted a chance at a fresh start. Market economics has shunted these concerns aside. Interest rates are determined by the law of demand and supply, just as the law of demand and supply determines the prices of apples and oranges.

But the competitive-market perspective is, at least in many instances, wrong: Credit markets are highly imperfect; borrowers typically have access to only a limited number of sources of credit, whereas creditors face a large number of potential borrowers. Borrowers typically are poorer than lenders, and often they turn to lenders in times of crisis, when their needs cannot be put off. Lenders have the opportunity to take advantage of the asymmetries in power to gain for themselves. Of course, charging an interest rate commensurate with risk is not usurious. But often the real interest rates charged are far higher than what would be required to adjust for the risk of repayment.

But even short of usury, the structure of international capital markets puts poor and developing countries at a marked disadvantage.

Forcing Developing Countries to Bear Risks

Richer countries are better able to bear the risks associated with interest rate and exchange rate volatility, and such volatility has been enormous during 1994–2004. But, in fact, debt contracts—even when the lending is done not by private creditors but by governments and multilateral institutions—place the risk burden on developing countries. In effect, lenders use their market power to force developing countries to assume risks *that in an efficient market would be borne by those more able to bear these risks*; that is, developed countries and the multinational institutions.[3]

The consequences have been disastrous. When the United States raised interest rates in the late 1970s and early 1980s, it explicitly paid little or no attention to the consequences this would have on others, including Latin American countries, who had been persuaded to borrow enormous amounts of money. (Because at the time at which the loans were made, real interest rates were low, or sometimes even negative, it may not have taken much persuasion.) This in turn led to the Latin American debt crisis and the lost decade of the 1980s. In 2002, Moldova, which has seen its income decline 70% since the end of communism, had to spend three-quarters of its meager public budget to service foreign debt. Moldova's debt burden had increased vastly when the Russian ruble, to which its currency was tied, devalued enormously in 1998. In both Latin America and Moldova, the major factor that led to an unmanageable debt burden came from outside their borders.

Ethical Failures in Excessive Lending

The more developed countries, and especially the multilateral institutions, are (or at least ought to be) in a position to advise countries on what levels of debt are prudent and on how to manage their risks. And, more importantly, they should do so in ways that are particularly sensitive to the consequences for the poor. But these lenders have not done so, and arguably, they have often provided advice that has exacerbated the risks to which developing-country borrowers are exposed. Most notable in this respect was the repeated advice to developing countries beginning in the 1980s to liberalize their capital markets, opening them up to destabilizing speculative capital flows and to short-term lending.

This is an instance in which lenders put aside their fiduciary responsibility and allowed embedded conflicts of interest to dominate their behavior. Wall Street speculators and international lenders may have made money from the opening of markets in developing countries, but there was at the time that the IMF and the U.S. Treasury advised countries to fully liberalize their capital markets no evidence or theory that capital market liberalization and the associated short-term capital flows led to faster growth. On the contrary, there was considerable evidence and theory that they led to greater instability and that the poor disproportionately bear the burden of this instability. More recently, even the IMF has recognized this—too late for those countries that were forced to follow its advice with such adverse consequences.

The reasons that such short-term lending contributes to instability should have been obvious—bank lending is procyclical; lenders lend when the economy is strong, and they want their money back when the economy is weak. The reasons that such short-term lending may not lead to increased growth should have been equally obvious: Factories cannot be built and long-term investments cannot be made with money that may have to be repaid at any moment. There are other reasons that capital market liberalization may be bad for growth—increased volatility makes investment riskier, and short-term foreign-denominated borrowing forces countries to put aside more money into reserves, money that has a very high opportunity cost. But whatever the reason, the evidence is clear: Capital market liberalization does not in general lead to faster economic growth, and those institutions that advised the developing countries knew this, or should have known this (Prasad et al. 2003; Stiglitz 2004).

By the same token, before the Russian crisis, the IMF advised Russia to convert more of its debt from ruble- to dollar-denominated debt. It knew, or should have known, that doing so was exposing the country to enormous risk and inhibiting its ability to adapt. It was clear that the exchange rate was overvalued. But with dollar-denominated debt, when Russia devalued, the benefit it got in increased exports and import substitution from the devaluation would be offset by the losses on the balance sheet.[4]

Rather than working to reduce the market failure or offset the consequences (i.e., to help markets develop incentive-compatible contracts in which the rich bear more of the risks associated with exchange rate and interest rate fluctuations), the IMF and other developed-country lenders have done what they could to make sure that those countries that have entered into these unfair contracts fulfill them, whatever the costs to their people.

Responding to Crises: Policy

Given the huge burden of risk that developing countries have borne, it is not surprising that they have faced repeated crises. Often these crises (as in the case of the Latin American crisis of the early 1980s or Moldova's more recent problems) are largely the result of events beyond their borders. There are then hard choices on how to respond. There are risks associated with different responses, and different policies affect which parties bear those risks. Ethics can help us decide whose interests to put first: for example those of the international banks or those of the poor people within the country.

Indonesia provides the most telling example, where the IMF together with the G7 provided some $22 billion (U.S.) in response to the crisis initiated by the Thai baht devaluation in 1997. The money was characterized as being used to bail out Indonesia, but a closer look at what happened shows that it was really the Western banks that were being bailed out. They got back more of the money that was owed to them than they would have otherwise (even if many still had to face some losses). The IMF did not give Indonesia the money; it only lent it the money. Hence, in effect, the money was designed to enable the Indonesian government to pay back private debts owed to the foreign banks (as elsewhere, effectively private debts were nationalized). Indonesia was not the beneficiary; the Western creditors were the real beneficiaries. This soon became clear when the IMF insisted that food and fuel subsidies to the poor be cut back—it argued that though there were billions of dollars to repay Western banks, there simply wasn't enough money to help the poor (though the costs were a mere fraction of what was provided for the bank bailouts). This came after unemployment had soared tenfold and real wages had plummeted—partly because of the policies that the IMF had insisted upon (Rodrik 2001). Evidently, welfare for the poor was not acceptable, whereas corporate welfare was not only acceptable but encouraged.

The IMF also insisted on contractionary fiscal and monetary policies, with the predictable result that the economic downturn became worse—indeed, it became a real depression (though the U.S. Treasury insisted that the word not be used)—with enormous hardship. The policies did mean that there was a trade surplus, enabling the countries of the region to repay the money that was owed. Again, the interests of foreign lenders were put ahead of those of the citizens of the borrowing country and especially the poor.

International institutions and other countries can decide on whether or how to help the crisis country. Japan provides an example of a model of what might be viewed as ethical behavior (which need not be disassociated from self-interested behavior) in the generous offer of $100 billion (U.S.) it made to its neighbors in East Asia during the crisis of 1997–98. It targeted that aid to help rejuvenate their economies (in contrast with the IMF money, which went to bail out Western creditors).[5] The contrast with the United States is striking. Putting what it viewed as geopolitical interests above the well-being of the people in the region, the United States did everything it could to squash Japan's initiative (and it was successful in doing so). Then, later, when Japan put forward the more modest, but still generous, $30 billion Miyazawa initiative, the United States tried to ensure that as much money as possible went to corporate restructuring—to bailing out Western investors and lenders.

Responding to Crises: Bankruptcy Regimes and Debt Forgiveness

Whenever there is lending, there is the risk that the borrower will not be able to repay what is borrowed or can only do so with enormous hardship upon himself and his family. How countries resolve these situations can be viewed as both an ethical and an economic issue. It is an ethical issue in part because it tests in the extreme how society balances the interests of the well off and powerful against those of the less fortunate. In ancient times, individuals who did not repay what they owed sometimes were thrown in the water with a stone tied around their feet: The punishment was severe. In nineteenth-century Britain, individuals were sent to debtor prisons, so graphically portrayed in some of Charles Dickens's novels. Sovereigns who did not repay were invaded by governments of creditor countries: Mexico was taken over jointly by Britain and France, as was Egypt. The practice continued even into the twentieth century, with the attack against Venezuela by European powers in 1902. Argentina's foreign minister at the time roundly condemned the attack on Venezuela, pointing out that lenders should have known that there was a risk of nonrepayment. Even more recently, the United States has used such defaults as part of the pretense for occupation of Caribbean and Central American republics.

Debt forgiveness has long been part of Judeo-Christian tradition, symbolized by the Jubilee, giving individuals the ability to make a fresh start. Bankruptcy can be viewed within the same tradition. Today, debtor prisons and military interventions are no longer viewed as acceptable. Yet the conditions under which individuals and countries are allowed to make a fresh start—and what exactly that means—remain questions of extreme controversy, with some arguing for more debtor-friendly regimes and some for more creditor-friendly policies.

Debt Relief for Highly Indebted Countries

Arguably, the easiest ethical case for debt forgiveness is a country that is so heavily burdened by debt that its governments cannot serve the basic functions of a state in a civilized society: to provide security and social services and maintain basic public infrastructure. These are cases where the consequences of forcing the debtors to repay what is owed are so onerous that even if the culpability of the lender is limited, debt forgiveness seems ethically compelling. Consider the plight of Moldova, mentioned earlier. In 2002, some 75% of its meager public finances went to service its foreign debt. Hospitals were without basic supplies. Public services were starved. Poverty was soaring so badly that many women were turning to a life of prostitution abroad. This would seem to present a compelling case for debt forgiveness. An ethical approach to global finance that prohibited rich countries from profiting at the expense of the poor would demand debt forgiveness where servicing debt conflicts directly with providing basic social services to a poor populace.

Bankruptcy

In both the East Asian and Latin American crises, critics of the IMF argued for greater reliance on bankruptcy—debt forgiveness effectively forced by the borrower's inability to repay—and less reliance on bailouts, which simply put the burden on future taxpayers in the borrowing country. Especially objectionable were the cases where governments were encouraged, in some instances effectively forced, to assume the liabilities of private borrowers. In effect, the IMF was bailing out the foreign lenders—putting their interests above those of workers and others in the developing country. Belatedly, after the failure of the sixth mega-bailout in almost as many years, the IMF finally recognized the need for greater reliance on bankruptcy and the development of systematic procedures. But its approach again raised ethical concerns. In the case of sovereign-debt restructurings, there are other claimants besides foreign (or even domestic) creditors, such as pensioners and children. These needs should, in fact, have primacy.[6] Yet the IMF has no systematic way to bring their concerns into the resolution process.[7]

Clearly, the nature of the bankruptcy regime affects incentives both for lenders to engage in due diligence in making lending decisions and to avoid excessive lending and for borrowers to repay what is owed and to take actions that enhance their ability to do so.

Lender Culpability

In the East Asian crisis, the IMF complained loudly about the behavior of the borrowers. However, every loan has both a borrower and a lender, and the lenders were thus potentially as much at fault as the borrowers. The lenders knew, or should have known, about the problems of the borrowers, including the lack of transparency and the potential risks. Previous bailouts of Western lenders may have created a moral hazard problem that encouraged lenders to engage in "excessive" lending because they would not have to bear some of the costs of the risks.[8]

An ethical approach should take into account not only the differing economic circumstances of the parties but also the origins of the problem of indebtedness. Most of us would say that if a lender, say a bank, provides a credit card to a child, and the child uses the credit card to run up huge indebtedness, then the child should not have to spend the rest of his or her life repaying the accumulated debt. The creditor was in a position to judge the consequences of making the loan, indeed in a better position than the child, and should bear some of the consequences of the child's inability to repay the debt.

There are other cases where the debt problem is caused, in no small measure, by policy decisions in the lending country. For instance, given the "market failures" in the debt instruments—which forced the developing countries to bear the risk of exchange rate and interest rate fluctuations—when the United States

raised interest rates, it imposed enormous costs on borrowing countries, effectively forcing them into bankruptcy. The United States (or U.S. banks) had
encouraged the lending—the borrowers had not been warned of the risks that
they might encounter from such marked changes in U.S. policy. And when the
United States raised interest rates, it focused only on the benefits of bringing
down U.S. inflation, not the costs imposed on others, such as a lost decade of
growth in Latin America. Given its culpability, the United States should have
moved quickly toward debt forgiveness; instead it dithered for almost a decade,
forcing Latin American countries to send money back to Washington—a procyclical policy that was at the center of ten years of stagnation.

Similarly, perhaps a key factor in the Argentinean crisis and the ruble crisis
was the mismanagement of the East Asian crisis by the IMF, which led to higher
global interest rates to emerging markets. These high interest rates made Argentina's debt difficult if not impossible to manage. The global slowdown that
resulted in low oil prices—combined with a policy strategy that contributed to
a shrinking GDP—was a central factor in Russia's inability to meet its debt
obligations.

The Case of Argentina

The sequence of events leading up to Argentina's crisis, and the unfolding events
afterward, provide a landscape on which to examine a host of ethical issues of
considerable complexity. There can be no doubt that great harm was done to
the people of Argentina. Starvation and malnourishment became widespread in
a country rich in natural and agricultural resources. The incidence of poverty
increased. There is shared culpability. Many contributed to the occurrence and
magnitude of the disaster, and there has been much finger-pointing. The IMF,
for instance, which had treated Argentina as its A + student, thereby earning
Argentina easy access to international capital markets, suddenly changed its
grade and began blaming corrupt politicians (many of them the same politicians
who had only shortly before been praised for their good judgment in following
IMF advice and paraded before the international community at the annual meeting of the IMF as exemplars for others to follow, without mention of their
corruption) and provincial governors for overspending. As is so often the case,
there is shared culpability. Yet the IMF's culpability is sufficiently large that
there is a strong case for debt forgiveness.

A quick look at the data helps put some perspective on the events. The federal
government of Argentina was not profligate—at the time of the crisis, its deficit
as a percentage of GDP was only 3%, and given the magnitude of the recession,
this was a remarkably small number. (Economists' usual benchmark is the structural, or full-employment, deficit; that is, what the deficit would have been had
the economy operated at full employment. In these terms, Argentina almost
surely had a surplus or at most a small deficit. By way of comparison, the United
States in 1992, during its last recession, which was far milder than that in
Argentina, had a deficit of close to 5% of GDP.) Indeed, Argentina could have
been blamed for not pursuing a sufficiently expansionary policy. The government

had in fact cut back primary expenditures (that is, expenditures net of interest) by 10% over the preceding two years, an impressive political feat but one that contributed to the economic contraction by shrinking public spending at a time when the economy demanded stimulation. The IMF also bears considerable responsibility for these excessively contractionary policies, upon which it had insisted.

A look at the sources of the deficit is also instructive. If the Argentine government had not privatized social security, it would have had a balanced budget, or even a slight surplus. If the government had pursued expansionary fiscal policies, or had devalued the currency, so that exports could start to grow and imports could be restricted, then there also would not have been a deficit, or it would have been much smaller. The country had been provided with policy advice that it followed and that earned it kudos in the early 1990s. But these policies led to the disastrous outcome. Providing this advice, without adequate warning of the likely consequences, can be argued to have been unethical, even more so when the same party provided several pieces of advice that worked together in the predictable way to the disadvantage of the country. For instance, privatization of social security essentially *always* worsens a government's budgetary position. In the United States, had social security been privatized, the deficit-to-GDP ratio would have been 8% in 1992. This, by itself, would not necessarily be a problem if the government were permitted to borrow the (now privatized) social security funds to match the (apparent) increase in the government deficit. But it is a problem if the government is told, as it goes into a recession, that it must maintain fiscal balance, regardless of the fact that it has privatized social security, because that imposes an additional large contractionary burden on the economy.

Recessions are inevitable, especially in today's highly volatile market economy. If recessions are inevitable, and if an institution (the IMF) has a policy of insisting on budget balance, or even near budget balance, even in a recession, *then* it follows that the act of privatizing social security will almost surely result in an increasingly severe economic downturn.

By the same token, the IMF itself lent and, by its praise, encouraged lending to Argentina, so that that country became the world's largest debtor. The funds, it was alleged, would enable Argentina to adjust to the structural changes that would enable it to grow faster in the future. In lending so much to Argentina, especially given its fixed exchange-rate system, the IMF exposed it to undue risks. With its exchange rate linked to the dollar and with considerable trade outside the dollar region, such as with Brazil and Europe, there was more than a small likelihood that Argentina's currency would become overvalued. Even apparently moderate levels of debt become untenable when interest rates increase enormously, sometimes through no fault of the borrower. As we noted, the developed countries have forced developing countries to bear the risk of interest rate and exchange rate volatility.

The East Asian crisis led to high emerging-market risk premiums, so that Argentina's interest rates rose and debt service increasingly became a problem. There was then a vicious circle: The overvalued currency and the high debt service both contributed to still higher interest rates, exacerbating that country's problems. Even a moderate devaluation might have led to an unbearable debt-to-GDP ratio; the actual devaluation led to a debt-to-GDP ratio in excess of 150%. Lenders should know that there is a reasonable risk of devaluation of any overvalued currency. In Argentina, the notion that the overvaluation might have been corrected by rapid improvements in productivity or large decreases in domestic prices was simply not very credible—and hence lenders should have realized the risk to which they were exposing Argentina.

One might say that it is the responsibility of the borrowers, not the lenders, but that is to ignore the ethical question of who ought to bear the cost of the catastrophic outcome of the IMF's economic program. Which party was in a better position to predict the outcome, and which party can assume the loss with the least human suffering? Lenders are supposed to be sophisticated in risk analysis and in making judgments about a reasonable debt burden. The lenders thus have more than a little culpability, as do others providing advice that could predictably lead to excessive indebtedness.

The world is stochastic, and an unforeseen turn of events may mean that even well-designed and well-intentioned lending may lead to excessive debt burdens. A sense of social justice in such situations should lead to debt forgiveness, *even if there was no lender culpability*.[9] In the case of Argentina, however, there was a prima facie case that the debt burdens were too high given the level of international volatility in exchange rates and interest rates: There was a significant probability of a default even if Argentina had acted "perfectly," with no corruption. When lenders have a high degree of culpability in the generation of excessive debt, the moral responsibility for debt forgiveness is even higher.

Further, if there is a moral imperative that prohibits generating or protecting wealth at the expense of the poor, then there is a responsibility to forgive debt when doing otherwise would increase the suffering of already poor people. However, that is not what the IMF did. Rather, it imposed strongly contractionary fiscal policies and encouraged the country to stick with the overvalued fixed exchange rate—a policy that had strong political support within the country, influenced no doubt by constant IMF lecturing on the topic and a concern that hyperinflation might break out once the constraint of the fixed exchange rate was abandoned, a fear that proved unfounded.

Surely, this "package" of acts caused, and could reasonably have been expected to cause, untold suffering; and given the predictability of the subsequent consequences, it could be considered "unethical."

The Global Reserve System

The global economic system has exhibited enormous instability. The IMF, which was set up to help stabilize the global economy and provide financing to enable countries to have countercyclical fiscal policies, has pushed policies (such as capital market liberalization) that have exacerbated that instability and led to unnecessary hardship.[10] It has, moreover, failed to address the problems of market failure that contribute to global instability at such great costs to developing countries. (As noted, poor countries wind up bearing the risk of interest rate and exchange rate fluctuations.)

Part of the problem lies with the global reserve system, which entails countries putting aside money in case of an emergency. The "reserves" are typically held in hard currencies—particularly in U.S. dollars. This implies that poor countries, in effect, lend to the United States substantial sums every year. Prudent requirements entail countries holding in reserve an amount equal to their short-term foreign-denominated liabilities; this means that if a firm within a country borrows, say, $100 million from a U.S. bank short term, the government of that country must set aside $100 million in reserves—that is, it must lend to the United States $100 million. Net, the country receives nothing. But when it borrows, it must pay, say, 18%, while when it lends, it receives less than 2%. There is a net transfer to the United States of more than $16 million a year— the United States benefits, but the developing country suffers.

The instabilities and inequities associated with the global reserve system impose high costs on the poor. There are reforms that would address these problems, including an annual emission of SDRs (special drawing rights, or "global greenbacks"), which could be used to finance development and other global public goods. The United States might be directly disadvantaged (it would no longer benefit as much from being the major global reserve currency), but it would gain from the greater stability of the world's financial system. In any case, clearly it is wrong for the United States to put its own self-interest ahead of the interests of those who suffer under the current arrangement.

Interactions among Policies

This chapter has focused on ethical problems arising in international financial markets. The consequences of these ethical lapses are, however, increased by problems elsewhere, such as in trade policy, where problems in one sphere interact with those in another. International trade agreements have advanced the interests of the advanced industrial countries, often at the expense of the less developed countries. Asymmetric trade liberalization makes the difficulties of adjusting to trade liberalization all the greater for developing countries, but when IMF policies and problems in global financial markets result in developing countries facing high interest rates, trade liberalization is especially likely to result in increased poverty and lower growth. Rather than resources being redeployed from low-productivity protected sectors to high-productivity export sectors, they simply move from the protected sectors into unemployment.

Similarly, the value-added tax (VAT) pushed on so many countries by the IMF is not only inequitable—it is equivalent to a proportional consumption tax—but also impedes development, as in practice it imposes a tax on the "formal sector," the sector that developing countries should be trying to strengthen because in most developing countries it is virtually impossible to tax the informal sector. But this policy has the effect of lowering the output price of the informal sector, including the raw materials that are inputs purchased by the developed countries, relative to the goods produced by the developed countries. In effect, goods that are substitutes for and competitive with those produced by developed countries are discouraged and those that are complements encouraged. Whether intentionally or not, such policies increase the welfare of the developed countries at the expense of developing countries.

The Ethics of Advice

This chapter has focused on ethical dimensions of global financial markets. Global financial markets are complex and often not well-understood. There is another set of ethical issues, those surrounding giving advice, that have already been alluded to. The advice given to borrowing countries by the IMF was often incomplete: There was not full disclosure either of the risks associated with the policy or the limited evidence in support of the policies. The advisers often did not analyze or disclose the full consequences of the policy, including the consequences for the poor. They tried to sell policies as if they were Pareto dominant when there were in fact trade-offs. In addition, by asserting that there was only a *single technocratic solution*, advisers undermined democratic processes. Their lack of transparency, often quite deliberate, undermined democratic processes in the developed countries as well as in the less developed. Finally, the international advisers typically did not fully disclose the conflicts of interest underlying some of their policies—the gains that they (their countries, and especially particular interests within their countries) would receive. As a result, the "minimal" aspect of the Hippocratic Oath—Do No Harm—has repeatedly been violated.

Conclusion

The issues described in this chapter can be, and have been, looked at through more neutral lenses. We can simply describe the market failures, the departures from efficiency in the design of credit instruments, and the consequences to the developing countries. We can describe the incidence of alternative policies. We can engage in economic and political analysis to explain why these failures have arisen. Does the normative-ethical vocabulary enhance these discussions? What is its role?

As noted in the beginning of the chapter, in a Smithian world, in pursuing one's interest one pursued the general interest. The pursuit of self-interest at least helped bring about a Pareto efficient outcome. Moral analysis entered in a much more circumscribed way in the choice among alternative Pareto efficient structures and how they might be maintained. Typically, there was little consideration of the moral weight to be given to alternative ways by which a particular goal could be achieved.

In the non-Smithian world with which we are concerned (and in which we all live), there are a host of other circumstances in which moral considerations ought to be brought to the table, in which we know that self-interest does not lead to socially desirable outcomes. In *this* world, if individuals thought about their fiduciary responsibilities, as well as their own interests, outcomes might be better. In short, ethics provides an alternative compass with which to guide behavior, and one that may be as or more certain than an undivided devotion to the simplistic pursuit of self-interest.

In a modern economy, individuals constantly face situations where there are asymmetries of information or of market power. Smith's advice in such situations is misguided. In such a situation, individuals do not necessarily advance the common interest by pursuing their own self-interest. There is room to think about the moral dimensions of one's actions, how the poor and weak are likely to suffer or benefit, without sacrificing economic efficiency.

Too often, however, the market failures have been matched by government failures. As we review the problems of globalization discussed in this chapter, it is clear that governments of the advanced industrial countries and the international institutions that they dominate have tried to manage globalization in ways that benefit themselves, and in particular special interests within their boundaries. Principles of social justice (or even of democratic processes) that have motivated political activity *within* countries have played little role in driving global economic policies or in shaping the global economic institutions. In a sense, economic globalization has outpaced political globalization, if by that we mean the creation of a polity in which shared values of democracy, social justice, and social solidarity play out on a global scale.

Globalization—the closer integration of the countries of the world—implies greater interdependence and therefore a need for greater collective action. Although determining the principles that should underlie this collective action is no easy matter, this much is clear: Given asymmetries of information and resulting market failures, processes in which each nation attempts to push for those policies that are narrowly in their own self-interest are not likely to produce outcomes that are in the general interest.

Ethics may be an uncertain and imprecise compass, but it at least provides some guidance in a world in which the only beacon, all too often, points in the wrong direction.

Acknowledgments This chapter is a revised version of a paper presented to the Vatican Conference at the Ninth Plenary Session of the Pontifical Academy of Social Sciences (Casina Pio IV, 2–6 May 2003). The author is indebted to his research assistants Nadia Roumani and Francesco Brindisi, and to Kira Brunner for editorial assistance. Financial support from the Ford Foundation, the Mott Foundation, the MacArthur Foundations, and SIDA is gratefully acknowledged.

Notes

1. For instance, at the high prices charged, sales of AIDS drugs would be minimal in poor countries, and accordingly, so would the revenue generated. The net effect on incentives to innovate would be small, whereas the human cost of the lack of availability of the drugs would be enormous.

2. The "power" of the international financial institutions, especially in the context of a crisis, means that developing countries typically believe that they ignore this advice at their peril. There are a variety of ways in which they can "force" developing countries to go along with their advice. They can not only withhold aid but also when the IMF withholds aid or strongly criticizes the economic policies of a country, others are likely to refuse to provide assistance or finance. See, for example, Stiglitz (2002).

3. The amount that borrowers would be willing to pay to divest themselves of these risks should exceed the amounts that the developed countries would require to compensate them for bearing the risks. Accordingly, in well-functioning capital markets, there should be this transfer of risk. Although there are moral hazard issues associated with some of the risks (e.g., exchange rates), much of the risk arises from events in the global economy for which such moral hazard problems do not arise. There is no satisfactory explanation for why the transfer of risks does not occur. In the case of lending from governments or multilateral agencies, particularly concessionary lending, the developed countries have little choice but to accept whatever terms are offered.

4. In addition, the way the IMF shut down 16 private banks induced a bank run, which weakened the financial system enormously, again with the predictable contractionary consequences.

5. This is not to say that it didn't have some self-interest: Not only was Japan's economy closely intertwined with those elsewhere in Asia but Japan may also have geopolitical aims in the region.

6. As is the case under Chapter 9 of the U.S. bankruptcy code.

7. Moreover, the IMF, a major creditor, proposed that it be at the center of the resolution, almost a bankruptcy judge, notwithstanding the conflict of interest inherent in such a role.

8. Defenders of the IMF often observe that the lenders bore some risk, but that is irrelevant: There will be excess lending as long as some of the risk is not borne by the lender.

9. Behind the "veil of ignorance" all would agree that in these adverse situations, arising from no fault on the part of the debtor, one should give the debtor a fresh start. In effect, there is an implicit "equity."

10. There are some who take a narrower view of the IMF's original mandate. They see it as enabling the fixed exchange-rate system to function. But clearly, underlying that desire was the more fundamental concern that the world not slip back into another global recession.

References

Prasad, E., Rogoff, K., Wei, S.-J., and Kose, A. M. 2003. Effects of Financial Globalization on Developing Countries: Some Empirical Evidence. IMF Occasional Paper No. 220. Washington, DC: IMF.

Rawls, J. 1999. *A Theory of Justice,* revised edition. Cambridge, MA: Belknap Press.

Rodrik, D. 2001. Development Strategies for the Next Century. In *Annual World Bank Conference on Development Economics,* ed. B. Pleskovic and N. Stern. Washington, DC: World Bank.

Stiglitz, J. E. 2000. Ethics, Economic Advice, and Economic Policy. Available online at: www.iadb.org/etica/Documentos/dc_sti_ethic-i.pdf. Italian translation: Etica, politica economica e paesi in via di sviluppo. *Rivista internazionale di scienze sociali,* 109(4)(2001): 1–16.

————. 2002. *Globalization and Its Discontents.* New York: W. W. Norton.

————. 2003a. *The Roaring Nineties.* New York: W. W. Norton.

————. 2003b. Ethics, Market and Government Failure, and Globalization, paper presented to the Vatican Conference at the Ninth Plenary Session of the Pontifical Academy of Social Sciences, Casina Pio IV (2–6 May).

————. 2004. Capital Market Liberalization, Globalization, and the IMF. *Oxford Review of Economic Policy.* Forthcoming.

8

HELPING THE POOR TO HELP THEMSELVES: DEBT RELIEF OR AID?

Serkan Arslanalp
Peter Blair Henry

Introduction

In the world's highly indebted poor countries (HIPCs), one in ten infants die at birth. For those who survive, life is an uphill battle. The unholy trinity of malaria, AIDS, and malnutrition conspire to deliver a life expectancy of 51 years—the average child born in Mozambique will be approaching his death bed as his counterpart in the United States enters middle age and the prime income-earning years of his life. Nor do the HIPCs' economies offer much hope of pulling their citizens out of grinding poverty anytime soon. Their average growth rate since the 1980s has been negative—things are getting worse, not better, for the indigent of the world.

Statistics such as these (see Table 8.1) are not easy to take. Civilized people find talk of death and destitution rather unpleasant. Something must be to blame, and the debt burden of the world's poorest countries—$169 billion (U.S.) in 1999—is a highly visible target. There have always been those who think that the debts of the world's poorest countries should be forgiven. But in 1996, debt-relief advocates redoubled their efforts. Catalyzed by the rock star Bono, there is an increasingly popular view—from NGOs to the pope to former U.S. Senator Jesse Helms—that the staggering level of debt is the primary obstacle to improved economic growth and living standards in the HIPCs.

Is debt relief a viable solution to worldwide poverty or a waste of time and money? The answer to this important question depends critically on another—

Disclaimer: The views expressed in this paper are solely those of the authors and do not represent the views of the National Science Foundation.

TABLE 8.1   Prospects are grim for the highly indebted poor countries (HIPCs)

Receiving debt relief[a]		Still under consideration	
Benin	Malawi	Angola	Kenya
Bolivia	Mali	Burundi	Lao PDR
Burkina Faso	Mauritania	Central African	Liberia
Cameroon	Mozambique	Republic	Myanmar
Chad	Nicaragua	Comoros	Somalia
Ethiopia	Niger	Democratic Republic	Sudan
Gambia	Rwanda	of Congo	Togo
Ghana	Sao Tome and Principe	Republic of Congo	Vietnam
Guinea	Senegal	Cote d'Ivoire	Yemen
Guinea-Bissau	Sierra Leone		
Guyana	Tanzania		
Honduras	Uganda		
Madagascar	Zambia		

	Infant Mortality (per 1,000 births)	Life Expectancy (years)	GDP per capita (current U.S.$)	GDP per capita growth (1980–2000)
HIPC countries	100	51	310	−0.2
United States	7	77	34,370	2.0

[a]These countries have reached the "decision point" under the Enhanced HIPC Initiative: Status as of January 2003.

Source: World Bank HIPC Initiative document: www.worldbank.org/hipc/progress-to-date/relief_and _outlook_Jan03.pdf; World Development Indicators Data Base.

does debt relief promote economic growth by improving efficiency and incentives for investment? Debt relief promotes investment and growth in circumstances where debt overhang—a term we later define more precisely—exerts a drag on economic performance. When a country suffers from debt overhang, debt relief can improve economic efficiency and make everyone better off, creditors as well as debtors. This chapter examines some important facts about 16 countries whose economies suffered from excessive debt during the 1980s: Argentina, Bolivia, Brazil, Bulgaria, Costa Rica, the Dominican Republic, Ecuador, Jordan, Mexico, Nigeria, Panama, Peru, the Philippines, Poland, Uruguay, and Venezuela. The debt overhang of these countries was alleviated by the debt-relief plan engineered by former U.S. Treasury Secretary Nicholas Brady. Under the Brady Plan, the international commercial banks agreed to write down a substantial fraction of the debt owed to them by the Brady countries.

The major problem for the Brady countries was that they ran into temporary difficulty servicing their debt in August 1982. A combination of adverse economic conditions and poor policy choices substantially increased the riskiness of the banks' loan portfolios in these countries. Creditors got worried and rushed to collect on their loans all at once, but the creditors' panic created an unmanageable short-term payment burden for the debtors. To make matters worse, new lending also ground to a standstill. With no new money coming in, scarce resources that would normally have funded investment were consumed by debt servicing. Growth came to an abrupt stop. Once some of the debt was relieved—seven years later—the path was clear for new funds to come from other sources. These new funds provided the impetus the countries needed to stimulate investment and growth.

It is tempting to conclude that debt relief for the HIPCs would produce similar results if only relief was forthcoming more quickly and in larger quantities. Unfortunately, the evidence does not support this conclusion. Debt relief is unlikely to stimulate investment and growth in the HIPCs because the HIPCs lack much of the basic infrastructure that forms the basis for profitable economic activity—things such as well-defined property rights, roads, schools, hospitals, and clean water. Because the principal problem of the HIPCs is a lack of infrastructure, there is little reason to believe that debt relief there will stimulate a sudden rush of private foreign capital that leads to higher investment and growth.

This is not an argument for leaving the HIPCs to wither on the vine. The point is that the HIPCs should be targeted not for debt relief but for direct aid that would assist their citizens in building the institutions and infrastructure that will eventually make them attractive places for both domestic and foreign investment.

Some argue that debt relief is equivalent to aid, but this is incorrect. Debt relief is not equivalent to aid because money is fungible. There is simply no reason to believe that writing down a government's debt by a billion dollars will translate into a billion dollars of additional infrastructure development. Having said that, aid is no panacea either, and we need to make sure that it is not wasted. The issue is not whether we should give aid but rather how to design aid programs that work more effectively.

The cruel irony of the current debate is that debt relief might be most efficient in a number of countries that are not being considered for such programs at all. These include highly indebted (but not so poor) less developed countries (LDCs) whose social infrastructure resembles those of the Brady countries: Colombia, Indonesia, Jamaica, Malaysia, Pakistan, and Turkey. Given their level of infrastructure, it is much more reasonable to expect that economies such as these might respond positively to debt relief.

The message here is ultimately a hopeful one. Debt relief works for relatively developed but highly indebted emerging economies that suffer from debt overhang. Aid is the most effective way of addressing the basic economic problems of the world's poorest countries. Our aim should be to make sure everybody gets what is most efficient.

Debt Relief Promotes Economic Growth When Countries Have Debt Overhang

Economic arguments for debt relief turn on the fact that there are circumstances in which too much debt exerts a drag on economic performance (debt overhang). When such conditions prevail, debt relief can improve economic efficiency, making both debtors and creditors better off.

Theory

There are two principal reasons why debt relief may be economically efficient.[1] First, it is good accounting practice to write off debts that cannot be collected. That way, future loans can be given on a sounder economic basis (Summers 2000). Advocates of this view demonstrated that during the debt crisis the stock prices of U.S. commercial banks reflected significant expected losses on the banks' loans (Sachs and Huizinga 1987). Because the market had already determined that the banks would be unable to recover the full value of their debt, Sachs and Huizinga argued that the banks should be willing to trade their LDC debt for a safe asset with lower face value.

Second, debt relief can make both borrowers and lenders better off when the borrower suffers from debt overhang. A corporation suffers from debt overhang when its existing stock of debt is so large that for a given project with positive net present value (NPV), the NPV of the project is less than the change in the value of the debt that will result from undertaking the project (Myers 1977). In other words, debt overhang exists when there is so much debt that the entire surplus of any new investment goes to the existing debt holders.

When a corporation suffers from debt overhang, equity holders will not finance new projects, even though undertaking the project would increase the value of the firm. The reason is that debt-overhang results in a transfer to existing debt holders that acts as an implicit tax on investment. Importantly, the debt overhang argument assumes that the corporation cannot issue new debt, which means that the cost of the project must be borne by the equity holders. An issue of new debt that has equal seniority with existing debt can alleviate the underinvestment problem.

The debt-overhang literature in international economics extends the tax analogy to a macroeconomic context. Because a sovereign government raises the money to service its debt by taxing firms and households, an increase in the government's obligation to external creditors implicitly constitutes an increase in the private sector's expected future tax burden. As in all tax problems, there is an optimal level of taxation. At reasonable levels of debt and debt servicing, increasing the face value of the debt increases its expected value. Beyond a certain level of debt, however, the tax burden becomes so large that it acts as a disincentive to investment. As current investment falls, future growth decreases and government revenues decline, along with the expected value of the debt.

Although debt overhang may arise when a country accumulates too much debt, just as importantly, it can also occur when a previously manageable stock of debt becomes intractable because of a change in a country's circumstances. To see the point, consider the net resource transfer (NRT)—the net flow of real resources into a country (debt, equity, and foreign direct investment minus debt servicing, dividends, and profit repatriation). In theory, LDCs should experience positive NRTs, as the rate of return in these countries should be higher than in rich ones. However, the NRT may suddenly turn negative if adverse economic shocks or poor economic management (1) drive creditors to call in existing loans and (2) make potential new creditors unwilling to lend. When the country's NRT suddenly turns negative, the private sector's tax burden once again increases sharply, with all of the previously mentioned consequences for investment, growth, and the value of creditors' claims.

Just as an infusion of new debt can solve a corporation's debt overhang, debt relief can also alleviate the problem in a sovereign context. Writing down the debt reduces the implicit marginal tax rate on expected future cash flows and raises the rate of return to private investment. Also, by forcing all creditors to accept some losses, debt relief removes the uncertainty associated with unresolved debt issues and paves the way for profitable new lending.[2] New lending in turn means more investment, growth, and total tax revenues. In other words, when a country suffers from debt overhang, the creditors can actually increase the expected value of their claims by forgiving some of the debt (Krugman 1988, 1989; Sachs 1989).

Facts

The theoretical arguments suggest that the crucial test of debt relief is whether it successfully restores positive net resource transfers to countries where international lending is profitable (Bulow 2002). Table 8.2 demonstrates that debt relief succeeded in restoring capital flows to the Brady countries. The table presents data on the average net resource transfer to Brady countries in event time. Year "0" is the year in which the Brady Plan was officially announced. The striking fact is that the sign of the NRT changes twice. The years "−19" to "−8" roughly correspond to the years 1970 through 1981. These were the boom years in international lending—U.S. commercial banks awash with liquidity from their OPEC clients were happy to lend to anyone who asked (Darity and Horn 1988). In every one of the years from −19 to −8, the average net resource transfer was positive for the Brady countries. In year −7, roughly the time of the onset of the debt crisis, the NRT turned negative and remained so until after the Brady Plan. After the Brady Plan, net resource flows became positive for the rest of the sample.

In order to fully appreciate the significance of these data, it is important to understand that debt relief has two effects on the debtor country—a direct effect and an indirect effect. The direct effect of debt relief is the actual reduction in the stock of debt. The indirect effect of debt relief is that it paves the way for new capital inflows.

The indirect effect of debt relief is more important than the direct effect. Under the Brady Plan, approximately $60 billion (U.S.) of debt was forgiven. Although significant—$60 billion (U.S.) is roughly 5% of the GDP of the Brady countries—this number pales in comparison with the sum of net resource transfers that the Brady countries received in new lending once outstanding debt problems were resolved.

Table 8.2 shows that during the five-year period after the Brady Plan, there was a total resource transfer of about $210 billion (U.S.) to the Brady countries.[3] In the following five years, there was an even larger resource transfer of $330 billion. The surge of capital following the Brady-induced resolution of the debt

TABLE 8.2   Debt relief restores positive net resource transfers (NRTs) to the Brady countries (the HIPCs have never experienced negative NRTs; group averages are in millions of U.S.$)

Year in event time	Brady countries	Highly indebted poor countries
−19	284	15
−18	388	41
−17	247	38
−16	385	45
−15	395	84
−14	778	108
−13	1197	95
−12	670	122
−11	819	159
−10	373	189
−9	73	220
−8	268	206
−7	−487	219
−6	−1179	183
−5	−1326	166
−4	−1335	182
−3	−1216	213
−2	−433	223
−1	−270	253
0	147	267
1	2369	321
2	1664	337
3	1505	344
4	3625	327
5	3749	346
6	6412	344
7	3528	322
8	5215	338
9	2448	312
10	3166	336

Net resource transfers are equal to net resource flows minus interest payments on long-term loans and foreign direct investment profits. The first column lists the years in event time. The number 0 represents the year in which its Brady Plan was announced. For heavily indebted poor countries (HIPC), 0 represents 1989. The next two columns show the progression of net resource transfers in event time to the Brady countries and the HIPC countries. The data on NRT are obtained from the World Bank's Global Development Finance Data Base.

crisis in these countries provides tangible support for the Dornbusch maxim that "Unresolved debt problems, not debt per se, are an obstacle to investment" (Dornbusch 1993: 103).

As a second barometer of the efficiency gains produced by debt relief, we also look at the stock market. The rationale for examining stock prices is clear. The stock market reflects expectations about future interest rates and cash flows. The surge in capital inflows documented in table 8.2 should have reduced in-

terest rates in the debtor country and improved future growth prospects. If interest rates went down and growth prospects improved, the stock market should
have increased (Arslanalp and Henry 2005).

Table 8.3 shows that the stock market did in fact go up in the ten countries
that have stock markets and reached debt-relief agreements between 1989 and
1995. On average, the stock market rose by 65% in the year prior to the official
announcement of debt relief—the period in which each country was outlining
its debt-relief strategy with the anticipation of acceptance under the Brady Plan.
Stated in U.S. dollar terms, the market capitalization of the Brady countries rose
by a total of $42 billion in anticipation of the Brady Plan.

Is the stock market increase spurious? In 1966, Paul Samuelson quipped that
"The stock market has predicted nine out of the last ten recessions" (Samuelson
1966: 92). Therefore, it is important to know whether the stock market reactions
are reliable predictors of real economic improvement or merely short-lived "ir-
rational exuberance" (to use the words of Federal Reserve Chairman Alan
Greenspan). After all, understanding why debt relief for the Brady countries led
to a large stock market appreciation is pivotal to understanding the mechanism
through which debt relief works and the circumstances under which it can be
expected to achieve efficiency gains. Specifically, if the Brady countries really
suffered from debt overhang, then, in addition to the stock market boom, we
should also have seen an increase in investment.

Table 8.4 shows that debt relief coincided with an investment boom. In the

TABLE 8.3   Debt relief drives up stock market values in the Brady countries

Country	Date of agreement	Change in stock market (percentage increase)	Change in market capitalization (billions of U.S. dollars)
Argentina	April 1992	121.2	19.8
Bolivia	March 1993	n.a.	n.a.
Brazil	August 1992	12.6	6.0
Bulgaria	November 1993	n.a.	n.a.
Costa Rica	November 1989	n.a.	n.a.
Dominican Republic	May 1993	n.a.	n.a.
Ecuador	May 1994	59.8	n.a.
Jordan	June 1993	39.0	0.9
Mexico	September 1989	58.2	8.6
Nigeria	March 1991	29.1	0.2
Panama	May 1995	n.a	n.a.
Peru	October 1995	1.1	1.4
Philippines	August 1989	49.2	1.7
Poland	March 1994	215.9	2.1
Uruguay	November 1990	n.a.	n.a.
Venezuela	June 1990	68.1	0.8
All countries		65.4	41.5

Sources: IFC, Emerging Markets Data Base, Cline (1995), and authors' calculations.

TABLE 8.4   Capital stock growth and GDP growth surge after the Brady Plan

	5 years before	5 years after
Investment	1.6	3.5
GDP growth	0.0	1.6

The second column lists the average GDP and capital stock growth five years before each country's Brady deal. The third column lists the average GDP and capital stock growth five years after the Brady deal.

five years prior to debt relief, the average growth rate of the capital stock was 1.6% per year. In the five years following debt relief, the capital stock grew at a rate of 3.5% per year. The difference between the two growth rates—1.9%—is not small. Assuming a standard production function in which capital accounts for about one-third of output, a 1.9% increase in the capital stock raises growth by almost 1% per year—0.63% to be exact (one-third times 1.9). As a final consistency check of the stock market's forecasting power, we also looked at the rate of economic growth. In the five years preceding debt relief, GDP per capita in the Brady countries grew at an average of 0% per year. In the five years following debt relief, it grew at 1.6% per year.

Debt relief produces rising asset prices, increased investment, and faster growth. Importantly, these changes seem to take place not so much because of the actual amount of debt relief itself but principally because of the new flow of lending to the private sector after the debt-overhang–induced lending standstill is over. These facts have important implications for the efficiency prospects of debt-relief efforts for the HIPCs.

Debt Overhang Is Not the HIPCs' Principal Problem

Debt relief worked for the Brady countries. If all else were equal, it might be reasonable to expect current debt-relief efforts in the HIPCs to produce similar results. The problem is that all else is not equal. Debt relief worked in the Brady countries because it eased a debt overhang that was inhibiting private lending, investment, and growth. But it is hard to argue that debt relief will generate investment and growth in the HIPCs because they do not suffer from debt overhang.

There are at least three pieces of evidence to suggest that debt overhang does not deter capital flows to the HIPCs. First, in contrast with the Brady countries, which suffered a sharp reversal in NRT during the 1980s, the HIPC countries have never suffered from a negative NRT. Table 8.2 shows that the NRT for the HIPC countries has always been positive. If debt overhang hinders capital flows to the HIPCs, then we would have expected to see a reversal of the sign of the net resource transfer at some point in time. This never happened. If the goal of debt relief is to restore positive NRTs in scenarios where it has turned negative, then it is not clear how this policy will help a set of countries that have experienced an uninterrupted stream of positive NRTs since 1970.

Second, although things went sour beginning with Mexico's default in 1982, creditors expected to make money by lending to the Brady countries. Presumably, this is why they did so in the first place. In contrast, there has never been any such expectation for the HIPCs. Table 8.5 shows that loans to the private sector (private debt + foreign direct investment + portfolio equity) comprised almost half of the total net resource flow to the Brady countries as early as 1974. On the other hand, international lending to the private sector has never been a significant fraction of the total net resource flows to the HIPCs. As a fraction of total inflows, loans to the private sector in the HIPCs have never exceeded 13% and have been as low as 4%.

Third, there has also been a shift in the composition of international lending to the Brady countries—away from the public sector and toward the private sector. Again, table 8.5 shows that at the peak of the debt crisis (1985–89) grants plus public and publicly guaranteed debt accounted for 73% of the net resource transfer to the Brady countries. By 1994, lending to the private sector constituted the chief source of net resource flows. No such shift has taken place in the HIPCs. In fact, the opposite has occurred—official flows and flows to the public sector have become more important, not less. The role of grants has increased to the point where they now constitute the majority of the net resource flows to the HIPCs.

The HIPCs' Principal Problem Is Weak Economic Institutions

Advances in law and finance help explain why private capital does not flow to the HIPCs. The degree to which a country's law protects the legal rights of minority shareholders exerts a significant influence on that country's access to external finance (La Porta, Lopez-de-Silanes, Shleifer, and Vishny (LLSV) 1997, 1998, 2002; Shleifer and Vishny 1997). Weak investor protection can lower the marginal product of capital and eliminate the incentive for capital to flow from rich to poor countries (Shleifer and Wolfenzon 2002; Henry and Lorentzen 2003). "If investors get poor protection, they will stay away, outside funds will dry up, and fewer resources will be available to finance growth" (Dornbusch 2000: 92).

The connection between investor protection and external finance is germane to the present discussion. Row 1 of table 8.6 shows that the median Brady country ranks lower than the median G7 country on the LLSV index of investor protection.[4] The private capital that does flow to the Brady countries pales in comparison with what we would see in a world where minority shareholders in those countries enjoyed the same legal protection as their U.S. counterparts. Although the median Brady country ranks low on the LLSV index, the HIPCs do not even make the list. If private capital trickles to the Brady countries because they fare poorly on the LLSV index, then woe to the HIPCs, whose

TABLE 8.5 The HIPCs have never received a significant quantity of private capital flows

	1970–74		1975–79		1980–84		1985–89		1990–94	
	Millions of US$	% of Total	Millions of US$	% of Total	Millions of US$	% of Total	Millions of US$	% of Total	Millions of US$	% of Total
HIPC										
Net Resource Flows	61	100.0	172	100.0	269	100.0	305	100.0	412	100.0
Public Debt	39	64.6	111	64.5	176	65.4	158	51.9	120	29.2
Private Debt	3	4.2	3	1.8	5	1.9	–1	–0.3	0	–0.1
FDI	4	5.9	12	7.0	11	4.0	14	4.4	50	12.2
PortfolioEquity	0	0.0	0	0.0	0	0.0	0	0.0	5	1.1
Grants	15	25.2	46	26.7	77	28.7	134	44.0	237	57.6
Brady										
Net Resource Flows	530	100.0	1562	100.0	1938	100.0	722	100.0	2645	100.0
Public Debt	264	49.8	1045	66.9	1346	69.4	443	61.4	309	11.7
Private Debt	133	25.1	219	14.0	212	11.0	–177	–24.5	466	17.6
FDI	116	21.9	253	16.2	305	15.7	365	50.6	982	37.1
Portfolio Equity	0	0.0	0	0.0	2	0.1	6	0.9	708	26.8
Grants	17	3.3	46	2.9	74	3.8	83	11.6	180	6.8

This table presents data on the composition of net resource flows for different groups of countries from 1970 to 2000. The first column lists the components of net resource flows. Net resource flows are the sum of net resource flows on public debt, private debt, foreign direct investment, portfolio equity, and official grants. The following columns display the data as averaged over intervals of five years. The HIPC countries are displayed in table 8.1. The Brady countries are displayed in table 8.3. The data on net resource flows and their components have been obtained from the World Bank's Global Development Finance Data Base.

TABLE 8.6   The HIPCs have much weaker social infrastructure than the Brady countries

	G7	Brady	HIPC	Group of 6
LLSV score	7.5	4.9	N/A	4.6
Hall and Jones (1999) rank	14	63	102	61
Heritage Foundation Index of Economic Freedom rank	14	59	110	58

The first row lists the median La Porta, Lopez-de-Silanes, Shleifer, and Vishny (LLSV) score of social infrastructure for the G7 countries, Brady countries, HIPCs, and the group of six countries. The countries in the group of six are Indonesia, Pakistan, Colombia, Jamaica, Malaysia, and Turkey. The second row lists the median Hall and Jones (1999) rank for each country group. The third row lists the median Heritage Foundation Index of Economic Freedom rank.

capital markets and investor protection laws are not sufficiently developed to even merit a ranking.

Having capital markets that are not sufficiently developed to make the LLSV ranking is probably correlated with weak economic institutions in general. In turn, economic institutions can be a crucial factor in determining the level of human-capital accumulation and the marginal product of capital (Kremer 1993). In other words, the rate of return on private lending in HIPCs is low because they lack the institutional development that is necessary to create an environment where (1) entrepreneurs can earn an economically fair rate of return on capital and (2) lenders have an incentive to extend capital to the private sector.

Row 2 of table 8.6 investigates this claim by using the Hall and Jones (1999) measure of social infrastructure to compare the HIPC and Brady countries. The social infrastructure measure ranks 130 countries and attempts to capture the extent to which a country has "an environment that supports productive activities and encourages capital accumulation, skill acquisition, invention and technology transfer" (Hall and Jones 1999: 84). The median G7 country ranks 14th, the median Brady country ranks 63rd, and the median HIPC country ranks 102nd. Moreover, all of the G7 countries are in the highest twentieth percentile; all of the Brady countries, except for Nigeria and the Dominican Republic, are in the highest seventieth percentile, and 27 of the 38 HIPC countries with available data are in the lowest thirtieth percentile.

Table 8.6 also compares the HIPC and Brady countries using the average value of their score on the Heritage Foundation Index of Economic Freedom from 1995 to 2002. The results are similar. Out of 161 countries, the median G7 country ranks Fourteenth, the median Brady country ranks Fifty-ninth, and the median HIPC country ranks one hundred tenth. Moreover, all of the G7 countries are in the highest twentieth percentile, all of the Brady countries, except for Bulgaria, are in the highest sixtieth percentile, and 24 of 39 HIPC countries with available data are in the lowest fortieth percentile over the same period.

It is interesting to note that six highly or moderately indebted countries that closely resemble the Brady countries have received no consideration for debt relief. The six are Indonesia, Pakistan, Colombia, Jamaica, Malaysia, and Turkey. The median LLSV score for this group of six is 4.6 out of 10. The median LLSV score for the Brady countries is 4.9. Similarly, the median country in the group of 6 ranks sixty-first on the Hall and Jones measure of social infrastructure; the median Brady country ranks sixty-third. Finally, the median country in the group of six ranks fifty-eighth on the Heritage Foundation Index of Economic Freedom; the median Brady country ranks fifty-ninth. Although we do not suggest that countries should receive debt relief based solely on their resemblance to Brady countries, the analysis does suggest that debt relief for the group of six might constitute a more efficient use of resources than debt relief for the HIPCs.

Put another way, the HIPCs' principal problem is an inadequate provision of public goods, stemming from the following kind of externality: It is in no individual's self-interest to build a road, so no one does; yet there would be large societal gains if someone did. In other words, in the HIPCs there are positive externalities to investing in projects that have high social, but low private, rates of return. The externality that debt relief is designed to address is quite different. When debt problems arise, the country and its creditors would be better off if all creditors would either extend new loans or reduce their repayment demands. But the externality—individual lenders acting in their self-interest will not take into account the effect of their inflexibility on the country and its other creditors—means that no rational lenders will do so of their own volition.

Distortions arising from an externality should be tackled with policy instruments that address the externality directly. Rich-country governments address the public-goods externality by collecting taxes. Poor countries, by definition, do not have the tax base to raise the resources they need, but this is the classic economic rationale for foreign aid—not debt relief (Bulow and Rogoff 1988; Bulow 2002). Undoubtedly, aid will not solve all of the HIPCs' problems. No amount of road building will convince entrepreneurs to invest if inflation is high, corruption rampant, and the exchange rate misaligned. But even in the face of sound micro- and macroeconomic policy, nobody is going to invest if they can't get their product to market. Later, we make the case for aid over debt relief more extensively, but first we look at the effect of debt relief on the HIPCs thus far.

It Is Not Clear That Debt Relief for the HIPCs Has Led to Faster Growth

We have argued that debt relief for the HIPCs is unlikely to produce the salutary economic effects that occurred with the passage of debt relief for the Brady countries. Table 8.7 evaluates the evidence to date. Row 1 shows that the HIPC countries that have begun receiving debt relief have seen a modest improvement in their growth performance. From 1990 to 95, the growth rate of these HIPCs was negative 0.5%. From 1996 to 2000, it was 1.5%—an increase of 2%. Os-

TABLE 8.7   The HIPCs receiving debt relief have not grown faster than those that have not

	1970–79	1980–89	1990–95	1996–2000
HIPCs (receiving debt relief)	0.6	−0.8	−0.5	1.5
HIPCs (all)	0.8	−0.6	−0.7	1.4

Source: World Bank World Development Indicators Data Base.

tensibly, this suggests that debt relief has worked. But there are three pieces of evidence that suggest the improvement in growth may not be attributable to debt relief per se.

First, row 2 of table 8.7 shows that the change in growth of those countries that have not yet begun receiving debt relief does not differ much from those that have. The growth rate of all the HIPCs from 1996 to 2000 is 2.1% higher than it was from 1990 to 1995.

Second, for the HIPC countries that have been receiving debt relief, the relief process did not actually begin until 2000. Therefore, it is not clear that the improvement in growth performance between 1996 and 2000 can credibly be attributed to debt relief. The original framework of the HIPC initiative was arranged so that countries would have to show a track record of reform for three years before they could reach a "decision point." At the decision point, a suitable debt-relief package would be arranged if the track record of reform was adequate. After no more than three more years of proven policy implementation, countries would reach the "completion point," at which time debt relief would be provided. Under this framework, only six countries reached their completion points from 1996 to 2000: Bolivia and Uganda in 1998; Guyana and Mozambique in 1999; and Burkina Faso and Mali in 2000. By late 1999, a consensus emerged that the HIPC framework was providing debt relief too slowly.

As a result, the original HIPC initiative was enhanced at the G7 meeting in Cologne during the fall of 1999. Under the enhanced HIPC initiative, countries began receiving debt relief as soon as they reached their decision points. Moreover, the enhanced framework made it easier to reach the decision point and provided more debt relief; 16 additional HIPC countries reached their decision points and began receiving debt relief in 2000.[5] In other words, most HIPC countries started receiving debt relief after 2000, and there are still a number of HIPC countries that have yet to receive debt relief.

Third, the reforms that were required as a precondition for debt relief may be the principal driving factor behind the modest improvement in growth performance. Perhaps the most important contribution of the HIPC initiative has been that it has induced HIPC governments to institute economic reforms. As table 8.7 shows, the growth performance of the HIPC countries improved during the period from 1996 to 2000. Because the HIPCs did not begin receiving debt relief until 2000, it would seem that the improvement in growth performance was mainly because of reforms.

Having said that, even with all the reforms in the late 1990s, GDP per capita has grown by only 1.5%. At that growth rate, it would take a country 46 years to double its standard of living—not exactly a growth miracle. In other words, reforms have helped replace economic contraction with slow growth, but the HIPC countries can only do so much without addressing the principal problem of poor economic infrastructure from which they suffer. As we have argued, aid, not debt relief, is the best way to tackle this problem.

Aid, Not Debt Relief

Even if debt relief will not promote investment and growth in the HIPCs, isn't it a kind gesture to relieve the debts of the world's poorest countries? Kind maybe, but not helpful. If the goal is to improve economic performance and reduce poverty, then aid may provide the most constructive way forward. The emphasis on aid over debt relief begs an obvious question: Is debt relief not a form of aid? The answer is that there are at least two reasons that aid and debt relief are not equivalent. First, debt relief may crowd out existing aid flows. Second, debt relief may have undesirable effects on the composition of existing aid flows. We now discuss each of these points in turn.

Debt Relief May Crowd Out Aid

In an effort to increase net resource transfers to the HIPCs, proponents of the HIPC initiative have been pushing for a reduction in debt servicing. But ironically, the HIPC initiative has actually reduced the net resource transfer to the world's poorest countries. Table 8.8 displays the point. Aid flows to the HIPCs increased continually from 1970 to the mid-1990s. Since 1996, however, aid flows have decreased significantly. As a share of GDP, the decline in aid flows is even starker. In the early 1990s, aid flows as a share of GDP were about 17%. Since 1996, they have only been about 12%. Together, the fall in aid flows and the postponed reduction in debt service have caused a significant decline in net resource transfers to the HIPCs.

Debt Relief May Change the Composition of Aid

Aid flows have declined since the beginning of the HIPC initiative, but this is not the only problem. Debt relief may also result in a shift in the composition of aid—away from multilateral inflows and toward bilateral inflows. To see why debt relief may induce this shift—which we will soon show to be undesirable—consider the net resource transfer identity.

By definition, the NRT is equal to capital inflows minus debt service. As we have shown in table 8.5, there are no significant private capital inflows to the HIPCs. Their capital inflows come principally from official sources in the form of grants: either bilateral or multilateral aid. To a first approximation, then, we can denote the NRT to the HIPCs as

TABLE 8.8 Aid flows to the HIPCs have fallen with the onset of debt relief

	1970–79		1980–89		1990–95		1996–00	
	Millions of U.S. dollars	Percentage of GDP	Millions of U.S. dollars	Percentage of GDP	Millions of U.S. dollars	Percentage of GDP	Millions of U.S. dollars	Percentage of GDP
HIPCs (All)								
Net resource transfers	90	5.8	213	6.2	337	9.3	320	7.1
Aid flows	88	5.7	247	7.2	436	12.0	364	8.0
Debt service	40	2.6	123	3.6	143	3.9	188	4.2
HIPCs (receiving debt relief)								
Net resource transfers	70	6.4	213	8.6	353	12.2	352	10.3
Aid flows	69	6.3	238	9.6	486	16.8	416	12.2
Debt service	36	3.3	94	3.8	124	4.3	146	4.3
Brady countries								
Net resource transfers	505	2.0	−550	−1.1	1,294	1.5	3,719	3.1
Aid flows	83	0.3	198	0.4	407	0.5	288	0.2
Debt service	926	3.7	2,769	5.4	3,022	3.5	7,953	6.5

Sources: The data on net resource transfers and debt service are obtained from the World Bank's Global Development Finance Data Base. The data on aid flows are obtained from the World Bank's World Development Indicators Data Base.

$$NRT = bilateral\ aid\ +\ multilateral\ aid\ -\ debt\ servicing$$

Now assume that, as a share of GDP, the NRT to the HIPC countries is constant. Table 8.8 shows this assumption to be reasonable. The NRT as a share of GDP has not increased substantially since the 1970s. This fact suggests that the developed countries are not prepared to increase their contribution of real resources to the development of the HIPC countries. Assume also that bilateral aid to the HIPCs is constant as a share of GDP. This may also be a realistic assumption because bilateral aid is largely based on the political and strategic considerations of the donor countries and is therefore exogenous to the current debt-relief operations (Alesina and Dollar 2000).

Under our assumptions, a fall in the HIPCs' debt servicing necessarily leads to a fall in multilateral aid. This shift from multilateral to bilateral aid is undesirable. The reason is that multilateral aid is released only when the multilateral agency pays for preapproved services rendered to the country. Bilateral aid, on the other hand, is like free cash flow to the recipient government. Because multilateral aid is generally spent more judiciously than bilateral aid, the alteration in the composition of aid could have important efficiency consequences.

Expressed differently, we are saying the following. Rich governments set aside a certain fraction of their budgets for aid (bilateral and multilateral). The bilateral portion of that aid budget will always be distributed on the basis of political, not efficiency, considerations. But given that the overall amount of aid resources is fixed, writing off the debt means that multilateral aid must fall.

Even if we relax the first assumption and assume instead that rich-country governments are willing to increase the size of the NRT, it is still relevant to ask whether the best way to do so is through more multilateral aid or more debt relief. We think that increased multilateral aid is likely to be more beneficial because the marginal multilateral aid dollar may go directly to building economic infrastructure (as we discuss further). Debt relief, on the other hand, is fungible—there is no guarantee that easing the government's budget constraint by a dollar will lead to an additional dollar of expenditure on infrastructure.

Making Aid Work

Aid critics argue that aid programs to poor countries have often been a failure. They point out that aid programs in general have not led to economic growth in recipient countries in the past (Boone 1995, 1996). More recent studies, however, have qualified this result by showing that aid may be effective under certain circumstances. A precise formulation of how to optimally allocate aid is beyond the scope of this chapter.[6] Nevertheless, we outline three basic principles that may be helpful.

First, aid has been effective when it was conditioned on the economic policies of the recipient country (Burnside and Dollar 2000).[7] Specifically, aid has a positive effect on economic growth if the recipient country has low inflation, a small budget deficit, and a high degree of trade openness. Because aid programs work best when implemented in countries that follow a sound macroeconomic policy, it is crucial that aid should be selective and disbursed only to the countries with a track record of good policies. In fact, one useful aspect of the HIPC initiative has been its emphasis on economic policy reform. The environment that the HIPC initiative is pushing for is the same environment in which aid can be effective. However, even though this makes HIPC countries more promising recipients of aid, as table 8.8 shows, aid flows to the HIPC countries have fallen since the HIPC initiative began.

Second, aid is more effective when managed multilaterally rather than bilaterally. Multilateral aid tends to favor countries that pursue sound economic policy (Burnside and Dollar 2000). As we argued earlier, political and strategic interests tend to drive bilateral aid flows. For instance, bilateral aid goes disproportionately to former colonies and military allies (Alesina and Dollar 2000). Given that more than half of total aid flows to the HIPCs have been bilateral, it is not surprising that past aid flows to these countries have been largely ineffective. Aid will be more effective if the composition of aid to the HIPCs shifts away from bilateral flows toward multilateral flows. Again, as we have argued, debt relief may have exactly the opposite effect.

Third, there should be more focus on the productivity of aid projects. Aid should be targeted toward projects where the social returns are the highest. Here are some salient examples. According to former U.S. Treasury Secretary Paul O'Neill, it would cost $1,000 (U.S.) to build a well for a village of 400 people.[8] Given that there are about 10 million people in Ghana that do not currently have access to clean water, he calculates that an aid budget of only $25 million can solve the whole problem. Another example is the Central Visayas Water and Sanitation project in the Philippines. This is a $30 million project, which will provide 500,000 people with clean water along with related improvements to their health. Another highly effective aid project would be the provision of simple bed nets for protection against malaria. For instance, when bed nets were distributed to the people living in Rufiji, a rural district of Tanzania, infant mortality fell by 28% in a year.[9] Yet, a bed net costs only three dollars. Given that malaria is estimated to reduce GDP growth by 1.3% every year in countries where it has a significant presence (Gallup and Sachs 2000: 85), providing these simple bed nets could produce significant benefits.

Providing access to clean water and protection against malaria are both worthy projects whose returns would more than justify their costs. But there is still a lingering question as to whether these projects can be established in countries where corruption is a major problem. There are three reasons why aid-in-kind might be a good idea in order to deal with corruption. First, corrupt governments are likely to prefer aid-in-cash over aid-in-kind. So, insisting on aid-in-kind may help select governments that are less corrupt. Second, aid-in-kind forces both the donor and the recipient to think harder about what kind of aid is in the best interest of the recipient. Third, fungibility may be less of a problem if aid is given in kind rather than in cash.

With rare exceptions, aid has not been effective. But the problem is not aid per se but the way that it has been disbursed in the past. There is much to learn from past failures that can lead to future successes. If disbursed judiciously—that is, according to the three principles we have outlined—aid can more than pay for itself through gains in economic efficiency. That was the case with the Marshall Plan and many other aid programs to countries such as Korea, Taiwan, and Japan (De Long and Eichengreen 1993).

Improving the efficiency of aid, however, is not sufficient. One of the Millennium Development Goals is to cut in half by the year 2015 the proportion of people living on less than one dollar a day. In order to reach this goal, a United Nations panel headed by the former president of Mexico, Ernesto Zedillo, estimated that the donor countries have to double the amount of aid that they are currently giving (United Nations 2001).

Conclusion

The world's poorest countries are deeply ill. Suggesting that debt is not the primary obstacle to their growth and development seems ironic, perhaps even cruel. But as the late reggae musician Bob Marley once said: "The truth is an offense, not a sin." Because the HIPCs do not suffer from debt overhang, they are not good candidates for debt relief. If the goal is to help poor countries build the economic infrastructure and institutions that best suit their development needs, then aid holds more promise than debt relief.

Acknowledgments Henry thanks the National Science Foundation's CAREER Program, the Stanford Institute of Economic Policy Research, and the Center for Economic Development and Policy Reform for financial support. Both authors thank Jeremy Bulow, Nick Hope, Diana Kirk, Fraser Preston, and Paul Romer for helpful conversations. Rania Eltom provided excellent research assistance.

Notes

1. Specifically, we discuss the circumstances under which debt relief yields ex-post efficiency. The question of whether debt relief is also ex-ante efficient is not explored in this chapter.

2. Forgiveness will not happen without coordination because any individual creditor would prefer to have a free ride and maintain the full value of its claims while others write off some debt. See chapters 11–13 for a discussion of how to overcome the free-rider problem.

3. The cumulative net resource transfer to the average Brady country during the five-year period after the Brady Plan was $13 billion (U.S.). In other words, there was a total net resource transfer of about $210 billion to all of the 16 Brady countries.

4. The index is a composite measure of shareholder rights, creditor rights, efficiency of the judicial system, the rule of law, and a rating of the accounting system.

5. Under the enhanced HIPC initiative, Benin, Cameroon, The Gambia, Guinea, Guinea-Bissau, Honduras, Madagascar, Malawi, Mauritania, Nicaragua, Niger, Rwanda, Sao Tome and Principe, Senegal, Tanzania, and Zambia reached their decision points in

2000. As of January 2003, four more countries have reached their decision points: Chad and Ethiopia in 2001 and Ghana and Sierra Leone in 2002.

6. See Easterly (2002) for a discussion of issues in designing effective aid.

7. Easterly (2003) and Easterly, Levine, and Roodman (2003) challenge this view.

8. Quoted from Paul Blustein, In Uganda, O'Neill and Bono Disagree About Success of Aid, the *Washington Post*, 28 May 2002.

9. *The Economist*. For 80 Cents More. 17 August 2002: 20–22.

References

Alesina, A., and Dollar, D. 2000. Who Gives Foreign Aid to Whom and Why? *Journal of Economic Growth,* Vol. 5, No. 1 (March): 33–64.

Arslanalp, S., and Henry, P. 2005. Is Debt Relief Efficient? *Journal of Finance,* Vol. 60, No. 2: 1021–1055.

Boone, P. 1995. The Impact of Foreign Aid on Savings and Growth. Working Paper. London School of Economics.

———. 1996. Politics and the Effectiveness of Foreign Aid. *European Economic Review,* Vol. 40, No. 2 (February): 289–329.

Bulow, J. 2002. First World Governments and Third World Debt. *Brookings Papers on Economic Activity,* No. 1: 229–55.

Bulow, J., and Rogoff, K. 1990. Cleaning Up Third World Debt Without Getting Taken to the Cleaners. *Journal of Economic Perspectives,* Vol. 4, No. 1 (Winter): 31–42.

Burnside, C., and Dollar, D. 2000. Aid, Policies, and Growth. *American Economic Review,* Vol. 90, No. 4 (September): 847–68.

Cline, W. 1995. *International Debt Reexamined.* Washington, DC: Institute for International Economics.

Darity, W., Jr., and Horn, B. 1988. *The Loan Pushers: The Role of Commercial Banks in the International Debt Crisis.* Cambridge: Ballinger Publications.

De Long, B. and Eichengreen, B. 1993. The Marshall Plan: History's Most Successful Structural Adjustment Program. In *Postwar Economic Reconstruction and Lessons for the East Today,* ed. R. Dornbusch, W. Nolling, and R. Layard, pp. 189–230. Cambridge, MA: MIT Press.

Dornbusch, R. 1993. *Stabilization, Debt and Reform.* New York: Prentice-Hall.

———. 2000. *Keys to Prosperity.* Cambridge, MA: MIT Press.

Easterly, W. 2002. The Cartel of Good Intentions. *Foreign Policy* (July/August): 40–49.

———. 2003. Can Foreign Aid Buy Growth? *Journal of Economics Perspectives,* Vol. 17, No. 3 (Summer): 23–48.

Easterly, W., Levine, R., and Roodman, D. 2004. New Data, New Doubts: A Comment on Burnside and Dollar's Aid, Policies, and Growth (2000). *American Economic Review,* Vol. 94, No. 3: 774–80.

Gallup, J., and Sachs, J. 2001. The Economic Burden of Malaria. *American Journal of Tropical Medicine and Hygiene,* Vol. 64 (1, 2) 5: 85–96.

Hall, R., and Jones, C. 1999. Why Do Some Countries Produce So Much More Output per Worker than Others? *Quarterly Journal of Economics,* Vol. 114, No. 1: 84–116.

Henry, P., and Lorentzen, P. 2003. Domestic Capital Market Reform and Access to Global Financial Markets: Making Markets Work. In *The Future of Domestic Capital Markets in Developing Countries,* ed. R. E. Litan, M. Pomerleano, and V. Sundararajan, pp. 179–214. Washington, DC: Brookings Institution Press.

Kremer, M. 1993. The O-Ring Theory of Economic Development. *Quarterly Journal of Economics,* Vol. 108, No. 3: 551–75.

Krugman, P. 1988. Financing Versus Forgiving a Debt Overhang. *Journal of Development Economics,* Vol. 29 (November): 253–68.

———. 1989. Market-Based Debt Reduction Schemes. In *Analytical Issues in Debt,* ed. J. Frenkel, M. Dooley, and P. Wickham, pp. 258–78. Washington, DC: International Monetary Fund.

LaPorta, R., Lopez-de-Silanes, F., Shleifer, A., and Vishny, R. 1997. Legal Determinants of External Finance. *Journal of Finance,* Vol. 52: 1131–50.

———. 1998. Law and Finance. *Journal of Political Economy,* Vol. 106: 1113–55.

———. 2002. Investor Protection and Corporate Valuation. *Journal of Finance,* Vol. 57: 1147–70.

Myers, S. 1977. Determinants of Corporate Borrowing. *Journal of Financial Economics,* Vol. 5: 147–75.

Sachs, J. 1989. The Debt Overhang of Developing Countries. In *Debt, Stabilization and Development,* ed. G. A. Calvo, R. Findlay, P. Kouri, and J. Braga de Macedo, pp. 80–102. Oxford: Basil Blackwell.

Sachs, J., and Huizinga, H. 1987. U.S. Commercial Banks and the Developing Country Debt Crisis. *Brookings Papers on Economic Activity,* No. 2: 555–606.

Samuelson, Paul A. 1966. Science and Stocks. *Newsweek* (19 September): 92.

Shleifer, A., and Vishny, R. 1997. A Survey of Corporate Governance. *Journal of Finance,* Vol. 52: 737–83.

Shleifer, A., and Wolfenzon, D. 2002. Investor Protection and Equity Markets. *Journal of Financial Economics,* Vol. 66, No. 1: 3–27.

Summers, L. 2000. Moving Forward with Millennial Debt Relief. Remarks at Reception to Celebrate HIPC, House Banking Committee Room, United States Congress, Washington, DC, 1 February 2000. Available online at: www.treas.gov/press/releases/ls363.htm.

United Nations. 2001. Report of the High-Level Panel on Financing for Development. Presented at United Nations Headquarters in New York, 28 June 2001. Available online at: www.un.org/reports/financing/recommendations.htm#cooperation.

Part III

Sovereign Debt: Prospects and Proposals

9

USING INTERNATIONAL FINANCE TO FURTHER CONSERVATION: THE FIRST 15 YEARS OF DEBT-FOR-NATURE SWAPS

William K. Reilly

In the 1980s, the debt burden of developing countries seemed to many of us in conservation a virtually insuperable obstacle to getting these countries to deploy adequate funds to protect their most important flora and fauna. Costa Rica, for example, presented a stark case of a country with a deep cultural attachment to its marvelous natural endowment and a government committed to conservation. Despite its intentions, the government was prevented by its agreement with the International Monetary Fund from adding to its budget for maintenance and protection of several stunning national parks, some under threats of poaching, logging, and encroaching settlement.

To address such needs without either repudiating debts or violating international agreements, World Wildlife Fund (WWF) conceived the idea of buying debt on the secondary market, where it was heavily discounted relative to its face value, and returning the debt to the indebted country in return for specific commitments to use the "new money" for its parks. During my tenure as president of WWF, Costa Rica benefited from several early swaps. From 1988 to 1991, nongovernmental organizations (NGOs) such as WWF and The Nature Conservancy (TNC), with support from private foundations and the government of Sweden, purchased $80 million (U.S.) face value of debt for $12.5 million. The result was a reduction in Costa Rica's foreign hard-currency obligations and $43 million in funding mostly dedicated to staffing, maintenance, and improvement of its parks administered by the National Parks Fund.

At the time we negotiated these deals with Costa Rica's natural resources minister, Alvaro Umaña Quesada, there was no set procedure—no formula for how such a deal would work, who would hold the funds, and who would enforce the deal's provisions. The model of having an NGO receive the money and administer project implementation was one that many subsequent debt-for-nature deals would follow, but it proved too much for some countries, such as Mexico under President Carlos Salinas de Gortari to swallow. Despite both the strong interest on the part of President Salinas in reducing Mexico's debt and his personal support for conservation, which he communicated to me repeatedly, the government's attitude toward its nongovernmental groups was so distrustful that it took several years before the Fundo Mexicano Para La Naturaleza (FMCN) was established as a privately run trust fund for nature protection.

The experience with debt-for-nature swaps is significant both for what these deals have achieved for nature protection and for the new sophistication demonstrated by conservationists in understanding and exploiting financial markets and financial instruments. Indeed, probably no other innovation, with the exception of trading credits for acid rain pollution in the 1990 U.S. Clean Air Act, has demonstrated a more successful reconciliation of economic interests and environmental objectives. That initial promise has blossomed. World Wildlife Fund's Center for Conservation Finance today enjoys ready access to bankers, lawyers, and other specialists in the world of high finance and continues to develop innovative ideas for funding conservation.

Debt-for-nature swaps thus merit attention and understanding. How do they work? What have they achieved? What is their potential?

Consider the peculiar conjunction between biological riches and economic penury that characterizes several countries of the developing world, particularly in the tropics. As anyone who has traveled there knows, tropical nations harbor a wholly disproportionate amount of Earth's flora and fauna, and much of it is under severe stress. One of the sources of this pressure is the need to service debt and ultimately pay it back to sources in developed countries—the World Bank, aid agencies, and commercial banks. The debt is commonly in hard currencies. To earn hard currency, many tropical countries have adopted economic strategies that favor large-scale, near-term extraction of natural resources. These strategies include intensive logging, mining, oil and gas development, and conversion of natural habitat for large plantations of a single food or wood commodity for export, whether this be replacing cleared rainforests with palm oil plantations or eliminating coastal mangroves in order to create shrimp ponds. Traveling for WWF, I've encountered this situation far too often. At the same time, even as the pressures from development mount, local endeavors to conserve biological diversity suffer from a severe lack of another key resource: money. A debt-for-nature swap contributes to both priorities—development and conservation.

A debt-for-nature swap in Peru offers an illustration of how this works: "New protection for some of the richest rainforests on Earth, thanks to a new agreement between Peru and the United States." So read the headline of a release announcing this swap. Signed in Washington, D.C., in June 2002, the accord commits the government of Peru to providing funds, in local currency, for conservation activities in that country. As a result, conservation groups will receive new funding for critical work in 10 protected areas covering more than 27.5 million acres of rainforest—an area the size of the state of Virginia in the United

States. The 10 protected areas to receive the new funding are in the heart of the western Amazon and among Peru's most pristine and biologically diverse. Peru has more than 20,000 species of vascular plants and nearly 1,800 species of birds, many of which are found nowhere else.

In this debt-for-nature swap in Peru, WWF and other leading U.S. conservation organizations contributed money to buy back an additional amount of discounted debt that Peru owed the U.S. government. Under the agreement, WWF, TNC, and Conservation International (CI) each committed approximately $370,000 (U.S.) for a total of $1.1 million. The U.S. government allocated $5.5 million to cancel a portion of Peru's debt to the United States. As a result, Peru will save about $14 million in debt payments over 16 years and will provide the local-currency equivalent of approximately $10.6 million toward conservation over 12 years. With in-depth technical expertise and many decades of experience working with Peruvian conservation organizations, these international conservation groups have exercised significant leverage, because of their contributions, in determining where and how the proceeds of the entire debt-swap transaction would be spent.

Peruvian conservationists will use the new funds for a variety of conservation activities, including establishing and maintaining protected reserves, training, research, and support for creating alternative livelihoods for indigenous people who live in the forests. The proceeds of the debt swap will offer a long-term source of dependable funding every year to support the activities of local conservation groups that have few other resources on which to draw.

An Idea Takes Hold

In 1984, WWF invented the concept of debt-for-nature swaps as a way of increasing funds for conservation of species and habitat in developing countries. The idea was based on the earlier model of debt-to-equity swaps. Under this model, private-sector interests would buy up discounted debt (denominated in U.S. dollars or another hard currency) that was owed by developing-country governments and corporations to large international commercial banks in developed countries and then exchange it into shares in privatized companies or local currency, which would be invested in the debtor country. In the case of debt-for-nature swaps, the local currency is used to invest in local conservation efforts.

We quickly learned that the effectiveness and in-country political support for swaps could be increased by actively involving local NGOs and communities as beneficiaries and as co-designers of the conservation programs. This proved to be the case in Costa Rica, Ecuador, and the Philippines, three countries where we negotiated some of the largest debt swaps between 1988 and 1993. Debt-for-nature swaps, we learned, had the added advantage of strengthening the institutions of civil society in countries where conservation initiatives typically had been handed down from government bureaucracies to a passive citizenry.

Some early critics of debt-for-nature swaps mistakenly believed that those deals would place national sovereignty in jeopardy by transferring ownership of land from national governments to foreign organizations. For this reason, one of the countries I thought would be most receptive to the potential, Brazil, initially opposed debt-for-nature swaps. Brazil's current president, Luiz Ignacio "Lula" da Silva, led the opposition at the time as leader of the Workers' Party.

I understand how the fear arose. Bolivia's first debt-for-nature swap, in 1987, was initially presented as a land acquisition and gave the false impression that land title had been transferred to a foreign group. In reality, the Bolivian government had retained control over the areas protected by the swap. In practice, there have been no instances where debt-for-nature swaps have resulted in a transfer of land title to a foreign entity. Although the objective of debt-for-nature swaps has been to secure conservation of areas already designated for protection, there have been relatively few cases where additional land has been set aside for conservation as a result of debt-for-nature swaps.

Critics argued, too, that debt-for-nature swaps violated the sovereignty of indigenous peoples living in places benefiting from the swaps. Local people, as I understand the Bolivian negotiations, had not been adequately consulted in the negotiations with respect to forestry concessions granted to logging companies and other access issues. The subsequent swaps we negotiated in the Philippines, Madagascar, and other places sought to address this point. We, along with other sponsors, learned from the Bolivian example the importance of ensuring that the proceeds benefited indigenous peoples directly through education and training.

To date, commercial debt-for-nature swaps, which involve privately held debt, have resulted in the cancelation of more than $150 million (U.S.), face value, of foreign commercial debt. This debt has been acquired at a total cost of $43 million—that is, for just over 28% of its face value—and has generated the equivalent of more than $100 million in new funds for conservation.

World Wildlife Fund's Center for Conservation Finance has carried out original research compiling data on all of the examples of commercial debt-for-nature swaps between 1987 and 2000, which are found in Table 9.1.

How Debt-for-Nature Swaps Work

A debt-for-nature swap involves the purchase of unpaid debt obligations of a developing country, conversion of that debt into local currency, and use of the proceeds to fund conservation activities (see Figure 9.1). The key to the transaction lies in the willingness of creditors—either international commercial banks (in the case of commercial debt-for-nature swaps) or the governments of developed countries (in the case of bilateral debt-reduction agreements)—to sell or cancel loans made to the government of a developing country for less than the full face value of the original loan. Why, you might wonder, would any creditor holding a promissory note for, say, $1 million, be willing to dispose of it for half that amount or less? The answer lies in a creditor's recognition that a developing country may never be able to fully repay its debts. As a result,

TABLE 9.1   Commercial debt-for-nature swaps, 1987–2000

Country	Date	Purchaser	Face value of debt (U.S. dollars)	Purchase price (U.S. dollars)	Conservation funds[a] (U.S. dollars)
Bolivia	Jul 87	CI	650,000	100,000	250,000
Bolivia	May 93	TNC, WWF	11,465,795	0	2,816,400
Bolivia total			12,115,795	100,000	3,066,400
Brazil	Jun 92	TNC	2,192,000	746,000	2,192,000
Brazil Total			2,192,000	746,000	2,192,000
Costa Rica	Feb 88	National Parks Foundation	5,400,000	918,000	4,050,000
Costa Rica	Jul 88	Netherlands	33,000,000	5,000,000	9,900,000
Costa Rica	Jan 89	TNC	5,600,000	784,000	1,680,000
Costa Rica	Apr 89	Sweden	24,500,000	3,500,000	17,150,000
Costa Rica	Mar 90	Sweden, TNC, WWF	10,800,000	1,900,000	9,600,000
Costa Rica	Feb 91	TNC/Rainforest Alliance	600,000	360,000	540,000
Costa Rica total			79,900,000	12,462,000	42,920,000
Dom. Rep.	Mar 90	TNC, PRCT	582,000	116,000	582,000
Dom. Rep. total			582,000	116,000	582,000
Ecuador	Dec 87	WWF	1,000,000	354,000	1,000,000
Ecuador	Mar 89	TNC, Missouri Botanical Garden	3,600,000	424,080	3,600,000
Ecuador	Apr 89	WWF	5,389,473	640,000	5,389,473
Ecuador total			9,989,473	1,418,080	9,989,473
Ghana	Jul 92	CI, SI, MUCIA, ICMS	1,000,000	250,000	1,000,000
Ghana	Jun 00	CI	120,000	104,000	120,000
Ghana total			1,120,000	354,000	1,120,000
Guatemala	Oct 91	TNC	100,000	75,000	90,000
Guatemala	May 92	CI	1,300,000	1,200,000	1,300,000
Guatemala total			1,400,000	1,275,000	1,390,000
Jamaica	Oct 91	TNC, PRCT	437,956	300,000	437,958
Jamaica total			437,956	300,000	437,958
Madagascar	Jul 89	WWF	2,111,112	950,000	2,111,112
Madagascar	Aug 90	WWF	919,364	445,891	919,364
Madagascar	Jan 91	CI	119,000	59,000	119,000
Madagascar	Oct 93	CI	3,200,000	1,500,000	3,200,000
Madagascar	Oct 93	WWF	1,867,500	909,412	1,867,500
Madagascar	Apr 94	WWF	1,340,469	0	1,072,376
Madagascar	May 94	CI	200,000	50,000	160,000
Madagascar	Feb 96	WWF	2,000,000	N/A	1,500,000
Madagascar total			11,757,445	3,914,303	10,949,352
Mexico	Apr 91	CI	250,000	183,000	250,000
Mexico	Aug 91	CI	250,000	0	250,000
Mexico	Jan 92	CI	441,000	355,000	441,000
Mexico	Jun 93	CI	252,000	208,000	252,000
Mexico	Jun 94	CI	280,000	236,000	280,000

(continued)

TABLE 9.1   (Continued)

Country	Date	Purchaser	Face value of debt (U.S. dollars)	Purchase price (U.S. dollars)	Conservation funds[a] (U.S. dollars)
Mexico	Jun 94	CI	480,000	399,390	480,000
Mexico	Nov 94	CI	290,000	248,395	290,000
Mexico	Dec 95	CI	488,000	246,000	336,500
Mexico	Jan 96	CI	391,000	191,607	254,000
Mexico	Jul 96	CI	495,674	327,393	442,622
Mexico	Nov 96	CI	670,889	440,360	560,752
Mexico	May 97	CI	265,714	186,000	243,494
Mexico	Jul 97	CI	310,000	237,661	299,499
Mexico	Jun 98	CI	311,000	249,000	311,000
Mexico total			5,175,277	3,507,806	4,690,867
Nigeria	Jul 91	Nigerian Conservation Foundation	149,000	65,000	93,000
Nigeria total			149,000	65,000	93,000
Paraguay	1991	TNC	9,000,000	2,000,000	5,000,000
Paraguay total			9,000,000	2,000,000	5,000,000
Philippines	Jun 88	WWF	390,000	195,975	390,000
Philippines	Mar 90	WWF	900,000	438,750	900,000
Philippines	Feb 92	WWF	9,646,606	5,000,000	8,815,946
Philippines	Aug 93	WWF	19,000,000	12,973,854	17,100,000
Philippines total			29,936,606	18,608,579	27,205,946
Poland	Jan 90	WWF	50,000	11,500	50,000
Poland total			50,000	11,500	50,000
Zambia	Aug 89	WWF	2,271,112	454,222	2,044,001
Zambia	Jul 94	IUCN	985,986	108,458	162,687
Zambia total			3,257,098	562,680	2,206,688
Grand total			167,062,650	45,440,948	111,893,684

[a]Conservation funds is the amount of money generated to support conservation programs as a result of the swap, usually paid in the form of local currency or local currency bonds.

CI = Conservation International.

IUCN = International Union for Nature and Natural Resources/World Conservation Union.

MUCIA = Midwest Universities Consortium for International Activities, Inc.

PRCT = Puerto Rico Conservation Trust.

SI = Smithsonian Institution.

TNC = The Nature Conservancy.

WWF = World Wildlife Fund/World Wide Fund for Nature.

Sources: WWF, Conservation International, Finance for Development, World Bank Global Development Finance.

creditors may do better by selling the debt at a discount today rather than waiting for the uncertain prospect of repayment sometime in the distant future.

Debt-for-nature swaps initially attracted attention, I believe, because they were the first example of conservation organizations mastering techniques of international finance. Yet, the debt swap itself is a means rather than an end. The ultimate success of a debt-for-nature swap depends on designing an effective

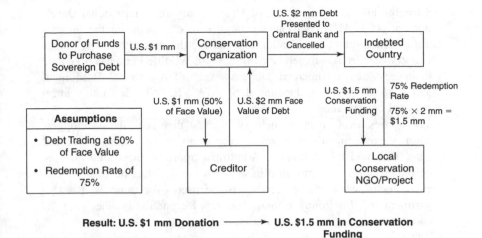

Figure 9.1. How a debt-for-nature swap works.

conservation program and strengthening the capacity of local organizations or communities to implement the program over the long term.

One of the most important achievements of debt-for-nature swaps has been their ability to provide long-term financing for conservation activities. Too often, conservation projects, which by their nature require years of sustained effort in order to yield results, have been crippled by continual uncertainty about whether funding would be available for more than one or two years into the future. Swaps often provide a long-term source of funding that is more certain than government park budgets because the payment of the proceeds of a swap may stretch out over 10 years or more.

Steps in a Commercial Debt-for-Nature Swap

No two commercial debt-for-nature swaps are the same. Yet, they generally follow a pattern. First, an indebted country needs to establish general guidelines for a commercial debt-for-nature program and then invite participation from conservation organizations. These guidelines often are modeled after existing debt-to-equity swap programs and may include:

- An international conservation organization and a developing country's private and public organizations dealing with nature conservation need to reach agreement on the conservation objectives and programs that will be funded by proceeds from a swap, ensuring that they are consistent with the priorities of the developing country.
- The international conservation organization then needs to secure sufficient funding to purchase the debt either from its own budget or by securing additional donations especially for this purpose. In some cases,

a foreign aid agency (such as the U.S. Agency for International Development (U.S. AID) contributes a large sum of money for the international conservation organization to purchase the discounted developing-country debt from commercial banks. World Wildlife Fund has been able to interest such commercial banks as Bank of America, J. P. Morgan, and Bank of Tokyo in donating debt to WWF, TNC, or another international conservation organization.

- The parties involved in the debt swap must then seek the developing-country government's approval for the swap, usually from its central bank and ministry of finance. Additional approvals are often also required from the government ministry that has jurisdiction over the relevant sector where the proceeds will be used—for example, the Department of Environment and Natural Resources in the case of conservation programs in the Philippines.
- The specific financial terms of the swap need to be negotiated. These include the rate to be used for exchanging the foreign-currency debt into local currency, the redemption rate (that is, the percentage of the original debt and interest that will be repaid by the developing country), and the local investment instrument (for example, inflation-indexed government bonds of the developing country). The combination of these variables will determine the financial attractiveness of the swap. Brazil, which had an active debt-to-equity program through 1990, never established attractive terms for debt-for-nature swaps and thus saw only one completed, a great disappointment given the country's extraordinary biological riches and its heavy indebtedness.
- Once all of the terms are agreed upon, the debt is acquired.
- The debt is presented to the indebted country's central bank, which cancels the debt and provides funds in local currency either in the form of cash or bonds.
- Finally, the agreed-upon conservation projects are implemented over the life of the program.

In order to avoid inflation and limit the budgetary impact of debt swaps, most debtor governments set limits on the amount of debt eligible for conversion during a given period. In addition, many debt-for-nature swaps have relied on bonds to spread payments over time to reduce the potential inflationary impact of swaps on the monetary supply. I believe the record now shows that debt-for-nature swaps have had a negligible impact on inflation in developing countries, partly as a result of good design and partly because the transactions have been small relative to the size of the economies affected. The organizations that benefited have also been concerned about inflation because of the risk of depreciation in the value of the local currency received from swaps. As debt-for-nature swaps have evolved, WWF and others have learned to pay greater attention to devising financial terms that are attractive for all parties to the transactions.

Bilateral Swaps: Conversion of Sovereign Government Debt

The first generation of debt-for-nature swaps involved commercial debt, and the swaps were initiated by NGOs. This successful experience led to debt swaps involving the conversion of government-to-government debt to fund conservation and other social sectors. The Peru debt-for-nature swap is a good example of a fairly recent bilateral swap.

In the United States, the financial mechanism of swapping debt in exchange for nature protection is now authorized by the Tropical Forest Conservation Act of 1998 (TFCA), which is modeled on an earlier program created during the first President Bush's administration called the Enterprise for the Americas Initiative (EAI). In a meeting with President-elect George H. W. Bush in December 1988, I recounted my experience negotiating a debt-for-nature swap in Costa Rica and proposed he commit the U.S. government to do on a large scale what WWF and conservation groups had demonstrated successfully: cancel hard-currency obligations owed the U.S. government in return for conservation commitments. Frequently, in 1989, he reminded me of his strong support for debt-for-nature swaps, and his administration incorporated the concept in the EAI. The innovation thus took off as the U.S. government became a committed player.

The EAI, which was enacted into law by the U.S. Congress in 1991, involved the partial forgiveness of debts owed by seven Latin American countries that were taking steps to open up their economies and promote democracy. The U.S. government forgave nearly 54% of the original $1.6 billion debt owed by these seven governments, or about $860 million. Much of the debt had been used to finance purchases of U.S. agricultural products under PL-480, the food-for-peace program. In return, each of these governments agreed to establish a local EAI fund and to pay annually into this fund an amount of local currency equivalent to a percentage of the yearly interest that otherwise would have been due the United States on the debt.

As a result of EAI, more than $150 million in funding has been generated for conservation and child-survival programs over a 10-year period. Although this amount represents but a small portion of outstanding developing-country debt, significant gains in conservation and social programs have resulted. These debt swaps have also influenced the way that conservation organizations, donors, and governments in developed and developing countries alike approach the topic of financing conservation, an enormously important result.

Based on the EAI's success, the U.S. government launched a broader bilateral debt–reduction-for-nature program under the 1998 Tropical Forest Conservation Act. This act authorized the establishment of tropical forest conservation funds in developing countries that have globally significant tropical forests and can meet other criteria such as having democratically elected governments and market-based economies. Although it was initially expected that hundreds of millions of dollars would be appropriated to fund this program, only $13 million (U.S.) a year was appropriated during FY 2000 and FY 2001, and only $11 million in FY 2002.

The International Experience with Debt Swaps

As table 9.2 shows, the United States is not the only developed country to have launched a bilateral debt-reduction program for conservation and sustainable development. In 1990, Switzerland established the 700 million Swiss franc Debt Reduction Facility (equivalent to approximately U.S. $400 million) to commemorate the 700th anniversary of the Swiss Confederation. Under Switzerland's bilateral debt-reduction program, environmental conservation is one of several social objectives for which the local currency saved as a result of debt swaps may be used (see figure 9.2).

The largest single bilateral debt-for-environment swap to date resulted from Poland's 1991 Paris Club debt-restructuring agreement. This led to the creation, in 1992, of an independent environmental fund called EcoFund, which finances private-sector investment projects in four target categories: reducing transboundary air pollution, reducing pollution in the Baltic Sea, lowering greenhouse gas emissions, and protecting Poland's biological diversity. Poland's 1991 Paris Club agreement canceled half of Poland's Paris Club debt. In exchange for cancelation of an additional 10% of each participating creditor's claims, Poland agreed to finance the EcoFund with an equivalent amount of hard-currency funding drawn down from an escrow account at the Bank for International Settlements. This is generating funds of $545 million (U.S.) for carrying out environmental projects between 1992 and 2010, with the cancelation of Polish debt to the United States accounting for just under three-quarters of the total and the rest consisting mostly of Polish debt owed to France, Italy, Norway, Sweden, and Switzerland.

Beyond Debt-for-Nature Swaps

In the long term, the success of a debt-for-nature swap depends less on the amount of money generated than on the success of the conservation programs and institutions the swap supports. With this in mind, leaders of the Philippine nongovernmental community, the Philippine government, WWF, and U.S. AID began planning in 1990 for a large swap to endow a major new institution for the conservation of the Philippines' unique biological diversity, the Foundation for the Philippine Environment (FPE). Its Board of Trustees is composed of representatives from Philippine development and conservation organizations, government representatives, the business community, academia, and one international NGO (initially WWF, later the World Resources Institute) (see figure 9.3). The intent here was not to finance a specific set of conservation projects already agreed to, as earlier debt-for-nature swaps by WWF in the Philippines had done. Rather, the aim was to provide FPE with an endowment whose earnings it could use to finance conservation efforts for decades to come, thus enabling FPE to establish its own long-term priorities free from the necessity of raising new outside money each year. As the result of two large swaps—$9.8 million (U.S.) in 1992 and $19 million in 1993—FPE's endowment grew to approximately $26 million, making it the largest-capitalized environmental NGO

TABLE 9.2 Bilateral debt-for-environment conversions by creditor government (values in US$)

Country	Date	Face value debt treated	Environmental funds paid
Creditor country: Canada			
Colombia	1993	12,800,000	12,800,000
Costa Rica	1995	16,600,000	8,300,000
El Salvador	1993	7,100,000	7,100,000
Honduras	1993	24,900,000	12,450,000
Nicaragua	1993	13,600,000	2,700,000
Peru	1994	16,210,000	354,919
Canada total		91,210,000	43,704,919
Creditor country: Finland			
Poland	1990	17,000,000	17,000,000
Peru	1996	24,620,000	3,679,020
Finland total		41,620,000	20,679,020
Creditor country: France			
Poland	1993	66,000,000	66,000,000
France total		66,000,000	66,000,000
Creditor country: Germany			
Bolivia	1997	3,700,000	1,150,000
Bolivia	2000	15,800,000	3,200,000
Ecuador	2002	9,500,000	3,081,400
Ecuador	2002	10,200,000	3,235,770
Honduras	1999	1,068,442	534,221
Jordan	1995	13,400,000	6,700,000
Jordan	1995	22,700,000	11,300,000
Jordan	2000	43,600,000	21,800,000
Jordan	2001	11,300,000	5,700,000
Madagascar	2003	25,092,262	14,843,007
Peru	1995	20,150,000	6,089,810
Peru	1999	5,140,000	2,060,000
Peru	1999	5,140,000	2,060,000
Philippines	1996	5,800,000	1,800,000
Syria	2001	31,700,000	15,900,000
Vietnam	1996	18,200,000	5,400,000
Vietnam	1999	16,400,000	5,000,000
Vietnam	2001	7,000,000	N/A
Germany total		265,890,704	109,854,208
Creditor country: Italy			
Poland	1998	32,000,000	32,000,000
Italy total		32,000,000	32,000,000
Creditor Country: The Netherlands			
Costa Rica	1996	14,100,000	14,100,000
The Netherlands total		14,100,000	14,100,000
Creditor Country: Norway			
Poland	2000	27,000,000	27,000,000
Norway total		27,000,000	27,000,000

(continued)

TABLE 9.2 (*Continued*)

Country	Date	Face value debt treated	Environmental funds paid
Creditor country: Spain			
Costa Rica	1999	5,222,302	2,180,594
Spain total		5,222,302	2,180,594
Creditor country: Sweden			
Poland	1997, 1999	13,000,000	13,000,000
Tunisia	1992	1,342,000	1,342,000
Tunisia	1993	477,300	477,300
Sweden total		14,819,300	14,819,300
Creditor country: Switzerland			
Bolivia	1993	35,400,000	1,365,000
Bulgaria	1995	16,200,000	16,200,000
Ecuador	1994	46,300,000	4,524,000
Egypt	1995	121,000,000	18,000,000
Guinea-Bissau	1995	8,400,000	400,000
Honduras	1993 & 1997	42,030,000	8,430,000
Peru	1993	131,000,000	32,700,000
Poland	1993	63,000,000	63,000,000
Tanzania	1993	25,600,000	190,000
Switzerland total		488,930,000	144,809,000
Creditor country: USA			
Argentina	1993	38,100,000	3,100,000
Bangladesh	2000	31,301,857	8,500,000
Belize	2001	8,584,692	9,289,560
Bolivia	1991	38,400,000	21,800,000
Chile	1991	39,000,000	1,400,000
Chile	1992	147,000,000	17,300,000
Colombia	1992	310,000,000	41,600,000
El Salvador	1992	335,000,000	25,600,000
El Salvador	1992	279,000,000	15,600,000
El Salvador	2001	38,400,000	14,000,000
Jamaica	1991	271,000,000	9,200,000
Jamaica	1993	134,400,000	12,300,000
Madagascar	1996	27,000,000	12,000,000
Peru	1997	350,000,000	22,844,235
Peru	2002	28,315,096	10,604,003
Philippines	2002	41,380,000	8,224,143
Poland	1991	370,000,000	370,000,000
Uruguay	1992	1,000,000	93,400
Uruguay	1992	33,400,000	6,100,000
USA total		2,521,281,645	609,555,341
Grand total		3,568,073,951	1,084,702,382

Source: WWF Center for Conservation Finance. For a detailed list of swaps and original sources, see www.worldwildlife.org/conservationfinance.

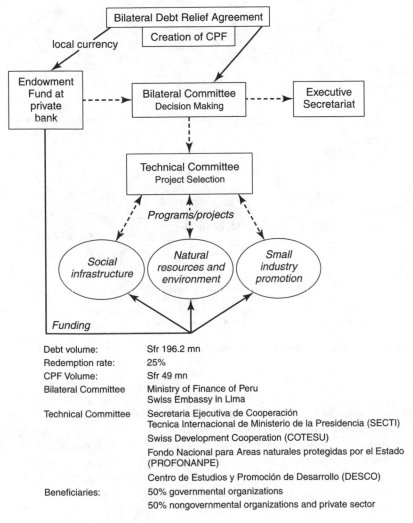

Figure 9.2. Swiss counterpart fund structure, Peru. Source: The Swiss Debt Reduction Facility.

in a tropical country at that time. Since then, at least 50 conservation trust funds have come into existence, including Mexico's FMCN and the Bhutan Trust Fund for Environmental Conservation. In Mexico's case, the initial reluctance President Salinas expressed to me was finally overcome as experience with debt swaps grew and negotiators devised safeguards the government considered appropriate.

The Foundation for the Philippine Environment provides the requisites for long-term financing and decision making to help conservation priorities survive

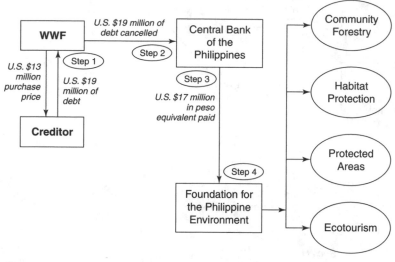

Steps
1. WWF pruchased U.S. $19 million face value of debt from creditor for U.S. $13 million.
2. WWF transferred U.S. $19 million debt to the Central Bank of the Philippines for cancellation.
3. Central Bank paid equivalent of U.S. $17 million in pesos and peso note to Foundation for the Philippine Environment.
4. FPE created endowment fund and disbursed grants for nature conservation.

Figure 9.3. Debt-for-nature swap for the Foundation for the Philippine Environment.

inevitable political and budgetary fluctuations. It has continued for over 10 years to finance a wide variety of conservation and development projects throughout the Philippines. These include programs for training local community leaders in natural-resource management, projects to conserve endangered species—the Philippine eagle comes to mind—through habitat conservation plans, and propagation of indigenous tree species that are suitable for agroforestry.

Participating nongovernmental groups have gained unprecedented opportunities to work with government departments, which, in turn, have taken advantage of greater opportunities to help set national conservation priorities and to apply the field experience of NGOs in carrying out programs. The interaction among these parties, including local residents and community organizations, has helped build a more broad-based conservation movement.

Debt swaps furthermore have proved to be an impetus for the growth and development of conservation groups and, importantly, for their ability to manage large financial transactions. The swaps also have brought into conservation activities other institutions, both public and private, that were previously uninvolved. Dr. Celso Roque, former Undersecretary of the Environment in the Philippines and former president of WWF-Philippines, once stated, "The debt-for-nature swap program is a tough act to follow. In the Philippines, it has made NGOs stronger and financially conscious and fostered the greening of financial institutions. It served as the catalyst for larger conservation programs from bilateral and multilateral donors. It encouraged productive partnerships between government, local NGOs, and international NGOs."[1] More recently, Philippine NGOs and WWF were instrumental in assisting the Philippine and U.S. governments in designing the new Tropical Forest Fund, which will be created as a result of a TFCA swap for the Philippines.

Where Do We Go from Here?

As the experience in the Philippines suggests, debt swaps have been the starting point for WWF and others to develop urgently needed new approaches for long-term financing of conservation. They also have benefited other social sectors. Debt-for-nature swaps have made important contributions to conservation directly, in countries such as the Philippines and Ecuador where they have generated substantial funding for conservation and helped foster new institutions, and indirectly, where they have provided lessons in establishing conservation trust funds and in undertaking other institutional reforms to encourage participation by diverse stakeholders, from finance ministers to grassroots community organizers. Debt-for-nature swaps and conservation trust funds represent long-term institutional responses to conservation challenges and an important departure from quick-fix remedies.

It is encouraging to see new proposals building on the debt-swap concept. In 2002, Congressman Mark Kirk of Illinois, for example, introduced a bill in the U.S. Congress called the Coral Reef and Coastal Marine Conservation Act. This act would allow tropical countries to apply repayment of interest and principal on their bilateral debt owed to the U.S. government to projects that promote the conservation of tropical reefs. The impressive biological diversity of coral reefs has led some people to call them the "tropical forests of the sea." Although coral reefs occupy less than 0.25% of the world's oceans, they contribute about one-fourth of the world's total fish catch, feeding as many as one billion people in Asia alone. Left unchecked, the destruction of coral reefs may have disastrous consequences for many poor nations in the tropics. If passed, this bill would apply the same principles that have made debt swaps effective for tropical forest conservation to protecting highly threatened coral reefs. Initiatives such as this can continue to play a catalytic role in slowing the downward spiral of environmental degradation and desperate poverty in some of the world's most unstable, albeit biologically rich, places. Elsewhere, in Jordan and Vietnam, we've seen that Germany negotiated debt swaps that addressed water and sanitation, indicating even broader potential for the concept in tackling a range of environmental needs.

Yet debt swaps and conservation trust funds have limitations because they are largely dependent on donor grants. In the case of debt swaps, the financial multiplier effect is what first generated donor interest. But beginning in the late 1990s, several factors have eroded the potential for multipliers and generally decreased opportunities for debt swaps. Some countries, such as Mexico and the Philippines, went through "Brady bond" restructuring of their external debt.

Under restructuring, the premium associated with debt conversions decreased substantially as the country's own debt situation improved. This was particularly true in the Philippines, where not only did debt prices increase (from 40% of face value in 1988 to around 70% in 1993 because of successful Brady bond restructuring) but also the redemption price offered by the government decreased sharply from 100% to a level about 10% above the debt price determined in a competitive auction. This meant that instead of debt-for-nature swaps being able to leverage donor funds by a factor of 2, they would merely leverage an additional 10–20% over a straight hard-currency donation, which barely justifies the significant time and effort that a complex debt-for-nature swap requires.

In other countries, opportunities for debt-for-nature swaps have been limited by the lack of local private conservation or development organizations with the capacity to administer the swap proceeds effectively.

Bilateral, or government-to-government, debt swaps surged in the early 1990s, with the proceeds usually being managed by boards of directors of local NGOs. These kinds of swaps also face constraints, however, because they ultimately rely on the foreign assistance budgets of developed countries at a time when foreign aid overall has been contracting and developing countries' own budgets are spread across numerous competing priorities. The Enterprise for the Americas Initiative illustrates the point. Although recognized as a successful form of hemispheric cooperation between the United States and several Latin American countries, the total annual budget appropriated by the U.S. Congress for debt-for-nature programs has dropped sharply since the early 1990s. This corresponds to the general decline in U.S. and other developed-country foreign aid since then. In Monterrey in March 2002, however, President George W. Bush pledged to reverse the decline in U.S. development assistance funding, committing new resources over the next several years. Yet the Bush administration requested that the U.S. Congress appropriate only $20 million for TFCA in FY2004. Given the continued relatively low level of funding for TFCA, it remains to be seen to what extent government-to-government debt swaps will play a role in newly reinvigorated U.S. development aid programs.

There are heartening signs elsewhere. Some European countries, for their part, are now taking a second look at debt-for-nature swaps. The government of the United Kingdom signed a Memorandum of Understanding with Indonesian President Megawati Sukarnoputri at the World Summit on Sustainable Development in Johannesburg in September 2002, providing authorization to negotiate up to 100 million British pounds (more than $150 million) for debt swaps in Indonesia. Britain's Export Credit Guarantee Department (ECGD) now applies strict environmental criteria in evaluating debt-swap transactions. The government of Germany also has negotiated debt-for-nature swaps in several countries, as noted, including a swap with Madagascar in support of that country's national parks. This July 2002 agreement was the first international accord signed by the new government in Madagascar. In April 2003, the two governments agreed that the swap proceeds would be used to endow the new Madagascar Foundation for Protected Areas and Biodiversity. Here, too, we will have to see whether these swaps will set a new trend in debt-for-nature transactions.

Conclusion

With the decline in debt-for-nature swap activity since its early years, it is reasonable to ask whether these swaps are still an attractive and viable option for debtor countries. Some critics have contended that debt swaps have failed because their contribution to debt reduction has been negligible in effect (amounting to approximately $1 billion for all countries, but half of this amount went to a single large debt swap in Poland). However, experience over the years has shown that debt-for-nature swaps, rather than offering a comprehensive solution to a country's debt problem, have proven most effective when they have been developed as a tool to accomplish specific environmental objectives. Unlike the heavily indebted poor countries (HIPC) initiative, which provides a comprehensive framework for debt relief on a global scale, debt-for-nature swaps have typically had much narrower objectives.

The HIPC initiative has resulted in outright cancelation of much of the bilateral debt owed by the world's poorest countries (most of which are in Africa), and this has removed the rationale for undertaking debt-for-nature swaps in those places. However, some developing countries—Madagascar and Mozambique, for example—have included the environment as one key sector in their "poverty reduction strategies" under the HIPC initiative. This means that the debt-relief savings generated as a result of HIPC debt reduction can be used for environmental protection projects as well as for more traditional types of "poverty alleviation" projects, which typically involve funding for education and health. Countries where commercial or bilateral debt-for-nature swaps could still play a role in the future are Argentina, Bolivia, Colombia, Ecuador, Indonesia, Jamaica, Nicaragua, Panama, and Paraguay.

In the summer of 1989, Chancellor Helmut Kohl of Germany, an early proponent of debt-for-nature swaps, agreed with President Daniel Arap Moi of Kenya to forgive outright a significant amount of government debt owed Germany by Kenya. At a meeting in the fall of 1989, I asked Chancellor Kohl why, given Kenya's magnificent but underfunded network of parks, he had not obtained a commitment to use some of the debt forgiven for these conservation purposes. The chancellor said he had tried but that President Moi wanted outright forgiveness. This points to yet another crucial contribution of debt-for-nature deals: They can cause developing countries to enhance the priority for nature conservation and to do things they would not otherwise consider. But often creditor nations must exert the proper pressure to obtain a conservation quid pro quo, for debtor nations naturally prefer complete forgiveness to conditional relief of loan obligations.

The Kenya example was disappointing. Yet, despite the complexity of debt swaps and despite the criticisms, directed particularly at the earliest examples, I remain a strong supporter. Hundreds of millions of dollars have been earmarked for conservation: for forests, for wildlife, and for protecting important biological resources. Local groups have benefited, strengthening their capability to take on increasingly challenging conservation priorities. There was little prospect, if any, for applying this level of resources to conservation in most of the places cited—

Ecuador, Madagascar, the Philippines, and elsewhere. In other words, the experience to date strikes me as nothing short of remarkable, resulting in some important accomplishments using imaginative and as yet not fully exploited approaches. Debt swaps are a responsible alternative to outright debt forgiveness. Finally, they have spawned a new generation of conservation finance tools, some of which are still taking shape. In an era in which resources for conservation are far from adequate, debt-for-nature swaps should be fully embraced.

Acknowledgments Special thanks go to Bruce Bunting and Melissa Moye, of WWF's Center for Conservation Finance, and Barry Spergel, for their help in preparing this chapter.

Notes

1. Celso Roque made this comment in person to Dr. Bruce W. Bunting, Vice President, World Wildlife Fund, 18 January 2000, in connection with a meeting at the global environment facility in Washington, DC.

10

ODIOUS DEBT

Seema Jayachandran
Michael Kremer

The campaign for sovereign debt relief is based on two ideas. First, certain countries are too poor to repay their loans. Second, some debts were illegitimate in the first place, and thus the country should not be responsible for repaying them. The first rationale for debt relief has been examined extensively by economists.[1] Several countries have been granted debt relief under the heavily indebted poor countries (HIPC) initiative, which considers the level of debt and the income of the country as the criteria for debt relief, but not the circumstances under which the debt was incurred. Thus, countries that are not as impoverished but have a plausible claim that their debts are illegitimate are not on the current list of debt-relief candidates.

The second rationale, which has received much less attention, is our focus. We lay out a mechanism that limits the ability of dictators to borrow internationally, loot the borrowed funds, or use them to finance the repression of their people and then saddle the people with the debt. Our starting point is the belief that debt incurred by a dictator for personal and nefarious purposes should be considered illegitimate and that the country's citizens should not be considered responsible for repaying this debt. Individuals do not have to repay money that others fraudulently borrow in their name, in the same way that a corporation is not liable for contracts that the chief executive officer or another agent enters into without the authority to bind the firm. If there were an analogous norm regarding fraudulent sovereign debt, banks would not issue loans to repressive or looting governments in the first place.

The United States argued along these lines during the 1898 peace negotiations after the Spanish-American War, contending that neither the United States nor Cuba should be responsible for debt the colonial rulers had incurred without the consent of the Cubans and not for the Cubans' benefit. Spain never accepted the validity of this argument, but the United States implicitly prevailed, and Spain took responsibility for the Cuban debt under the Paris peace treaty. This episode inspired legal scholars to elaborate a legal doctrine of "odious debt" (Sack 1927; Feilchenfeld 1931). They argued that sovereign debt is odious and should not be transferable to a successor government if it (1) was incurred without the consent of the people and (2) did not benefit the people. Because both conditions must hold for debt to be considered odious under this definition, debts of a regime that loots but rules democratically or of a nondemocratic regime that spends in the interests of the people would not be considered odious. Some scholars also added the requirement that creditors be aware of these conditions in advance (Sack 1927).

However, this doctrine has gained little momentum within the international law community, and countries are held responsible for repaying illegitimate debt under the international system's current norm. South Africa is a case in point. The apartheid regime in South Africa borrowed from private banks through the 1980s, while a large percentage of its budget went to finance the military and police and otherwise repress the African majority. The South African people now bear the debts of their repressors. Whereas the Archbishop of Cape Town has campaigned for apartheid-era debt to "be declared odious and written off," and South Africa's Truth and Reconciliation Commission has voiced a similar opinion, the post-apartheid government has deferred to the current international norm and accepted responsibility for the debt. South Africa seems to fear that defaulting would hurt its chances of attracting foreign investment and wants to be seen as playing by the rules of capitalism. Its top ministers have denounced a lawsuit seeking reparations from banks that loaned to the apartheid regime because "we are talking to those very same companies named in the lawsuits about investing in post-apartheid South Africa."[2]

Similarly, although Anastasio Somoza was reported to have looted $100 million to $500 million (U.S.) from Nicaragua by the time he was overthrown in 1979, and the Sandinista leader Daniel Ortega told the United Nations General Assembly that his government would repudiate Somoza's debt, the Sandinistas reconsidered when their allies in Cuba advised them that repudiating the debt would unwisely alienate them from Western capitalist countries.[3]

There are a number of other cases in which dictators have borrowed from abroad, expropriated the funds for personal use, and left the debts to the population they ruled. For example, under Mobutu Sese Seko, the former Zaire (now Congo) accumulated over $12 billion (U.S.) in sovereign debt while Mobutu diverted public funds to his personal accounts (his assets reached $4 billion in the mid-1980s) and used them in his efforts to retain power (e.g., payments to cronies, military expenses).[4] Similarly, when Ferdinand Marcos lost power in 1986, the Philippines owed $28 billion to foreign creditors, and Marcos's personal wealth was estimated at $10 billion (Adams 1991; World Bank 2003).[5]

Policies to Curtail Odious Debt

We argue for empowering an independent institution to assess whether regimes are legitimate and declare any sovereign debt subsequently incurred by illegitimate regimes odious and thus not the obligation of successor governments. This could restrict dictators' ability to loot, limit the debt burden of poor countries, reduce risk for banks, and hence lower interest rates for legitimate governments that borrow.

Currently, countries repay debt even if it is odious because if they failed to do so, their assets abroad might be seized and their reputations would be tarnished, making it more difficult for them to borrow again or attract foreign investment.[6] However, if there were an institution that assessed whether regimes are odious and announced its findings, this could create a new equilibrium in which countries' reputations would not be hurt by a refusal to repay illegitimate debts, just as individuals' credit ratings are not hurt by their refusal to pay debts that others fraudulently incur in their name. In this equilibrium, creditors would curtail loans to regimes that have been identified as odious because they would know that successor governments would have little incentive to repay them. This argument draws upon a well-known result in game theory that repeated games have many possible equilibria, and simply making some information publicly known can create a new—and, in this case, better—equilibrium. Clarity about which regimes are odious can engender a new international norm that a country is not responsible for the debt incurred by a dictatorial regime and its reputation will not be tarnished if it repudiates this type of debt.

Although a public announcement that a regime is odious might curtail lending to such regimes, there is no guarantee that everyone would coordinate on this new equilibrium without some means of enforcement. Two enforcement mechanisms could ensure that lending to odious regimes is eliminated. First, laws in creditor countries could be changed to disallow seizure of a country's assets for nonrepayment of odious debt. That is, odious debt contracts could be made legally unenforceable. Second, foreign aid to successor regimes could be made contingent on nonrepayment of odious debt. For example, the International Monetary Fund (IMF) and World Bank could adopt a policy of not providing assistance to governments who are repaying creditors for illegitimate loans. If the foreign aid were valuable enough, successor governments would have incentives to repudiate odious loans, so banks would refrain from originating such loans.

Advantages over Traditional Trade Sanctions

When the international community wants to put pressure on a government that suppresses democracy and human rights, a common approach is to impose economic sanctions. Limiting an odious regime's ability to borrow can be considered a new form of economic sanction that has several attractive features relative to traditional trade sanctions. Like other sanctions that the international community uses to pressure governments without resorting to war, the threat of limits on borrowing could create incentives for regimes to reform. Governments might loot less to retain the ability to borrow. Would-be dictators might even be discouraged from seeking power if sovereign borrowing were not one of the spoils of office.

Traditional sanctions, however, are often criticized as either ineffective or inhumane. Limiting borrowing avoids these two shortcomings. First, when trade sanctions are deployed, smugglers and even some national governments will likely flout them, enticed by profits boosted by the sanction itself. Curtailing odious debt, in contrast, is a self-enforcing sanction. The key difference is that banks cannot break this sanction unilaterally because they rely on others to enforce the reputational punishment. Whereas trade sanctions are eviscerated by one or a few defectors even if there are a large number of abiders, with the "loan embargo," a few creditors and investors who are willing to lend to and invest in a country that has repudiated odious debt would eliminate any incentive for the country to repay the debt. A private bank would think twice before lending to a regime if the world's leading powers, international organizations, and financial institutions had declared the regime odious and announced that they would consider successor governments justified in repudiating any new loans the odious regime incurs. For example, when the United Nations imposed trade sanctions against the apartheid government of South Africa in 1985, it also could have declared that it would not consider debt incurred by the apartheid government as a legitimate obligation of the successor government. If banks doubted that successor regimes would repay loans issued after the announcement, they likely would have been unwilling to make such loans.

Second, when trade sanctions are not evaded, they are thought to impoverish the people they were intended to help because of the loss of national income. For example, if firms in the country are prevented from selling their products abroad, the loss of revenue might cause them to fire workers or decrease wages. In contrast, curtailing dictators' ability to borrow, loot, and saddle the people with large debts would hurt illegitimate regimes but help their populations. The burden of repaying the debts would almost certainly outweigh any short-run benefit the population would obtain from proceeds of the loan that trickled down to them. (If a regime loots only a small amount and most of the proceeds flow to the people, the regime probably should not be considered odious.)

More countries engage in foreign trade than in sovereign borrowing, so limits on borrowing could only be applied as a sanction in certain cases. Nonetheless, it could have a significant impact in these cases. For example, Franjo Tudjman of Croatia was arguably an odious ruler, having instigated violence against political opponents and looted public funds. In 1997, the International Monetary Fund (IMF) cut off aid that was earmarked for Croatia at the behest of the United States, Germany, and Britain, who were concerned about the "unsatisfactory state of democracy in Croatia." Despite this, commercial banks lent an additional $2 billion (U.S.) to the Croatian government between the IMF decision and Tudjman's death in December 1999.[7] If the proposed institution existed, creditors might not have granted Tudjman the subsequent $2 billion in loans, and the Croatian people would not bear the debt today. Such potential applications suggest that limits on borrowing should be part of the toolkit of policies available to the international community.

Incentives for Truthfulness

There is clearly room for discretion in assessing whether loans to a particular regime are odious. Governments lie on a continuum in the extent to which they do or do not have the consent of the people and do or do not spend for their benefit. Someone could argue that Mexican debt incurred during the era of domination by the Partido Revolucionario Internacional, or debts incurred in the United States before the passage of the Voting Rights Act of 1965, qualify as odious debt.

For a limit on borrowing to improve upon the status quo, it is necessary to provide incentives for the institution assessing the legitimacy of debt to do so truthfully. An institution that cares about the welfare of the people of developing countries more than that of banks and other creditors might be tempted to declare legitimate debt odious as a way to redistribute resources from creditors to the debtor country. However, if creditors anticipate being unable to collect even on legitimate loans, they will be wary of lending at all, and the available capital to borrowers will diminish. This danger is one of the main reasons why the doctrine of odious debt has gained little support within the legal community. An institution with the opposite bias of favoring banks over debtor nations might also make false rulings; in this case, it might fail to designate debt as odious in order to help the creditors.

To overcome these risks, the institution could be empowered only to rule on future loans to a government and not on existing debt. Then creditors would not face the uncertainty that loans they issue will be declared odious later. Moreover, the institution will have stronger incentives to be truthful. Even if the institution is more concerned with the welfare of debtors than that of creditors, it would have incentives to judge a regime honestly because honesty benefits the population. If the institution falsely calls a legitimate government odious, it deprives a country of profitable investments financed by loans. If it falsely calls an odious government legitimate, the government can borrow and loot the country.

Requiring an institution to judge the legitimacy of loans before they are incurred also limits the potential for favoritism toward creditors. An institution that favors creditors and rules on existing debt might fail to declare some debts odious. However, if it rules only on future loans, even a small degree of concern for truthfulness or for the welfare of people in borrowing countries should be sufficient to prevent an institution from calling an odious government legitimate. This is because before a loan is issued, the expected profits of a loan are very small for banks, as they have many alternative uses for their capital. In contrast, outstanding debt is a "zero-sum game" between creditors and debtors, so a biased institution can help whichever party it favors. Because false rulings about future debt hurt the population of borrowing countries and cannot substantially help creditors, an institution empowered only to block future lending is unlikely to make biased judgments in order to help debtors or creditors.

There remains a possibility that an institution that rules on future debt may be biased for or against certain governments. If the major powers regard a country as an important trade partner or strategic ally, the institution might fail to brand the government odious regardless of potential misdeeds. For instance, it is unlikely that an institution would brand either China or Saudi Arabia as odious. Because such regimes with powerful friends can borrow presently, biased decisions in their favor would simply maintain the status quo. If instead the institution disfavors a government for foreign policy reasons, even though the government has the consent of the people or spends for their benefit, the institution might falsely term it odious, thus cutting it off from lending. For example, the United States might wish to block loans to the current government of Iran, independent of whether the regime satisfies the definition of odiousness. If this happened, citizens of the country would be worse off than under the status quo. The institution could be designed under a "do no harm" principle. Requiring unanimity or a two-thirds vote to declare a regime odious could safeguard against the possibility that a country would falsely be branded odious because of the biases of a few members of the institution, as the decisive voter would be less biased against the government than under a simple majority rule. Some illegitimate, self-serving regimes would continue to receive loans under this rule, but it would be an improvement on the status quo if even one such regime were denied loans.

Other Issues

Inherited Debt

It also is important to consider how the new policy would affect an odious regime that inherits legitimate debt from the previous government. Even under the status quo, an odious regime likely would prefer not to repay its creditors and instead keep the repayment money for itself. It would be difficult to extract these resources from the regime; the best it may be possible to do is to prevent it from procuring more resources. To reduce the probability that the regime will default on its obligations, the international community might consider providing specific exemptions for the rollover of existing loans.

Long-Lasting Dictators

If a dictator stays in power for a long time, banks might issue short-term loans as long as they believed that the dictator would be in power long enough to repay the loans. Even in this case, the dictator is worse off with the policy than without it because the risk that the odious regime will lose power before he can repay even a short-term loan will increase the interest rate he faces. Also, because the interest rate will be set so that, in expectation, the dictator repays the value of the loan, the dictator can loot only the surplus from borrowing, and the population is not saddled with the debt.

Good Regimes Can Turn Bad and Bad Regimes Can Reform

It also may be the case that a government is nonodious at first but becomes odious. For example, Mobutu in Zaire became more corrupt over time. In practice, regimes could be monitored repeatedly or continuously, perhaps in response to complaints, and a regime might at first be judged nonodious but then be considered odious at a later time. Only loans made after the revised judgment would be considered odious.

Illegitimate Regimes and International Law

The doctrine of odious debt has no formal status in international law. For example, the United Nations convention related to sovereign debt under state succession makes no mention of odious debt. Nonetheless, there are some examples in which indebted countries have invoked the concept of illegitimate debt. In addition, the doctrine's main premise—that some rulers are illegitimate representatives of the people they rule, and that these rulers are personally responsible for actions taken while in power—appears often in international legal arguments.

Twenty years after the newly independent Cuba renounced the debt incurred by its Spanish rulers, the Soviet state followed suit and repudiated the tsarist debt in 1921. They argued that "no people is obliged to pay debts that are like the chains it has been forced to bear for centuries" (International Law Commission 1977: 72). In 1923, Costa Rica claimed in an arbitration case that loans issued by the Royal Bank of Canada to its former ruler Frederico Tinoco were illegitimate. The arbitrator in *Great Britain v. Costa Rica*, U.S. Chief Justice Taft, rejected the relevance of Tinoco's nondemocratic status but nullified the debt on the grounds that "the bank knew that this money was to be used by the retiring president, F. Tinoco, for his personal support after he had taken refuge in a foreign country" (Williams et al 1933). Iran invoked the doctrine of odious debt in an arbitration case about debts to the United States incurred by the former imperial government in 1948. In 1997, the Iran-U.S. Claims Tribunal ruled that the current government of Iran was liable for the debts, but the Tribunal wrote that in doing so it "does not take any stance in the doctrinal debate on the concept of 'odious debts' in international law" (Iran-U.S. Claims Tribunal 1997).

More recently, public campaigns for debt relief for countries such as South Africa, Indonesia, and Iraq have argued that the debt was odious.

The view that some uses of power by government officials are illegitimate or criminal seems to be gaining favor in other areas of international law. The prosecution of Slobodan Milosevic for war crimes is one example. In addition, there have been lawsuits against human rights abusers brought by their victims in U.S. courts under the Alien Torts Claims Act (*Filartiga v. Pena-Irala* 1980). This trend suggests that the international community may now be more receptive to the doctrine of odious debt than when it was originally proposed, especially if it is implemented in a way that mitigates the potential problems.

How Should These Policies Be Implemented?

An obviously important question in implementing the doctrine of odious debt is which institution would judge odiousness. The United Nations Security Council already imposes sanctions against governments, so it is a natural candidate. The United States and the other permanent members of the Council (China, France, Russia, and the United Kingdom) might prefer this option because they would have veto power. Another option is an international judicial body that hears cases brought against particular regimes and is composed of professional jurists representing several countries, similar to the International Court of Justice or the newly established International Criminal Court in the Hague.

It is also conceivable that the United States carries sufficient weight in the international system to implement such a judicial system on its own. For example, U.S. law could be amended to define odious debt and to disallow seizure of a foreign government's assets when the government repudiates odious debt; and the United States could announce that it would not provide foreign aid to countries that were repaying odious debt and would not support IMF or World Bank aid to such countries. Then even banks outside the United States would likely be reluctant to lend to that regime, fearing that successor governments would not repay, and creditors' recourse to that country's assets would be impaired.

It might also be possible for civil society to begin putting pressure on banks not to lend to illegitimate governments. If a well-respected nongovernmental organization identified odious regimes and promulgated a list of them, creditors might be reluctant to lend to governments on the list.

The most likely way that the institutional structure would take shape is that the international community, led by a few influential countries, would apply the loan embargo for a specific case, and then the precedent would evolve into a general policy. The policy need not be adopted wholesale and in the abstract. For example, the United States has pressured the ratings agency Moody's to withdraw its favorable credit rating of Iran. Iran planned to issue sovereign bonds, with European banks as the target bondholders, and the United States wished to limit Iran's ability to borrow as part of its economic sanctions program.[8] However, eliminating the Moody's rating is unlikely to compel European banks to fall in line with the U.S. position. Suppose, though, that the hardliners in the Iranian government launched a coup and there was international consensus that the Iranian government was neither representative of the people nor intending to spend in the people's interests. The UN Security Council could issue a declaration that Iran was odious and its bonds were unenforceable. The permanent members could vow to back foreign aid to a successor Iranian government that repudiated the bonds. Would-be bondholders would almost certainly fall in line with this sanction.

Or the case that triggers the new policy might involve the nullification of outstanding debt. There has been much debate about whether the estimated $100 billion (U.S.) in debt incurred by Saddam Hussein should be the responsibility of the Iraqi people now. Iraq can make a fairly strong case that Saddam Hussein borrowed without the consent of the Iraqi people and then spent much of the money to finance violence and repression. The argument that Iraq should not be expected to repay the debt has gained momentum partly because Iraq is unlikely to be *able* to repay it. Its debt burden far exceeds its gross domestic product. The United States, for example, might welcome an Iraqi decision to repudiate its debt because an Iraq burdened with debt would be more dependent on American aid. If the Iraqi government decides to renounce Saddam Hussein's debt, this might spur the creation of a system that discourages lending to repressive rulers such as Saddam Hussein in the first place. We would have taken our first step toward creating a new norm under which a country is not responsible for odious debt.

This new policy could help legitimate debtors and their creditors. Creditors would benefit from knowing the rules of the game in advance. Currently, it is hard for creditors to anticipate which loans will be considered odious in the future. If odiousness were declared in advance, banks would avoid lending to odious regimes in the first place and no longer face the risk of large losses if a successful campaign nullified their outstanding loans. Accordingly, with greater certainty, interest rates could fall for legitimate governments. Most importantly, dictators would no longer be able to borrow, loot the proceeds—or use them to finance repression—and then saddle their citizens with the debts.

Appendix: When Debt Is Not Odious: An Approach to Bailouts

In cases where legitimate governments borrow to finance economically disastrous policies, an approach similar to the one we propose for odious debt might be useful. If the population of a country chooses such a government, some would argue that it is their prerogative, and it would be a breach of international sovereignty to block the government's ability to borrow. However, many contend that the international financial institutions (IFIs), such as the World Bank and the IMF, subsidize wasteful spending in the form of international aid packages to countries whose economies have collapsed. This is the familiar moral hazard argument: The expectation of bailouts from IFIs encourages commercial banks and bondholders to make loans that governments could not reasonably repay on their own.

The IFIs could discourage this type of opportunistic lending by private creditors in the following way: The IFIs could, after assessing the creditworthiness of a government, announce that the government's policies are likely to make it unable to fulfill its debt obligations.[9] The IFIs could also announce that they would be willing to provide aid to the country once it resumes pursuing sound policies but not to help repay debt issued after the announcement. In particular, a condition of future IFI assistance would be that countries not simultaneously repay any loans made after the IFI announcement. In this way, the IFIs would avoid encouraging private lending to the country that was motivated by antici- pation of a bailout. Unlike in the odious debt case, loans would not be consid- ered illegitimate and unenforceable. If creditors thought the country could repay without an IFI bailout, they would continue to lend.

With this approach, the IFIs would be able to continue to give aid packages to countries that followed good policies but suffered bad luck. However, they would not bail out creditors who had opportunistically lent to countries that were following risky policies.

Acknowledgments This chapter is based on Jayachandran and Kremer (2006).

Notes

1. In the first rationale, Krugman (1989) and Sachs (1989) describe a debt-overhang problem caused by negative shocks. In the second rationale, Adams (1991) and Hanlon (2002) argue the case that much developing-country debt is illegitimate, and Khalfan et al. (2002) discuss related legal issues. The philosopher Thomas Pogge (2001) proposes that a panel assess the democratic status of governments in order to deter lending to autocratic regimes. We differ from earlier work in discussing the multiple equilibria of the debt market—which are what make assessments potentially efficacious—and the trade-offs between ex ante and ex post assessments.

2. S. Africa Shuns Apartheid Lawsuits, *Guardian*, 27 November 2002: 19.

3. Somoza Legacy: Plundered Economy, *Washington Post*, 30 November 1979: A1; Cuba's Debt Mistakes: A Lesson for Nicaragua, *Washington Post*, 5 October 1980: G1.

4. The *Financial Times* reports the $4 billion (U.S.) figure as the estimate of the United States Treasury and International Monetary Fund. An *FT* investigation found that Mobutu's wealth peaked at this value ("Mobutu Built a Fortune of $4 Billion from Looted Aid," 12 May 1997: 01). Others report his 1997 wealth as $9 billion ("Superstar Eclipsed by Greed," *Times* [London], 5 May 1997: 03, Overseas sect.).

5. Other examples: Sani Abacha was reported to have $2 billion (U.S.) in Swiss bank accounts in 1999 after five years as Nigeria's ruler. ("Going after 'Big Fish,' new Nigerian President trawls for Corruption," *International Herald Tribune*, 25 November 1999: 03). Jean-Claude Duvalier's successors in Haiti claim he took $900 million (U.S.) with him when he left power in 1986. Haiti's debt was $700 million at the time ("Haiti in Life and Debt Struggle," *Guardian*, 17 June 2000: 22). Debt figures are from Hanlon (1998).

6. In the few cases where a government has repudiated the debts of previous regimes as illegitimate, such as after the Russian revolution, the new government presumably had few plans to deal with foreigners and had few assets overseas subject to creditor countries' legal systems, so it had little to lose by defaulting.

7. UK Warns Croatia it Risks Losing Aid, *Financial Times*, 31 July 1997: 02; Croats Find Treasury Plundered; State Says Former Regime Stole or Misused Billions, *Washington Post*, 13 June 2000: 01.

8. Moody's, Citing U.S. Concern, Cancels Ratings on Iran Debt, *New York Times*, 4 June 2002: 7, sect. W.

9. Note that although the charters of the IFIs proscribe their judging governments on political grounds when making funding decisions—and hence they could not be the

judges of odiousness—in this case their judgments would be on economic grounds, and no independent panel would be needed.

References

Adams, P. 1991. *Odious Debts.* London: Earthscan.

Feilchenfeld, E. 1931. *Public Debts and State Succession.* New York: Macmillan.

Filartiga v. Pena-Irala (1980). 630 F.2d 876.

Hanlon, J. 1998. *Dictators and Debt.* London: Jubilee 2000. Available online at: www .Jubilee2000.org.

Hanlon, J. 2002. Defining Illegitimate Debt and Linking Its Cancellation to Economic Justice. Mimeo, Norwegian Church Aid.

International Law Commission. 1977. *Yearbook of the International Law Commission.* New York: United Nations.

Iran-U.S. Claims Tribunal. 1997. Case No. B36. King of Prussia, PA: Mealey Publications.

Jayachandran, S. and Kremer, M. 2006, forthcoming. Odious Debt, *American Economic Review.*

Khalfan, A., King, J., and Thomas, B. 2002. Advancing the Odious Debt Doctrine. Working Paper. Center for International Sustainable Development Law, McGill University.

Krugman, P. 1989. Market-Based Debt-Reduction Schemes. In *Analytical Issues in Debt,* ed. J. A. Frenkel, M. P. Dooley, and P. Wickham, pp. 258–78. Washington, DC: International Monetary Fund.

Pogge, T. 2001. Achieving Democracy, *Ethics and International Affairs,* Vol. 15: 3–23.

Sachs, J. 1989. The Debt Overhang of Developing Countries. In *Debt Stabilization and Development: Essays in Memory of Carlos Diaz-Alejandro,* ed. G. Calvo, R. Findlay, P. Kouri, and J. Braga de Macedo, pp. 80–102. Oxford, UK: Basil Blackwell.

Sack, A. 1927. *Les Effets de Transformations des États sur Leur Dettes Publiques et Autres Obligations Financières.* Paris: Recueil Sirey.

Williams, J. F., Lauterpacht, H., Lauterpacht, E., Greenwood, C., and Oppenheimer, A. 1933. *International Law Reports: Volume 2: Annual Digest of Public International Law Cases 1923–1924.* Cambridge: Cambridge University Press.

World Bank. 2003. Debtor Reporting System and Joint BIS-IMF-OECD-World Bank Statistics on External Debt. Available online at: www.worldbank.org/data.

11

DEALING COMPREHENSIVELY, AND JUSTLY, WITH SOVEREIGN DEBT

Jack Boorman

Virtually everyone has signed on to the general proposition that relief from unserviceable debt is sometimes needed for countries, as it is for bankrupt individuals and corporations, even though the concept and legal structure of domestic bankruptcy do not translate well to sovereign governments. A major push toward more effective means of dealing with unsustainable debts came from the recognition that the absence of such measures has been extremely costly both for the citizens of the debtor countries and for the countries' creditors. The experience of so many countries in Latin America in the 1980s—the lost decade of stagnant economies—convinced many that insistence on full repayment in the face of a genuine incapacity of governments to honor their obligations was self-defeating. Ultimately, the debt of these countries to international banks had to be written down—to levels below what might have been necessary if that action had been taken earlier. Similarly, the practices of the Paris Club of official creditors, whereby debt was piled on debt through repeated reschedulings of creditor-country claims on poorer countries, also came to be seen as self-defeating.

Whatever the motivation, strong coalitions were forged and, eventually, significant progress was made in dealing with sovereign debt. The path of progress was, however, uneven and halting. The Brady Plan helped deal with the debt to international banks owed by many Latin American countries (Rieffel 2003). The increasing effectiveness of the London Club in dealing with unserviceable bank claims on countries broadened the process and facilitated workouts for many of the countries that were hit by financial crises in the 1990s. The World Bank's program to assist the poorest countries in buying back their commercial bank claims at deep discounts (the "Fifth Dimension") significantly expanded the scope of relief from commercial bank debt. The increasing willingness of official creditors, acting through the Paris Club, to write off a portion of their claims on the poorer countries and, eventually, the call for relief for the poorest from the claims of the international financial institutions—culminating in the heavily indebted poor countries (HIPC) initiative—took debt relief to a new level and facilitated a more comprehensive treatment of countries' debts.

Some of the initial debates and arguments that took place in light of the evident need for action to lighten the burdens of excessive sovereign debt focused on the economic and financial fundamentals of the indebted countries and on the prospects for recovery if they were provided with debt relief. But over time the debate was broadened by those calling for a "just" treatment of the debtor countries—and their populations—culminating in the call by Jubilee 2000 to write off the debts of the poorest countries. And it has been complicated by the changing profile of sovereign debt, by the different economic—and sometimes political—circumstances of the countries involved, and by a lack of clarity and lack of agreement on what the precise aim of debt relief for such governments should be. Thus, although much progress has been made in developing mechanisms to deal with sovereign debt problems, a number of important issues remain.

First, the objectives of debt workouts and debt relief need to be more clearly delineated. For example, the calls for greater justice in the provision of debt relief are welcome. But justice is not a precise concept, it is not immediately operationally meaningful, and it cannot be judged simply by the metric of the extent of relief provided.[1] Moreover, can one ever hope to determine justice in the context of only one aspect of a country's economic situation (i.e., its debt and the burden of that debt)? And who has the right to decide what is just, whatever the context?

Second, because of the changing nature of debt, and of the markets on which debt is traded, the mechanisms available for the provision of debt relief must evolve. They must be sufficiently diverse and flexible to deal comprehensively with the very different debt profiles of crisis countries.

These are not easy issues. This chapter will try to deal with them and will argue: (1) that justice in the provision of debt relief, especially for the poorer countries, should not be judged solely on the precise amount of that relief but rather in the broader landscape of that country's economic relations with the rest of the world and, in particular, the wealthy nations' willingness to provide aid resources and a fair trading environment for such countries; and (2) that the mechanisms now available to deal with sovereign debt crises are not sufficiently comprehensive and that the void that exists could be filled if a proposal by the International Monetary Fund (IMF) for a sovereign debt restructuring mechanism (SDRM) were to be pursued.

The role of the IMF in all of this will be touched upon at various points in the chapter.

More Generous Relief for the Poorer Countries?

Certainly the record of the 1980s in providing debt relief to the poorer countries—as was the case with the treatment of the commercial bank debt of the emerging-market countries in Latin America and elsewhere during that period—was pretty dismal. The rescheduling through the Paris Club of official bilateral debt owed by low-income countries produced little long-term relief and, in fact, led to a snowballing of debt as a result of the accumulation of interest on rescheduled claims. Similarly, repeated support packages from the IMF, the World Bank, and other multilateral organizations significantly increased the claims of those organizations on the poorer countries. Absent sufficient growth rates in the affected countries, debt profiles worsened and became increasingly unsustainable.

But things began to change in the late 1980s. The World Bank's Fifth Dimension provided resources to poorer countries to buy back their commercial debt at very large discounts—effectively eliminating medium- and long-term commercial bank debt for many of these countries. On bilateral official debt, the Paris Club—grudgingly and with undue delay—instituted progressively more generous restructuring terms under initiatives agreed upon at various G7 summits.[2] Moreover, under the HIPC initiative, the claims of the multilateral financial institutions, including the World Bank and the International Monetary Fund, were brought into the debt-reduction process for the first time (Ross and Abrego 2001). Finally, during the latter part of the 1990s a number of industrial countries, including the United Kingdom and France, began to write off completely their, Official Development Assistance (ODA) claims on some of the poorest countries.

There have been positive and significant results from these initiatives. As of the end of March 2003, for example, debt relief under the HIPC initiative has been committed to 26 poorer countries. Overall HIPC debt relief, together with bilateral debt relief under the traditional mechanisms and additional bilateral debt forgiveness beyond that of the HIPC initiative, amounts to about a two-thirds reduction in the overall stock of debt of these countries. That relief has cut the debt service of these countries relative to government revenue from over 27% in 1998 to 15% in 2003 and will take it to below 11% in 2005. It has also helped these governments increase social expenditures from less than 6% of GDP in 1999 to over 9% in 2002—an amount four times that spent on debt service.

These are important achievements. But calls continue for greater debt relief for these countries. Why has more not been done? There are differences in philosophy, and there are the realities of international politics behind these developments. On the philosophy, some have argued that the creation of a credit culture is important if these countries are to have access to appropriate levels of borrowed resources in the future. Responsible borrowing for productive purposes is in a country's interest. But that requires a culture that bases borrowing decisions on effective analysis of the potential payoff from such borrowing, and it requires a genuine and credible commitment to honor the claims taken on.

Leaving these heavily indebted countries with some sustainable level of debt to service creates the institutions and the mindset for managing debt. Without that, the future will see only repeated rounds of overborrowing, overlending, and repeated initiatives to resolve the resulting debt problems.

On the political front, the constraints on funding debt relief have been severe and the generosity of some of the major creditor countries has been limited. The initiatives launched by the IMF and the World Bank to assist the poorer countries—the enhanced structural adjustment facility (ESAF) (now the poverty reduction and growth facility, PRGF) and HIPC initiative—are illustrative in this respect. A glance at the financial accounts of the IMF will reveal an amazingly complex structure of loan accounts, subsidy accounts, special trust funds, gold sales proceeds accounts, and more. Few beyond those directly involved as these arrangements were put into place fully comprehend the structure. But the reasons that this structure was created are clear. To mobilize anywhere near the resources that were projected to be required to successfully fund these initiatives, it was necessary to cater to the particular needs of each creditor and donor and then, in the end, even to tap resources within the IMF itself to secure the amounts sought. Greater generosity on the part of some of the wealthier countries would have made this unnecessary. But that was not to be! The calls by many to provide more generous debt relief have to confront this reality. The result has been that, although the initiatives have been fully funded, they provide relief only up to the amounts projected as needed. And the projected needs themselves were cautiously derived and were not blind to the realities regarding likely available financing. Yes, there is a vicious circle here. If there was a real hope of securing more resources, the analytic case for those resources could have been made at the more generous end of the margins of what economics can do in the current state of the science.

What of the Ethics or Justice in All of This?

"Dealing justly with debt" has become an increasingly emphasized theme. One would presume little objection to the general proposition that debt (especially that of the poorer countries) should be dealt with "justly." That's the simple, and positive, part. The real issue turns on what that means in practice and how it is to be achieved.

Is there any guidance to be had from the dictionary on how to deal justly with debt? Merriam Webster's (11th Edition) and Oxford (2nd Edition) define "just" as "reasonable" (a just but not generous decision) and as "conforming with what is morally upright or good" and "rendering everyone his due." They define "justice" as "the quality of conforming to law" and "the administration of what is just, especially by the impartial adjustment of conflicting claims."

The spirit of these words is unassailable. However, they do not provide much in the way of operational guidance. If "justice" means "conforming to law," that could be taken as an endorsement of the sanctity of contracts and leaves little room for seeking anything other than the full repayment of debt—assuming, of course, that the contracts are valid! If "just" refers to "mostly upright," that would seem to open a wide variety of views and approaches, but they would probably lead quickly to conflicting views as to what is morally correct or acceptable and consistent with "rendering everyone his due."

Notwithstanding the lack of operational guidance here, the reality is that there is a broad acceptance of the proposition that debt can become unpayable and a recognition that certain circumstances may warrant a change in even perfectly legally grounded claims. Bankruptcy legislation, which exists in almost all domestic legal systems, is one such recognition of this reality. Domestic bankruptcy law, and the practices associated with it, help deal with the unpayable debt of corporations and individuals and permit a modification of the original contracts under which creditors would have a right to full repayment. These systems by no means work equally well in all countries, but that is being improved. Even in the best of systems, however, difficult judgments are required regarding the capacity of the individual or the corporation to service its debt.[3]

But even these difficulties pale in comparison with those confronted when the debtor is a sovereign government that borrowed internationally under the law of another country, as has been the case in so many financial crises during the 1990s. Here, domestic bankruptcy law generally does not apply. Moreover, there are few hard rules or guidelines about how to measure capacity to pay or to determine what concessions must be made by the many parties involved.

What is an unpayable debt in the context of a sovereign government? For any government, its capacity to service its debt is a function of its revenue-generating capacity and the decisions made regarding expenditures other than debt service. A government can, in some sense, always tax more or spend less to make resources available to service its debt. But where does one draw the line? Too much taxation can, in the end, be economically inefficient and counterproductive. Reducing expenditures can cut into basic services that many would rank morally preferable or in some way more desirable than debt service.

Here, although one can have great sympathy and respect for some of those in the NGO community and elsewhere arguing the case for debt relief, the case they make is not always helpful operationally. The issue is especially complicated in the case of poorer countries, where it must be seen in the broader context of the entire package of financial assistance that the country may be receiving. Part of the motivation for this assistance is to help the country promote its own development and to help it finance needed social services for its public before it is capable of providing for those needs from its own resources. Debt relief can free up budgetary resources that would otherwise be used to service that debt. Other forms of aid increase the total resources available to the country. There are advantages and disadvantages to each of these forms of assistance. But it is also the reality that they are, at least in part, substitutes for each other. More debt relief provided by creditor and donor governments can and sometimes does reduce the resources available to support other forms of assistance.

Thus, the question of justice should not be seen simply in terms of debt relief. It should be seen instead in the context of all the various instruments through which the richer countries of the world assist the poorer countries. The canvas is, of course, broader than this and needs to encompass all of the actions of the richer countries that impact the economies of the poorer countries, including trade policy (e.g., agricultural protection), procurement policies, military sales policies, and the like. This makes the task of helping these countries more complicated than simply calling for greater debt relief. Most people in the official international community see the issue in this broader context. In this view, the objective tends to be seen in terms of getting the countries' debt to a sustainable position and dealing with the broader needs of the country through increased aid and other mechanisms.[4]

This is the issue on which all should concentrate. There is an urgent need to get those among the wealthier countries that are falling increasingly behind any reasonable transfer of aid resources to the poorest countries—chief among them the United States—to dramatically increase their assistance.[5]

Do various proposals put forward by some in the NGO community and by others help to put flesh on the concept of justice in providing debt relief? Two ideas, in particular, warrant consideration: The first is the suggestion that debt reduction should be determined through an arbitration process; the second is the proposal that debt relief, in part, should rely on judgments about what is called "odious" debt.

The Jubilee USA Network says that "debts whose service causes impoverished people to be denied access to education, health care and clean drinking water" should be declared invalid through an arbitration process (Jubilee USA Network 2003: 2). This is emotionally appealing. But is it operational? Consider even the situation in the United States. There are unquestionably impoverished people—and, in fact, a growing number—in the United States who are receiving inadequate schooling, with devastating effects on their capacity to reach their potential and as a result a loss both to themselves and to the country. Should the U.S. government cease servicing some of its (rapidly increasing) debt and devote that money to education? Most people, I suspect, would say no, but may argue that, to the extent there is a real issue here, it should be dealt with through increased taxes or lower government expenditures elsewhere. Although these are areas where there may be little scope for action in the poorer countries, it does not follow that debt relief is the answer. Other actions, including increased aid flows from the richer countries, less distortive trade policies, and the like, may be more effective in providing the increased resources needed to provide the services needed in the poorer countries. One could make an additional argument here that may be particularly relevant to poorer countries (i.e., that tampering with the debt, especially if done in a way that unjustly imposes a cost on creditors, will reduce the future access of the government to financial markets, thereby reducing the potential to invest in schools and hospitals and, more generally, adversely affect medium- and long-term growth prospects, hurting those that the debt relief is intended to help).

There is a further problem with the idea of "arbitration." The NGOs do not want the IMF to set the financial hurdle for debt relief, nor do they accept that it should be left to the debtor and its creditors, who they seem to fear may negotiate a deal hurtful to the poor. Hence, they propose a neutral arbitration, informed by civil society, and instructed to find a "just" haircut to be applied to the creditors. They say this is what occurs under Chapter 9 of the United States bankruptcy code and that this should be the model. But that is not the case. Under Chapter 9, the court can only approve a plan that has the support of the debtor and at least one class of creditors. Moreover, neither creditors nor the debtor would accept the concept of a third party vetoing a decision on debt restructuring that had been agreed to by the debtor government and its creditors.[6]

Beyond this, there is the fact that, for most of the poorer countries, finding this neutrally determined point for debt relief does not solve the real problem. As Jeff Sachs (2002), among others, has noted, even a complete write-off of these countries' debts leaves them with large unmet needs that have to be addressed primarily through new aid flows. It is the comprehensive picture of the needed resource transfers to these countries that must be the focus of efforts to help improve their lot.

The second approach suggested by some in the NGO community comes at the issue from a different angle and calls for action to void what is referred to as "odious debt." Again, I quote from Jubilee USA Network, which defines such debt as:

> loans to dictators who stole the money; debts corresponding to corrupt and wasteful "development" projects; loans that were made with the purpose of purchasing the tools of repressing democracy; debts contracted in combination with policy conditions which aggrevated poverty, reduced living standards, and/or otherwise undermined the debtor country's capacity to achieve independent economic and financial development and thus the ability to repay the loans; and other illegitimate and odious debts. (Jubilee USA Network 2003: 2)

One can have few illusions about the existence of something like odious debt. The world is replete with examples of what neutral observers may agree is debt that might be so characterized. But the real issue is how to deal with debt more generally when it becomes unpayable. And this goes well beyond any notion of odious debt. The international community has shied away from mechanisms built on concepts such as odious debt and has concentrated on the broader issue. In the case of some creditor governments, it appears they eschew that kind of an approach for political reasons—governments may not want to recognize or defend some of the things they have done in the past! Others won't accept an approach that requires such Solomonic decisions! There is also a case to be made that dealing with debt in this way could introduce a new source of risk that could seriously affect the workings of the secondary market and its corollary, the ability of sovereigns to mobilize new money. Who will lend to these countries or buy their debt in secondary markets if there is a chance that, down the road, the claims will be declared odious and uncollectible?

Again, the question to ask is whether the NGO approach is operational. Who decides which debt falls into these categories? What are the values or criteria to be applied? If the odious debt deals were cut between one government and another, who decides—and by what criteria—on the balance to be struck between the wronged citizens of the debtor country and the taxpayers of the creditor country, who will absorb the cost of the debt relief. Are the latter not, in some sense, also victims?

The issue of odious debt has been taken one step further by Michael Kremer and Seema Jayachandran (Kremer and Jayachandran 2002). They try to advance the debate by focusing only on future debt. In essence, they call for an independent institution to assess whether (government) regimes are legitimate and to declare future debt incurred by such regimes odious. Any such debt would not enjoy the protections usually granted to international debt (i.e., creditors would not be permitted to seek judgments or to attach assets in the event of default). This has some appeal. In particular, it might help limit the obvious problems associated with declaring debt odious ex post and the debilitating effects such a practice could have on markets.

However, there remain a number of major stumbling blocks to this approach. First, is it reasonable to believe that a mechanism can be established to determine which regimes are odious and, therefore, effectively deny them credit? Perhaps there are some regimes that are so extreme, and so unimportant geopolitically, that wide agreement could be struck regarding their odious nature. However, it is difficult to see a construct that would permit a line to be drawn that captured all of the odious regimes (by whose definition?) and only the odious regimes. Realistically, international politics will intervene. The United States supported Mobutu, Marcos, and a host of others. Is there anything to cause us to believe that there will not always be such examples in the world of international politics as we know it? Moreover, if there were effective mechanisms to deliver debt relief when it was needed, would such a politically intractable device be needed? Presumably, the more odious a regime and the more credit is misused, the greater the relief that will be required when the regime collapses. Hopefully, this will occur earlier if creditors know they will get caught up by those mechanisms if they are so foolish as to lend to such regimes.

The Missing Element for a Comprehensive Solution: Dealing with Private Claims on the Sovereign

The preceding arguments suggest that the mechanisms now in place are reasonably robust and sufficient to deal with excessive sovereign debt problems—commercial bank debt, official bilateral debt, and even the claims of the multilateral institutions—for the poorer countries. They have even proven their worth in the context of the emerging-market countries facing excessive claims of commercial debt and bilateral official debt. But, there is still something missing in all of this. Markets have changed. Countries—and especially the emerging-market countries—rely much less on commercial bank credit and much more on securitized debt issued in the international bond markets. It is this latter debt that has been at the heart of the debt problems in countries such as Ukraine, Pakistan, Russia, Ecuador, and, most recently, Argentina and Uruguay. There are cases in which familiar mechanisms, such as debt exchanges, may be sufficient to provide the relief needed by a country. This has been the case in the debt exchange for Uruguay. However, there are other cases where currently available mechanisms may not be up to the task.

The international markets lack a reasonably predictable and orderly means to deal with the bonded debt of emerging-market countries when that debt becomes excessive. It is this void that led Anne Krueger, the First Deputy Managing Director of the IMF, to propose the SDRM in November 2001 (Krueger 2002).

The major motivation for the proposed SDRM is to help reduce the unacceptably large costs associated with disorderly defaults to private creditors by sovereign governments whose debt burden has become unsustainable. The collapse that has taken place in Argentina and the enormous cost paid by so many people in that country—and, yes, also by the creditors of Argentina—from the massive financial and economic dislocation and disruption that has occurred has renewed interest in this problem. What has occurred in Argentina was not inevitable.

The dislocation and disorder that occur in such cases are often the result of a reluctance on the part of the country's authorities first to confront the underlying policy problems or, subsequently, to approach the country's creditors for relief when its debt has become unsustainable. In too many cases, the authorities gamble for redemption through ever less credible policy measures rather than face the uncertainty of approaching the country's private-sector creditors for the needed relief. Argentina in the summer and fall of 2001 is all too dramatic an example of this phenomenon.

Why the hesitancy to approach creditors? There are, of course, reputational reasons: No government or individual minister wants to admit the reality of the country's debt problem. In some cases, of course, these will be the same people who oversaw the accumulation of that debt! There is also the concern regarding future access to capital markets. But, importantly, it is also the fact that there is simply no mechanism to reasonably assure the country that, upon approaching its creditors, there will be an orderly, reasonably predictable, and transparent process for reaching a negotiated settlement with creditors to restructure the country's debt in line with its prospective capacity to service that debt.

This reality inevitably puts the official community and the IMF, in particular, in a difficult position in deciding whether to continue to support the country's policies in the absence of a restructuring of its debt. In the face of unsustainable debt burdens, continued IMF lending would be no panacea. Perhaps it could buy a little time. But increasing the burden of debt that benefits from the IMF's preferred creditor status may only increase the magnitude of the debt adjustment that must eventually be borne by private-sector creditors and bilateral official creditors in situations where there is no underlying improvement in the country's capacity to service its debt.

Quite obviously, the preferred course of action is to prevent such crises from occurring in the first place, and many of the initiatives in the IMF and elsewhere have been aimed precisely at that objective. Stronger economic and financial policies have been combined with improving the environment for private-sector decision making in ways that should facilitate the assessment and management of risk. This offers the best prospect for allowing countries to reap the potential gains from globalization while minimizing the likelihood, and potential severity, of crises. Robust assessments of the strength and soundness of banking systems and a country's financial system more generally; a cautious opening of countries' domestic capital markets commensurate with development of its domestic financial institutions; encouragement of the adoption of internationally recognized standards and codes and of best practices in numerous areas of economic policy making and institution building; and better surveillance or monitoring of country policies by the authorities themselves, as well as by the IMF, are all part of these efforts.

Unfortunately, despite best efforts, crises will still occur, and there is a case that better mechanisms are needed to reduce the costs of these crises. Bankruptcies occur domestically, and there is virtually no one who argues against the adoption of legal mechanisms to deal with such events. Similar capacity is needed for sovereign governments in an increasingly complex international financial system (Rogoff and Zettelmeyer 2002).

So what is needed? In the first instance, a way needs to be found to deal with the well-known collective-action problem. The existing system fails in this respect, and this market failure provides the rationale for public intervention. Collective-action problems complicate the process of reaching agreement on a restructuring. There is a danger that individual creditors will decline to participate in a voluntary restructuring in the hope of recovering payment on the original contractual terms, even though creditors—as a group—would be better served by agreeing to such a restructuring.

The problem of collective action is most acute prior to a default, where individual creditors may have some reasonable hope of continuing to receive payments under the terms of their original contracts. A debtor that had reached agreement with the bulk of its creditors on a restructuring would no doubt hesitate to default on a small amount of the original debt simply to secure unanimity in the restructuring. But if a significant proportion of creditors elect not to participate in a restructuring, each hoping to be part of a small minority, the restructuring will inevitably fail.

Following a default, the options facing creditors—particularly those who have no interest in litigation—are more limited, and so the problems of collective action may be less acute. But they are still present!

However, there is a trap in believing that default is a good solution to collective-action difficulties. Of course, there is no doubt that, following default, agreement on a restructuring would eventually be reached. But default—and the associated uncertainties regarding creditor–debtor relations—generally leads to widespread economic dislocation. Proposals for strengthening arrangements for debt restructuring are intended to increase the likelihood that early agreement—preferably before default occurs—can be reached on a restructuring that can restore viability. It is in no one's interest for either debtors or their creditors to bear unnecessarily large costs in these crisis situations.

As an aside, if Argentina and its creditors reach a settlement in a reasonable time—after policies become better defined and more acceptable and a genuine dialogue begins—some will declare success. However, that outcome can already be declared a failure—and a massive failure—because of the loss and suffering that has already occurred, at least arguably as a result of the absence of a robust mechanism that would have allowed the authorities and the country's creditors to deal with the looming debt problem in a timely and less disruptive manner.

Many have come to believe that these weaknesses of the current system can be resolved only through a mechanism that has the features of the proposed SDRM. Although collective-action clauses (CACs) and some of the other proposals now also being pursued could help, they can only be complementary to an SDRM. Both are needed.

The SDRM proposal that has been developed by the IMF would have the following major features:

1. A supermajority of creditors could vote to accept new terms under a restructuring agreement. Minority creditors would be prevented from blocking such agreements or enforcing the terms of the original debt contracts (i.e., they would be bound by the decision of the majority).[7]
2. A dispute resolution forum would be established to verify claims, assure the integrity of the voting process, and adjudicate disputes that might arise.

Other features that could facilitate a more orderly process during the period of negotiation might include:

1. Provide protection for the sovereign debtor from disruptive legal action by creditors. This could be provided, in appropriate circumstances, through a stay on litigation, preventing creditors from seeking court decisions for repayment while negotiations are under way. The possible automaticity and the triggers for such possible stays have been a widely discussed point in the debate on the SDRM.
2. Provide assurances to creditors that the debtor will negotiate in good faith and will pursue policies—most likely to be designed in conjunction with seeking financial support from the IMF—that help protect the value of creditor claims and help limit the dislocation in the economy. The IMF's policy on lending into arrears is key in this regard.
3. Creditors could agree to give seniority and protection from restructuring to fresh private lending, to facilitate ongoing economic activity through the continued provision of, inter alia, trade credit (something akin to debtor-in-possession financing).

The development of the SDRM has been guided by a number of principles: First, the mechanism should only be used to restructure debt that is judged unsustainable. It should neither increase the likelihood of restructuring nor encourage defaults. Second, any interference with contractual relations should be limited to those measures that are needed to resolve the most important collective-action problems. Third, the framework should be designed in a manner that promotes greater transparency in the restructuring process and encourages early and active creditor participation during the restructuring process. It should not increase the role of the IMF in this regard. Fourth, the integrity of the decision-making process under the mechanism should be safeguarded by an efficient and impartial dispute-resolution process. Fifth and finally, the SDRM should not give rise to an expansion of the IMF's legal powers.

The proposal that has been put forward—formulated in specific terms in a statement from the managing director of the IMF to the International Monetary and Financial Committee (IMFC) and discussed at the meetings of that body in Washington in April 2003—has evolved since Anne Krueger first brought up this issue (Krueger 2002). That evolution has been guided by what has been the most ambitious consultative process ever engaged in by the IMF on an important policy proposal. These modifications include the way in which a stay on litigation may be activated while negotiations are under way with creditors, the way in which members of the dispute resolution forum (DRF) would be selected so as to assure their independence from the IMF, the powers that may be exercised by the DRF and its rule-making authority, the role of the IMF in activation of the mechanism, and others. These modifications reflect the very helpful discussions that have taken place in a wide diversity of forums with the official sector, bankruptcy practitioners, the international legal community, NGOs, and many others. As always, of course, some have welcomed the modifications made and others would have been happier to stick with certain elements of the original proposal. Nevertheless, virtually all of the changes have improved the proposal and have helped to secure greater support for it—support that within the IMF includes over 70% of the membership.

The debate on SDRM has also contributed in other ways. First and foremost, there is far greater understanding of all these issues, and the related legal and institutional complexities, than existed before. Secondly, the discussion has given new impetus to the push in the official community to encourage the use of collective-action clauses in sovereign debt issues. That push began with the Rey report of the G10 in the mid 1990s but had accomplished very little until new life was breathed into the effort in the context of this discussion. Similarly, there is now support in some quarters—at least in principle—to develop a voluntary code of good conduct that would, among other things, foster greater transparency, provide guidance to debtors and creditors regarding procedures for contact and negotiations, and help provide greater predictability to the restructuring process under any legal framework. Such a code could be made applicable to a broad set of circumstances, ranging from periods of relative tranquility to periods of acute stress, and could constitute an established set of best practices. In contrast, proposals for strengthening arrangements for debt restructuring have a more limited scope and purpose (i.e., to facilitate the resolution of financial crises).

By its very nature, a voluntary code, although potentially helpful, could not resolve collective-action problems. Moreover, a code could only be effective to the extent that it is able to attract broad support among debtors and their creditors. Accordingly, the most promising approach to developing a code that could form the basis of a broad consensus would be for it to be developed jointly by debtors, their creditors, and other interested parties (including the IMF).

In the end, however, these initiatives are best seen as complementary to SDRM. It is unlikely that either collective-action clauses or a code of good conduct would be sufficiently powerful by themselves to provide what is needed to deal with the more complex and potentially damaging crises that may occur. Nevertheless, a system with reasonably comprehensive and robust CACs and a well-defined and widely supported code of conduct will be an improvement on the system that currently exists.

Some Challenges to the SDRM

One might have thought that in putting forward a proposal to fill in a missing element in the mechanisms available to deal with foreign debt problems, the IMF would have struck a sympathetic chord with the NGO community. After all, Argentina was in the midst of a default that was wreaking havoc on its economy and throwing a significant portion of the population into poverty. But that sympathy, let alone support, was not forthcoming. At a conference held at the IMF in January 2003, a number of criticisms of the SDRM were put forward by representatives of the NGOs. As an example, the proposal was faulted because only private creditors would have to reduce their claims (Pettifor and Raffer 2003). This is not correct. It is true that the proposal assumes continuance of the preferred creditor status of the IMF and some other multilateral organizations, but bilateral official creditors would be expected to provide relief on their claims on the country. Private creditors absolutely insist on this; it was always foreseen in the proposal that bilateral official creditors would share the burden; and the means by which to accomplish this participation was actively discussed by official creditors in the Paris Club.

Another criticism was that "SDRM would not return poor, indebted countries to viability/sustainability" (Pettifor and Raffer 2003). I believe there is some confusion here. The SDRM is not aimed at the poorest countries. It may be relevant to a very few of them that have large amounts of debt outstanding to private creditors (such as Nigeria). But for the low-income countries generally, there is the HIPC initiative and other mechanisms discussed earlier in this chapter. These are the mechanisms to be brought to bear on the debt problems of those countries—in the context of appropriate levels of other forms of aid.

There are also some in the NGO community who fault the proposal for not including a process through which countries can be discharged of their obligation to repay "odious debt." As indicated earlier, it would be difficult to argue that there is no odious debt in the world! But that is not the point. The point is that the SDRM has a quite specific purpose (i.e., to help deal with the problems of market-access countries whose debt has become unsustainable and to establish a system for more orderly and coordinated negotiation between the country and its creditors for debt relief in such circumstances). As in economics, where there is an axiom that there should be one policy instrument for each economic objective, so here, too, it is worth keeping in mind the single objective of the SDRM. It is interesting to note that neither private creditors, many of whom would presumably have to give less relief if so-called odious debt were set aside, nor the emerging-market countries themselves, have voiced any support for this proposal to write off odious debt.

Questions and challenges have also been raised about the role of the IMF under the SDRM and, more generally, in all cases where decisions about debt relief need to be made in the context of judgments about debt sustainability. In the particular case of the SDRM, there are several dimensions to this. For example, it is proposed that the SDRM be created through an amendment to the IMF's Articles of Agreement rather than through a new international treaty. The rationale is straightforward. Helping countries manage their debt problems and the economic and certain institutional aspects of their interface with international capital markets falls squarely under the IMF's mandate, and SDRM fits within the boundaries of that mandate.[8]

As proposed, the amendment would create no new legal powers for the IMF itself. Among other things, it would permit majority voting by creditors to bind minority or dissenting creditors to a debt-relief plan that the creditors themselves negotiate with the debtor country. And it would establish a DRF, independent of the IMF, with powers to assure the integrity of the process and help resolve disputes that may arise.

Apparently most controversial in the eyes of some NGOs and other critics of the proposal is that the IMF would continue to have a role in assessing the sustainability of the country's external position, including its debt. Some see this as putting the IMF in the position of dictating the terms of any settlement between the country and its creditors.[9]

The major aspect of this criticism pertains to the IMF's role in policy formulation and judgments regarding debt sustainability. In the report cited previously on the SDRM conference held at the IMF, the claim is made that the Fund would play a preemptive role in shaping the outcome of any debt crisis resolution negotiations. They will do this by setting the country's level of debt sustainability. In addition, the Fund will continue its existing role of determining the debtor's economic policies. The IMF effectively disempowers the debtor, all other creditors and civil society (Pettifor and Raffer 2003). This is an important critique because it goes to the heart of one of the important functions of the IMF and has implications not just in the case of a country that was to appeal to the SDRM if such a mechanism existed but to the role played by the IMF in all cases of debt restructuring. At a technical level, this function is draped in the language of debt sustainability and the capacity of a country to service its debts, including debts to the IMF itself. However, at the moral level or as a matter of justice, this involves judgments about the relative burden to be placed on the citizens of the country and on its creditors.

The Role of the IMF in Assessing Debt Sustainability

When a country finds itself with a balance-of-payments problem—even one well short of default in a debt crisis—it may request financial assistance from the

IMF. The role of the IMF here is the classic one of providing temporary financial assistance to the country to help finance its balance of payments over the period needed to design and implement policies to correct the underlying problems. The availability of such financing is motivated by the desire of the international community to assist the country so that it can avoid or limit the destructive measures sometimes taken by countries facing such problems, including import restrictions, aggressive currency devaluations, and other measures that may adversely affect its trading partners and that are "destructive of national and international prosperity."[10]

In such cases, the quid pro quo for the financial assistance provided by the IMF is agreement on a set of policies mutually agreed upon by the IMF and the country as sufficient to correct its balance of payments and related macroeconomic problems. This is one of the "adequate safeguards" called for in the IMF's Articles. These policies may include demand-restraint measures—fiscal restraint, credit and monetary tightening, and the like—to reduce the pressures on the balance of payments, as well as measures to induce a switch in production from nontradable goods to tradable goods—through, for example, a change in the exchange rate or other export-growth–enhancing measures. There should also be more general growth-promoting measures in the package, not least to help ensure both economic and political sustainability for the often difficult policy measures that may be needed. There is no template for such policies; there are many ways—and a multitude of specific policies—that may be selected and combined to bring about the desired correction. The specific program must be tailored to the country's individual circumstances and agreed to by the authorities and accepted by the population more broadly. Without such broad ownership and understanding, the difficult policy-adjustment process is unlikely to be fully implemented or sustained.[11]

But here is a key point. The policy package must be sufficient to correct the underlying problems and to put the country in a position to repay the IMF and manage its other payment obligations. In the most serious cases—those addressed in this chapter—those other debt-service obligations themselves may be restructured either by rescheduling, to spread the burden over time and perhaps remove humps in the debt-service profile, or by debt reduction. Especially in the latter case, the forces at work are multiple and highly complex. But in a single phrase, it comes down to a question of how much policy adjustment and how much debt relief. How much will the country have to sacrifice and how much loss to the creditors will there be? And who is to decide this?

Some critics of the IMF would charge that it dictates the degree of adjustment, the policy package, and does so with a bias toward protecting the claims of the creditors. This is the view of the IMF as debt collector. Reality, however, is much more complex. Countries and their populations can bear only so much in the adjustment process. This is well-recognized. But creditors have legitimate claims and rights as well. This is clearly the case under law, wherein creditors confronted with default can sue for repayment and, if successful, can attach assets and seek other forms of compensation.[12] But is this not the case morally as well? Is there not a matter of justice here as well? Sometimes those calling for the forgiveness of debt lose sight of the identification of the ultimate source of credit and the cost to the ultimate providers of credit. Behind official credits—say, by a country's export credit agency—are taxpayers. Behind private-market credits, from banks or through bond issues, are a host of individual creditors—depositors, bondholders, and the like. Perhaps there is little sympathy for such creditors in some quarters, and perhaps that is based on a perception of the situation of such individuals relative to that of the poor who may be affected by adjustments in the debtor country. But look, for example, at the profile of holders of Argentina's bonds. More than 40% of such debt is reported to be held by retail investors in countries such as Germany, Italy, and Japan, and these investors do not always fit the profile of wealthy "coupon clippers"; they are often pensioners who invested their savings in Argentine bonds. The rights of such individuals to repayment—like the rights of the coupon clippers—must be weighed against the pain of adjustment for the Argentine citizen.

In sorting all of this out, someone needs to judge the feasible, politically sustainable degree of adjustment. In the first instance, this is the responsibility of the country authorities to propose. But it is also the responsibility of the international community acting through the IMF to assess in judging the authorities' proposals. This does not mean dictating policies. It means discussing the alternatives, analyzing their impact, and measuring the implications for losses that may be taken within society, as well as by creditors. There is no way to avoid these judgments. At the same time, given the capacity of economic analysis, this is by no means an exact science.[13]

How then can the process unfold in a way that gives appropriate attention to the capacity of the economy and the population to adjust—for example, to pay more taxes or receive fewer services through government spending—and the capacity of creditors to absorb losses. The latter is relevant both because creditors also have rights and because these rights can be converted into legal judgments that, at the least, can complicate the efforts of the country to deal with its problems. And here lies one of the keys to a solution. The more orderly the adjustment and the sooner the benefits of that adjustment materialize, the more there will be to share between the country and its creditors.[14]

This view of the process may also hold the key to responding to the call from the NGOs and others—including the IMF itself—for civil society to have a role in the discussions leading to a debt-relief plan. Surely a better way needs to be found to provide that voice when considering how much adjustment is appropriate. The extremes are untenable. Minimum adjustment, for example through a full renunciation of the claims of creditors, will marginalize the country and prevent it from accessing financial resources needed to promote growth in the future. It also tramples on the rights of creditors. Similarly, full servicing of debt at the cost of unacceptable cuts in domestic services—including health, education, and other social programs—is also unacceptable. These extreme alternatives are also likely to be economically damaging in that they will adversely impact longer-term growth and development. The issue of justice returns here, and perhaps it is best achieved by assuring that the voices of all are heard. Civil society must have a role. The question is not whether they should participate—

especially in democratic societies—but the form and mechanisms through which that participation should be organized. And this goes to the issue of how policies and debt sustainability are really determined. In this context, the government budget is the key instrument of policy. That is where debt-service capacity will in the first instance be determined. And, contrary to the views of some in the NGO community, the country's budget is not dictated by the IMF when a country seeks its assistance. In most countries, and increasingly so, the budget is the result of a parliamentary process that determines the overall framework of the budget, spending priorities, judgments about taxing capacity, and all the other aspects of the final budget presentation. The IMF is part of that process through its discussions with the government. Civil society should certainly be part of that process as well through representations to the government, participation in parliamentary debate, the giving of testimony, lobbying, and through all other means traditional to the specific culture of each country. That is where effective participation is required; that is where transparency is needed; and that is the process through which the trade-offs that ultimately help determine sustainability will be made.

However, this is also the nexus of very difficult decisions by the international community and by the IMF. Should the international community endorse a country's budget—and the implicit haircut to be taken by creditors—if the government refuses to impose a fair tax burden on its own citizens? Should it endorse demands of creditors that would result in cutting critical expenditures on social programs below some measure of what is required and appropriate in the country's circumstances? These are devilishly difficult judgments to make. But the international community, acting through the IMF, cannot avoid making these judgments. Decisions about IMF lending to a country in the context of debt relief to be provided by private or public creditors cannot be made in the absence of such judgments. Viewed in those terms, the burden to find a "just" solution lies squarely in the hands of that community.

But this does not remove the need for judgment! Here the burden on the IMF is a very serious and a very difficult one. All parties can be expected to argue their interests—less adjustment wanted by the country, more adjustment wanted by the creditors. As noted, a key means by which to help bring the parties together is to minimize the disruption stemming from a crisis and preserve or restart growth as quickly and effectively as possible. This limits the loss and reduces the burden on everyone, but there will still be losses to be shared, and the international community acting through the IMF has the responsibility to help define the corridor—not the exact solution point—down which that sharing will likely have to take place.

What Will Become of the SDRM Proposal?

Finally, what are the prospects for the SDRM? The proposals made regarding SDRM have stimulated an extremely important and productive debate that has vastly increased everyone's understanding of these issues. The atmosphere created by the prospect of an SDRM has also been the single most important factor in the progress that has been made to formulate and to encourage the use of collective-action clauses and, more recently, the impetus given to work on a code of good conduct for those operating in the international capital markets. Some have hinted, prematurely, at its death, but one should not rush to judgment at this time! Bankruptcy legislation took many years to enact in the United States and in other countries. These are not easy concepts, and people need to be persuaded. As indicated, over 70% of the executive board of the IMF, supports the SDRM. Even those now opposed support much of the substance of the proposal. More work and more thinking is called for, and that is what has been requested by the IMF's governing body.

Notes

1. The U.S. Declaration of Independence holds that "it is self-evident that all Men are endowed . . . with certain unalienable Rights . . . Life, Liberty, and the Pursuit of Happiness." But how far do those rights extend? Life—a healthy one? Is that an entitlement with implications for the role of government in the provision of health care? Liberty—the freedom to shout "fire" in a crowded auditorium? The Pursuit of Happiness—if it involves a cost to others or impinges on their rights? Some of these questions are reasonably well-answered. But others remain subject to intensive political debate and, presumably, will never be definitively resolved. The same is true of the concept of justice in the context of debt relief.

2. During 1975–88, the Paris Club creditors rescheduled debt but did not cancel debt or reduce present value through reductions in interest. But debt reduction began under initiatives announced at Toronto in 1988 (up to one-third), London in 1991 (up to 50%), Naples in 1994 (up to 67%), Lyon in 1996 (up to 80%), and Cologne in 1999 (up to 90%).

3. Take the airline insolvency cases now under negotiation in the United States. What kind of concessions are necessary from the various unions, let alone from the chief executives!, that will help determine the future cost structure of the companies before creditors should agree to a reorganization that involves a writedown of their claims? And how is this to be done in a way that does not leave the restructured company with an unfair cost advantage over its competitors who have not sought relief by filing for bankruptcy?

4. Jeff Sachs (2002: 23) makes this point quite dramatically. Citing the Commission on Macroeconomics and Health of the World Health Organization (WHO), which he chaired, he notes that "For low-income countries in Sub-Saharan Africa, for example, it was found that spending on health care services needs to increase from 3.9 percent of GNP in 2002 to 13.2 percent of GNP in 2015, in order to extend the coverage of essential health services to roughly two-thirds of the population." He then notes that "Annual debt service owed by a HIPC rarely exceeds 5 percent of its GNP. Thus, even if all of the HIPCs' debt were cancelled, the savings would not be enough to fund the increased outlays needed just for health, much less the sums also needed for expanded education and basic infrastructure, such as water and sanitation, and feeder roads to villages."

5. Here, too, Jeff Sachs is right on the mark. In an article, "A Rich Nation, A Poor Continent," in the *New York Times* on 9 July 2003, at the time of President Bush's visit

to Africa, Sachs noted that "According to a recent report from the Internal Revenue Service, some 400 super rich Americans had an average income of nearly $174 million each, or a combined income of $69 billion, in 2000 . . . more than the combined incomes of the 166 million people living in four of the countries that the president is visiting this week: Nigeria, Senegal, Uganda and Botswana" (A21). Furthermore, and incredibly, "Suppose the super rich applied their tax savings (under the Bush tax cuts) towards Africa's survival. That . . . would provide a huge chunk of the $8 billion that the United States should contribute to the global health care effort" (A21). Imagine what could be done if Sachs's point were extended beyond just the 400 richest and beyond just those in the United States!

6. This could be a possible outcome under the approach suggested by some NGOs because the debtor government might be willing to tighten policies in the near term to accelerate reaccess to capital markets.

7. The statutory basis of the SDRM approach would provide the legal framework under which a debtor and its creditors could act as if common collective-action clauses were included in all relevant debt instruments.

8. Creating a new international treaty would likely be a much more complicated and uncertain undertaking than amending the IMF's Articles of Agreement. The Articles have been amended before, and therefore this process is familiar to the membership. Moreover, an amendment can take effect when three-fifths of the members having 85% of the voting power have accepted the amendment. Upon such acceptance, the amendment becomes binding on all members and therefore universally applicable immediately. Amending the IMF's Articles rather than creating a new international treaty would also provide the framework with greater stability. Withdrawing from a free-standing treaty may have little cost to the withdrawing country. Withdrawing from the IMF, however, deprives the country of the benefits of membership in the IMF as provided for under the Articles of Agreement and is an action no country has ever voluntarily taken.

9. Some also see this role as incompatible with the IMF's role as a creditor, and indeed a preferred creditor. The IMF has traditionally been treated as a preferred creditor by debtor countries and by other creditors (i.e., by the private banks and capital markets and by bilateral official creditors). It is widely accepted that, as the institution providing finance to a country in times of crisis and in times when other sources of credit have often disappeared, it is appropriate for the IMF to have preferred status. The argument is simply that crisis financing would not likely be forthcoming without that protection; hence, crises would almost certainly be deeper, more protracted, and more costly both to the involved country and to its neighbors and the international community more generally. This preferred status, of course, means that, in the event debt relief is sought, the other creditors must provide a greater share of the needed relief than would be the case if the IMF reduced its own claims also. It seems odd that this preferred status of the IMF is accepted as appropriate by private and official creditors affected by it in the way just described, whereas others, such as NGOs, which are not so affected, are opposed to it.

10. This is stated in Article I of the Articles of Agreement of the IMF, which lists the purposes of the Fund. Article I (v) states: "To give confidence to members by making the general resources of the Fund temporarily available to them under adequate safeguards, thus providing them with opportunity to correct maladjustments in their balance of payments without resorting to measures destructive of national or international prosperity."

11. This search for ownership and broad-based support was one of the motivations for the development of the poverty reduction strategy paper process, which seeks to assure

the participation of a broad spectrum of civil society in the development of a country's economic policies.

12. The judgments made in cases of sovereign debt under the laws of the countries in which financial centers are located are based on the rights of the creditors under those laws; the courts in such cases do not—as they do under domestic bankruptcy law pertinent to individuals and corporations—make judgments about the capacity of the country to make the contractual payments.

13. Perhaps the clearest example of the IMF playing this role is in the context of the HIPC initiative. The IMF, clearly working with the World Bank and others, effectively sought the agreement of the international community—including both official and private creditors—that the capacity of the poorest heavily indebted countries to adjust was not sufficient to permit full repayment of their debt and that relief from all creditors was needed. Here, the case may have been obvious, and the IMF was working in concert with creditors who, for the most part, had come to the same conclusion. Although less obvious or less accepted in other cases, the essence of the IMF's role is the same.

14. This is, of course, the appeal of the SDRM to many of its advocates.

References

Jubilee USA Network. 2003. *Statement on Arbitration.* Available online at: www .jubileeusa.org/arbitration.pdf.

Kremer, M., and Jayachandran, S. 2002. *Odious Debt.* Policy Brief. Washington, DC: The Brookings Institution.

Krueger, A. 2002. *A New Approach to Sovereign Debt Restructuring.* Washington, DC: International Monetary Fund.

Pettifor, A., and Raffer, K. 2003. *Report of the IMF's Conference on the Sovereign Debt Restructuring Mechanism,* 22 January 2003. London: Jubilee Research.

Rieffel, L. 2003. *Restructuring Sovereign Debt.* Washington, DC: The Brookings Institution.

Rogoff, K., and Zettelmeyer, J. 2002. Early Ideas on Sovereign Bankruptcy Reorganization: A Survey. Working Paper WP/02/57. Washington, DC: International Monetary Fund.

Ross, D., and Abrego, L. 2001. Debt Relief under the HIPC Initiative: Context and Outlook for Debt Sustainability and Resource Flow. Working Paper WP/01/144. Washington, DC: International Monetary Fund.

Sachs, J. 2002. Resolving the Debt Crisis of Low Income Countries. Brookings Papers on Economic Activity, No. 1. Washington, DC: The Brookings Institution.

12

THE IMF'S SDRM—SIMPLY DISASTROUS RESCHEDULING MANAGEMENT?

Kunibert Raffer

After nearly two decades of fierce opposition to the idea of sovereign insolvency, the International Monetary Fund (IMF or the Fund) has performed a remarkable and sudden U-turn and fully embraced it. In November 2001, its then First Deputy Managing Director, Anne Krueger, unexpectedly joined those proposing a solution to the sovereign debt problem based on domestic insolvency laws:

> [T]he lack of adequate incentives to ensure the timely and orderly restructuring of unsustainable sovereign debts has remained an important weakness. Staff and management of the IMF have been considering in recent months how to fill this gap, helped by suggestions from academics, the private creditor community, nongovernmental organizations, national authorities, and our Executive Board. (Krueger 2002b: v)

Although the titles of Krueger's first papers speak of a "new approach," the idea of sovereign insolvency is not new at all (Krueger 2001a, 2001b, 2002a, 2002b).[1] This chapter reviews the history of sovereign insolvency and critiques the IMF's proposed approach. It then describes a more promising model based on Chapter 9, Title 11, of the U.S. Bankruptcy Code (known simply as Chapter 9).

History of Sovereign Insolvency

Before Krueger, Adam Smith recommended in *The Wealth of Nations* a fair and open bankruptcy as the solution least dishonorable to sovereign debtors and least hurtful to creditors. In 1981, an international lawyer, C. G. Oechsli, published a proposal to use the principles of corporate insolvency, specifically Chapter 11, Title 11, of the U.S. Bankruptcy Code (known as Chapter 11 for short) to renegotiate the debts of developing countries. Soon after, a British banker, David Suratgar, proposed a similar idea, and another banker, the late Alfred Herrhausen, was among the most vocal advocates of negotiated debt reduction at that time. Their proposals were later supported by a number of economists, among them Nobel Laureate Lawrence Klein, Jeffrey Sachs, and myself. The United Nations Conference on Trade and Development (UNCTAD) advocated Chapter 11 in 1986. Thomas Kampffmeyer was the first to draw attention to the German example of a de facto insolvency and proposed the application of corporate insolvency to Southern debtors (Kampffmeyer 1987).

The U.S. Treasury and both the World Bank and the International Monetary Fund strongly opposed sovereign insolvency, operating on the illiquidity theory: Countries should be considered temporarily illiquid, not bankrupt. Debtors would "grow out of debts." These institutions dismissed the Chapter 11 approach with the technicality that it fails to address the question of sovereignty and is therefore inapplicable to sovereign countries.

In 1987, I responded to this argument by proposing to internationalize Chapter 9, which is applicable to municipal insolvencies (Raffer 1989). Chapter 9 takes into account the issue of governmental powers (comparable to sovereignty), and its principal features can be applied directly to sovereigns. Eichengreen correctly saw the main obstacle of this proposal as being the lack of political will to implement it (Eichengreen 1999)—a problem significantly redressed once the Fund itself proposed sovereign insolvency.

After the Mexican crash of 1994–95, Alan Greenspan publicly contemplated the concept of international insolvency. But this apparent official interest quickly subsided. Jubilee 2000 UK, which started the growing international debt-reduction movement, took up the Chapter 9 proposal and campaigned for cancelation of unpayable debts under an international arbitration process based on Chapter 9 principles. Other campaigns followed. The German Erlaszjahr 2000 first demanded "an international Chapter 9." Jubilee 2000 Red Guayaquil (Ecuador) and the Tegucigalpa Declaration of Latin American Jubilee movements did so, too.

Around 2000, the proposal received additional support from the Organization for Economic Co-operation and Development (OECD) (in the *Reports on the International Financial Architecture* published after the Asian crisis) and in statements by employees of the Bank of England and the Bank of Canada, arguing that sovereign debtors need the safe harbor that bankruptcy law provides in a corporate context (Haldane and Kruger 2001). Just before Krueger's first speech, the U.S. Treasury Secretary, Paul O'Neill, the British Chancellor of the Exchequer, Gordon Brown, and the Canadian Finance Minister, Paul Martin, spoke out in favor of a solution modeled on Chapter 11.

Thus, although laudable, Krueger's approach is hardly new. Her merit was in finally breaking the taboo at the IMF and bringing about a long-needed change in its attitude. She provided credibility at 19th and H Streets. Her approach—now called the sovereign debt restructuring mechanism (SDRM)—dif-

fers perceptibly from earlier proposals.[2] It is totally shaped by the IMF's institutional self-interest, and, understandably, strong reservations were lodged
against it by creditors (including the U.S. Treasury) (Taylor 2002), NGOs, and
academics.

By proposing the SDRM, the IMF finally admitted the long-denied obvious.
On the basis of debatable data, the IMF and the World Bank had claimed that
their programs would restore sustainability and overcome the debt problem. The
first HIPC initiative's officially declared objective was reaching overall debt
sustainability by coordinated action, allowing countries to exit from continuous
rescheduling (IBRD 1997: 44). The very existence of the enhanced HIPC proves
that the original HIPC was unable to do so, and the two HIPC initiatives underscore the failure of IMF and World Bank strategies generally in the poorest
countries. Finally joining the ranks of those demanding sovereign insolvency
over the years, the IMF admitted the failure of traditional debt management in
middle-income countries. Krueger (2001a) rightly stresses that an orderly workout "would clearly reduce the costs of restructuring," and the unnecessarily
heavy economic costs imposed by present debt strategies on countries "themselves, and on the international community that has to help pick up the pieces."
She fails to mention why countries did not opt for that solution in spite of such
costs: Creditors had not allowed debtor countries to opt for it. Most notably, the
IMF and the World Bank forced countries "with insurmountable debt problems"
not to do so. The heavy costs of delay rightly deplored by Krueger are "creditor
caused" damage (Raffer 1998).

Although this chapter agrees that sovereign insolvency procedures are urgently needed to fill a gap in the international financial architecture, it argues
against the IMF's specific approach. Reflecting strong institutional self-interest
on the part of the IMF, the SDRM is unfair, in particular to private creditors
and debtors. If implemented, it is likely to become another unsuccessful IMF
attempt at debt management, a "Simply Disastrous Rescheduling Mechanism."

The Essence of the SDRM

After 2001, the IMF staff churned out SDRM variations and new acronyms at
a speed that made description of *the* SDRM difficult. Nevertheless, some fundamental points have remained unchanged, although a host of alternatives regarding details obfuscate the picture.

Starting Proceedings

Krueger's proposal gives the IMF much discretion over the insolvency process.
A technically insolvent country would "come to the Fund and request" a stay,
getting "implicit support to a temporary standstill" (Krueger 2001a: 5). The
debtor could "negotiate a rescheduling or restructuring with its creditors, given
the Fund's consent to that line of attack" (Krueger 2001a: 5). The Fund would
thus be given the right to endorse the stay triggered by the debtor's demand for

insolvency relief, and thus there would be no SDRM "attack" without the IMF's permission.

Krueger continues: "Like an IMF-supported adjustment program, the stand-still could be endorsed for limited periods and renewed following reviews of the country's economic policies and its relations with creditors" (Krueger 2001a: 7). She suggests a "maximum period beyond which the stay could not be maintained without the approval of a required majority of creditors." Krueger's proposal allows for more than one renewal. Creditors might have to wait before getting a chance to vote on a stay, and during this period the Fund alone would decide. Creditor majorities endorsing legal protection from the start—the IMF could be understood this way (see e.g. IMF 2002c: 5)—is clearly unrealistic. Forming creditor committees takes time.

The passage on relations with creditors raises the question of why the Fund would have to evaluate them. Are creditors themselves unable to judge whether their relations with a debtor are good? What if their view differs from the IMF's? What happens if—for the sake of argument—all creditors accept a stay but the IMF does not agree? Would the IMF cooperate if a solution it disliked were agreed on by all—or a supermajority (e.g., majorities across all debt instruments)—of creditors and the debtor?

The IMF eventually stated that: "Activation [of a stay] would not automatically trigger any suspension of creditor rights. There would be no generalized stay on enforcement and no suspension of contractual provisions" (IMF 2002d: 9). The IMF proposes the application of the "hotchpot" rule: Any amount recovered through litigation would be deducted from the sum the creditor would finally be entitled to receive (with legal expenses, successful litigants could be worse off than those not litigating). However, quick-acting creditors might be able to collect more through litigation than their share of a final settlement, and forcing successful litigants to surrender money would be impractical. Therefore, the IMF proposes that its sovereign debt dispute resolution forum (SDDRF) should, upon the debtor's request and subject to the approval of creditors, have the authority to require courts outside the sovereign's territory to enjoin specific enforcement actions that might seriously undermine the restructuring process. Creditors would have an incentive to urge the debtor to demand a stay, as any money recovered over and above the amounts resulting from the SDRM would come at their expense. The IMF suggests that representative creditors' committees could have the authority to vote on behalf of the majority of creditors until creditors are sufficiently well-organized to act collectively. These two mechanisms assure that, in the absence of a lucky, speedy litigant actually collecting, the same amount of money will be recovered without and under automatic stays. The economic effect would be equal.

The ability to restrict litigation already exists. The IMF explains that debtor countries may further limit their vulnerability to litigation by depositing assets in jurisdictions where enhanced protection from legal processes is already available. The IMF suggests that a creditor "who has obtained a judgment—but has not yet collected on it—could still have its claim restructured through a vote of a qualified majority" (2002d: 34). Because litigation is seldom quick, and, as some commentators note, U.S. courts are inclined to delay if negotiations are under way between creditors and a debtor, the possibility of a quick hit seems virtually zero in practice. Retaining the right to litigation—a concern expressed by many Wall Street investors—is thereby reduced to a meaningless formality without any consequences but additional costs (Raffer 2003).

As a fundamental legal principle, creditors must not be the judge over their own cause, and insolvency laws demand neutral entities—courts—to decide on stays. The IMF's proposal that it alone endorse the stay would mean that one creditor alone could decide against everyone else, including a creditor majority and the debtor.

Similarly, the IMF states that interest would continue to accrue after the SDRM started "to limit any interference with contractual relations" (IMF 2002d: 42). However, "some of the interest that may have accrued after activation may be written off when the final restructuring agreement is negotiated." If a uniform interest rate were applied—as the Fund suggests—the result of adding first to reduce later is the same as that of stopping interest accrual.

Which Claims?

It is not clear which debts would be affected by the SDRM. The IMF suggests that debtors may choose which debts to include in the SDRM (IMF 2002c: 8), a choice that would be "influenced" by the Fund, whose conditionality would "enhance" the "incentives to assure equitable treatment" of creditors (IMF 2002c: 16). The IMF proposes to create many creditor classes with classification rules part of the amendment of its Articles of Agreement and "each class vested with effective veto power over the terms offered to other classes" (IMF 2002c). This would most likely result in at least one of the many classes blocking the proceedings. The IMF would certainly offer its "good services" to overcome such deadlocks, employing additional people if necessary.

The IMF consistently insists that multilateral debts, including its own claims, must be privileged. Under the SDRM, the present de facto preference for international financial institutions (IFIs) would be converted into a de jure preference. Preferential treatment of IFIs makes the ongoing discussion about bailing in the private sector particularly misleading.[3] The Miyazawa–Brady initiatives in Mexico and Ecuador, for example, foundered despite large and disproportionate reductions from private creditors. There is also an economic-efficiency argument in favor of equal treatment of creditors to guard against misallocation of funds and antimarket behavior by the IFIs.

With regard to Paris Club members, the situation remains unclear. The IMF suggests that these debts could be included in the SDRM (possibly in a separate class). These important IMF shareholders might fare better, as they "would presumably continue their current policy of requiring that the debtor seek comparable treatment from private creditors when private claims on the sovereign are judged to be material, and would also continue to assess whether the agreement of private creditors meets this requirement" (IMF 2002c: 21).

Essential Decisions

The IMF's executive board alone decides on the most important issues under the SDRM: sustainability (and thereby the amount of debt reduction) and the adequacy of the debtor's economic policy. These decisions cannot be challenged. Throughout the SDRM's variations, this has always remained clear and unchanged. In contrast with Chapter 9, which allows overindebted municipalities to present a plan, under the SDRM, the Fund, not the debtor, would submit the plan. The IMF even suggests that "it may be preferable for the Executive Board to be given the final authority to determine whether a member has breached its obligations and what sanctions should apply" (IMF 2003d: 54).

Amending the Articles of Agreement

The SDRM mechanism down to quite some detail is to be enshrined in the IMF's statute, which smacks of institutional self-interest. Krueger (2001a: 7) argues that laws barring "vultures" from interfering with the mechanism "must have the force of law universally." Otherwise, creditors would deliberately seek out jurisdictions where they can enforce claims against creditor majorities. Because "[g]etting every country to amend its domestic bankruptcy law—let alone to enforce it in a uniform way—would be a heroic undertaking," Krueger recommends an amendment of the IMF's Articles (Krueger (2001b: 3). This would oblige all member states to change their domestic laws in such a way that the opposition of creditor minorities can be overruled. "Super majorities" would then be able to bind dissenting creditors.[4] This "statutory approach" would firmly and officially install the IMF as the overlord of sovereign debt relief.

The argument in favor of the statutory approach is altogether flawed. Not all countries and territories are IMF members. The Cayman Islands, for example, is not a member but enjoys enough autonomy to offer itself as a place for creditors shopping for jurisdictions where unanimity is not required.[5]

Krueger (2002c: 4) reassures skeptics that the statutory amendment would be used "only as a tool to empower creditors and debtor, not as a way to extend the IMF's legal authority." This is difficult to believe, considering that there is an easy way to assure that "vultures" cannot disturb negotiations between creditors and the debtor. Krueger herself (Krueger 2001a: 4) points out that it is not absolutely clear whether the tactics of Elliot Associates (a classic "vulture fund") would "survive legal challenge in future cases." Legally, there are several ways to preclude vulture funds from operating and at least one watertight way of doing so (Raffer 2002).

Fortunately, neither universality nor an international treaty is needed; just the co-operation of big creditor governments would suffice. Loan agreements are heavily concentrated in very few jurisdictions. Most are governed by New York and British laws. If the United States and the United Kingdom changed their sovereign immunity laws slightly, the problem of disruptive litigation would be solved for most existing contracts; and if followed by those few "exotic" places such as Frankfurt, whose laws are occasionally stipulated, the problem would disappear. By revising these laws such that the start of international insolvency procedures would suspend all waivers of immunity relating to a case, the respective courts of these jurisdictions would have to refuse to hear disruptive litigation. Additional provisions stating that "the confirmation of an international solvency plan voids such waivers of immunity" would foreclose litigation after successful proceedings. Such minor changes would not affect domestic laws.

Collective-action clauses (CACs) in future loan contracts could bar disruptive litigation from the start. They could include any of the useful CACs proposed so far or agree on arbitration instead of waivers of immunity, as already stipulated by some contracts between countries and private creditors. One could agree on a traditional waiver of immunity combined with the stipulation that no creditor be allowed to sue during insolvency proceedings. Any of these options would put an end to the interference of vulture funds.

The statutory approach would increase the IMF's importance dramatically. It would end the long turf war between the International Bank for Reconstruction and Development (IBRD) and the IMF about who is in charge of debt management, at least for insolvent countries. Unlike past debt-management strategies, where the IBRD and the IMF have jointly played the leading role, the IBRD would be out. Present unjustified preferred creditor treatment would be legally guaranteed by treaty. This is one important difference between the SDRM and all earlier proposals.

The (SD)DRF

In spite of Krueger's initial assertion (Krueger 2001a) that the IMF should not adjudicate disputes, verify claims, or confirm the integrity of voting, a new organ of the IMF, initially called the dispute resolution forum (DRF) and later the sovereign debt dispute resolution forum (SDDRF), is to chair SDRM proceedings. The executive board could not play this role because of the perception that its decisions would be guided by the IMF's creditor interests or by the debtor country's IMF membership. Krueger proposed a "new judicial organ" with "very limited functions," established by amending the IMF's Articles of Agreement and operating independently from the executive board and the board of governors: "The amendment would provide that the decisions of the judicial organ would not be subject to review by any of the IMF's other organs, and that, more generally, the judges appointed . . . would not be subject to the interference or influence of the staff and management of the IMF" (Krueger 2002b: 35).

Conspicuously, interference and influence of the Board are not excluded. This new IMF organ has no "authority to challenge decisions made by the Executive Board regarding, inter alia, the adequacy of a member's policies or the sustainability of the member's debt" (Krueger 2002b: 35). It "would enjoy limited but exclusive powers for the orderly conduct of the restructuring process, including the resolution of disputes between a sovereign debtor and its creditors . . . and amongst creditors" (Krueger 2002c: 4). It should operate "independently not only of the Executive Board, but also of the governors, management and staff of the IMF. The flipside of this independence is that the role of the dispute resolution forum should be strictly limited" (Krueger 2002c: 4).

Apparently, Krueger sees a necessary trade-off between independence and authority. The SDDRF would also verify claims, oversee voting, and certify key decisions by the debtor and creditor supermajorities. Its decisions resolving disputes between the debtor and its creditors or among creditors could not be challenged (IMF 2002c). Although the possibility of appeal was proposed later, the SDDRF would have substantial powers over private creditors and the debtor.

In spite of the SDDRF's limited role, Krueger (2002c) proposed a complicated, clumsy, and unnecessary five-stage process dominated by the IMF. All member countries were to nominate one person. These nominees were then to be vetted (with outside advice) by a "neutral" committee established by the IMF's executive board in order to reduce the roster from 183 names to 21. The vetted and reduced list was to be passed to the governors for a vote on the entire list as a package. If approved, the managing director would appoint the members for a renewable term. The appointed would elect a president, who—when needed—would "impanel" three members of the roster to form the panel for actual cases.

The IMF's weighted voting structure establishes clear creditor majorities. They would be able to determine the committee and to dismiss its proposal. Once again, debtors would be under the thumb of their official creditors. Barry Herman devised interesting proposals to alleviate the concern that creditors would choose the committee and determine the members of the SDDRF. One could introduce the one-country-one-vote rule for the special case of selecting the SDDRF. Alternatively, one could hold a two-stage election allowing only candidates with more than a certain percentage of the vote to pass to stage two, which would give both creditor and debtor sides a veto. Of course, one could go further than Herman by eliminating voting altogether. The affected creditors and the debtor could simply choose from the whole list of 183 persons, which of course would reduce the control of the IMF and official creditors.

Soon, different variations were proposed, all similarly complicated (IMF 2002d). Either the executive board would choose 7–11 representative member countries and ask each to forward the name of one judge to form a selection panel, or the managing director would appoint 7–11 independent and qualified persons to the selection panel based on external advice by respected organizations. The latter is preferred by the Fund's staff.

This panel would then select a pool of 12–16 candidates from which judges would be "impaneled" when a crisis arose. The Fund recommends that its members and "any other persons or organizations" could nominate SDDRF members (IMF 2002d: 59). The selection panel could also search for candidates. Advice of independent, international professional associations that are expert in insolvency and debt restructuring, and the views of private creditors' associations, member countries, executive directors, and any other interested parties, are to be considered (IMF 2002d). Apparently, this catch-all phrase does not include the affected debtor population.

The panel would have to adhere to selection criteria specified in the amendment to the IMF's Articles of Agreement in producing the list and proposing a president and alternate president. The list would have to be accepted by consensus and be forwarded to the board of governors, through the executive board, for approval. The board of governors could get authority to enlarge the number of nominees that can be designated by the selection panel. Again, the board of governors would only be able to accept or reject the list. If rejected, the process would start all over again. If approved, the managing director would appoint the members for renewable terms. An appeal process was added. All of these detailed provisions would be part of the IMF's amended statute (IMF 2002c, 2002d).

Krueger (2002c: 5f) asserts: "Just as importantly, if [the SDDRF] would have no authority to override the decisions of a qualified majority of creditors on such issues as the terms of the restructuring plan or the length of a stay." In fact, because the IMF determines sustainability and economic policies, only one practically important decision is left to creditors. Creditor majorities can refuse to accept the result, leaving the problem unsolved, however, and possibly encouraging the IMF to support the debtor. All remaining decisions on terms can only affect relatively minor issues, such as repayment schedules of n or $(n+k)$ years. In spite of repeated assertions to the contrary, the IMF would be left with all important decisions.

Reservations about the SDRM

The open discussion triggered by the Fund was commendable. Reservations about the SDRM come from all sectors. Because the IMF will continue to determine sustainability and dictate the debtor's policies, the fundamental problem that characterized past debt reductions will remain unchanged.

Understandably, Krueger's "statutory approach" has met substantial reservations. Even quite a few executive directors of the Fund identified concerns about a significantly extended role for the IMF. John Taylor, the U.S. Treasury's undersecretary for international affairs, opposed an increase in the IMF's importance, proposing as an alternative a package of new CACs (Taylor 2002). In fact, CACs fit perfectly with sovereign insolvency. Enhancing the creditors' ability to act collectively would allow more efficient and quicker results. Taylor sees the need to limit official sector support and sees reform of sovereign debt restructuring as a means to do so. He does not object to arbitration as a means of handling inconsistencies between different types of issues or jurisdictions. One may thus conclude that Taylor is opposed to one specific model but is not necessarily against an insolvency mechanism generally. Obviously, he is not against arbitral awards as such but against centralizing the process with the IMF.

Private creditors expected to take another haircut oppose Krueger's approach fiercely, and rightly so. The SDRM discriminates against them and totally disempowers them with respect to the most important decisions. Private creditors have already complained about undue preference of multilaterals. Even before the SDRM, private creditors voiced concern that the IMF and the World Bank "will be concerned with protecting their own balance sheets rather than with fair 'burden sharing,' " and therefore are "not suited either as arbitrators or as objective regulators of sovereign insolvency procedures" (Commerzbank 1999). This holds equally for the SDRM.

Understandably, debtor countries oppose the SDRM. The SDRM is unlikely to solve their problems and will increase the IMF's already crushing weight. The SDRM does not take the debtor's justified interests properly into account. Likewise, civil society and NGOs oppose the scheme because it would not restore the debtor's economic viability. The misery of debtor-country populations and the inefficiency of present debt management would continue even though private creditors might be asked to grant considerable debt reduction. The SDRM would enshrine an increased role for the IMF in international law.

Which Domestic Model?—Chapter 9 versus Chapter 11

First, Krueger was unclear which U.S. bankruptcy laws should be the model for SDRM—Chapter 9 (municipalities) or Chapter 11 (corporations). Later, Chapter 11 was declared the blueprint, although Krueger saw Chapter 9 "in many respects . . . of greater relevance in the sovereign context" (Krueger 2002b: 12ff). But she sees important differences between municipalities and sovereigns that would have implications on the design of the SDRM:

> Chapter 9 legislation acknowledges—and does not impair—the power of the state within which the municipality exists to continue to control the exercise of the powers of the municipality, including expenditures. This lack of independence of municipalities is one of the reasons why many countries have not adopted insolvency legislation to address problems of financial distress confronted by local governments. (Krueger 2002b: 12ff)

Quoting neither legal sources nor academic literature, Krueger's only short passage on Chapter 9 manifests her apparent dislike of it. The fact that municipalities are subject to constitutional rights of states is presented in a misleading way. It appears to be based on §903, "Reservation of State power to control municipalities":

> This chapter does not limit or impair the power of a State to control, by legislation or otherwise, a municipality of or in such State in the exercise of the political or governmental powers of such municipality, including expenditures for such exercise, but
>
> 1. a State law prescribing a method of composition of indebtedness of such municipality may not bind any creditor that does not consent to such composition; and
> 2. a judgment entered under such a law may not bind a creditor that does not consent to such composition (Chap. 9, 11 USC).

Responding to the need to reconcile constitutional rights of the federation and states, §903 simply states that insolvency procedures do not invalidate state laws and state rights regarding a "political subdivision or public agency or instrumentality of a State" (§101(34) 11 USC) deriving all its rights and powers from the state (Kupetz 1995). Filing for bankruptcy protection does not void the Constitution or the law—neither in the case of municipalities nor in the case of corporations. If justified, Krueger's reservation against Chapter 9 would also be valid against Chapter 11. Logically, domestic laws could no longer be a source of international law just because they do not deal with sovereigns.

Section 903 does not disturb constitutional arrangements.[6] As laws on the subject of bankruptcy are constitutionally reserved to Congress (Article I, Section 10) and states are prohibited from passing laws impairing the obligation of contracts, a state can basically suggest a solution. If creditors agree, this might be useful. Because the U.S. Constitution is not the constitution of every country, it is unlikely that U.S. constitutional concerns are the reason for the lack of municipal insolvency procedures in other countries. Hungary, on the advice of private Western consultants, adopted an insolvency law for public debtors after the demise of communism.

The difference between the Chapters 9 and 11 is fundamental. Chapter 9 is the only procedure protecting governmental powers and thus applicable to sovereigns. Section 904 ("Limitation on Jurisdiction and Powers of Court") clearly states:

> Notwithstanding any power of the court, unless the debtor consents or the plan so provides, the court may not, by any stay, order, or decree, in the case or otherwise, interfere with
>
> 1. any of the political and governmental powers of the debtor
> 2. any of the property or revenues of the debtor; or
> 3. the debtor's use or enjoyment of any income-producing property.

The concept of sovereignty does not contain anything more than what §904 protects. The court's jurisdiction depends on the municipality's volition, beyond which it cannot be extended, similar to the jurisdiction of international arbitrators. Unlike in other bankruptcy procedures, liquidation of the debtor or receivership is not possible. No trustee can be appointed (§926, avoiding powers, if seen as an exception, is very special and justified). Section 902(5) explicitly confirms that " 'trustee', when used in a section that is made applicable in a case under this chapter . . . means debtor." Change of "management" of U.S. municipalities (i.e., removing elected officials) by courts or creditors is not possible—nor should it be in the case of sovereigns. If any regulatory or electoral approvals are necessary under nonbankruptcy law in order to carry out a provision of the plan, §943(b)(6) states that this must be obtained before the court can confirm the plan, a point clearly adaptable to sovereigns. Obviously, similar guarantees are absent from Chapter 11.

Public interest in the functioning of the debtor safeguards a core of municipal activities. Municipalities in the United States are allowed to maintain basic social services essential to the health, safety, and welfare of their inhabitants. The affected population has a right to be heard. The procedure is as transparent as befits a public entity. The U.S. Chapter 9 provides viable solutions protecting the governmental sphere of the debtor as well as the interests of creditors. This is essential, as only a totally fair mechanism would be universally accepted, and rightly so. Naturally, only the basic principles, not all details, of Chapter 9 should form the basis of arbitral proceedings. Evidently, some important and necessary details of Chapter 9 are unnecessary and inapplicable internationally. Eligibility and authorization to be a Chapter 9 debtor—fundamental and necessary within the United States for constitutional reasons—is one example.

Compared with the SDRM, the Chapter 9 model has one major drawback for the IMF—the additional protection of sovereignty, governmental powers, public interest, and rights of other creditors would limit the Fund's absolute dominance.

Advantages of an International Chapter 9

An international insolvency mechanism based on Chapter 9 has clear advantages over the proposed SDRM, as described in the following sections.[7]

Respecting the Rule of Law

The SDRM violates the fundamental legal principle that one must not be a judge in one's own cause. All major legal systems require a neutral entity without self-interest to preside over legal conflicts, deciding if and when necessary. This is also economically sensible, as someone with a vested interest is unlikely to decide objectively and thus efficiently. The IMF's role in debt management since the mid-1970s drives this point home. One important and fundamental principle preached to debtor countries by creditors, not least the IMF, is brushed aside when it comes to dealing with Southern debts and increasing the IMF's influence. Under the SDRM, the IMF, a creditor with a creditor voting majority, would assume the role of a judge in determining issues vital to its own self-interest.

This also results in unfair treatment of other creditors, as the SDRM perfectly illustrates. The IMF has shaped the economic policies of debtor economies over decades, has been a leading institution in all debt-management schemes, and is thus co-responsible for present problems. Countries such as Argentina or Indonesia were held up as models right until their respective crashes, when quick and comprehensive reassessments of each country's performance occurred. What has been lauded as efficient and healthy is condemned as inefficient and corrupt a split second later. In spite of the IMF's co-responsibility the SDRM allows it to get out scot-free and even rewards the Fund with an increased role in debt management. To reach sustainability, other creditors have to lose more compared with equal treatment of all creditors. Rather than bailing in the private sector, the SDRM bails out the IMF.

Under an international Chapter 9 process, by contrast, ad hoc arbitration panels, a traditional mechanism of international law, would be nominated by both sides. Creditors and debtors would nominate one or two persons, who in turn would elect one further member to reach an uneven number. All the IMF's clumsy selection processes are unnecessary. The parties, debtor and creditors, would establish panels—the IMF would not be needed. A treaty, although possible, is not necessary. Ad hoc arbitration, used over centuries, allows greater flexibility than treaties and solves problems adequately when they come up. If the major creditor governments against whose opposition no proceedings would be possible agreed to participate and sovereign immunity laws were changed as described, proceedings could start. Lawsuits against the debtor would no longer be legally possible in participating creditor countries, as the debtor's sovereign immunity would have been restored. Verdicts by courts from other countries could not be executed in participating countries. Creditors could no longer enforce their claims and protect their interests outside insolvency proceedings. This is not different from the SDRM—once the IMF's statute is amended, creditors would no longer be able to defend their interests outside the SDRM.

Unsurprisingly, the IMF has tried to find an argument against ad hoc panels. As claims would have to be verified first "to be recognized for participation in decision-making . . . the selection of a panel would have to follow, not precede, the verification process. But then who would resolve disputes arising from verification if there was [sic] no panel already in place?" (IMF 2002d: 63).

The answer is simple: All registering creditors nominate their arbitrators, who immediately decide on the recognition of claims. Collective-action clauses would be helpful to organize this process more quickly. Recognized creditors could either confirm their nominees or replace them. The latter could theoretically become necessary if so many claims are excluded that different arbitrators were nominated by the remaining creditors, which—though possible—seems unlikely to be the normal case. Because creditors are known and organized, endorsing or replacing them could be done quickly. Creditors whose claims are dismissed are parties to the case and should have the same right to nominate arbitrators judging their case as anyone else. To back up a weak point, the IMF adds that creditors might each wish to appoint their own arbitrator, which would make the case unmanageable and "could distort the balance of power between the debtor- and creditor-selected arbitrators." This seems to hold only if the nominees are not impartial arbitrators but actually represent and defend the interests of certain groups. In this case, of course, anyone would like to have their own "defenders." This problem never occurred in the few cases so far where private creditors and sovereign debtors agreed on arbitration on debt issues. Compared with having to accept the IMF's choice, my proposal of ad hoc panels definitely confers more rights on creditors.

Naturally, the debtor government may choose to leave the task of nominating panel members either to the Parliament or the people. Arbitrators could be elected from a roster by voters. Anyone reaching a minimum of supporting signatures by voters would have to be on it. Alternatively, one arbitrator might be chosen by Parliament and the other by voters. The Parliament might establish a special committee for this purpose, including members of the cabinet, as proposed in a bill drafted on the initiative of Congressman Mario Cafiero by the Argentine opposition party ARI. The bill would establish a "Comisión Representativa del Estado Nacional." Consisting of members from both houses and the executive power, it would nominate panel members and represent Argentina during the proceedings. In case of a change of government, which has occurred quite often in indebted countries, a new incoming government might be prepared to opt for one of these democratic possibilities.

Arbitrators would have the task of mediating between debtors and creditors, chairing and supporting negotiations by advice, providing adequate possibilities to be heard for those affected by the plan, and—if necessary—deciding the case. This would be done while obeying the main principles of Chapter 9, such as protection of the debtor's governmental powers and the right of the affected population to voice their views, but also the best interest of creditors. The entities and NGOs representing the population, such as trade unions, entrepreneurial associations, and religious or nonreligious NGOs, would present their views, argue their points, and present their data in an open procedure before the panel. Sustainability would emerge from the facts presented and discussed. It would not be determined by the IMF, whose record of estimating sustainability is anything but good.

I suggested that the procedure start with a verification process of claims as is usual in all domestic insolvency regimes, applying the same legal standards as in the North (Raffer 1990: 309). Representatives of official creditors, especially of IFIs, declared this to be utopian and impossible. Meanwhile, verification became part of Krueger's "new approach." The IMF demanded specific checks regarding "for example, the authority of an official to borrow on behalf of the debtor."[8] (IMF 2002d: 68). The panel would have to terminate the proceedings if activation is unjustified or deny approval of a plan if the debtor has the means to honor all its obligations. There is no need to involve the IMF to obtain "an appropriate means for the Fund to signal its disapproval" (IMF 2002d: 26).

Because facts would be presented by both parties and the representatives of the population in a transparent procedure before the panel, the debtor's capacity to pay and sustainability would emerge fairly reliably from this process. Defending their legitimate self-interests, anyone could present data and arguments to corroborate their position, thus narrowing down the set of feasible options considerably. Decisions—if needed—are unlikely to affect substantial sums of money but rather solve deadlock situations. For obvious reasons, justified opposition by creditors should not be simply overruled. "Agreements between debtor and creditors would need the confirmation of the arbitrators, in analogy to Section 943" (Raffer 1990: 305). The panels would have to take particular care to ensure fairness and to safeguard the human dignity of the poor—similar to the protection enjoyed by a municipality's inhabitants.

One question is whether to form ad hoc panels or to establish a specialized institution. Theoretically, institutionalized bodies (e.g., special panels at the International Court of Justice or the International Chamber of Commerce) or rosters of arbitrators at UNCITRAL (UN Commission on International Trade Law) could work as well. Barry Herman suggested a special body elected in a way comparable with that of UNCITRAL (where the UN General Assembly elects members), or individuals could be elected by the UN General Assembly and the UN Security Council. The debtor majority in the General Assembly might make creditor states skeptical, even though this would only invert the debtor–creditor relation compared with Krueger's proposal. Paulus proposes a "model law" formulated by UNCITRAL or UNCTAD for example, to be copied by countries in order to avoid different national laws dealing with sovereign insolvency combined with a neutral entity (Paulus 2003). The latter could either be a member of the UN family or the International Court of Justice. The proposal by Acosta and Ugarteche (2003) is probably the most far-reaching—an international arbitration tribunal working on the basis of the Chapter 9 principles, to which I would additionally propose codifying a legal framework of international financial relations.

Practically, however, both speed and their self-dissolving quality strongly recommend ad hoc panels—at least for the present debt overhang. Once the backlog of cases has been dealt with, it is to be hoped that there will be no more need for a body. The existence of an international Chapter 9 would be both a disincentive to loose lending and an incentive to find solutions "in the shade of the law," as Krueger put it. Any standing body with the exclusive mandate to chair sovereign insolvency cases would thus hopefully soon be underemployed. If so, one may suppose that the IMF would search for new activities for its SDDRF to justify its existence.

The Principle of Debtor Protection

The idea of internationalizing the basic ideas of U.S. municipal insolvency reflects the basic function of any insolvency procedure, solving a conflict between two fundamental legal principles: the right of creditors to interest and repayments, and the human right recognized generally (not only in the case of loans) by all civilized legal systems that no one must be forced to fulfill contracts at the cost of inhumane distress, life, health, or human dignity. In the case of insolvency, these principles collide. Although their claims are recognized as legitimate, insolvency exempts resources from being seized by bona fide creditors. Debtors—unless they happen to be developing countries—cannot be forced to starve their children in order to pay (see Hanlon, Chapter 5, this volume; Jochnick, Chapter 6, this volume). Human rights and human dignity are given priority over repayment, even though insolvency only deals with claims based on a solid and proper legal foundation. A fortiori this is valid in the case of less well-founded claims.

None of the IMF's documents so far contains the smallest hint of any kind of debtor protection. Neither the affected population nor vulnerable groups have any possibility of voicing their views. Considering that HIPC II recognizes—at least verbally—the participation of affected people and the protection of the poor, the SDRM is rooted in the ideas of the failed HIPC I and the "structural adjustment" model of the 1980s.

Besides preserving essential services to the population, Chapter 9 also gives the affected a right to be heard. Internationally, it would have to be exercised by representation (Raffer 1990). Taxpayers who have to pick up the bill should indeed have a right to know and to comment on proposed solutions. Participation and transparency, other important demands of public creditors vis-à-vis their debtors, are guaranteed within the United States. It should be added that within the United States the court may, but need not, grant the right to be heard to anyone with a direct legal interest in the case—a legal standard that is a far cry indeed both from IMF practice and the SDRM. Nongovernmental Organization representing the population would thus not be "arbitrators" as Rogoff and Zettelmeyer (2002a) wrongly believe.

Exempting resources necessary to finance minimum standards of basic health services, primary education, and other needs can only be justified if that money is demonstrably used for its declared purpose. Not without reason, creditors as well as NGOs are concerned that this might not be the case. The solution is quite simple—a transparently managed fund financed by the debtor in domestic currency. The management of this fund could be monitored by an international board or advisory council consisting of members from the debtor country as well as from creditor countries. They could be nominated by NGOs and governments (including the debtor government). Because this fund is a legal entity of its own, checks and discussions of its projects would not concern the government's budget, which is an important part of a country's sovereignty. Aid could also be channeled through the fund, changing its character of money just set apart from the ordinary budget toward a normal fund for the poor.[9]

Preferential Treatment of Multilateral Debts

One cornerstone of the SDRM is the unconditional exemption of the IMF's own and other multilateral claims, thus legalizing present unjustified practice. Commercial banks and bondholders usually have not interfered with their clients' economic policies. International financial institutions have strongly influenced the use of loans, exerting massive pressure on debtors—to the extent of provoking doubts whether countries "owned" their economic policies. They have routinely taken economic decisions but refused to participate in the risks involved. They insist on full repayment, even if damages negligently caused by their staff occur, which have to be paid by borrowers. A high rate of failure of IFI loans renders adjustment programs necessary, which are administered by IFIs, as long as unconditional repayment to IFIs is upheld. This logical mechanism might be described somewhat cynically as "IFI-flops securing IFI-jobs" (Raffer 1993a: 158). This perverse incentive system is totally at odds with any market economy—with unsurprising results. The famous story on the IMF told by Stiglitz (2000) "of one unfortunate incident when team members copied large parts of the text for one country's report and transferred them wholesale to another," leaving the initial name in some places, underlines the need for financial accountability.

Like any other creditor, IFIs must carry the risk of losses. But, in addition, like consultants they should observe professional standards and must be financially responsible for their decisions in order to connect decisions and the risks involved. The most basic condition for the functioning of the market mechanism demands it. If this link is severed, market efficiency is severely disturbed, as former communist economies clearly prove. Economic efficiency, but also fairness to the debtor and to other creditors, demands that IFIs, which are at least partially responsible for the mess, should no longer be treated with preference.

Because conditionality initially was not foreseen for IMF drawings, loan-loss provisions were unnecessary. When conditionality was introduced, no appropriate changes regarding the Fund's financial accountability were made. This became particularly problematic once the IMF started massive debt-management operations. Introducing financial accountability for its own decisions is thus all the more important. Equal treatment if a debtor acting on IFI-provided advice becomes insolvent is the easiest way to do so.

The statutes of all multilateral development banks foresee default of sovereign borrowers. Article IV.6 of the IBRD's Articles of Agreement, for example, demands a special reserve to cover what Article IV.7 calls "Methods of Meeting Liabilities of the Bank in Case of Defaults." Detailed rules exist on how to proceed if sovereign debtors become insolvent or distressed. Because the IBRD is only allowed to lend either to members or nonmembers if member states fully guarantee repayment (Article III.4), the logical conclusion is that default of member states was definitely considered possible, and maybe even an occasionally necessary solution. Unaware of any preferred creditor status, a legal concept that cannot be found in its Articles of Agreement and does not formally apply to the IBRD, the IBRD's founders wanted it to be subject to some market discipline rather than totally exempt from it. Mechanisms allowing it—and regional development banks—to shoulder risks appropriately were designed. Thwarting its founders' intentions, the IBRD has refused to obey its own constitution. It wrongly claims that accepting loan losses would make development finance inoperative. By contrast, the European Bank for Reconstruct and Development recognizes losses and survives. The IMF has already reduced its claims in the case of HIPCs and started provisioning against expected losses. It is therefore difficult to argue that this is legally or technically impossible. There is no reason why IFIs should be protected from the market mechanism at the expense of other creditors and the debtor. In the case of HIPCs, sustainable levels of debt are unlikely to be achieved without considerable reductions of multilateral claims.

Generally, all creditors of one sovereign debtor—including domestic creditors—should be treated strictly equally. One possible exception may be other heavily indebted developing countries. It would not make sense to push country A into bankruptcy by relieving country B. In such cases, preferential and differential treatment, strictly according to objective criteria, such as claims affected, the creditor's GDP per capita, or export income, seems worth considering. Regarding some types of domestic debts, exceptions should be discussed, such as for pension funds forced by law to buy government bonds. Securing decent pensions (which does not necessarily mean total exemption) in spite of losses resulting from forced investments should be part of debtor protection. When negotiating the resources for the fund financing the protection of the poor, money could be earmarked for this purpose. Unpaid wages of civil servants should be paid—as the IMF suggested as well.

Speed

Unlike the SDRM, which suffers from a complicated structure, an international Chapter 9 could be implemented at once if the important creditor nations agree. Panels could be formed immediately, starting with the basic principles of U.S. Chapter 9 and making their own procedural rules as needed. Eventually, a body of case law would develop.

Regulatory Changes

Although not a necessary part of an international Chapter 9 process, the intro-duction of Chapter 9 could also be used as an opportunity to introduce stabilizing regulatory changes into the international financial architecture. One virtually costless (economically) stabilizing feature would be the universal introduction of tax-deductible loan-loss reserves, as practiced on the European continent (Raf-fer 2001). This would also avoid taxation of illusory profits, which presently occurs in countries where these reserves must normally be formed after taxation.

Conclusion

The rejection of the SDRM during the 2003 spring meeting by the United States and emerging markets precluded the introduction of an unfair, self-serving, and inefficient system. The search for a viable solution is not over. The discussion will definitely erupt again with the next big crisis, especially if and when the sums needed for further bailouts are large. Unfortunately, political actors go on delaying, imposing those unnecessary costs on debtors and the international community, which Krueger rightly decried.

There is a strong and convincing case for one specific type of insolvency appropriate for sovereign debtors, an arbitration process based on the principles of Chapter 9 of the U.S. bankruptcy code. Unlike the SDRM, it could be im-plemented quickly and would be fair to all concerned.

Notes

1. Rogoff and Zettelmeyer (2002a, corrected in 2002b) compiled an impressively comprehensive—but not always accurate—survey of earlier publications. Rogoff explains their motive: "First, we noticed in the press that many people were rushing forward to take credit for First Deputy Managing Director Anne Krueger's proposal as soon as it started to receive acclaim. Note that success has many fathers" (IMF 2002a: 198). Perhaps customary citations of prior authors would have prevented this "rush" for credit. For surveys and bibliographies, see Raffer (2001), Rogoff and Zettelmeyer (2002a, 2002b), and Malagardis (1990).

2. See chapter 11 this volume.

3. See chapter 13 this volume.

4. Because both changing the Fund's statutes and the process of ratification would take time, Krueger's proposal would have "no implications for our current negotiations with member countries—Argentina and Turkey, for example" (Krueger 2001b: 2).

5. It should be recalled that these three minuscule islands have routinely been used as an argument against the Tobin Tax, vehemently opposed by the IMF. It was argued that the tax could not be introduced because universal acceptance could not be assured. "Tobin Tax paradises," such as the Cayman Islands, would preclude implementation. The same concern would logically hold with regard to Krueger's "forum shopping."

6. Cf. Kupetz 1995: 582.

7. This model, described in greater detail elsewhere (especially Raffer 1990, 2001), is also called FTAP (Fair Transparent Arbitration Process) by some NGOs.

8. This demand echoes my words from ten years before (Raffer 1993b: 68).

9. The importance of debtor protection can be illustrated in the example of Malawi. The IMF and IBRD were accused of having forced Malawi to sell maize from its National Food Reserve to repay debts. The IBRD encouraged the country "to keep foreign exchange instead of storing grain" (quoted from Pettifor 2002). In a BBC interview, Malawi's president said the government "had been forced [to sell maize] in order to repay commercial loans taken out to buy surplus maize in previous years" (Pettifor 2002). The IMF and the World Bank had insisted on it. Malawi sold a substantial amount of maize. In 2002, famine struck. Seven million of a population of 11 million were severely short of food according to Action Aid. Creditor interest was given priority over survival. Horst Köhler insisted that the "IMF was part of this process of giving advice to the Malawi government and the IMF may also not have been attentive enough . . . but it was not the responsibility of the Fund to implement the advice" (House of Commons' Treasury Select Committee 2002: 11ff and 18f). Repayment was preferred over the right to life. This would no longer be possible under my model.

References

Acosta, A. and Ugarteche, O. 2003. A Favor de Un Tribunal Internacional de Arbitraje de Deuda Soberana (TIADS), unpublished paper.

Commerzbank. 1999. Emerging Markets This Week, Vol. 26 (October).

Eichengreen, B. 1999. *Toward a New International Financial Architecture: A Practical Post-Asia Agenda.* Washington, DC: Institute for International Economics.

Haldane, A., and Kruger, M. 2001. The Resolution of International Financial Crises: Private Finance and Public Funds. Mimeo (November).

House of Commons Treasury Select Committee. 2002. Treasury—Uncorrected Evidence. 4 July 2002. Available online at: www.publications.parliament.uk/cmselect/cm treasy/uc868-iii/uc86801.htm.

International Bank for Reconstruction and Development (IBRD). 1997. *Global Development Finance,* Vol. 1. Washington, DC: IBRD.

International Monetary Fund (IMF). 2002a. Success of SDRM Idea Has Many Fathers—Interview with Rogoff and Zettelmeyer, *IMF-Survey,* Vol. 31, No. 12 (June): 197–200.

———. 2002b. IMF Board Holds Informal Seminar on Sovereign Debt Restructuring, PIN No. 02/38 1 April 2002. Available online at: www.imf.org/external/np/sec/pn/2002/pn0238.htm.

———. 2002c. Sovereign Debt Restructuring Mechanism—Further Considerations Mimeo (14 August).

————. 2002d. The Design of the Sovereign Debt Restructuring Mechanism—Further Considerations. Mimeo (27 November).

Kampffmeyer, T. 1987. *Toward a Solution to the Debt Crisis: Applying the Concept of Corporate Composition with Creditors.* Berlin: German Development Institute.

Krueger, A. 2001a. International Financial Architecture for 2002: A New Approach to Sovereign Debt Restructuring. 26 November 2001. Available online at: www.imf .org/external/np/speeches/2001/112601.htm.

————. 2001b. A New Approach to Sovereign Debt Restructuring. 20 December 2001. Available online at: www.imf.org/external/np/speeches/2001/122001.htm.

————. 2002a. New Approaches to Sovereign Debt Restructuring: An Update of Our Thinking. 1 April 2002. Available online at: www.iie.com/papers/krueger0402.htm.

————. 2002b. Sovereign Debt Restructuring and Dispute Resolution. 6 June 2002. Available online at: www.imf.org/external/np/speeches/2002/060602.htm.

————. 2002c. Sovereign Debt Restructuring and Dispute Resolution. 6 June 2002. Available online at: www.imf.org/external/np/speeches/2002/060602.htm.

Kupetz, D. S. 1995. Municipal Debt Adjustment under the Bankruptcy Code. *The Urban Lawyer,* Vol. 27, No. 3: 531–605.

Malagardis, A. 1990. *Ein "Konkursrecht" für Staaten? Zur Regelung von Insolvenzen souveräner Schuldner in Vergangenheit und Gegenwart.* Baden-Baden: Nomos.

Paulus, Ch.P. 2003. Staatsbankrott in einem rechtlich geordneten Verfahren, unpublished paper.

Pettifor, A. 2002. Debt Is Still the Lynchpin: The Case of Malawi. Available online at: www.jubileeplus.org/opinion/debt040702.htm.

Raffer, K. 1989. International Debts: A Crisis for Whom? In *Economic Development and World Debt,* ed. H. W. Singer and S. Sharma, pp. 51–63. London and Basingstoke: Macmillan. (Selected Papers from a conference at Zagreb University 1987.)

————. 1990. Applying Chapter 9 Insolvency to International Debts: An Economically Efficient Solution with a Human Face. *World Development,* Vol. 18, No. 2: 301–13.

————. 1993a. International Financial Institutions and Accountability: The Need for Drastic Change. In *Trade, Transfers and Development: Problems and Prospects for the Twenty-First Century,* ed. S. Murshed and K. Raffer, pp. 151–66. Aldershot: Elgar. Available online at: http://homepage.univie.ac.at/kunisert.Rafferk.

————. 1993b. What's Good for the United States Must Be Good for the World: Advocating an International Chapter 9 Insolvency. In *From Cancún to Vienna: International Development in a New World,* ed. Bruno Kreisky Forum for International Dialogue, pp. 64–74. Vienna: Bruno Kreisky Forum.

————. 1998. The Necessity of International Chapter 9 Insolvency Procedures. In *Taking Stock of Debt: Creditor Policy in the Face of Debtor Poverty,* ed. EURODAD, pp. 25–32. Brussels: EURODAD.

————. 2001. Solving Sovereign Debt Overhang by Internationalizing Chapter 9 Procedures, Working Paper No. 35. Vienna: Austrian Institute for International Affairs. Updated version available online at: homepage.univie.ac.at/kunibert.Raffer.

————. 2002. Shopping for Jurisdictions—A Problem for International Chapter 9 Insolvency? 24 January 2002. Available online at: www.jubilee.org/raffer.htm.

————. 2003. To Stay or Not to Stay—A Short Remark on Differing Versions of the SDRM. Available online at: www.jubileeplus.org/latest/raffer310103.htm.

Rogoff, K. 1999. International Institutions for Reducing Global Financial Instability. *The Journal of Economic Perspectives,* Vol. 13, No. 4: 21–43.

Rogoff, K., and Zettelmeyer, J. 2002a. Early Ideas on Sovereign Bankruptcy Reorganisation: A Survey. IMF Working Paper WP/02/57. Washington, DC: International Monetary Fund.

————. 2002b. Bankruptcy Procedures for Sovereigns: A History of Ideas, 1976–2001, *IMF Staff Papers,* Vol. 49, No. 3: 470–507.

Stiglitz, J. 2000. What I Learned at the World Economic Crisis. *The New Republic* (17 April).

Taylor, J. 2002. Sovereign Debt Restructuring: A US Perspective. 2 April 2002. Available online at: www.iie.com/papers/taylor0402.htm.

13

DEALING WITH SOVEREIGN DEBT: TRENDS AND IMPLICATIONS

Arturo C. Porzecanski

The history of international finance is littered with instances of governments that declared themselves unable to meet their financial obligations on a timely basis. For example, it has been documented that Spain defaulted on its debt 13 times from the sixteenth through the nineteenth centuries, a period during which France defaulted eight times and Portugal and Germany (or rather, its predecessor states) did so a half dozen times. Latin American governments defaulted frequently during the 1800s, not just the 1900s. Turkey and its predecessor, the Ottoman Empire, were often in default during the nineteenth and twentieth centuries (Reinhart et al. 2003).

This chapter provides an overview of the reasons behind sovereign debt defaults. It discusses trends in external indebtedness (public and private) and in government indebtedness (domestic and foreign). It describes the manner in which private lenders and investors, and official bilateral and multilateral agencies, have dealt with sovereign defaults during the 1980s and 1990s. And it closes with an in-depth consideration of the case of Argentina post-2001, which promises to be the most complex sovereign default and workout in contemporary history.

The main arguments are, first, that private lenders and investors have been, and continue to be, able to deal promptly and effectively with instances of sovereign default, such that new, supranational bankruptcy procedures are not necessary. Second, official lenders have not proven to be similarly capable of coping with and resolving instances of sovereign overindebtedness, and thus they should not be relied upon to play an even larger role in the international financial architecture. And third, Argentina's lingering debt woes are not the result of shortcomings in market practices or international norms but rather stem largely from that country's self-inflicted wounds and from its government's ideological unwillingness to negotiate a practical solution.

Reasons for Sovereign Defaults

Events of sovereign default have clustered around times of armed conflict, political upheaval, or global economic distress—times during which governments incurred deficits they could not finance because economic activity and public confidence were disrupted. World Wars I and II, the Great Depression, the oil price shocks of the 1970s, and the collapse of the Soviet Union all gave rise to economic and political stresses that paved the way to sovereign defaults. Moreover, defaults have often followed the abandonment of rigid exchange-rate regimes, be it the various gold standards typical of the 1800s and early 1900s or the managed currency regimes that were prevalent in the emerging markets until the 1990s. Governments with a poor track record, little credibility, and limited political resolve—especially when their own financial woes were aggravated by widespread corporate and bank failures—have been particularly susceptible to default (figure 13.1).

Governments tend to default specifically when they must increase spending quickly (for instance, to prosecute a war), experience a sudden shortfall in revenues (because of a severe economic contraction), or face an abrupt curtailment of access to bond and loan financing (e.g., because of political instability). It is usually very difficult for governments in such trouble to take the necessary offsetting actions, such as hiking tax collections or cutting spending on an emergency basis, and governments generally do not have the deep cushion of cash

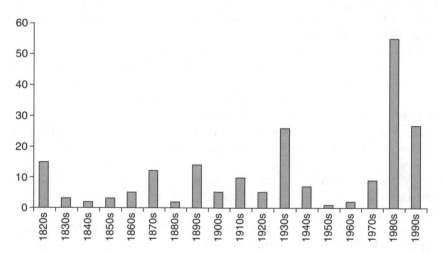

Figure 13.1. Number of government defaults declared on foreign-currency debt. Source: Standard & Poor's, *Sovereign Defaults: Heading Lower into 2004*, 18 September 2003, pp. 15–17.

reserves that could allow them to forestall a default. The sudden exit from a given currency regime, for its part, can lead to a default because the typically large currency depreciations that follow often generate confidence crises that reduce the demand for government bonds and money, generating inflation and capital flight. The resulting spike in domestic interest rates and bond yields sometimes scares rather than entices investors and lenders to provide funds to the government out of concern that a "debt trap" will soon exhaust the authorities' capacity or willingness to keep servicing their obligations. Governments with large exposures to currency mismatches and interest rate or maturity risks are, of course, particularly vulnerable.

The governments that have defaulted during the past three decades have had a more burdensome public debt in relation to current revenues and GDP, a higher proportion of external debt in relation to total indebtedness, and a shallower domestic financial market than those that have not defaulted (IMF 2003a). The much-quoted ratios of public or external debt to GDP often do not convey the degree of vulnerability of a sovereign to default risk because a great deal depends upon the currency denomination, floating-rate nature, and maturity structure of the liabilities.[1] The creditworthiness of governments with a high proportion of debts in or indexed to hard currencies (e.g., U.S. dollars, euros, or Japanese yen) is dependent upon the exchange value of their local currency, such that a sharp depreciation can seriously undermine their ability to pay or even refinance obligations. The finances of sovereigns that issue debt indexed to inflation, or sell bonds with floating or adjustable coupons, are similarly vulnerable to a sudden rise in inflation or hike in market interest rates. Governments that place mostly short-dated securities are exposed to refinancing or liquidity risks—even if they are otherwise creditworthy (Porzecanski 2004).

The unreliability of debt-to-GDP ratios explains why they correlate less well with the risk classifications assigned to sovereigns by the credit-rating agencies than do the ratios of government debt to revenues, especially given the wide range of ratios present in each creditworthiness category. The credit ratings awarded by Fitch Ratings (see table 13.1) and Moody's Investors Service, for example, are consistent with a multiplicity of debt ratios—and especially debt-to-GDP comparisons.

Trends in External Indebtedness

The focus of most media coverage, academic research, and policy studies has been on defaults involving the external indebtedness of nations. This indebtedness consists of the financial obligations of the government and the private sector to foreign lenders and investors. Defaults on the external debt of governments have usually but not always caused the private sector to default on its own foreign indebtedness. Sometimes causality has run the other way, with private-sector bank or corporate defaults, or near defaults, affecting the government's own wherewithal. In any event, it is estimated that at least two-thirds of the total external indebtedness of developing countries consists of government obliga-

TABLE 13.1   Government debt ratios by Fitch sovereign rating categories[a]

	Debt as % of GDP		Debt as % of revenues	
	Average	Range	Average	Range
Investment grade				
AAA	44.5	6–68	109.8	12–168
AA	45.2	0–150	108.1	0–514
A	36.5	5–105	148.4	13–239
Chile	36.5		148.4	
BBB	38.7	15–61	125.5	40–238
Malaysia	45.6		197.5	
Mexico	45.6		202.1	
Poland	47.5		123.2	
South Africa	38.0		125.5	
Noninvestment grade				
BB	48.6	18–81	222.2	74–528
Bulgaria	53.6		146.7	
Colombia	55.1		196.1	
Peru	46.7		274.8	
Philippines	70.0		497.7	
Russia	42.4		113.5	
B/C/D	79.8	22–181	301.5	95–825
Argentina	166.7		934.8	
Brazil	85.7		227.3	
Ecuador	62.8		242.1	
Turkey	90.9		337.9	
Venezuela	57.2		273.3	

[a]General government debt ratios for 2002, sovereign ratings as of September 2003.
Source: Fitch Ratings, *Sovereign Data Comparator*, 30 September 2003, p. 6.

tions, whether to official creditors (bilateral or multilateral agencies) or private creditors (foreign banks, bondholders, and suppliers). This proportion has not changed much since the 1970s.[2]

The total external indebtedness of developing countries (figure 13.2 multiplied very rapidly during the 1970s and then quadrupled between 1980 and 1998 when measured in current U.S. dollars, but it has stabilized since then at about $2.6 trillion (IMF 2004, p. 228). In relation to rising exports of goods and services, this external indebtedness has diminished from the equivalent of 1.7 times in 1998 to an estimated 1.2 times as of 2003. As will be seen, however, the decline has been much smaller, or nonexistent, in relation to GDP.

Once broken down by region, it is apparent that the trends are quite dissimilar. On the one hand, the external indebtedness of African countries has fallen since 1995 in nominal terms (see table 13.2) by 9%, or a cumulative $27 billion (U.S.), and especially in relation to total exports and GDP—mainly the combination of debt forgiveness on the part of official and private creditors and constrained access to international capital of any sort. At the other extreme, the

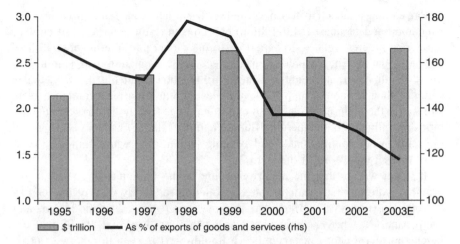

Figure 13.2. External indebtedness of emerging markets. Source: IMF, *World Economic Outlook*, September 2003 (Washington, DC: IMF, 2003), pp. 228–29.

external indebtedness of Eastern European and former Soviet Union countries has grown most rapidly in absolute terms (by almost 55%, or $155 billion) since the mid-1990s, declining relatively little in relation to export earnings. The foreign debt of Asian developing countries has grown in nominal terms (by 18%, or $106 billion) during this time but has dropped quite markedly in relation to both exports and GDP—to ratios that are rock bottom, in fact. The foreign debt of the Asian countries is now equivalent to less than 77% of export earnings and to a mere 25% of GDP, whereas the respective averages for all emerging markets are close to 118% (exports) and 38% (GDP).

In the Middle East, the increase in external indebtedness has been meaningful (by 38%, or $139 billion) since 1995, but an impressive reduction in ratios to

TABLE 13.2   Absolute size of external indebtedness by region

	$ Billion (U.S.)			Change 1995–2003	
	1995	2000	2003E	$ billion	%
Africa	295.3	272.8	267.9	−27.4	−9.3
Developing Asia	577.5	673.9	683.8	106.3	18.4
Middle East and Turkey	369.5	493.9	508.9	139.4	37.7
Latin America	622.3	761.3	758.6	136.3	21.9
Emerging Europe[a]	282.9	384.0	438.5	155.6	55.0
Total	2,147.5	2,585.9	2,657.7	510.2	23.8

[a]Central and Eastern Europe, Russia, and former members of the USSR.
Source: IMF, *World Economic Outlook*, p. 228.

export earnings and GDP has nevertheless been achieved. Latin America reg-
isters more indebtedness ($136 billion) but a mixed result in terms of its burden,
with good progress relative to export performance but not in terms of GDP. The
reason is that currency depreciations and economic stagnation were common in
many South American countries during 1999–2003, reducing the U.S. dollar
value of their economic output. Nevertheless, Latin America's foreign debt is
still by far the highest in relation to export earnings (nearly 210%)—double the
ratios prevailing in both emerging Europe and the Middle East, and nearly triple
the ratio in developing Asia—and is quite burdensome when compared with
GDP as well (above 40%) (table 13.3).

It is noteworthy that the maturity profile of the foreign debt has been improving, with long-term indebtedness accounting for nearly 90% of the total as
of 2003, up from 85% in 1995. The improvement is most dramatic in Asia and
Latin America, where governments learned the hard way in 1997–98 that too
much short-term debt can precipitate a liquidity crisis even in otherwise creditworthy countries. With regard to the degree of reliance upon the private capital
markets, the regions show a remarkable disparity. Whereas on average the developing countries rely upon private sources for around 60% of their total external financing, the range varies from a low of 25% in the case of African

TABLE 13.3   Characteristics of external indebtedness by region

	% of exports of goods and services			Difference	% of GDP			Difference
	1995	2000	2003E	1995–2003E	1995	2000	2003E	1995–2003E
Africa	249.4	174.2	151.1	−98.3	72.1	63.0	49.2	−22.9
Developing Asia	126.9	96.3	76.9	−50.0	32.6	30.7	25.3	−7.3
Middle East and Turkey	172.9	146.8	136.4	−36.5	58.5	59.2	54.8	−3.7
Latin America	253.2	212.3	208.1	−45.1	36.9	38.7	44.1	7.2
Emerging Europe[a]	110.4	115.1	96.4	−14.0	N/A	N/A	N/A	N/A
Total[b]	166.6	137.2	117.6	−49.0	41.5	40.6	37.7	−3.8

	Long-term debt (% of total)			Difference	Owed to private creditors (% of total)			Difference
	1995	2000	2003E	1995–2003E	1995	2000	2003E	1995–2003E
Africa	90.7	93.3	93.1	2.4	28.8	25.2	25.0	−3.7
Developing Asia	81.5	90.9	90.6	9.1	57.6	56.8	56.4	−1.1
Middle East and Turkey	88.4	87.1	90.1	1.7	53.4	65.7	63.6	10.1
Latin America	84.8	87.6	87.2	2.5	69.0	78.3	72.9	3.9
Total	85.4	89.3	89.6	4.2	56.0	62.6	59.9	3.9

[a]Central and Eastern Europe, Russia, and former members of the USSR.
[b]Totals of debt to GDP exclude the countries of Emerging Europe because of the unavailability of comparable data.
Source: IMF, *World Economic Outlook*, pp. 229–233.

countries to a high of 73% in emerging Europe and Latin America. Debt of countries in emerging Europe to official sources used to account for nearly half of the total. Now it represents less than one-fourth of the total. Reliance on private sources of financing has also increased meaningfully in the Middle East (up from less than 53% in 1995 to 64% in 2003). The African countries have been notoriously dependent upon concessional aid from official bilateral and multilateral agencies, and so have a number of poor countries in South Asia. It is interesting that the regional average for Asia is little changed despite the graduation of several countries in East Asia from reliance upon financing from foreign official agencies.

Trends in Government Indebtedness

Trends in external indebtedness do not tell the whole story, however. In the past decade, governments in most emerging markets have allowed for, and often fostered, the development of local bond markets.[3] In Latin America, for example, the development of bond markets has followed from the partial (or, in the case of Chile, wholesale) privatization of pension regimes and also from the growth of other financial intermediaries such as mutual funds and insurance companies. The emergence of private pension funds and private insurance companies, in particular, has created a natural demand for long-term assets such as government and corporate bonds. The fact that, during the 1990s, Latin American governments and central banks managed to vanquish hyperinflation and stabilize their currencies has encouraged these institutional investors to purchase bonds. Initially, most government and corporate bonds were denominated in U.S. dollars or else their principal was adjusted by the cost of living, and they all had short maturities. Increasingly, however, domestic bonds are being denominated in the local currency, bear a fixed interest rate, and feature lengthening maturities.

In other parts of the world, such as in East Asia and Turkey, governments have been turning for funding to local banks or, in the wake of massive bailouts, they have recapitalized domestic banks by issuing government bonds to them, which count as subordinated debt. Considering the number of bad experiences involving reliance on external indebtedness, it should not be surprising that many governments have increasingly chosen to meet more and more of their financing needs domestically—albeit often at higher cost and with shorter maturities, at least initially.

As noted at the start, however, external-debt data include the foreign liabilities of both the public and private sectors, but many times they do not evolve in a similar manner—nor do they suffer the same fate in the event of great economic or political stress. In the wake of the 1997–98 financial crisis, for example, many banks and corporations throughout East Asia have been paying off the bulk of their external obligations.[4] This has generally not been the case in Latin America. In emerging Europe, in contrast, there has been a quantum leap in private-sector foreign indebtedness—starting from next to nothing, of course, before the 1990s. Therefore, it is worthwhile to separate out trends in the foreign debt of governments from trends in the cross-border liabilities of banks and corporations.

Regional variations are again considerable. In the Asian developing countries, domestic government indebtedness has increased most rapidly—by nearly 20 percentage points of GDP between 1995 and 2002—such that the average ratio of domestic debt to GDP stood at around 45% by 2002. Latin America follows with an increase worth some 12 percentage points of GDP during the same seven-year period, to a regional average debt-to-GDP ratio of almost 25%. In the Middle East and Africa, domestic government indebtedness has risen from 35% to a heavy 41% of GDP. In emerging Europe, in contrast, there has been a relative drop in domestic indebtedness, such that the regional ratio has fallen from 30% to 21% of GDP. On an unweighted regional average basis, domestic government debt has increased from 21% to 30% of GDP since the mid-1990s (see table 13.4).

The foreign debt of governments has tended to increase relative to GDP in Asia and in Latin America, such that total public indebtedness now exceeds the equivalent of 60% of GDP, up from less than 45% of GDP in the mid-1990s. In the countries of the Middle East and Africa, government foreign debt has decreased marginally relative to GDP, and given the aforementioned rise in domestic indebtedness, the overall liability position of governments has worsened slightly to around 94% of GDP—an exceedingly high ratio, indeed, for countries with a usually low revenue base. In the sample of emerging European countries, the cross-border obligations of governments have dropped off substantially as a proportion of GDP, following mostly successful economic transformations that have boosted per capita incomes, mirroring the trend in domestic debt. Consequently, the burden of public debt in that region has plunged since 1995 from the equivalent of 80% to 55% of GDP. All regional trends considered, emerging-market governments are more indebted, both domestically and abroad, than they were in the mid-1990s (see figure 13.3).

TABLE 13.4   Domestic and external government debt (% of GDP)

	Domestic			External			Total		
	1995	2000	2002	1995	2000	2002	1995	2000	2002
Developing Asia	25.5	42.1	44.1	17.0	23.0	22.1	42.5	65.1	66.2
Latin America	12.1	17.5	23.7	30.2	26.7	36.8	42.3	44.2	60.5
Middle East and Africa	34.9	40.7	40.9	55.3	48.7	53.1	90.2	89.4	93.9
Emerging Europe	30.3	17.0	21.1	49.5	41.2	33.6	79.8	58.3	54.7
Total[a]	21.4	26.7	30.3	37.2	33.2	36.0	61.4	64.5	71.4

[a]Unweighted regional averages; the domestic and external debt subcomponents do not sum to the total for all emerging markets because only countries for which continuous data were available are included.

Source: IMF, World Economic Outlook, p. 116.

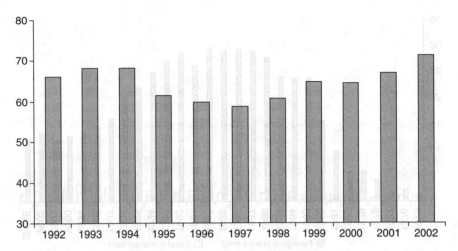

Figure 13.3. Government indebtedness in emerging markets (% of GDP). Source: IMF, *World Economic Outlook*, p. 17.

The rise in domestic government indebtedness relative to GDP witnessed in all regions with the exception of emerging Europe raises the issue of whether future defaults might not affect mostly domestic rather than international investors. An examination of the pattern of defaults since the mid-1970s suggests that instances of default involving foreign-currency debt have been far more numerous than those involving local-currency obligations (see Figure 13.4). Furthermore, the 1980s leap in events of default involving foreign obligations was not accompanied by a noticeable increase in domestic debt defaults from their low base.

At first sight, the impression is that governments respect their domestic financial obligations more than they do their international obligations. It is no wonder, therefore, that local-currency government bonds tend to be rated higher than foreign-currency bonds. Yet in a few countries where runaway domestic government debt is potentially the main source of financial instability, at least one of the major rating agencies (Moody's) has been awarding a lower grade to the local debt obligations of governments such as India, Japan, and Turkey.

To be sure, the globalization of financial markets means that foreign investors are increasingly purchasing domestic government debt, whether denominated in local currency or indexed to inflation or to the exchange rate, as opposed to bonds payable in hard currencies and subject to contracts under European or U.S. law. By the same token, domestic investors—from wealthy individuals to mutual and pension funds—are frequent buyers of their country's international bonds because they afford greater liquidity, legal protection, and other benefits, such as anonymity and tax sheltering. Therefore, it is difficult to conclude that even if sovereign defaults were to affect just one category of indebtedness, they would have an impact on but one group of investors.

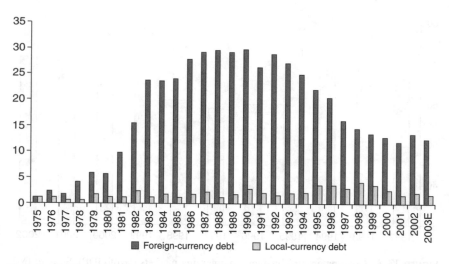

Figure 13.4. Incidence of sovereign defaults on foreign-currency and local-currency debt (% of all sovereigns). Source: Standard & Poor's, *Sovereign Defaults*, pp. 4–5.

Moreover, governments tend to shun defaults on domestic debt because they can have devastating consequences for banks, pension funds, and insurance companies, triggering a major destabilization of the domestic financial system. It is in any case much easier for governments to lean on domestic institutional investors to roll over or purchase additional public debt, either through moral suasion, raising liquidity requirements, or altering the investment criteria that pension funds must observe. Governments can also declare a default on foreign obligations while appealing to nationalism without fear that the gunboats of old will arrive to collect, whereas defaulting on domestic obligations is much more likely to provoke a run on banks and a backlash among voters. All things considered, defaults on domestic government debt should continue to occur less frequently than defaults on international obligations.

The implication is that the sovereign debt defaults of the future will probably keep impacting cross-border lenders and investors, and go on involving—directly or indirectly—the official bilateral and multilateral lending agencies. Therefore, how best to deal with governments in default will likely remain a challenge to the international financial community, and the prevention and cure of said defaults will continue to be the subject of considerable academic, market, and policy debate.

Dealing with Sovereign Defaults: Proposals

Bankers and bondholders all over the world have been dealing with sovereign debt defaults for centuries. Yet policy makers in Washington and other G7 capitals have been promoting the idea that the functioning of the world's financial markets must be improved by making it easier for insolvent governments to obtain debt relief from their foreign creditors (Rogoff and Zettelmeyer 2002).

Two high officials appointed in late 2001 made this project their top priority: Anne Krueger, first deputy managing director of the IMF, and John Taylor, then undersecretary for international affairs at the U.S. Treasury. Ms. Krueger's ideas were formalized into a detailed proposal for a statutory mechanism to facilitate the bankruptcy of nations—the so-called sovereign debt restructuring mechanism, or SDRM (Krueger 2002). This proposal has yet to gain the necessary political support among a number of governments, including that of the United States. Its earlier versions envisioned a powerful role for the IMF that would have allowed it to make decisions that limit creditors' rights. In the face of universal criticism from private-sector lenders and investors, the IMF's role was later toned down to the equivalent of the sole expert witness, whereby the IMF would pass judgment on how much debt any government could reasonably be expected to service. In this capacity, the IMF (and thus its G7 and other government shareholders represented on its board of directors) would have a procedural advantage. They would be in a privileged position to protect the claims of official bilateral and multilateral lenders by insisting that a greater-than-otherwise amount of debt relief be granted by private creditors.

Mr. Taylor's approach, on the other hand, involved the voluntary modification of bond contracts to include clauses facilitating changes in payment and other terms by a qualified majority of bondholders (Taylor 2002). The main idea is that every bond contract should designate a bondholder representative to act as an interlocutor with the sovereign debtor; require the sovereign to provide more key financial information to its bondholders; allow for a supermajority of bondholders to amend payment terms, now often requiring unanimity of consent; and include enforcement provisions that concentrate the power to initiate litigation in a single jurisdiction (Group of Ten 2002). These new clauses have become widely known as collective-action clauses (CACs), and although several already exist in bonds issued under English law, most new and outstanding bonds of emerging-market sovereigns are issued in other jurisdictions, such as New York and Frankfurt, where such clauses have not been customary.

Most emerging-market issuers and investors were initially reluctant to introduce CACs in new bond contracts for fear of signaling that they contemplate or countenance an eventual default. Besides, even if such clauses were introduced voluntarily in all new debt issues, the stock of outstanding bonds would still be governed by preexisting legal arrangements such that the practical effect of CACs would be marginal for years to come. Under strong pressure from the U.S. Treasury, however, the governments of Mexico and Brazil were persuaded in early 2003 to issue new bonds with CACs, and they were successfully placed with institutional investors at no measurable extra cost. Governments such as those of South Africa, South Korea, and Venezuela followed suit later in the year, although each new sovereign bond tended to include its own particular clauses, meaning that a uniform market standard in CACs is yet to develop.[5] On the whole, nearly half of all new sovereign bonds (measured by value) issued in 2003 under New York law included CACs, whereas none of them had done so the previous year (Koch 2004).

In contrast with G7 and IMF policy makers, most institutional investors and lenders feel that any international reforms should focus on making contracts easier to enforce and facilitating the constructive involvement of bondholders and other private-sector creditors in debt-restructuring negotiations (IIF 2001b). Yet the G7 has not called for any actions or penalties against irresponsible governments, such as the attachment of their official international reserves when they are on deposit with central banks such as the U.S. Federal Reserve or with the Bank for International Settlements (BIS), the central banks' central bank. Thus, the investors who have filed suits and won judgments against Argentina in New York and other jurisdictions, because of the default that took place there starting in December 2001, cannot get their hands on the billions of dollars that the government of that country has sheltered at the BIS.

Although various proposals for resolving debt crises have been advanced, they all suppose that the lack of collective action among private-sector lenders and investors is the main obstacle to the smooth functioning of the international financial system.[6]

Yet there is little if any empirical support for this assumption. On the contrary, private creditors have been much more progressive, flexible, and quick in dealing with sovereign insolvency situations than official lenders have been—and the gap in the effectiveness of their approaches appears to be growing. In fact, private lenders have provided a good example for how official bilateral and multilateral lenders themselves might deal more fairly and effectively with sovereign insolvency situations.

Dealing with Sovereign Defaults: The Record

The absence of innovative mechanisms has not impeded several landmark workouts of sovereign indebtedness. The governments of Ecuador, Pakistan, Russia, and Ukraine, for example, have all been able to restructure their bonded debt—and have done so in record time. Substantial debt-service relief and even sizable debt forgiveness have been obtained through the use of exchange offers, often accompanied by bondholder exit consents that encourage the participation of as many investors as possible in take-it-or-leave-it settlements. Rather than amending bond covenants, the exchange offers typically entail the debtor government presenting its private creditors with a menu of voluntary options, such as accepting new bonds for a fraction (for example, 60%) of the principal owed but paying a market interest rate, or new bonds for the original principal but paying a concessional interest rate. Experience has demonstrated that neither the threat of litigation nor actual cases of litigation have obstructed these debt restructurings, which have involved large institutional investors as well as small retail investors throughout the world (World Bank 2003a).

For example, in early 2003, the government of Uruguay asked local and international investors to consider a debt-restructuring request, and more than 90% of them agreed, enabling the operation to be consummated in a matter of several weeks.[7] The Uruguayan authorities previously spent many months debating the nature of the restructuring with the IMF. The IMF wanted Uruguay to default on its obligations to bondholders as Argentina had done at the end of 2001, with the intention of likewise demanding massive debt forgiveness from private creditors, but the Uruguayan authorities refused to go down this potentially ruinous path. The government there wanted to pursue instead a market-friendly debt exchange with the sole purpose of stretching out the maturities falling due in 2003 and the next several years while respecting both the original amounts owed and the initial coupons. It was only after the Uruguayan authorities sought and obtained support from the Federal Reserve and the U.S. Treasury that the IMF staff backed down and agreed to support a voluntary debt exchange.[8] Once an understanding between the IMF and Uruguay was reached, matters moved quickly. Informal discussions with private creditors were held in March 2003, a concrete proposal was put forth in April, investor replies were received in May, and by June Uruguay's bonded debt had been successfully restructured. This was accomplished despite the fact that the investor base was diverse and scattered around the globe: from retail investors in Argentina and Japan to institutional investors in the United States and Europe, all of whom were bound by contracts written in several jurisdictions, each with its own currency and distinct legal features. In the wake of the successful restructuring, Uruguay's debt rallied strongly, and before six months had passed, the government was able to return to the international capital markets, placing a new bond issue in October 2003 and subsequently other bonds in 2004 and 2005.

Historically, countries in financial trouble have followed one of three routes.[9] The first is the negotiated route, whereby governments sit down to hammer out a debt-restructuring deal with a representative committee of either bondholders or commercial bankers, depending on which group holds a majority of the claims on the sovereign. This is the typical approach followed by dozens of governments from Argentina in the early 1980s to Vietnam in the late 1990s. They all negotiated with a bank advisory committee (BAC), or so-called London Club (because most of the negotiating sessions took place either in London or in New York), in contrast with the so-called Paris Club of official creditors (which meets under the aegis of the French Treasury). The BAC would then recommend to other private creditors that they accept the terms agreed to with the government in question, and most would usually do so (Rieffel 2003). Those unwilling to participate (e.g., small regional banks) would generally be paid but with the understanding that they would not be welcome to do new business in that country.

The second route is the unilateral exchange offer, whereby governments engage one or more commercial or investment banks to consult privately with a critical mass of lenders or investors about the possible shape of an acceptable settlement, which is then crafted and presented to all creditors on a take-it-or-leave-it basis. As mentioned previously, these exchange offers are accompanied by bondholder exit consents that encourage the participation of as many investors as possible by leaving nonparticipants in a disadvantageous position, for example, with less liquid securities. This is the approach that has become more popular and was used successfully by Pakistan (1999), Ecuador (2000), Ukraine (2000), and Uruguay (2003).[10] In recognition that the ideal should not become the enemy of the good, governments will then, if necessary, quietly pay off any recalcitrant creditors when their original claims come due.

The third route is the unilateral demand, whereby a government comes up with a proposed restructuring on the basis of what it feels it can pay going forward—no matter that it may not be what the market will bear. There are few instances of this approach, but the precedents are not promising because the absence of a negotiated solution tends to lead to international financial isolation and also to prompt litigation, which can be successful in eventually securing payment in full.

The best example is Peru during the 1980s. In 1984, a round of debt nego- tiations between the government and its bankers failed, the country imposed restrictions on the use of foreign exchange to prevent the depletion of its inter- national reserves, and this led to the accumulation of arrears. A year later, in 1985, newly inaugurated president Alan García stated that he would not nego- tiate with bankers and the IMF and that the government would pay in debt service the equivalent of no more than 10% of export earnings, or about $300 million (U.S.) per year. At the time, interest arrears were already worth $500 million, and debt-service payments due in 1985 exceeded 50% of expected ex- port earnings. García's government ended up authorizing payments equivalent to some 20% of export earnings for a while but then stopped making any pay- ments at all.

Having been in partial arrears to the IMF since September 1985, Peru was declared ineligible for further IMF funds in August 1986 and was later threat- ened with expulsion from the organization (Boughton 2001). The government ended up in arrears not just to private creditors but to virtually all official cred- itors, including the Inter-American Development Bank (IADB) and the World Bank. Many of Peru's commercial lenders filed lawsuits to preserve their legal claims because they worried that, if they did not do so, the statute of limitations would expire on the outstanding debts.

In 1990, after Alberto Fujimori was elected Peru's new leader, the country's economic policies and attitudes changed radically for the better. President Fu- jimori initiated a major market-friendly reform of the economy and adopted sound fiscal and monetary policies agreed to with the IMF, though initially without the benefit of new loans. Beginning in late 1991, the government paid off its arrears to the IADB, IMF, and World Bank with bridge loans provided by Latin American, the Japanese, and the U.S. governments, paving the way for debt relief from the Paris Club and resumed lending from the IMF and other multilaterals. Meanwhile, the authorities switched to a negotiated approach with private creditors, convening a bank advisory committee and signing an agree- ment to stay all pending lawsuits to promote negotiations to resolve the entire problem of unpaid foreign debts. The country would eventually (in 1997) com- plete a debt-restructuring process under the Brady Plan, becoming current with all creditors. However, after pursuing a claim in U.S. courts for several years, a lone disgruntled creditor (*Elliott v. Peru*) was able to obtain full payment in 2000 on a small amount of unrestructured obligations after posing a credible threat of attachment to payments made by the government to Brady bond-holders.[11]

The case of Peru illustrates that when a sovereign is willing to negotiate a realistic debt-relief formula in good faith, in the context of efforts to improve its capacity to service post-restructuring obligations, then the overwhelming majority of private lenders and investors can be persuaded to accept some losses and move on. In contrast, official lenders are very unwilling to grant debt forgiveness and often even to reschedule maturing obligations. The multilateral agencies, in particular, deem themselves to be preferred creditors who must be paid in full at the originally contracted interest rates and maturities no matter the circumstances. They claim that because they are willing to lend to governments in trouble when private lenders are not, they should receive top priority in the chain of payments. And yet, the lending programs of the multilaterals to governments cut off from the international capital markets are often insufficient to cover even the obligations coming due to the agencies themselves. Besides, all disbursements are highly conditional on stabilization policies and structural reforms, such that funds arrive in installments with many strings attached. The foreign aid and export credit agencies, for their part, are usually so slow to grant any debt relief that governments in dire need often start running arrears to them in the hope that those payments will be restructured down the road—and eventually, they usually are.

The cases of Bolivia, Nicaragua, and Ecuador, with which this author had some involvement, highlight the difference between how private and official creditors have treated governments in serious financial trouble.[12] In 1988, commercial bank creditors first forgave nearly 90% of what the government of Bolivia owed them, and in 1993 they wrote off nearly 85% of the then-remaining principal (IIF 2001a).

In contrast, the country became eligible for debt relief from official bilateral and multilateral creditors under the original heavily indebted poor countries (HIPC) initiative a full decade later, in September 1998, and under the enhanced HIPC initiative only in June 2001 (World Bank 2003b).

In 1995, commercial bank creditors forgave more than 90% of what the government of Nicaragua owed them. In contrast, official bilateral creditors represented by the Paris Club canceled less than 70% of the eligible debts at about the same time, with no debt relief coming from the multilateral agencies. The country never became eligible for debt relief under the original HIPC initiative, although Paris Club creditors agreed to cancel 70% of Nicaragua's remaining debt obligations in December 2002.[13] The country finally qualified for the comprehensive debt-forgiveness benefits of the enhanced HIPC initiative in early 2004.

In 1995, private creditors also granted a mix of debt and interest forgiveness to the government of Ecuador as part of a comprehensive Brady-style settlement. Creditors accepted the choice of either writing off 45% of the principal owed while stretching out the maturity dates for repayment of the remainder for thirty years, or charging highly concessional interest rates for thirty years. The holders of nearly 60% of the total debt chose to provide principal relief, and the remainder chose to provide long-term interest-rate forgiveness.

When Ecuador experienced acute economic difficulties again in 1999, the IMF made it clear to the government that it would not get any help from the official community unless it defaulted to private creditors and obtained debt forgiveness once again.[14] Shut out of IMF and other official financial support, the government had no choice but to declare default even though very small amounts were coming due on outstanding Brady and Eurobond debt.[15] Before long, Ecuador's bondholders were formally requested to grant permanent debt relief—and by August 2000 they had forgiven about 40% of what was owed to them.

In contrast, official bilateral and multilateral lenders have not granted any debt forgiveness to Ecuador. The country was twice deemed by the IMF to be insolvent enough to deserve write-offs from private creditors—but not poor enough to deserve write-offs from the official development community. Paris Club creditors therefore have agreed merely to reschedule about one-third of debt-service payments coming due (those originally maturing between May 2000 and May 2001 and between March 2003 and March 2004) according to the Houston terms, the least generous of all Paris Club poor countries' debt treatments. This means that Ecuador has continued to be charged mostly market interest rates by its official creditors and is expected to repay the bulk of its obligations when they come due.[16]

Meanwhile, it is still business as usual at the multilateral agencies: They have not rescheduled, never mind forgiven, any of Ecuador's debt, and they have provided little new money. In fact, from 2000 to 2002, amortization payments by Ecuador to the multilateral agencies exceeded disbursements from those agencies (IMF 2003b). Once interest payments made to the multilateral agencies are factored in, it becomes clear that Ecuador has made substantial net transfers to the official community.

In conclusion, bondholders and commercial and investment banks in Japan, Europe, and the United States should be recognized rather than castigated for their track record in dealing with sovereign debt problems. They have helped to resolve expeditiously and even generously the sovereign debt crises in which they have been involved in various parts of the world. Official bilateral and multilateral agencies, on the other hand, cannot make a similar claim, even though they are charged with fostering development and the alleviation of poverty conditions. The insistence of multilateral creditors on the sanctity of originally contracted amounts and payment terms combined with their highly conditional and often modest new lending, plus the unwillingness of bilateral creditors to make substantial concessions quickly, means that official lenders are often part of the problem rather than part of the solution. This is true in the case of the poorest countries in the world, and it is also true in the case of Argentina.

The Case of Argentina: Background

The international financial community is currently witnessing the aftermath of the largest sovereign debt default in contemporary history—that declared by Argentina in late December 2001. It has involved nearly $90 billion (U.S.) of mostly bonded debt plus more than $20 billion in overdue interest payments through the end of 2004. The default was declared at a time when the country had lost the confidence of its domestic and international investors. Deposits had been withdrawn from the banking system on such a large scale that a freeze on deposits was imposed, the refinancing of even a small amount of maturing domestic government debt had become nearly impossible, and the IMF had refused to keep providing emergency financial support.[17]

During the 1990s, Argentina's capacity to service its debt obligations became inextricably tied to the peculiar exchange-rate regime adopted in early 1991 and ditched officially in January 2002 whereby the value of its currency (the peso) was set equal to that of the U.S. dollar. The public debt had grown during the 1990s for a variety of reasons (such as deficit spending by the central and provincial governments, massive bond issuance to settle old liabilities, and losses incurred by the central bank) from the equivalent of less than 35% of GDP in the early part of that decade to over 50% of GDP by 2001. The one-to-one regime encouraged the government, and also the private sector, to take on mostly foreign-currency–denominated debt. By late 2001, in fact, only 3% of the total public debt, and a mere 2% of total government bonds, were denominated in Argentine pesos (figure 13.5), whereas more than 70% of obligations were contracted in U.S. dollars and the remainder in other hard currencies.

This extremely skewed currency composition of the public debt represented a huge potential risk because when one peso was equal to one dollar, the public debt was roughly equivalent to some 50% of GDP, as noted, but if ever one peso (ARS) no longer purchased one dollar (USD), then the country's debt ratios

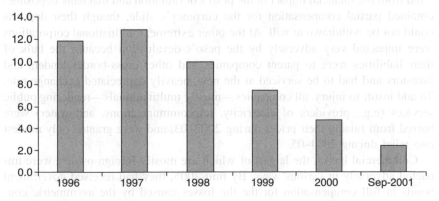

Figure 13.5. Argentina: government bonds denominated in local currency. Source: Argentina Ministerio de Economía y Producción.

would instantly spiral out of control. At an exchange rate of 2 ARS/USD, the burden of the mostly foreign-currency–denominated public debt would double to the equivalent of about 100% of GDP, and at 3 ARS/USD it would balloon even more to an unviable 150% of GDP.[18]

How could a government that collected tax revenues only in pesos, that had long ago sold all of its assets that could attract dollars, and that was legally prevented even from printing pesos—the then-autonomous central bank was authorized to issue pesos only in exchange for dollars—end up with only a token amount of its liabilities denominated in pesos? And yet, this patently irresponsible currency mismatch, which was overlooked by the financial markets and was blessed by the IMF, with which Argentina maintained a very close working relationship throughout the 1990s, ensured that if there was ever a change in the currency regime involving a major devaluation, the public sector would be rendered instantly insolvent.[19]

To lighten the government's debt burden and also that of most households and corporations in the face of a deepening economic depression, the incoming administration of President Eduardo Duhalde passed an Economic Emergency Law in early January 2002 forcibly converting most obligations denominated in U.S. dollars into Argentine pesos at one-to-one parity. A decree issued in February of that year further ruled that bank deposits would be converted into pesos at a more favorable exchange rate of 1.4 ARS/USD and that the government would issue bonds to the banks to compensate them for the mismatch of having their assets and liabilities converted at different exchange rates. New measures announced that March offered bank depositors the option of receiving government bonds in exchange for frozen deposits and specified that all government debt issued under Argentine law would be converted into pesos at the more favorable 1.4 ARS/USD rather than at 1:1. Shortly thereafter, the Central Bank of Argentina issued regulations making it clear that debts related to foreign trade transactions, future and forward contracts, or governed by foreign law were not subject to any conversion and remained denominated in U.S. dollars.

The results of these measures were that most Argentine debtors were sheltered from the financial impact of the peso's devaluation and that bank depositors obtained partial compensation for the currency's slide, though their deposits could not be withdrawn at will. At the other extreme, multinational corporations were impacted very adversely by the peso's devaluation because the bulk of their liabilities were to parent companies and other cross-border lenders and investors and had to be serviced at the new, heavily depreciated exchange rate. To add insult to injury, all companies—mostly multinationals—rendering public services (e.g., providers of electricity, telecommunications, and water) were barred from raising their prices during 2002–03, and were granted only modest rate relief during 2004–05.

Commercial banks, the largest of which are mostly foreign-owned, were impacted adversely in various ways. By mid-2005, they had received government bonds in full compensation for the the losses caused by the asymmetric conversion of assets and liabilities from USD into ARS. They had not been compensated by the value of deposits that were paid out in full, in USD or its ARS equivalent at the new exchange rate, under court orders obtained in 2002–04 by many depositors. And they faced a yield mismatch that resulted in heavy operating losses during 2002–03 stemming from the fact that many of their assets (e.g., government bonds and personal and mortgage loans) pay low interest rates indexed to inflation or wages, whereas many of their liabilities (deposits that are no longer frozen) pay higher, market-based interest rates. As a result, most of the banks operating in Argentina in 2005 remain financially vulnerable and undercapitalized.

The financial condition of the government initially improved somewhat as a result of the conversion of some of its obligations from dollars into pesos, but it soon deteriorated significantly because of the issuance of substantial amounts of new debt to banks and their depositors. Therefore, excluding arrears of principal and interest, the stock of public debt, which had amounted to the equivalent of $144 billion (U.S.) at the end of 2001, dropped to $113 billion by end of March 2002 but proceeded to increase thereafter and by the middle of 2003 had reached $153 billion, the equivalent of more than 120% of GDP. Once arrears were included, the public debt stood at approximately $185 billion by the end of 2003 (table 13.5), which represented about 140% of that year's GDP. By the close of 2004, the public debt had further increased to over $190 billion due to accumulation of interest arrears, but because of the economy's strong recovery, this was equivalent of about 125% of that year's GDP.

TABLE 13.5 Argentina: Public sector debt (U.S.$ billions, 2003E)

	Principal	Past-due interest and other arrears	Total	% of total
To be restructured				
Bonds	81.2	18.2	99.4	53.7
Loans	6.8	0.5	7.3	3.9
Bilateral agencies	4.9	0.4	5.3	2.9
Commercial banks	1.6	0.1	1.7	0.9
Other creditors	0.3	0.0	0.3	0.2
Subtotal	**88.0**	**18.7**	**106.7**	**57.6**
To be excluded from restructuring				
Bonds	30.6	0.0	30.6	16.5
Guaranteed	10.0	0.0	10.0	5.4
Other (BODENs)	20.6	0.0	20.6	11.1
Loans	47.9	0.0	47.9	25.9
Guaranteed	14.6	0.0	14.6	7.9
Multilateral agencies	30.8	0.0	30.8	16.6
Other	2.5	0.0	2.5	1.3
Subtotal	**78.5**	**0.0**	**78.5**	**42.4**
Total	**166.5**	**18.7**	**185.2**	**100.0**

Source: Argentina Ministerio de Economía y Producción. Available online at: www.mecon.gov.ar/finance/sfinan/reest-deuda/road-show-cwg-oct-03.pdf.

During the course of 2002–03, the governments of President Duhalde and his elected successor, Néstor Kirchner, made it clear that whereas about two-fifths of debt obligations would be honored under certain conditions, the remainder would not be paid pending a restructuring that had to involve a massive amount of debt forgiveness. The senior debt being serviced, with a face value of nearly $80 billion (U.S.), consists of the new bonds issued mainly to banks and their depositors (the so-called BODENs); new bonds and loans guaranteed by tax revenues resulting from a distressed-debt exchange in late 2001; and old and new loans from the multilateral agencies (the IMF, Inter-American Development Bank, and World Bank). However, the Duhalde and Kirchner governments let it be known that debts to these official agencies would only continue to be serviced if the agencies themselves started disbursing new loans in amounts equivalent to what was coming due.[20] The junior debt in arrears, with a face value of over $90 billion, is made up largely of bonds issued in various foreign jurisdictions, plus a small amount of loans from official bilateral agencies and private-sector commercial banks, all dating from before the end of 2001.

The Case of Argentina: Prospects and Implications

The restructuring of Argentine government debt has posed a complex and daunting challenge to the international financial community. Beyond the fact that no other sovereign had defaulted on so huge a volume of indebtedness, there was the sheer dimension of the task at hand. According to the authorities, the securities they wished to restructure encompassed more than 150 individual bond issues denominated in seven different currencies and subject to eight distinct governing jurisdictions.[21] Moreover, it was estimated that almost 45% of the debt up for restructuring was in the hands of hundreds of thousands of scattered individual investors, mostly in Italy and Germany. This was a departure from the norm, which is that a few dozen institutional investors (e.g., mutual and pension funds, insurance companies, and commercial and investment banks) account for the vast majority of debt to be restructured. Therefore, the legal and ownership features of the Argentine case promised to make any debt restructuring particularly difficult to achieve.

To make matters worse, the Argentine authorities made it known that they aimed to obtain a massive write-off. At the unveiling of their initial proposal during the IMF/World Bank annual meetings in Dubai in September 2003, they requested that 75% of eligible principal and 100% of past-due interest be forgiven. At follow-up meetings that took place in Europe and the United States during October 2003, they further proposed issuing new bonds with coupons as low as 0.5% per year and with maturities as long as 42 years (Argentina Ministry of Economy and Production 2003). This implied degree of desired relief, on the order of more than 90% on a net-present-value basis, has no parallel in the country's checkered financial history, which includes defaults in the nineteenth century but no interruptions of debt servicing during the nearly 90 years until 1982.[22]

Indeed, the combination of principal, interest rate, and maturity relief desired by the Argentine government was only comparable with—and for the most part exceeded—that sought by the poorest countries in Africa and Latin America during restructurings that took place in the 1980s and 1990s. The threshold of pain that the authorities proposed to inflict on bondholders was very difficult to justify given the country's relative income and wealth. Indeed, as of 2003, per capita income in Argentina stood at an estimated $3,400 per year, temporarily depressed in the wake of the massive currency devaluation of 2002 from its usual level of $6,000–$8,000 per year. Even so, the depressed figure put the country in a league far above that of the poorest countries in Africa and Latin America, where per capita incomes hover around $1,000 per year or less. Not surprisingly, most investors willing to be quoted reacted very negatively to the initial Argentine proposal.[23]

The extraordinary degree of debt and debt-service forgiveness sought by the Argentine authorities was derived by calculating unilaterally a maximum fiscal effort deemed to be sustainable politically and economically. This effort is measured by the so-called primary fiscal surplus, namely the excess of current revenues over current and investment outlays before consideration of interest payments. The higher the primary fiscal surplus, the more nonborrowed resources are available to meet interest payments on the public debt—and to possibly amortize some principal as well.

According to the authorities, a primary fiscal effort equivalent to 2.4% of GDP (figure 13.6) for the federal government, plus an extra 0.6% of GDP generated by provincial governments, is all that was compatible with fostering an economic recovery with GDP growth averaging 4% per year during 2004–06. By Argentine standards, the proposed primary fiscal effort was meaningful, because this measure averaged 0.5% of GDP during 1994–2002. However, other

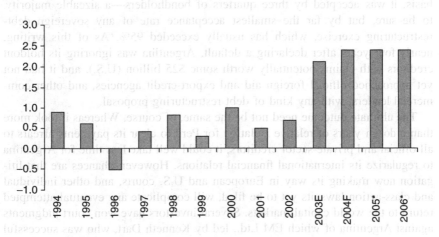

Figure 13.6. Argentina: primary fiscal balance (% of GDP). Source: Argentina Ministerio de Economía y Producción.

countries in similar straits have pledged to make, or have been making, even greater fiscal efforts, on the order of 4–6% of GDP (e.g., Brazil, Ecuador, Turkey, and Uruguay) to minimize the degree of otherwise necessary debt forgiveness. Therefore, many creditors were unlikely to find acceptable the fiscal effort that the Argentine authorities envisioned.

The desired extent of debt relief was also shaped by unilateral calculations of debt sustainability, namely the necessary improvement in key solvency ratios such as debt to GDP and annual debt service to fiscal revenues. This improvement was designed to enable Argentina to obtain upgrades in its rock-bottom sovereign credit ratings and renewed access to the international capital markets in the not-too-distant future. According to official projections, even assuming that the debt restructuring proceeded as intended, that the multilateral agencies refinanced all of Argentina's maturing principal repayments during 2004–13, and that the government could place new bonds domestically to offset the scheduled redemption of performing debt, there would be a meaningful residual financing gap in every year starting in 2005 and at least through 2010. Therefore, while the government was aiming to come back to the capital markets as quickly as possible after the debt restructuring was completed, experience from the African and Latin American governments that had previously obtained debt forgiveness anywhere near the magnitude that Argentina was expecting showed that they had not been able to return to the international financial markets.

Beyond the many obstacles to a prompt and successful restructuring of Argentina's obligations, there is the matter of how the government proceeded in terms of a negotiating strategy. The Kirchner administration has pursued a confrontational, unilateralist approach that is reminiscent of Peru's Alan Garcia. It has not been willing to negotiate in good faith with its creditors, and the assumptions behind its proposal for massive relief have been widely questioned.[24] After the government put forth a finalized bond exchange proposal in early 2005 seeking debt relief on the order of a less extreme 70% on a net-present-value basis, it was accepted by three quarters of bondholders—a sizeable majority, to be sure, but by far the smallest acceptance rate of any sovereign debt-restructuring exercise, which has usually exceeded 95%. As of this writing, nearly four years after declaring a default, Argentina was ignoring its holdout creditors with claims potentially worth some $25 billion (U.S.), and it had not yet approached official foreign aid and export-credit agencies, and other commercial lenders, with any kind of debt restructuring proposal.

The ultimate outcome need not be the same, of course. Whereas it took more than a dozen years of relative isolation for Peru to clear its payments arrears to all official and private-sector creditors, it could well take less time for Argentina to regularize its international financial relations. However, chances are that litigation now making its way in European and U.S. courts, and other individual and class-action lawsuits yet to be filed, will complicate any eventual attempted return to the world capital markets. Several investors have won court judgments against Argentina of which EM Ltd., led by Kenneth Dart, who was successful in taking on Brazil when that country went through its Brady bond restructuring, is the largest with a $724 million ruling in its favor courtesy of the U.S. District Court (for the Southern District of New York).

The fact is that distressed-debt investors, including vulture funds, have been attracted to defaulted emerging-market debt, buying paper (bank loans, supplier credits, or bonds) with the intention of suing for full recovery. According to Singh (2003), most of these investors have been successful in their litigation or in forcing out-of-court settlements, or are holding favorable judgments and orders of attachment (table 13.6). They have averaged recovery rates of about three to 20 times their investment, equivalent to returns net of legal fees (often recouped from the sovereign) of 300–2,000%. However, litigation is a protracted affair in which many lawsuits take between three to ten years to settle. Sovereigns are exposed to the greatest vulnerability when they make or receive payments through existing systems such as Euroclear and Clearstream, as evidenced by the cases of *Elliott v. Peru* and, more recently, *LNC Investments v. Nicaragua*. Therefore, there is a risk that by failing to reach a friendly understanding with virtually all of its creditors, any funds that the Argentine government may attempt to obtain in the future in the international capital markets may be attached by disgruntled or opportunistic bondholders.

Does the case of Argentina suggest that the international financial architecture has proved to be deficient? Our answer is decidedly in the negative. Different rules of international financial engagement would not have avoided the traumatic

TABLE 13.6   Recent cases of litigation against sovereigns

Debtor	Face value of claim	Outcome
Brazil	$1.48 billion (U.S.)	Paid in full
Cameroon	ECU3.8 million	Partial attachment; attempted retrial
Cameroon	$19.9 million (U.S.)	Under appeal
Congo	$27 million (U.S.)	Settled for 30% of face value
Congo	$7 million (U.S.)	Settled
Cote d'Ivoire	$10 million (U.S.)	Settled
Ecuador	$6 million (U.S.)	Paid in full
Ethiopia	$100 million+ (U.S.)	In arbitration
Guyana	$6 million (U.S.)	In arbitration
Honduras	$1.7 million (U.S.)	Not settled
Madagascar	$55 million (U.S.)	Paid in full
Nicaragua	$96 million (U.S.)	Attempting to attach assets
Panama	$48 million (U.S.)	Settled
Peru	$64 million (U.S.)	Paid in full
Poland	CHF5 million	Settled
Turkmenistan	$3.8 million (U.S.)	Paid in full
Uganda	$5.5 million (U.S.)	Ordered to pay $20.6 million (U.S.)
Uganda	$1.8 million (U.S.)	Ordered to pay $2.7 million (U.S.)
Uganda	$10.5 million (U.S.)	Ordered to pay creditors
Yemen	$8.2 million (U.S.)	Settled for ⅓ of face value
Zambia	$45 million+ (U.S.)	Settled for $100 million (U.S.)

Source: Singh (2003).

exit of a heavily indebted and currency-mismatched government out of an artificial exchange-rate regime, and they would not hasten the country's financial rehabilitation.

Specifically, the existence of a supranational SDRM back in 2001, or the presence of CACs in all of the country's bonds, would not have made matters any easier. Because a substantial proportion of the Argentine government's debt obligations was held by local banks, pension funds, and insurance companies, any announcement of a payment standstill with the intention of seeking meaningful debt forgiveness via an SDRM or the activation of CACs would surely have triggered a stampede of bank depositors for the exits and a collapse of the pension and insurance industries. This would have led to a run on the central bank's official reserves, rather quickly precipitating a devastating currency devaluation, the imposition of limits on bank withdrawals and capital outflows, and thus the same economic implosion, political fallout, and popular discontent that was witnessed in late 2001 and early 2002. Those who believe that Argentina could have defaulted, obtained debt forgiveness, and returned to "business as usual" in no time at all—if only the government could have trampled on the rights of investors protected by foreign law as easily as it trampled on those operating under its own laws—are engaging in wishful thinking.

All debate regarding the extent of debt forgiveness that was appropriate for Argentina to receive would likewise not have been avoided—not without adverse consequences, in any case—by the existence of an SDRM or the widespread application of CACs. In either case, a debtor government must still persuade the vast majority of its creditors to accept a proposed debt-relief formula. We doubt that bondholders would have accepted the kind of massive debt forgiveness that the Argentine government requested in September 2003 or thereafter, even if the SDRM had been operational and the IMF had given the Argentine demand its full blessing.

It is true, however, that individual creditors would find it still more difficult to collect from an errant government such as Argentina's if it were under the protection of an SDRM-administered restructuring plan. But if creditor rights were curtailed relative to the status quo compliments of an investor-unfriendly reform of the international financial architecture, surely Argentina would not be able to come back to the capital markets for a very long time, and other weak sovereign credits would lose their present-day level of access to international private capital. Argentina would probably become a ward of the official multilateral agencies—the ones that are already heavily exposed there, have been bullied by the government into making substantial new loans, and cannot possibly be objective about how much debt forgiveness the country is entitled to obtain from junior creditors.

As considerable experience has taught, only international and domestic reforms that strengthen rather than weaken the enforcement of contracts, and that encourage dialogue and cooperation rather than the imposition of unilateral "solutions," are likely to speed up the rehabilitation of countries in financial trouble. A highly complex sovereign debt restructuring such as Argentina's can only be handled by a meeting of the minds between the government and its mostly private-sector creditors, accomplished either through face-to-face negotiations with a representative committee of bondholders or through an extensive, informal consultation process that leads to an acceptable exchange offer. These are the tried and tested avenues to eventual success.

The missing ingredient is willingness on the part of the Argentine authorities to help themselves. In the context of a negotiated solution to their over-indebtedness conundrum, this willingness would have translated into committing a greater share of rapidly rising tax revenues to future debt service and to using a portion of accumulating international reserves to make some up-front payments on account of past-due interest.[25] These are the kinds of concessions that many governments—Argentina's and others—have made in past debt-restructuring negotiations in return for permanent debt forgiveness on the part of private lenders and investors. The alternative is a long, drawn-out "dialogue of the deaf" that will encourage more litigation and that has the potential to tie up in knots the implementation of the restructuring deal reached in early 2005 with the majority of creditors. A *deus ex machina* sovereign bankruptcy solution imposed by the G7 governments is not a realistic alternative.

Acknowledgments Two sections of this chapter draw heavily on material that appeared in "The constructive role of private creditors," *Ethics and International Affairs*, 17: 2 (2003), 18–25.

Notes

1. An analysis of the ratios of external debt to GDP in the year when a default episode occurred shows that, at least during the 1980s and 1990s, many emerging-market countries experienced an adverse credit event despite the fact that their ratios were below 50% of GNP. See Reinhart, Rogoff, and Savastano, "Debt Intolerance," pp. 11–12.

2. The World Bank estimates that the external debt of developing countries reached $2.43 trillion (U.S.) as of the end of 2003, of which $2.07 trillion, or 85% of the total, consisted of long-term government and government-guaranteed obligations, including the use of IMF credit. It is not known what percentage of the short-term external indebtedness of $364 billion was owed or guaranteed by governments, but chances are that most of it was owed by private-sector banks and corporations. See World Bank, *Global Development Finance 2004*, 2 vols. (Washington, DC: World Bank, 2004), 2: 2.

3. The notable exception is Africa, where it is really only in South Africa that there is a thriving domestic bond market.

4. According to the World Bank, the long-term external indebtedness of the private sector in the East Asia and Pacific region was cut back from a peak of $159 billion (U.S.) in 1998 to $115 billion as of the end of 2003, and the region's short-term external indebtedness, which involves mostly private-sector obligors, has was reduced from a maximum of $132 billion in 1997 to $63 billion as of the end of 2000, though it is estimated to have crept back up to $112 billion by the end of 2003. See World Bank, *Global Development Finance*, 2: 6.

5. The Institute of International Finance (IIF), a Washington-based research and advocacy group that represents the world's largest private financial institutions, was first to announce its support of CACs. However, it also called for the establishment of a private-sector advisory group to work with troubled debtors and the official community, and a

partnership between private financial institutions and governments to limit disruptive creditor litigation (see www.iif.com/data/public/icdc0402.pdf, 9 April 2002). The pursuit of such market-based approaches was later endorsed by five other private-sector organizations (Emerging Markets Creditors Association, Emerging Markets Traders Association, International Primary Market Association, Securities Industry Association, and The Bond Market Association; see www.emta.org/ndevelop/oneill.pdf, 3 June 2002). These industry representatives later went on to draft a set of model collective-action clauses that could be included in future bond contracts, but they took care not to weaken the rights of bondholders for the sake of expediency (see www.emta.org/ndevelop/ Finalmerged.pdf, 31 January 2003). For a review of the application of CACs under New York law, see Sergio J. Galvis and Angel L. Saad, "Collective Action Clauses: Recent Progress and Challenges Ahead," 20 February 2004. Available online at: www.law .georgetown.edu/international/documents/Galvis.pdf.

6. According to the first deputy managing director of the IMF, a new approach to sovereign debt restructuring is needed because "in the current environment, it *may* be particularly difficult to secure high participation from creditors as a group, as individual creditors *may* consider that their best interests would be served by trying to free ride. . . . These difficulties *may* be amplified by the prevalence of complex financial instruments . . . which in some cases *may* provide investors with incentives to hold out . . . rather than participating in a restructuring" (emphasis added). See Krueger, *A New Approach*, and p. 8.

7. Cleary, Gottlieb, Steen, and Hamilton (U.S. attorneys for Uruguay). 2003. "Press release: Uruguay in Groundbreaking $5.2 Billion Debt Restructuring, 29 May 2003. Available online at: www.cgsh.com/newsworthy-categories.cfm?strNwsCatName=Re structurings.

8. Television interview with President Jorge Batlle of Uruguay, "El Default Significaba el Quiebre Institucional de Uruguay," 4 July 2003. Available online at: www .presidencia.gub.uy/sic/noticias/archivo/2003/julio/2003070404.htm. This version of events had previously been revealed by Vice President Luis Hierro of Uruguay but had been denied by the IMF's spokesman; see IMF, "Transcript of a Press Briefing by Thomas C. Dawson," 26 June 2003. Available online at: www.imf.org/external/np/tr/2003/tr030626 .htm.

9. There is a fourth approach followed by various French kings in the 1500s and 1600s—that of beheading the creditors—but thankfully it has gone out of style in recent centuries. See Reinhart, Rogoff, and Savastano, "Debt Intolerance," p. 8.

10. Interestingly, the government of Pakistan followed this route even though its bonds were governed by U.K. law and included CACs. Therefore, its obligations could have been amended after a negotiation process with the requisite qualified majority of bondholders.

11. Hedge fund Elliott Associates L.P. paid $11 million (U.S.) in 1996 on the secondary debt market to buy $21 million of Peru's sovereign debt and then sued for full repayment plus capitalized interest. The U.S. Court of Appeals eventually ruled in its favor, and it obtained enforcement orders from courts in several countries, including Belgium. It was the Brussels court's stance that discouraged members of Euroclear from accepting payments from the government of Peru on account of Brady bonds, which forced Peru to settle with Elliott by paying at least $58 million. The individuals involved in Elliott Associates reportedly have conducted similar actions against several other sovereigns. For a discussion of the legal ramifications of such actions, see G. Mitu Gulati and Kenneth N. Klee, "Sovereign Piracy," 01-7 (2001). Available online at: http:// papers.ssrn.com/sol3/delivery.cfm/SSRN_ID272194_code010604510.pdf?abstractid=272194.

12. The case of Russia, not detailed here, likewise illustrates these differences. Whereas private creditors agreed to provide substantial debt relief in early 2000, the Paris Club of official creditors only rescheduled a small amount of arrears and other payments coming due up to the end of 2000—some $8 billion (U.S.) out of a total of $51 billion of indebtedness to bilateral creditors represented by the Club. Available online at: www.clubdeparis.org/en/countries/countries.php?IDENTIFIANT = 89&POSITION = 0& PAY_ISO_ID=RU&CONTINENT_ID=&TYPE_TRT=&ANNEE=&INDICE_DET=.

13. Paris Club. 2002. Press release: The Paris Club and Nicaragua Agree to a Debt Restructuring under the Enhanced Heavily Indebted Poor Countries Initiative. 13 December 2002. Available online at: www.clubdeparis.org/rep_upload/PR01.pdf.

14. This is based on frank, off-the-record conversations with IMF and Ecuadoran officials. For the IMF's version of the events, see Stanley Fischer, "Ecuador and the IMF," 19 May 2000. Available online at: www.imf.org/external/np/speeches/2000/051900.htm.

15. After speaking to numerous IMF and Ecuadoran officials privately, another author concluded that "the IMF appears to have chosen to make Ecuador a guinea pig for a more aggressive approach to bailing in private creditors." See William R. Cline, "The Role of the Private Sector in Resolving Financial Crises in Emerging Markets," in *Economic and Financial Crises in Emerging Market Economies*, ed. Martin Feldstein (Chicago: University of Chicago Press, 2003), p. 482.

16. Paris Club. 2000. Press release dated 15 September 2000. Available online at: www.clubdeparis.org/en/press_release/pagep_detail_commupresse.php?FICHIER = com 9889887550; Paris Club. 2003. press release dated 13 June 2003. Available online at: www.clubdeparis.org/en/press_release/page_detail_commupresse.php?FICHIER= com10554999350.

17. For useful background on Argentina's economic woes, see Arturo C. Porzecanski, "Argentina: the Root Cause of the Disaster," *ABN AMRO Emerging Markets Fortnightly*, 24 July 2002, pp. 15–20. Available online at: www.nber.org/~confer/2002/argentina02/porzecanski.pdf; Michael Mussa, *Argentina and the Fund: From Triumph to Tragedy* (Washington, DC: IIE, 2002); Ricardo Hausmann and Andrés Velasco, "Hard Money's Soft Underbelly: Understanding the Argentine Crisis," in *Brookings Trade Forum 2002*, ed. Susan M. Collins and Dani Rodrik (Washington, DC: Brookings Institution Press, 2003), pp. 59–119; Andrew Powell, "Argentina's Avoidable Crisis: Bad Luck, Bad Economics, Bad Politics, Bad Advice," in Collins and Rodrik (eds.), *Brookings Trade Forum 2002*, pp. 1–58; and Guillermo A. Calvo, Alejandro Izquierdo, and Ernesto Talvi, "Sudden Stops, the Real Exchange Rate and Fiscal Sustainability: Argentina's Lessons," in Alexander et al. (eds.), *Monetary Unions and Hard Pegs* (New York: Oxford University Press, 2004) pp. 151–181.

18. Once freed, the exchange rate jumped to as much as 3.86 ARS/USD in late June 2002 before settling at around 2.80–3.00 ARS/USD after March 2003. To be sure, the dollar value of GDP has since recovered somewhat, but as of 2003 the estimated value of Argentina's GDP ($125 billion) remained a fraction of its predevaluation level ($270 billion).

19. As the former chief economist of the IMF during the 1990s has admitted, "the Argentine case is particularly revealing because the Fund was deeply involved with Argentina for many years before the emergence of the present crisis. In this important respect, Argentina is different from most other cases where the Fund has provided exceptionally large financial support. . . . [The] failures of the Fund are clearly associated with the core of the Fund's most intense involvement with a member: when it is providing financial assistance and when the policies and performance of the member are sub-

ject to the intense scrutiny of Fund conditionality." See Mussa, *Argentina and the Fund*, pp. 2–3.

20. To make this point crystal clear, in late 2002, the Duhalde administration briefly went into arrears with the World Bank, and in mid-2003 the Kirchner government briefly went into arrears with the IMF, when these institutions dragged their feet in terms of authorizing new disbursements. The Washington agencies, faced with the possibility of mounting arrears and potentially huge loan-loss provisions—and possibly massive write-offs down the road—quickly caved in and disbursed new funds to the government of Argentina in both instances, whereupon the government immediately cured its defaults to the multilateral agencies.

21. It is estimated that 53% of the obligations were denominated in U.S. dollars and 33% in euros, with the rest in other currencies, and that 51% of the debt was governed by U.S. law, 18% by English law and 17% by German law, with the rest subject to other jurisdictions including Argentina's (11% of total). See Argentina Secretariat of Finance, Ministry of Economy and Production, "Argentina's Restructuring Guidelines," 22 September 2003. Available online at: www.mecon.gov.ar/finance/sfinan/reestr-deuda/dubai _22-9_english.pdf.

22. Argentina is one of the few countries of significance in Latin America that did not default during the Great Depression. For background on prior departures from fixed exchange-rate regimes and associated defaults or avoidance of defaults, see Gerardo della Paolera and Alan M. Taylor, *Straining at the Anchor: The Argentine Currency Board and the Search for Macroeconomic Stability, 1880–1935* (2001). For background on debt servicing during the Great Depression, see Erika Jorgensen and Jeffrey Sachs, "Default and Renegotiation of Latin American Foreign Bonds in the Interwar Period," NBER Working Paper #2636, June 1988. Available online at: www.earthinstitute.columbia .edu/about/director/pubs/w2636.pdf.

23. Agence France-Presse. 2003. Argentine Creditors Left Fuming with Debt Restructuring Proposal, 22 September 2003. Available online at: http://quickstart.clari.net/qs _se/webnews;wed/cu/Qargentina-debt-imf.RulU_DSM.html.

24. The Argentina Bondholders Committee (ABC) presented an alternative restructuring proposal in December 2003, and while it accepted most of the government's assumptions, it demonstrated that a somewhat greater fiscal effort up front, and a greater willingness to roll over maturing obligations to domestic bondholders, could result in a drastically lower need for permanent debt forgiveness. See ABC, *Argentina Bondholders Committee Restructuring Guidelines*, 3 December 2003. Available online at: www.emta .org/ndevelop/ABC_Final_Restructuring_Guidelines_12-3-03.pdf.

25. In 2003, central government tax revenues jumped by 43% in peso terms and by 53% in U.S. dollar equivalents. See Argentina Secretaría de Hacienda, Subsecretaría de Ingresos Públicos. Available online at: www.mecon.gov.ar/download/rec_trib/2003 -diciembre.xls. Official international reserves, for their part, increased by 35% in 2003 from $10.5 billion (U.S.) to $14.1 billion. See Banco Central de la República Argentina. Available online at: www.bcra.gov.ar/hm000000.asp.

References

Argentina Ministry of Economy and Production. 2003. Consultative Working Groups Meeting. October 2003. Available online at: www.argentinedebtinfo.gov.ar/docu mentos/road-show-cwg-oct-03.pdf.

Argentina Secretariat of Finance, Ministry of Economy and Production. 2003. Argentina's Restructuring Guidelines. 22 September 2003. Available online at: www.mecon.gov.ar/finance/sfinan/reestr-deuda/dubai_22-9_english.pdf.

Boughton, J. 2001. *Silent Revolution: the International Monetary Fund, 1979–1989.* Washington, DC: International Monetary Fund.

Calvo, G., Izquierdo, A., and Talvi, E. 2004. Sudden Stops, the Real Exchange Rate and Fiscal Sustainability: Argentina's Lessons. In *Monetary Unions and Hard Pegs,* eds. V. Alexander et al. New York: Oxford University Press.

Cline, W. 2003. The Role of the Private Sector in Resolving Financial Crises in Emerging Markets. In *Economic and Financial Crises in Emerging Market Economies,* ed. M. Feldstein. Chicago: University of Chicago Press.

della Paolera, G., and Taylor, A. 2001. *Straining at the Anchor: The Argentine Currency Board and the Search for Macroeconomic Stability, 1880–1935.* Chicago: University of Chicago Press.

Fischer, S. 2000. Ecuador and the IMF. Available online at: www.imf.org/external/np/speeches/2000/051900.htm.

Galvis, S., and Saad, A. 2004. Collective Action Clauses: Recent Progress and Challenges Ahead. *Georgetown Journal of International Law,* Vol. 35: 4. Washington, DC: Georgetown University Law Center.

Group of Ten. 2002. Report of the G-10 Working Group on Contractual Clauses. 26 September 2002. Available online at: www.bis.org/publ/gten08.pdf.

Gulati, G., and Klee, K. 2001. Sovereign Piracy. UCLA School of Law Research Paper #01-7. Available online at: http://papers.ssrn.com/sol3/delivery.cfm/SSRN_ID272194_code010604510.pdf?abstractid=272194.

Hausmann, R., and Velasco, A. 2002. Hard Money's Soft Underbelly: Understanding the Argentine Crisis. In *Brookings Trade Forum 2002,* ed. S. M. Collins and D. Rodrik. Washington, DC: Brookings Institution Press.

Institute of International Finance (IIF). 2001a. Survey of Debt Restructuring by Private Creditors. Washington, DC: IIF (April).

———. 2001b. Principles for Private Sector Involvement in Crisis Prevention and Resolution. Washington, DC: IIF (January). Available online at: www.emta.org/ndevelop/iif-psi.pdf.

International Monetary Fund (IMF). 2003a. *World Economic Outlook September 2003.* Washington, DC: IMF.

———. 2003b. Ecuador: Selected Issues and Statistical Appendix. IMF Country Report No. 03/91. Washington, DC: IMF. Available online at: www.imf.org/external/pubs/ft/scr/2003/cr0391.pdf.

Jorgensen, E., and Sachs, J. 1998. Default and Renegotiation of Latin American Foreign Bonds in the Interwar Period. NBER Working Paper #2636 (June). Available online at: www.earthinstitute.columbia.edu/about/director/pubs/w2636.pdf.

Koch, E. B. 2004. Collective Action Clauses—The Way Forward. *Georgetown Journal of International Law,* Vol. 35: 4. Washington, DC: Georgetown University Law Center.

Krueger, A. 2002. *A New Approach to Sovereign Debt Restructuring.* Washington, DC: IMF.

Mussa, M. 2002. *Argentina and the Fund: From Triumph to Tragedy.* Washington, DC: IIE.

Porzecanski, A. 2002. Argentina: The Root Cause of the Disaster. *ABN AMRO Emerging Markets Fortnightly,* (July): 15–20. Available online at: www.nber.org/~confer/2002/argentina02/porzecanski.pdf.

————. The Constructive Role of Private Creditors. *Ethics and International Affairs,* Vol. 17: 2. New York: Carnegie Council on Ethics and International Affairs.

————. 2004. Sovereign Liquidity Risk: An Update. *ABN AMRO Emerging Markets Fortnightly,* 17 March, pp. 13–21.

Powell, A. 2002. Argentina's Avoidable Crisis: Bad Luck, Bad Economics, Bad Politics, Bad Advice. In *Brookings Trade Forum 2002,* ed. S. M. Collins and D. Rodrik. Washington, DC: Brookings Institution Press.

Reiffel, L. 2003. *Restructuring Sovereign Debt: The Case for Ad Hoc Machinery.* Washington, DC: Brookings Institution Press.

Reinhart, C., Rogoff, K., and Savastano, M. 2003. Debt Intolerance. *Brookings Papers on Economic Activity,* No. 1. Washington, DC: Brookings Institution.

Rogoff, K., and Zettelmeyer, J. 2002. Bankruptcy Procedures for Sovereigns: A History of Ideas, 1976–2001, *IMF Staff Papers,* 49: 3. Washington, DC: IMF.

Singh, M. 2003. Recovery Rates from Distressed Debt: Empirical Evidence from Chapter 11 Filings, International Litigation, and Recent Sovereign Debt Restructurings. IMF Working Paper WP/03/161 (August). Washington, DC: IMF.

Taylor, J. 2002. Sovereign Debt Restructuring: A U.S. Perspective. Washington, DC: U.S. Treasury. 2 April 2002. Available online at: www.ustreas.gov/press/releases/po2056.htm.

World Bank. 2003a. *Global Development Finance 2003,* 2 vols. Washington, DC: World Bank.

————. 2003b. HIPC Initiative: Status of Country Cases Considered under the Initiative (September). Available online at: www.worldbank.org/hipc/progress-to-date/status _table_Sep03.pdf.

14

THE JUBILEE 2000 CAMPAIGN: A BRIEF OVERVIEW

Ann Pettifor

> *We hope that the international community will come to realize that the poorest countries cannot develop their potential without total debt cancellation within the framework of Jubilee 2000.*
> —President Chissano, Mozambique (Barrett 2000)

> *I thank Jubilee 2000 for the sweep of your achievements so far and, yes, the scale of your ambitions that we are summoned to meet. . . . Your vision is of a new climate of justice across the world, a new climate of justice that will liberate nations from unsustainable debt.*
> —Chancellor Gordon Brown, March 1999

> *In Peru and the rest of Latin America, where millions of people struggle against poverty and in the name of democracy, Jubilee 2000's presence and actions at an international level have given us a reason to believe in the effectiveness of collective action and in the greatness of human solidarity.*
> —Ismael Muñoz, General Coordinator of Jubilee 2000 Peru (Barrett 2000)

Introduction

In this chapter, I hope to shed some light on how advocacy of an arcane development issue, Third World debt, was transformed in just four years by a huge, effective global campaign—Jubilee 2000. This campaign demonstrated that the constituency in rich western countries in support of the poorest, most indebted nations is much bigger than the narrow memberships of traditional aid agencies and nongovernmental organizations (NGOs); that many millions of citizens could be mobilized behind a global economic justice campaign; and that this could be achieved through international coordination and cooperation by national autonomous campaigns.

In my view, it is still too early to fully evaluate the impact of the Jubilee 2000 campaign, as much of the debt relief promised has not so far been delivered or allocated to development. Nevertheless, at the time of writing (April 2004), $43 billion (U.S.) of debt relief has been delivered to 28 of the world's poorest countries—the first tranches of a promise by G8 leaders to cancel $100 billion of debt for a total of 42 countries. Although this debt relief has been delivered at an agonizingly slow pace and with the burden of discredited IMF conditions, it nevertheless represents a substantial transfer of resources to heavily indebted poor countries—resources that are more directly available to the governments of these countries than much foreign aid. Furthermore, in a Jubilee Research study of 10 African countries that benefited from the campaign, evidence suggests that funds released by debt cancelation are being used productively (Blackmore and Greenhill 2002). Our research shows these funds are channeled into increased social spending—particularly in health and education.[1]

The success of Jubilee 2000 has in turn pushed sovereign debt and the injustice of relations between rich and poor countries to the top of the global political agenda, so that, for instance, the debt dimension to the Iraq crisis moved to the forefront of debate immediately after the occupation of that country. Debt and development issues are now routinely discussed at international summits—and the IMF and World Bank have come under considerable pressure to modify their economic policy prescriptions. Furthermore, Jubilee 2000 laid the foundations for new challenges to the phenomenon known as "globalization" by a wider community than that of antiglobalization activists, most notably the millions who are members of Western faith communities.

A word of caution: I am a co-founder of the international Jubilee 2000 campaign and played a leadership role both in Britain and also internationally between 1995 and 2000. This account is based on that experience. It will attempt to be frank, honest, and objective, but given my particularly Northern, British perspective, it will necessarily be selective. Aspects of the campaign not always visible to others will be revealed, but because of my own bias, other aspects will be obscured. Jubilee 2000 was and still is a phenomenon. It is part of a complex and diverse global social movement, responding to and resisting the transformation of the global economy that has made finance dominant over all aspects of the economy and in the process greatly enriched the few and impoverished and indebted the many. No single account of this particular resistance by a large segment of humanity to the delusional ambitions of globalization's advocates can be comprehensive, nor can it do the international movement of Jubilee 2000 full justice.

Jubilee 2000—A Brief Overview

In a grass roots campaign reminiscent of the drive against South African apartheid, the debt-relief movement, particularly the faith-based Jubilee 2000 coalition, has jarred the highest levels of power.

—*Washington Post*, April 1999

The idea of linking the new millennium to the ancient biblical mandate of Jubilee (Lev. 25: 28) originated with Martin Dent, an academic at Keele University in Britain, in 1990. Martin Dent wrote extensively about the biblical concept of Jubilee and throughout the duration of the campaign provided inspiration and philosophical insights for campaigners. He built up some support for his idea but on the whole met with skepticism. After a few years, Dent and his friend Bill Peters approached the Debt Crisis Network (DCN), an alliance of the biggest British aid agencies coordinating work on Third World debt. Most rejected Dent's idea as "corny" or "too religious" for their constituencies.

However, the DCN believed that linking a campaign for debt cancelation to the Jubilee year, the year 2000, a "kairos time" to use Dent's words, was likely to resonate with, and therefore mobilize, large numbers of people of faith in Western creditor nations. But Martin Dent's big idea was brilliant for other reasons, best known to advertising and marketing agencies. Most successful communication comes from linking two ideas that may appear bizarrely different but that actually, in combination, have a terrific dynamic, or synchronicity. In this case, Dent linked, first, a huge, almost global celebration of the passing of time, and second, an (apparently) obscure biblical mandate to periodically cancel debts, free slaves, and restore land to its rightful owners. The effect was to be electrifying.

At the time, I was coordinator of the Debt Crisis Network and heavily engaged in lobbying the World Bank and IMF for more debt relief. In February 1996, determined to provide a platform for people from debtor nations to put their case to communities in Britain, we had assembled a group of African leaders, led by ex-President Kenneth Kaunda of Zambia, to tour Britain. This tour culminated in an event hosted by Britain's Catholic Cardinal Hume, who invited another prominent Catholic, Michel Camdessus, managing director of the IMF, to attend the meeting on Third World debt. This invitation and the event itself brought Mr. Camdessus face to face with the hostility of world Catholic leaders toward the institution he led and its economic policies. That meeting led directly to the IMF (a "preferred creditor") undertaking the historically unprecedented step of writing off debts by participating in the World Bank's heavily indebted poor countries (HIPC) initiative of 1996.

Even with this change in approach by the international financial institutions (IFIs), we believed that broader public pressure had to be applied to achieve both substantial debt cancelation and a shift in the IMF's deflationary economic policies. So, beginning in 1995–96, Martin Dent and I gathered together a group of people supportive of the Jubilee 2000 concept. We analyzed the problem in depth, discussed different, radical approaches to the debt, and began to design and structure a campaign, that we hoped could be internationalized and would initially run parallel to the DCN. Ultimately, we hoped to persuade all the members of DCN to integrate their debt work with this new campaign.

Jubilee 2000's first key supporters, and fellow attendees at these early meetings, were mainly evangelical Christians organized around the aid agency TearFund. The Debt Crisis Network's approach to debt cancelation was radical by their standards, as indeed was the political analysis of the injustice of global finance. Nevertheless, fired up by the biblical mandate outlined in Leviticus 25, they prepared to take on a new role—engaging in public advocacy on an issue of political economy. By the spring of 1997, 1,000 days before the millennium, we had raised enough money to launch the campaign by erecting a neon-lit clock in Piccadilly Circus, London, that proclaimed Jubilee and counted down the days to the new millennium.

The Campaign Begins to Roll

We were clear from the start that Jubilee 2000 would only be successful if we could persuade campaigners and aid agencies both in the United Kingdom and in other countries to join us in advocacy. Thus began a heavy travel schedule, first within the United Kingdom itself and then in endless rounds of meetings with NGO representatives in the United States, Latin America, Africa, and Europe. In June 1997, the Maryknoll sisters in Washington, led by Marie Dennis, helped launch a similar campaign in the United States at the G8 summit in Denver; in September, the German Protestant and Catholic churches, led by Jurgen Kaiser, launched a campaign; in October, an alliance of NGOs in Scotland, led by Liz Hendry, the Church of Scotland, and the Anglican Church, launched their campaign; and in February 1998, the Italian campaign, Sdebitarsi, led by Paola Biocca and Luca de Fraia, was launched. At the same time, Jubilee 2000 campaigns unknown to us were emerging as far as away as Japan but also in countries such as Peru, Honduras, and Kenya. Eventually, after just three years, thanks in large part to the movements against the debt already well-established in developing countries, and thanks in part to the work of Catholic and Protestant missionaries and aid agencies, there were Jubilee 2000 coalitions and campaigns in 69 countries around the world (Barrett 2000).

After an initial hesitant start, the British campaign quickly gained momentum, thanks largely to the support of evangelical Christians. The immediate and extraordinary success of their work on debt advocacy was surprising and galvanized (and sometimes antagonized) other Christian organizations. By October 1997, we had attracted the support of the British medical profession, the Mothers Union, the Trades Union Congress (TUC), the National Black Alliance, the Muslim Council of Britain, Comic Relief (a charitable fund led by British comedians), all the major aid agencies (except Oxfam), and all the major faiths. At this point, we prepared to formally upgrade the loosely organized Jubilee 2000 campaign and its uncertain governance structure into a more democratic and accountable national coalition. This was done in cooperation with the Debt Crisis Network, which, in the summer of 1997, agreed to dissolve itself and help establish a broad national Jubilee 2000 coalition.

The Jubilee 2000 coalition was launched in the Jubilee Room of the House of Commons on Monday, 13 October 1997. We were determined to break with much NGO practice and inject a democratic dimension into the coalition, so an electoral college was designed for the annual *election* of a board. Its purpose was to provide for the fair representation of the diverse strands of the coalition, so although seats were reserved for the election of grassroots activists supporting the campaign, there were also elected places reserved for the large membership organizations, such as the aid agencies, and the TUC, which represented 12 million British workers. Election to the board was very competitive in that first year, and its balanced composition nearly always ensured measured, fair, and informed decision making and accountability. Elections were held each year, with membership of the board remaining stable. Two sound people were at the helm: Ed Mayo of the New Economics Foundation as chair, and Michael Taylor, previously director of Christian Aid, as president. Although there were many tensions within the broad British coalition, the board remained, on the whole, united and consistent in its support of the overall direction of the campaign and of the staff. The board, however, saw itself as accountable only for the conduct of the British campaign—and preferred to keep ambiguous the issue of relations with the other national Jubilee 2000 campaigns.

1998: The Campaign Is Internationalized

We had already targeted the world's most powerful leaders and resolved to mobilize thousands to protest at the forthcoming summit of the G8 in Birmingham (U.K.) on 16 May 1998. In October 1997, although we had begun to win the support of the aid agencies, with their large budgets and numerous staff, we had very few paid staff at the center, and only intermittent income, made up of small donations from supporters. To make things more challenging, the big aid agencies represented on the board of Jubilee 2000 placed constraints on our ability to fund-raise—concerned that we would poach their members and, more importantly, their members' financial contributions.

After hurriedly appointing a small team, preparatory work began for the great "human chain" at the 1998 summit. Our success in mobilizing 70,000 people (a police estimate; we counted 100,000) for that event is still one of the campaign's greatest achievements. In comparison, the 1999 Seattle protest against the World Trade Organization mobilized only 35,000. Jubilee 2000's achievement is even greater when one considers that it was mobilized on a (shaky) shoestring budget, with very little capacity at the center; but with our organization and mobilization amplified by coalition members. We made skillful use of scarce resources, deployed our publicity and marketing skills fairly well, and made our demands radical. Coalition members, led by Christian Aid, the TUC, MEDACT (an organization of medical professionals), the Mother's Union, the Catholic aid agency CAFOD, and the evangelical agency TearFund contributed resources and deployed people into the mobilization. We won the support of Britain's *Guardian* newspaper, which produced a centerfold spread on Third World debt on the weekend of the demonstration and helped build public support for the human chain not just in the United Kingdom, but internationally.

Part of the explanation for our success rests with the extraordinary response from grassroots supporters to the campaign's educational work and radical analysis and strategy. Highly motivated, and almost spontaneously, these supporters set up autonomous and self-financed coalitions in their localities. They used the model of the national coalition to unite people of different faiths, aid agencies, political parties, trade unions, and community organizations behind the single demand that the debts of the poorest countries be canceled by the year 2000.

The massive 9 km "human chain" at the Birmingham summit on 16 May 1998 was an extraordinary and memorable event for all who attended, not least the world leaders themselves. It placed Third World debt very firmly on the international political agenda—in particular in the rich, developed countries. Thereafter, the Jubilee 2000 movement gained terrific momentum—both in the United Kingdom and internationally—as we set out to achieve the goals of the campaign "to cancel the unpayable debts of the poorest countries by the year 2000 under a fair and transparent process."

The secretariat of the coalition in the United Kingdom, although linked to and supported by much larger organizations, remained a small, under-resourced body of people that nevertheless managed to assemble and prepare research and data on debt and make it available in an easy and popular style—often translated into Spanish and French. This was disseminated to campaigners the world over via a relatively new but vital tool in our armory—the Internet—which we exploited fully. Our Web site in the last years of the campaign was visited by more people than visited those of the IMF and World Bank!

Between 1998 and the end of 2000, we organized regular events using our two key campaign themes: first, the theme of time, counting down to a deadline; and second, the theme of chains—the oppressive kind that bind but also human chains that unite and link up people—locally and internationally. The slogan "400 days to the Millennium" became a hook on which to launch some campaign activity or a new report, or to highlight developments in debtor nations. And we worked hard to build human chains across the world—particularly through the Internet.

The campaign was given a remarkable public relations boost in Britain when, during the Honduran and Nicaraguan floods of October 1998, we explained that Britain was giving aid with one hand and taking debt payments with the other. This shocked and energized British journalists, and we became headline news on BBC bulletins.

Organizing Internationally

Between 15 and 17 November 1998, the Italian and Swedish campaigns organized an international meeting of Jubilee 2000 campaigners in Rome. It was a tense but successful event in which campaigners from 58 countries in which Jubilee 2000 was active and the representatives of 12 international organizations working on Jubilee 2000 met for the first time. It was an event at which campaigners from the North were evenly matched by those from the South.

The Southern campaigns caucused and mandated that the movement as a whole demand tough conditions for debt cancelation—so that resources from debt relief were not corruptly diverted but instead put to productive use in reducing poverty. Moreover, the Southern campaigners insisted that these conditions had to be set locally, by communities and organizations within the debtor nation who would also take responsibility for monitoring the use of the funds.

That way, debt relief could be used to strengthen and deepen democracy—by holding to account both debtor governments and foreign creditors in debtor nations. See, for example, the following extract from the declaration by Jubilee 2000 campaigns in Rome in November 1998:

We have united in calling for the cancellation of the debt by 2000 including:

- The un-payable debt, which cannot be paid without imposing sacrifices on the poor people;
- Debt that in real terms has already been paid;
- Debt accrued as a result of badly designed programs or projects;
- "Odious Debt" and debt accrued under repressive governments.

Creditor governments, the international financial institutions and the commercial banks—which bear the major responsibility for the debt crisis—cannot be the ones to set conditions for debt cancellation.

Civil society in southern countries must play a significant and influential role in a transparent and participative process. This process will define and control the use of the resources freed from debt cancellation for the benefit of the poor.

The future processing of lending and re-negotiation of debt must correspond to a just relationship between borrowers and lenders. For the cancellation of debts there has to be an independent and transparent arbitration process.

We urgently call for action. Human lives are being lost and there is widespread destruction. At the beginning of the new millennium, the moment for a new beginning has arrived.

Arriving at the final resolution was a tough process. There were tensions between the British delegation and a small group of activists, led by Alessandro Bendana of Nicaragua, who were critical of Northern Jubilee 2000 campaigns for failing to take on the character of a politicized, revolutionary movement. We in turn were adamant: Jubilee 2000 was part of a broad *social* movement, which was pluralistic and had within it, at times, conflicting ideological viewpoints. However, the movement as a whole was united in its resistance to debt "as systemic a by-product as pollution or global warming of a global political economy locked into inequality and unsustainability" (Pettifor 2003: preface).

To maintain its integrity and appeal, and its character as a broad social movement, we were determined that Jubilee 2000 would not be captured or directed by any single political party or any single political strand. This obstinate commitment did not make me popular in some circles. At the Rome meeting, however, those who were politically motivated were not able to galvanize the other Southern campaigns, so tensions and disagreements were resolved, with the conference backing the final resolution overwhelmingly. However, tensions deepened over the next few years, as some within the international movement characterized disagreement around strategy and tactics as a North–South ideological divide. The South African NGO AIDC and leaders of the Philippine "Freedom from Debt Coalition" were subsequently to challenge Jubilee 2000's North–South alliance by launching a much more politicized organization—"Jubilee South."

The Cologne G8 Summit 1999

In June 1999, the international campaign assembled at Cologne for another G8 summit. This time the event was organized by the team at Erlassjahr, the highly effective German Jubilee 2000 campaign. About 30,000 people were mobilized, including hundreds of campaigners from debtor nations.

At this event, as thousands of campaigners swarmed through the narrow streets of Cologne attracting worldwide attention from the media, the gap between the approach of leaders of "Jubilee South" and the Northern Jubilee 2000 campaigns widened. The former withdrew to a small hall to hear and make speeches to an NGO audience while, nearby, the G8's communiqué on debt was being hammered out and fought over. Jubilee 2000 campaigners from the G8 countries concerned with influencing the outcomes and press reports of the summit (by limiting the "spin") used the opportunity to engage and challenge their leaders, their "sherpas," advisers, and the powerful and varied media professionals present at the summit. We felt, rightly or wrongly, that we were engaged in hand-to-hand fighting, whereas our colleagues from "Jubilee South" preferred to disengage from battle and to debate with the already converted. They, in turn, were critical of our statements at that summit, which welcomed G8 progress on debt relief. History will judge whether the Jubilee 2000 campaigns of Germany and the United Kingdom adopted the correct strategy and tactics at Cologne. No doubt, we made errors; but we were convinced that for a global social movement to have impact, there had to be tolerance, space, and opportunity for advocacy at all levels and in all available political forums.

At that Cologne summit, Bono of U2, Youssou N'dour, and Bob Geldof (one of the organizers of the Live Aid benefits) attended to give support, which lifted our profile with the media and helped us communicate to a mass audience our concern that (1) the G8 communiqué was being "spun" to suggest deeper debt relief than was in fact being offered; and (2) that the G8 were using the debt-relief initiative to extend and deepen controversial IMF economic conditions. Nevertheless, it was at this summit that the leaders of eight of the world's richest countries agreed to build on the 1996 HIPC initiative and provide what they claimed would be $100 billion (U.S). of debt relief to 42 countries.

Thereafter, the campaign became unstoppable, boosted everywhere by myriad manifestations of grassroots activism. These were complemented by national and international media events that helped integrate, amplify, and magnify the work of local activists. Jubilee 2000's headlines and the backing of global figures such as Muhammad Ali and the pope made it that much easier for local campaigners to knock on doors and approach politicians.

Clinton Promises 100% Debt Cancelation

Jubilee 2000's visit to the pope in September 1999 ensured global press coverage and resulted in the pontiff issuing a radical statement of anger and frustration at the delaying tactics of rich creditor countries. The pope's intervention was to have a significant impact, later that week, on President Clinton of the United States.

The Jubilee 2000 delegation we led had gathered at the pope's summer palace, Castel Gandolfo. It was an extraordinary gathering. Included were musicians, rock stars, activists, and economists—from both the North and South. Quincy Jones, Bono of U2, Bob Geldof, and Willie Colon from Puerto Rico attended. The economists were Prof. Jeffrey Sachs and Prof. Adebayo Adedeji of the University of Ibadan, Nigeria. Laura Vargas, leader of Jubilee 2000 Peru, and the leaders of international Catholic organizations were present, too.

From there, part of the delegation flew to Washington to meet with African finance ministers and to participate in the annual meetings of the IMF and World Bank. On day two of that conference in September 1999, a small group of us were relaxing in the coffee shop, half listening to long speeches delivered by presidents and finance ministers in the huge adjoining Convention Hall. Unexpectedly, we heard President Clinton announce that the United States would write off 100% of the debts owed it by the countries defined by the World Bank as heavily indebted. Thus began the scramble by world leaders to write off 100% of the "bilateral" debts owed to their countries by the year 2000. Jubilee 2000 was building on its Cologne summit achievement.

By this time, the campaign had a momentum of its own, and its deep roots in the South helped ensure that 24 million people in 166 countries signed what had by now become the first-ever global petition, one that was to enter the Guinness Book of Records.

We took the petition to the gathering of world leaders at the Millennium General Assembly of the United Nations in New York in early 2000. There, thanks to the graciousness of the president of Nigeria, Olusegun Obasanjo, and with the support of Bono, we were able to formally hand over the Jubilee 2000 petition of 24 million signatures to world leaders–represented by UN Secretary General Kofi Annan.

The G8 Summit in Okinawa

The climax of our campaigning was the Okinawa G8 summit of 2000. After the experience of Birmingham, G8 leaders arranged to meet at venues farther away from public scrutiny and demonstrations, and Okinawa was to prove to be the most remote.

By then, Jubilee 2000 had built up considerable influence with G8 finance ministers. Aided by the enormously energetic and well-organized Japanese Jubilee 2000 campaign (led by Yoko Kitazawa) and working jointly with Jubilee 2000 campaigns in other G8 countries, we began to apply pressure on G8 leaders to invite leaders of debtor nations to their "fireside chat." As a result, President Obasanjo, accompanied by the presidents of South Africa and Algeria, was invited to meet with President Bill Clinton, Prime Minister Tony Blair, and others in Tokyo. It was considered inappropriate to invite these leaders to the real "fireside chat" on the island of Okinawa. Nevertheless, a precedent was established, that would become another of the campaign's great achievements. The invitation to Southern leaders has been repeated by the G8 every year since then.

Because of Okinawa's remoteness, it was not possible to bring large numbers of campaigners to the summit. Nevertheless, a troop of intrepid British Jubilee 2000 supporters arrived by bicycle, having cycled across Europe and China to be at the event![2] Such was the commitment and dedication of our supporters. We despaired about whether we could make an impact with such small numbers, but by good fortune the Japanese authorities chose to announce that they had spent $750 million (U.S.) on hosting the event. To be fair, much of this was investment in Okinawa itself, and the Japanese were trying to indicate pride in the sacrifices they had made to entertain the world's leaders well. However, their message rebounded. Media organizations from around the world were appalled to find that $750 million could have written off the entire debts of Haiti and the Gambia. So, once again, we made prime time TV, commenting on and condemning G8 extravagance while making the case for the indebted countries.

The Institutional Radicalism of the British Campaign

Jubilee 2000's principles were radical, but so, too, in the United Kingdom, was our organization. The Jubilee 2000 UK coalition had been conceived of as a short-lived, time-limited campaign, with a very clear deadline for its goals and a specific date for closure. This decision to build an organization with a short lease on life was deliberate and was intended to prevent the campaign from becoming a bureaucracy. Having witnessed so many campaigns becoming institutionalized and bureaucratic, we were determined to avoid the same fate. We wanted to build an organization that would exist for the campaign and not vice versa. Furthermore, we believed that the time deadline was fundamental to the dynamics of the campaign and could not be compromised. So, at the end of 2000, the staff at the British office undertook the difficult task of closing down the campaign.

There were weaknesses in the decision to set up a limited-life campaign, but there were great strengths, too. The clear deadline and the sense that Jubilee 2000 would not, like some campaigns, be interminable added immensely to its dynamism and impact. It was also important to recognize that Jubilee 2000 was simply a *campaign* that had succeeded in broadening, deepening, and focusing the energies of an already existing international *movement*—a movement that could not be closed down.

Nevertheless, at the time of closure of the British office, we, the staff, all had a profound sense of unfinished business. Our colleagues from Africa and Latin America found the decision to close inexplicable and were very critical. Many thought we were simply dilettantes—prepared to abandon the struggle long before debt relief had been secured.

At the same time, divisions in the international movement were setting in, so it may have been timely for the UK campaign to withdraw from the dominant role it had played and to pass the torch to others, particularly campaigners from the South.

What Were the Key Elements of Jubilee 2000's Success?

There were various elements that explain the Jubilee 2000 campaign's extraordinary success, including:

1. radical analysis of the debt crisis;
2. the theological principles underpinning the campaign;
3. political principles of national and global coalition-building; and
4. emphasis on education and effective communication with a wide range of audiences.

A Radical Analysis

One of the key elements behind Jubilee 2000's success, not just in Britain but internationally, was the radical nature of the analysis we made of the problem of Third World debt. For a campaign to be successful and capable of uniting a range of social forces, research, deep thought, and careful preparation must go into the analysis of the campaign's central issues. The process is similar, I would argue, to that of cutting a diamond. An expert diamond-cutter can spend two years staring at and examining a stone before deciding on the angle at which it is to be cut—an angle that if struck accurately will be "true" and will maximize reflection of all the stone's many aspects. This is similar to the problem addressed by a campaign: "cutting it" in such a way as to enhance all aspects of the issue and maximizing support for all aspects of the campaign. This "cutting" or analytical exercise should, as far as possible, arrive at and promote what is most true about an issue. A campaign that is poorly analyzed and that does not reflect different facets of the truth at the heart of the issue will not, in my view, mobilize significant numbers. Of course, defining what is "true" is not straightforward, but the point is to aim for it. There is nothing that galvanizes campaigners more.

Prior to Jubilee 2000, most (but certainly not all) Northern campaigns on debt tended to give the impression that this was a charitable issue; that poor countries had fallen into financial difficulties through, it was often implied, a combination of incompetence and corruption and that their debts had to be "forgiven." We found this phrase quite unacceptable because "forgiveness," like "redemption" (originally an economic term), has come to have a religious meaning in common usage. Applied to debtors today, "forgiveness" implied that one party to the debt were sinners and needed to be pardoned by their creditors. Furthermore, this analysis led international creditors to transfer the burden of adjustment in a debt crisis overwhelmingly onto the debtor. Therefore, the analysis had to be challenged.

The Jubilee 2000 campaign insisted instead on the *co-responsibility* of both debtors and creditors for the crisis—both needed to admit culpability and share in the liabilities. In the North, our emphasis was even more marked. By switching the emphasis away from debtor nations and demonstrating how creditor governments had encouraged borrowing by engaging in "loan-pushing," often corruptly and often to promote military exports, we were able to switch the focus away from debtor nations and toward powerful *perpetrators* of the crisis. This enabled campaigners in Britain and other countries to challenge, through local, accessible democratic processes, government lenders such as the Export Credit Guarantee Department.

This switch of emphasis away from debtors and toward the culpability of creditors empowered British and other Western campaigners. Many campaigns on development issues encouraged campaigners to feel pity for the poor on the one hand and guilt on the other. Neither of these are empowering. On the contrary, they paralyze and immobilize campaigners. What *is* empowering is understanding on the one hand and a sense of responsibility on the other. A sense that a campaigner can challenge injustice and can influence and achieve change by holding elected politicians to account (i.e., that he or she *can* make a difference).

In the South, campaigners were used to having their countries and governments demeaned as victims on the one hand while being culpable on the other for incompetence and corruption. It is remarkable how ordinary people all over the world take responsibility for their governments and feel the pain and humiliation of failed, corrupt government and debased currencies and impoverished communities. Jubilee 2000 blamed the powerful. This analysis was one of the reasons, in my view, that we were able to build such extraordinary solidarity across North/South campaigns and communities—and quickly weld together a global social movement.

The analysis was radical, too, in that it did not pull punches. The core of the campaign was the emphasis on the deliberate, *structural* nature of global economic injustice—injustice that was neither "natural" nor the result of accident. If the truth was to be unveiled, then all the dirty secrets of the international financial system had to be brought to light—and challenged. Jubilee 2000 UK tried to do this through rigorous analysis of World Bank and IMF data; by showing that IMF "structural adjustment" policies are designed to extract and transfer resources from debtors to international creditors; by exposing the role of Export Credit Guarantee Departments; and by obliging the secretive Paris Club of international governmental creditors to account for and make public their role and activities.

The Jubilee Principle

The Jubilee principle was at the heart of the campaign and was one of the key reasons for its appeal not only to Jews and Christians but also people of other faiths. It is a profound and deeply entrenched principle of economic justice, underpinning almost all of Western civilization's economic practice.

Fundamentally, the Jubilee principle (or Sabbath economics) reflects Judaic and Christian belief that there should be embedded within social and economic relations systems or regulations for periodic corrections to imbalances and in-justices (Myers 1998a) and that these corrections (to economic, political, or environmental imbalances) are best achieved through the regulatory framework of the Sabbath. Under the regime of the Sabbath, every seven days, the popu-lation was (and still is in many economies) expected to cease exploitation of the land and of labor and to refrain from consumption. Every seven years, tilled land was rested and given a full year to recover from exploitation. Similarly, hard workers were, and still are in some academic institutions, granted "sab-baticals"—a year off from work every seven years.

Every seven times seven years (i.e., in the 49th year), the Torah or Old Testament commanded that slaves be freed, debts canceled and land restored to its rightful owners. In the 50th year, this correction to imbalances would be celebrated as the "Jubilee year" (Myers 1998a): "And ye shall hallow the fiftieth year, and proclaim liberty throughout all the land unto all the inhabitants thereof; it shall be a jubilee unto you; and ye shall return every man unto his possession, and ye shall return every man unto his family" (Leviticus 25: 10).

Ched Myers argues that, in the New Testament, Sabbath principles balance abundance and need. "Give us enough bread for today, and forgive us our debts as we forgive others" (Matthew 6: 11–12) (Myers 1998b). In a world of abun-dance, all reasonable needs can be met. In this sense, the Sabbath principles challenge neo-liberal economic principles, which stress scarcity—not abun-dance—of finance, goods, and services. At the same time, contemporary eco-nomic systems encourage unlimited consumption and the lifting of all constraints on the demand for loans, goods, and services. So whereas goods are scarce, needs and consumption, it is argued, can be unlimited. "Sabbath economics" and the Jubilee principle directly challenge this ideology.

The Jubilee principle in particular has long inspired liberation struggles. These include the struggle of black slaves in the Deep South, as well as the American struggle for independence. Part of the Leviticus text is engraved on Philadelphia's Liberty Bell ("Sound the trumpet of Jubilee, and declare liberty throughout the land").

"Sabbath economics" is also reflected in principles central to Islamic and Buddhist thought and civilization. The Qur'an outlines, in the longest verse in the whole book, "instructions on how to arrange for a loan . . . and the rules governing the relationship between the lender and the borrower . . . the lender is entitled only to the amount he lent, no more and no less. If the borrower is unable to repay the debt when it matures, then the payment must be put off until s/he is able to pay" (Zaki Badawi 1998).

One of the chief reasons for the success of Jubilee 2000 was that its eco-nomic, political, and spiritual principles originated, and resonated deeply, with millions of Jews, Christians, Muslims, and Buddhists all over the world.

The campaign was launched at a time when these fundamental principles were being overturned by globalization. As a result of the transformation of the global economy that began in the 1970s, values and economic systems that had been in place for thousands of years faced fundamental challenges. One of these was the ancient form of regulation known as the "Sabbath." Sunday was a day decreed to be free of consumption and free of exploitation of both land and labor. The forces of globalization, the drive to deregulation and liberalization, required an end to this form of periodic regulation of consumption and exploitation. Today, in its stead we have the 24/7 phenomenon, caused by the removal of regulation and limits over the exploitation of land, labor, and consumption.

The transformation of the global economy since the 1970s meant effectively that the "money-changers had taken over the temple." This was reflected in the new dominance of the finance sector—and the power of this sector over the "real" economy (New Economics Foundation 2003). As a result, there has been huge growth in the world's financial assets held mostly by the finance sector—banks and other creditor institutions, investment funds, pension funds, and mutual funds—all forms of financial intermediaries. With this explosion of financial assets, the stock of credit—and with it the burden of debt—has grown exponentially. And so, too, has inequality—as those with assets grow richer partly by extracting further assets from those indebted to them.

Market liberalism balks at the kinds of constraints placed on the rich by the system of Sabbath economics; in particular, the principle of periodic correction to debt imbalances through the Jubilee principle of "debt-release" and the New Testament's appeal for the forgiveness of debts as we forgive others. For this reason, as well as many others, Jubilee 2000 represented a major ideological challenge to the market fundamentalism practiced by major creditors represented by the IMF, the World Bank, and other Western financial institutions. And in making this challenge, Jubilee 2000's millions of Christian, Jewish, Muslim, and Buddhist supporters believed they were acting out their faith, fulfilling the mandates of key scriptures, and confronting the revolutionary, secular, and divisive world of finance. It was this faith, in my view, that gave Jubilee 2000 its extraordinary dynamism.

The Political Principles of National and Global Coalition Building

Unison has a strong tradition of international solidarity work, and for me, one of the great results of Jubilee 2000 was the lasting networks that were built up between people north, south, east and west, as we came together to challenge the injustice of the debt. Cooperation within the international trade union movement certainly has been strengthened in the process and I know we will continue to campaign on this crucial issue until justice is achieved.
    —Rodney Bickerstaffe, General Secretary, Unison, at the UNCTAD meeting in
                                                    Bangkok, February, 2000

Important lessons for Jubilee 2000 emerged from the labor, trade union, and anti-apartheid movements in Britain during the 1980s. These struggles yielded the bitter experience of the divisiveness that can fester at the heart of most well-meaning, progressive organizations, packed invariably with very good people.

It was vital that Jubilee 2000 not fall victim to such divisions. On the contrary, for an issue of this importance, requiring the building of political will on a global scale, the broadest possible alliances had to be constructed—and held together. This could only be done, we concluded, on the basis of a narrow principle. In other words, a broad campaign or movement could only be built up around a simple, principled proposal, which should have the power of uniting, not dividing, communities locally, nationally, and also internationally. Adherence to the principle (embodied in the simple words of the short Jubilee 2000 petition) would be strict—but that would be all that would be required of our supporters.[3] We would not ask their views on other matters; we would not "expel" them for failing to share our views on all issues; and we would certainly never "discipline" them—something, for example, that all political parties engage in. In other words, we would not build a political party but instead would help deepen an existing, broad social movement by providing clear focus. As President Clinton put it, "When you get this many people from this many different backgrounds pointing in the same direction, you can be pretty sure it's the right direction" (Barret 2000).

Unity was difficult to maintain. Internally, the British coalition suffered tensions because of perceptions on the part of aid agencies that Jubilee 2000 represented a substantial threat to their profiles, their fund-raising, and their membership recruitment. This was ironic because the campaign mobilized many millions more than the narrow memberships of aid agencies and in the process "raised the seas on which many (development) ships sailed." The fears of aid agencies proved to be misplaced because far from reducing their income and memberships, Jubilee 2000 helped build a much bigger constituency for development issues and thereby increased their fund-raising and recruitment. Nevertheless, this end result was not always certain and caused great unease.

Balancing the varied interests, skills, and levels of participation of diverse coalition members was tough. It was particularly difficult to ensure the inclusion of those affiliated organizations that had less experience with campaigning on debt and development issues (such as the trade unions and medical profession).

There were also "political" tensions, as Jubilee 2000's analysis was more radical than that of some of our U.K. partners, many of whom were cautious about challenging the New Labor government. There were also tensions between those with policy expertise and the many who joined the coalition but lacked expertise in the finer points of international debt and finance. Much credit must go to the staff and the board members for insisting on unity around the simple principles of the petition and for ensuring that divisions were mendable and never spilled over into the public domain.

North–South tensions were less easy to manage. Jubilee 2000 began with a commitment to the rights of people in *debtor* nations to organize autonomously. Equally important, in our view, was the need for people in *creditor* nations not to speak for others but instead to speak for themselves and hold their elected representatives accountable for the way in which their governments acted in international forums and for the way in which taxpayer revenues were used both in lending and in debt write-offs. In other words, our governments were part of the problem, and we as citizens had a responsibility to do something at home about their activities in the IMF, the UN, the World Bank, and the WTO.

We hoped that the international movement would unite different social forces, working within their own spheres—North and South—to hold governments, the World Bank and IMF, and international financiers accountable.

Of course, matters were not so straightforward. Although autonomy is something we all favor, autonomy for campaigners in poor countries often means isolation and poverty. In the absence of resources, with governments that were at best remote and at worst repressive, and with the pressure of domestic priorities, campaigners in debtor nations found it hard to mount campaigns on the same scale as Northern campaigns. For our colleagues in these countries, it was much more challenging to hold governments and international financial institutions accountable. Jubilee 2000 UK resisted becoming a grantor to these partners mainly because we believed that this would fundamentally alter the nature of our relationships. And so we urged faith and development organizations to support debt-campaigning work in Africa and Latin America. For some campaigns, these resources were made available, but many struggled to make ends meet.

Jubilee 2000 Challenged the Idea of "Global Civil Society"

For better or worse, we in the British campaign had not backed, and indeed opposed, the idea of an international "Steering Committee" for Jubilee 2000. We believed that the principles of autonomy and self-organization for each national campaign were fundamental. This belief arose from our analysis that democratic accountability could only be achieved within the context of the state and its borders. Attempting to build a democratic and accountable body that was global, borderless, and outside the framework of the state was, we concluded, a delusional and utopian ambition. For the purposes of building a global social movement, all that was required (we believed) was the need to cooperate and coordinate our activities internationally. That coordination could only take place on the basis of agreement by individual national campaigns, challenging *their* governments and accountable to *their* supporters at home. We also doubted whether an international body could be representative and whether only those with time and resources to attend international meetings would be active. We were convinced that such a body would quickly become highly politicized and be taken over by one faction or another.

North–South Tensions

North–South relationships in a broad social movement are complex and fraught with imbalances, injustices, and a lack of understanding. However, we believed it was vital to overcome these inherent tensions and build a *united* social movement that would challenge the highly effective, powerful, and on the whole *united* "Washington consensus" of international creditors. We found the same determination to build international unity among those who were victims of the debt—our active campaigning partners in Africa, Latin America, and Asia. The reasons for this dedication to unity were straightforward. First, as mentioned earlier, we needed to be strong enough to challenge the unity of powerful international creditors. Second, international unity empowered campaigners on the ground. In Britain, we were empowered when the finance minister of Guyana, Mr. Bharratt Jagdeo, accompanied us to a meeting with Tony Blair during the Birmingham G8 summit. His presence and his direct experience enormously enhanced the authority of our delegation, intensifying pressure on our prime minister. Similarly, campaigners in Peru, challenging dictatorial President Fujimori, were strengthened and protected by international alliances at times when they could very easily have been victimized by their elites—the fate of a number of Jubilee 2000 campaigners in Africa.

As a result, for most of the duration of the campaign, Jubilee 2000 achieved an extraordinary north–south alliance—an alliance that I know intimidated and impressed World Bank and IMF officials who encountered our unity of purpose in 69 countries. Sadly, this unity, which continued up until 2000, did not survive the campaign.

Education and Communication

[Jubilee 2000] has managed to put a relatively arcane issue—that of international finance and development—on the negotiating table throughout the world. The pledges Clinton and Brown have made would not have happened without Jubilee 2000. It's one of the most effective global lobbying campaigns I have ever seen.
    —World Bank spokesman, *PR Week*, 16 April 1999

Jubilee 2000 was first and foremost an education campaign. At the heart of the campaign was a belief that ordinary people, in both debtor and creditor countries, could get a grip on complex international finance issues—and once they understood these issues would be empowered to act. This belief motivated us to communicate and to do so in the most appropriate and effective ways with a diverse range of audiences—at every level of society. Above all, we wanted to expose and democratize knowledge and information on this, a matter of public, not private, finance. We did this in Britain, for example, by preparing and distributing high-quality reports, well-evidenced research and briefings, hard-hitting fact sheets, punchy press releases, or the briefest sound bites for broadcast at an event such as the annual Brit Awards.[4] We were willing and keen to communicate in ways that would best enable our varied audiences to hear and understand our message. We were driven to communicate and educate at every level possible.

This approach to our supporters, and to our varied audiences, was one of the key elements at the heart of Jubilee 2000's success. We refused to keep information exclusive or to patronize supporters, and we remained confident that ordinary people could come to grips with complex economic issues that were usually confined to the exclusive domains of "policy wonks," academic analysts, and experts. We particularly targeted women, arguing that most women, wherever they lived, managed household budgets and therefore understood the rudiments of economics. Empowering them to understand national and international economics became a central mission of the campaign.

A great deal of hard work and energy went into explaining, teaching, and communicating with individuals and audiences about international finance and debt. In Britain, this initially took the form of endless talks, workshops, and briefing sessions in churches, trade unions, and community halls up and down the country. The secretariat initially prepared several PowerPoint® presentations that carefully marshaled arguments and facts and outlined data relating to individual debtor nations. These were copied and widely circulated to our "BMs"—"ballistically motivated" activists—who used them to brief themselves and then spread the word in talks and briefings to numerous groups. As one of the richer campaigns in the international coalition, we were able to afford the World Bank's annual *World Debt Tables* (since renamed *Global Development Finance*), purchased at $300 (U.S.) an issue. We used this and other data to regularly churn out briefings and circulate them to an enormous e-mail list or sent them by post to supporters. Our Web site became an authoritative and up-to-date source of information and data on Third World debt. In the process, we educated activists and campaigners but also politicians, officials, and journalists. For example, Alistair Campbell, Prime Minister Blair's official spokesman, stated that "A lot of change has been achieved by people getting together. Jubilee 2000 and the part played by the entertainment industry has had an effect. At Downing Street we get a huge flow of letters."

The education of activists was enormously empowering. Campaigners regularly engaged in detailed correspondence with Treasury, World Bank, and IMF staff over aspects of developing-country debt. Hundreds of thousands of letters were sent to the British government and to the offices of the World Bank and the IMF in Washington. Additional civil servants had to be appointed to deal with the deluge. One expressed incredulity in a private conversation with me. He explained that he had received a letter complaining about the arbitrary nature of the debt-to-export ratio used to calculate the sustainability of poor-country debts and in particular the arbitrary "cut-off point" chosen for calculating how much of Uganda's total debt was eligible for cancelation. "This letter was written on pink paper, with a bunch of roses in the corner," said the civil servant, who went on to ask "Who *are* these people? . . . and how do they *know* about Uganda's cut-off point?" According to the Judges' appraisal after granting Jubilee 2000 First Prize at One World Media Awards in June 1999, "This was a truly inspirational campaign that delivered its message with flair and simplicity."

Campaigning and Education in Debtor Nations

The education of activists in the South was equally impressive. One of the most effective examples was the Jubilee 2000 Peru campaign, led by Laura Vargas, a key figure in the networks of the Peruvian Catholic church. Jubilee 2000 Peru produced sophisticated briefings, wittily illustrated and simply explained in small, colorful, cheaply produced magazines. In a complex logistical operation, organized from Lima, thousands of these magazines were distributed to parishes in the coastal, desert, and jungle regions of the country. A series of regional and then parish council-based meetings were planned and convened, where Peru's debt and that of other poor countries was discussed and debated in packed meeting halls and clubs. (The Peruvian campaign collected 1,850,060 signatures for the Jubilee 2000 petition.) As a result, millions of ordinary Peruvians came to understand the nature of their country's debt, the variety of its creditors, and the role debt payments played in diverting precious resources from development.

Archbishop Rodriguez, Archbishop of Honduras, at the launch of Jubilee 2000 Latin America in January 1999, said that "There is a great hope when ordinary people put their hands together. Nothing can stop us. The campaign has started something that will change many things in the next century."

In Kenya, Wangaari Mathaai, the leader of "Greenbelt," a national environmental campaign, combined with church leaders to brief and educate hundreds of thousands of Kenyans. On a tour of Kenya, she addressed endless church meetings and tirelessly explained the facts of Kenya's foreign debts. As a result, Kenyans learned just how much was owed by their government to foreign creditors, how this debt had often been corruptly incurred, and how much of the government's annual budget was devoted to repaying it.

Zie Gariyo, leader of the Ugandan Jubilee 2000 campaign, recounts the story of a peasant farmer who had been briefed by members of his church and marched into the local offices of the municipal government demanding to know why the Ugandan government was prioritizing debt repayments over expenditures on a school for the area. The official he confronted was angry and, upon hearing that the peasant farmer had learned all he knew from Jubilee 2000, rang Zie in Kampala to complain: The government's budget was being misinterpreted, and anyway it was not for a peasant farmer to express opinions on something as complex as the country's foreign debt! According to President Jagdeo of Guyana, "Jubilee 2000 has done wonderful work and has made foreign debt a global issue. In the North and in the South, Jubilee 2000 has helped people understand the impact of foreign debt on daily life" (Barrett 2000).

Educating the Media

Our mission to educate, inform, and communicate began among our grassroots supporters, but we were also determined to extend this work to politicians, academics, and thousands of journalists in the broadcast and print media both nationally and internationally.

Briefing journalists is a thankless task. They work fast and shift quickly from one subject to another. Turnover on press desks is high. As a result, our small media team worked very hard and for long hours. Fortunately, the culture within Jubilee 2000 UK of maintaining high standards of professionalism, even on a shoestring budget, and of integrating policy, research, advocacy, and communication, meant that we were able to guarantee accuracy and were "fleet of foot" in dealing with and responding to the media. Journalists were treated with great respect; we went to great lengths to simplify and précis information for them so that they could digest it in the short time they had to write up or prepare stories. And we always made certain that they had a quote, riposte, or rebuttal each time the Paris Club, World Bank, IMF, or G8 issued a statement on debt.

This groundwork and hard graft of always educating was at the core of Jubilee 2000's success.

Conclusion

Jubilee 2000 was a brief, highly focused campaign assembled with minimal resources that, thanks to the Jubilee principle and its adherents in faith communities, exploded into a global campaign within four years. It was designed as a short-lived, goal-oriented campaign that would unite diverse social forces within an existing social movement. It was not intended as a vessel for the development of global civil society, a goal we considered utopian. Although we made many mistakes, Jubilee 2000's principled approach to self-organization and international cooperation provided a framework, and perhaps a model, for the mobilization of millions of people in varied and diverging societies, enabling them to unite and resist the dominance and power of unaccountable financial and corporate institutions.

Notes

1. For details of how debt-relief funds have been used, for example, in Tanzania, see the letter to Jubilee 2000 from President Mkapa at www.jubileeresearch.org.
2. The weekend of the Okinawa G8 meeting (in 2000) was the prompt for hundreds of local debt campaigns to take to the streets with stunts and activities across the United Kingdom and around the world. At home in London, I turned on Radio 4 to hear the national noon news bulletin. The debt protests were the lead item, and to illustrate them the bulletin reported that "members of the World Development Movement in Brighton have taken to the sea in Tony Blair masks to demonstrate that world leaders are 'up to their necks in Third World debt'." An action by WDM local members had worked its way up the massive BBC newsgathering ladder to lead the national bulletin because it was a fine idea with a strong message. It reminded me that Jubilee 2000 was never about the secretariat in London or the headquarters of the coalition members. But it is a campaign whose strength came from dedicated local groups who understand the campaigning power of a good idea and the undeniable moral argument for debt relief.
3. "We, the undersigned call on world leaders to cancel the unpayable debts of the poorest countries by the year 2000, under a fair and transparent process."
4. Britain's biggest music industry awards—with a huge live audience and a global TV audience.

References

Barrett, M., ed. 2000. *The World Will Never Be the Same Again*. London: Jubilee 2000.
Blackmore, S., and Greenhill, R. 2002. *Relief Works*. London: New Economics Foundation. Available online at: www.jubileeresearch.org.
Pettifor, A., ed. 2003. *Real World Economic Outlook*. London: New Economics Foundation and Palgrave Macmillan.
Myers, C. 1998a. Godspeed the Year of Jubilee! The Biblical Vision of Sabbath Eco-

nomics, *Sojourners Online* (May–June). Available online at: www.sojo.net/index
.cfm.

———. 1998b. Balancing Abundance and Need. Available online at: www.the
otherside.org/archive/sep-oct98/myers.html.

Zaki Badawi, M. 1998. The Ethics of Debt Forgiveness. Paper presented to the Irish
School of Ecumenical Studies, February 1999.

INDEX

Page numbers in italics refer to figures and tables.